STRAYS

Thank you to Miki and my family.

First published in English in 2021
by SelfMadeHero
139–141 Pancras Road
London NW1 1UN
www.selfmadehero.com

Written and illustrated by Chris W. Kim

Publishing Director: Emma Hayley
Editorial & Production Director: Guillaume Rater
Publishing Assistant: Stefano Mancin
Designer: Txabi Jones
UK Publicist: Paul Smith
US Publicist: Maya Bradford
With thanks to: Dan Lockwood

A CIP record for this book is available from the British Library

ISBN: 978-1-910593-99-8

10 9 8 7 6 5 4 3 2 1

Printed and bound in Slovenia

STRAYS

CHRIS W. KIM

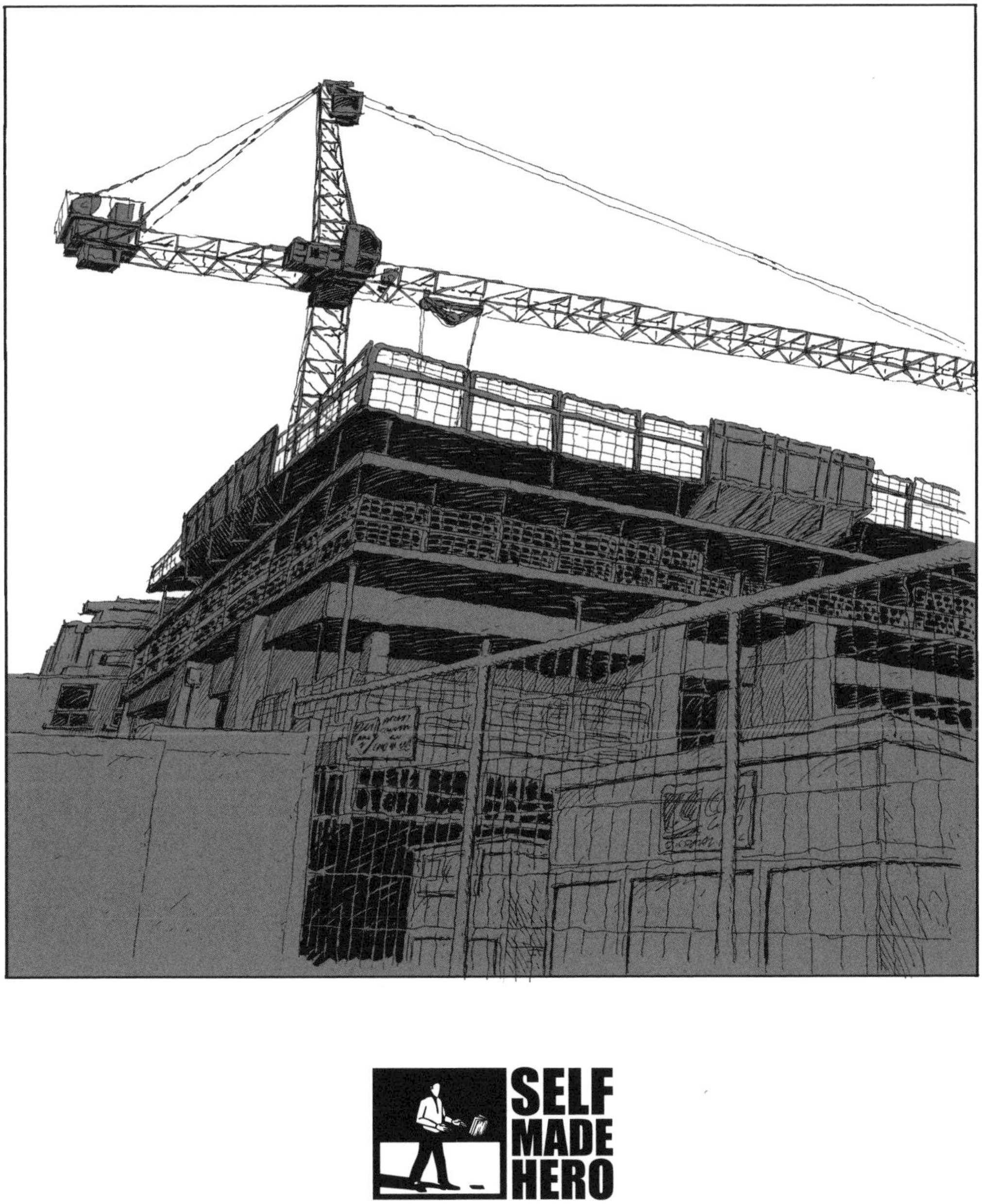

SELF MADE HERO

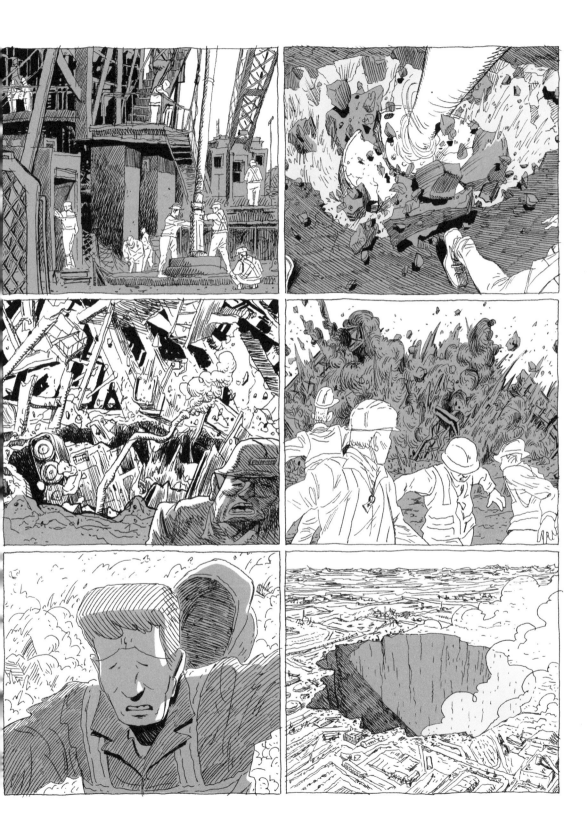

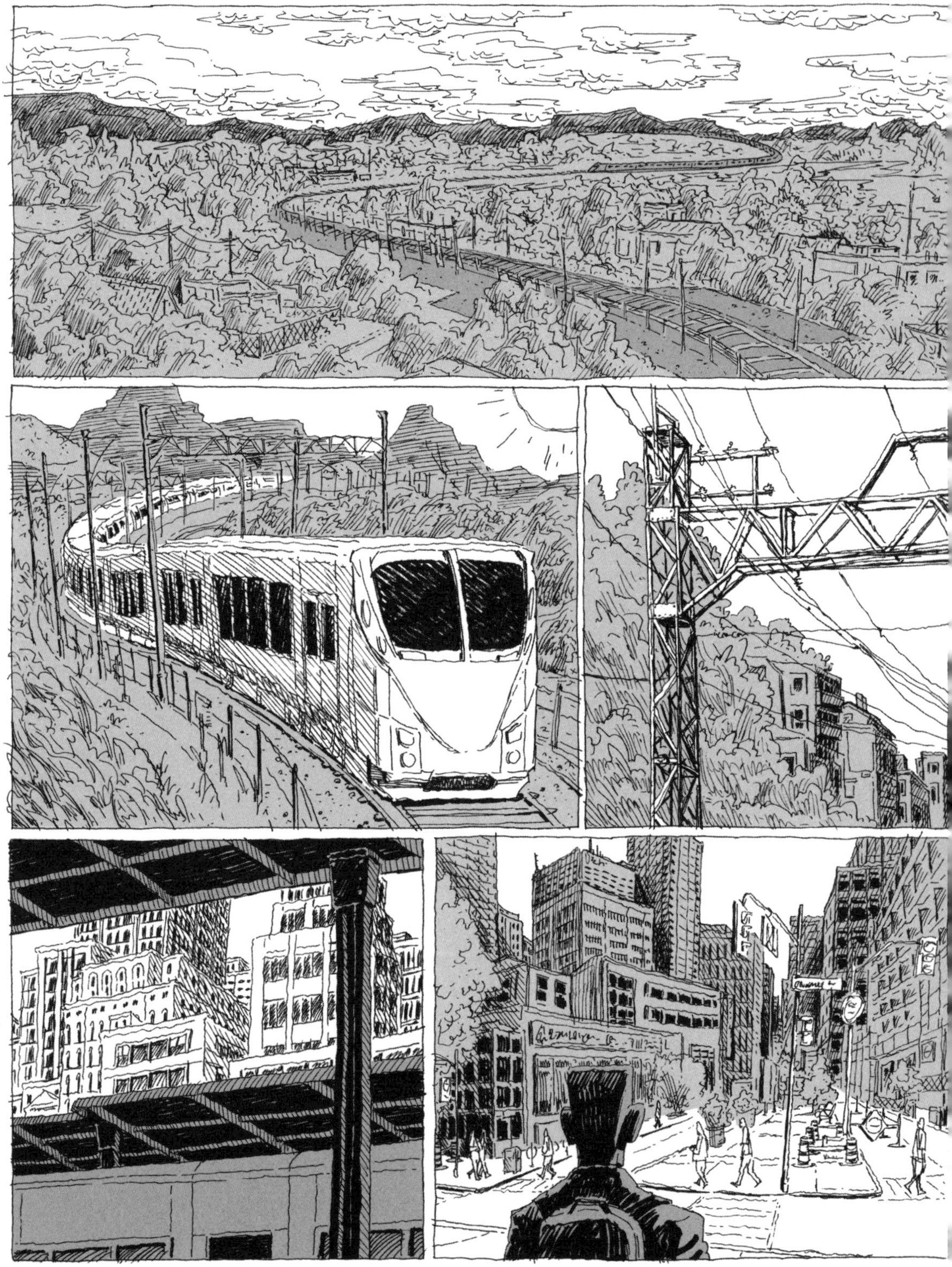

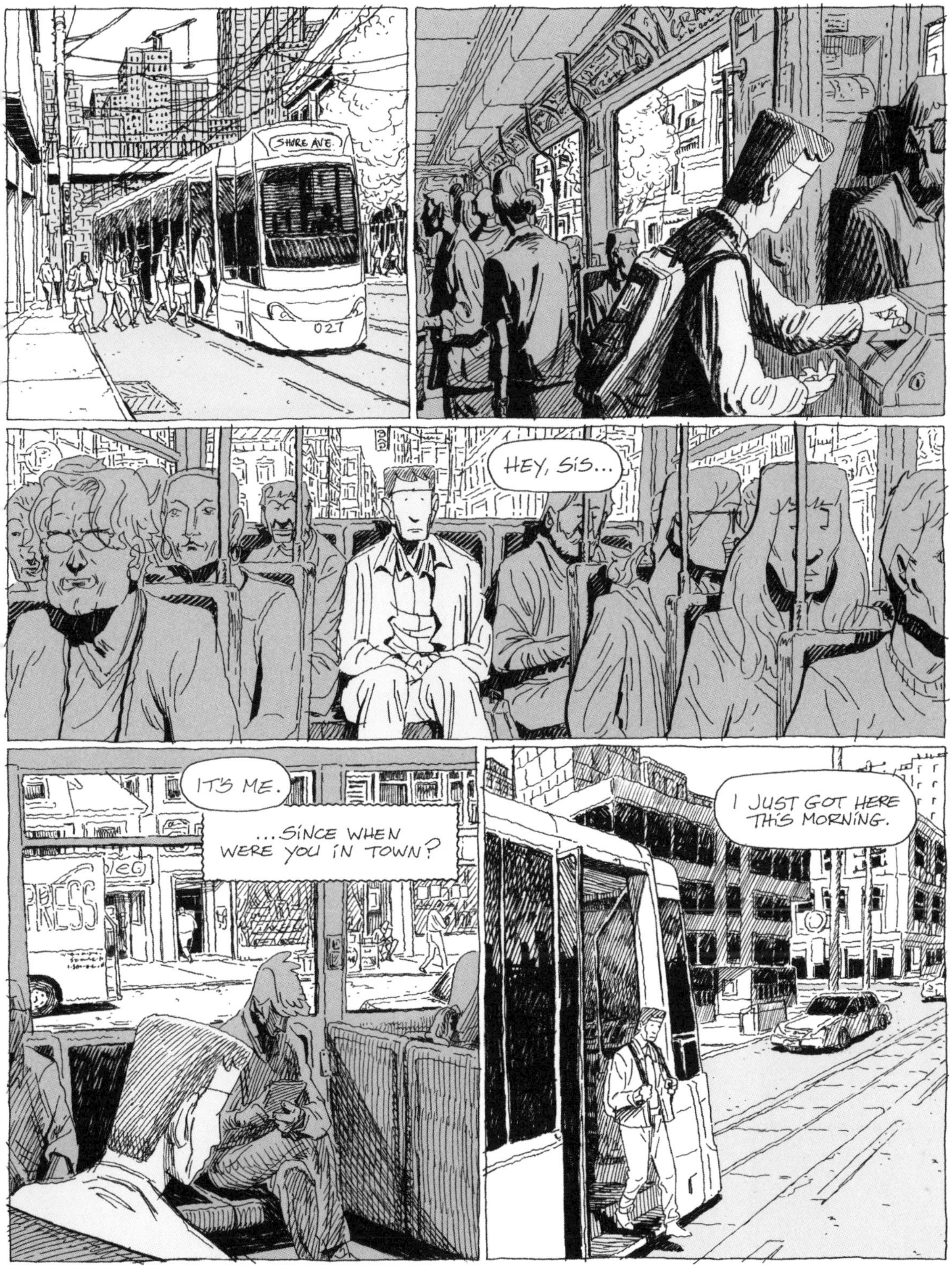
SHORE AVE.
027
HEY, SIS...
IT'S ME.
...SINCE WHEN WERE YOU IN TOWN?
I JUST GOT HERE THIS MORNING.

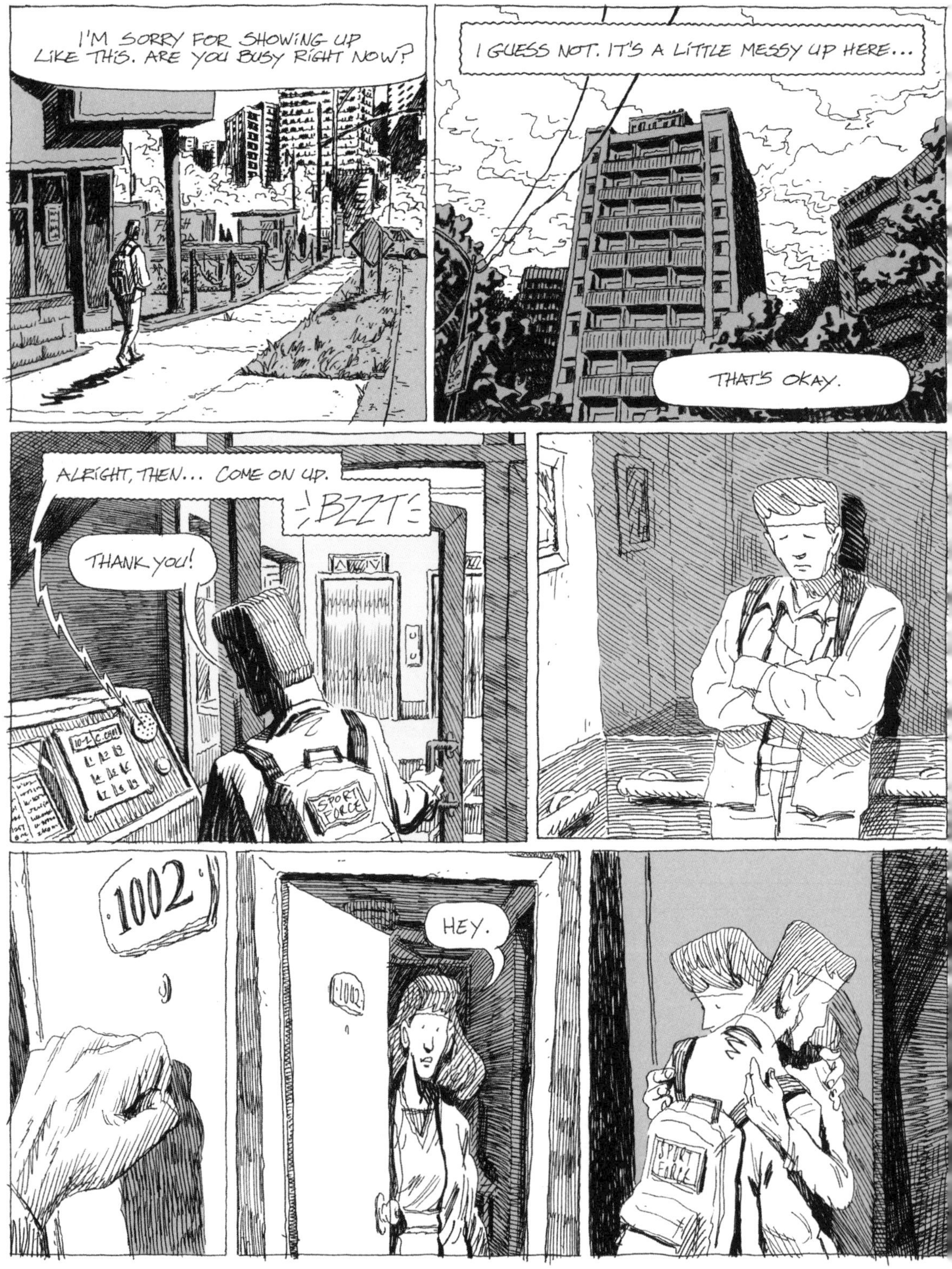
I'M SORRY FOR SHOWING UP LIKE THIS. ARE YOU BUSY RIGHT NOW?
I GUESS NOT. IT'S A LITTLE MESSY UP HERE...
THAT'S OKAY.
ALRIGHT, THEN... COME ON UP.
BZZT
THANK YOU!
SPORT FORCE
1002
HEY.
SPORT FORCE

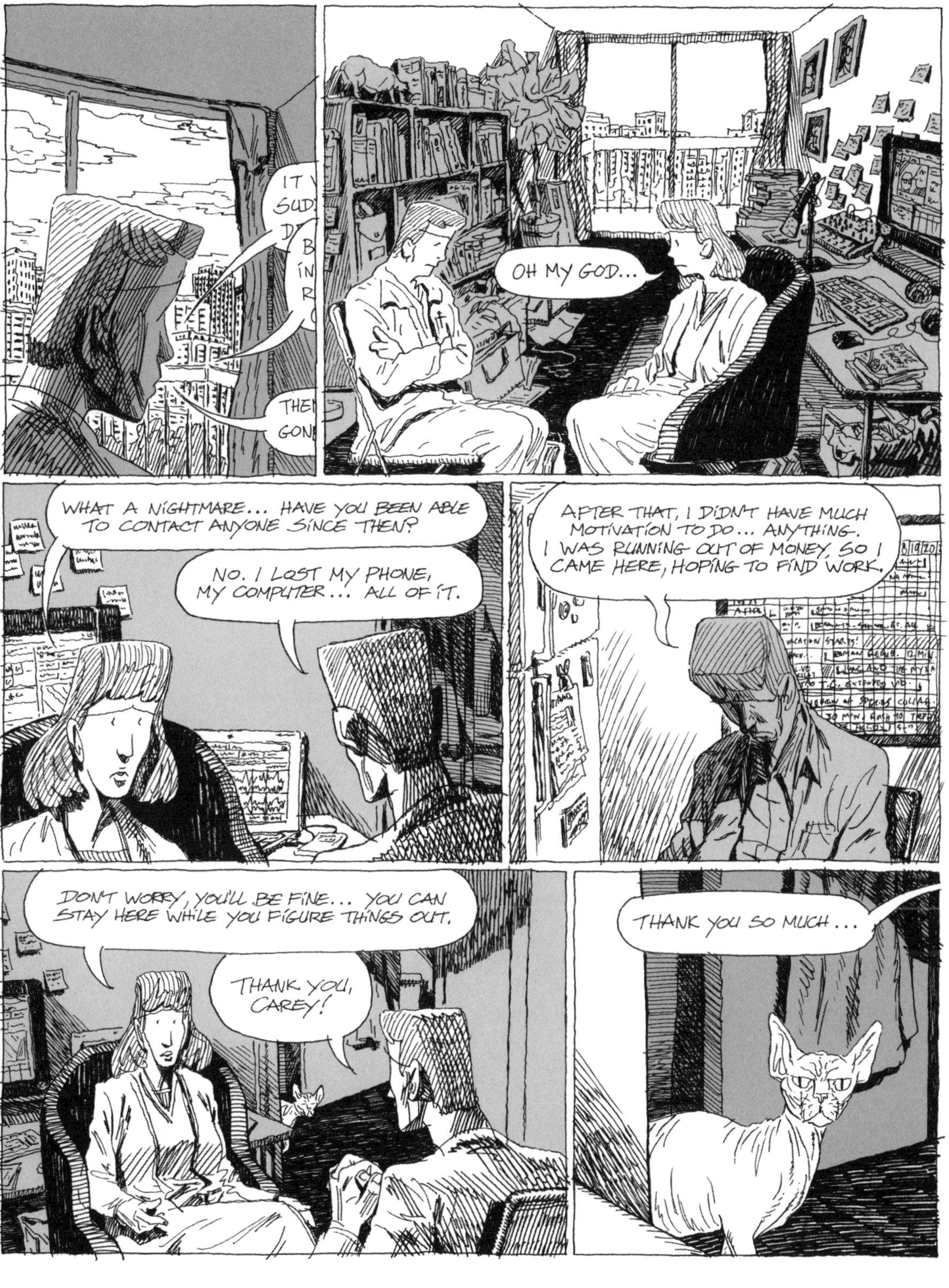
OH MY GOD...
WHAT A NIGHTMARE... HAVE YOU BEEN ABLE TO CONTACT ANYONE SINCE THEN?
NO. I LOST MY PHONE, MY COMPUTER... ALL OF IT.
AFTER THAT, I DIDN'T HAVE MUCH MOTIVATION TO DO... ANYTHING. I WAS RUNNING OUT OF MONEY, SO I CAME HERE, HOPING TO FIND WORK.
DON'T WORRY, YOU'LL BE FINE... YOU CAN STAY HERE WHILE YOU FIGURE THINGS OUT.
THANK YOU, CAREY!
THANK YOU SO MUCH...

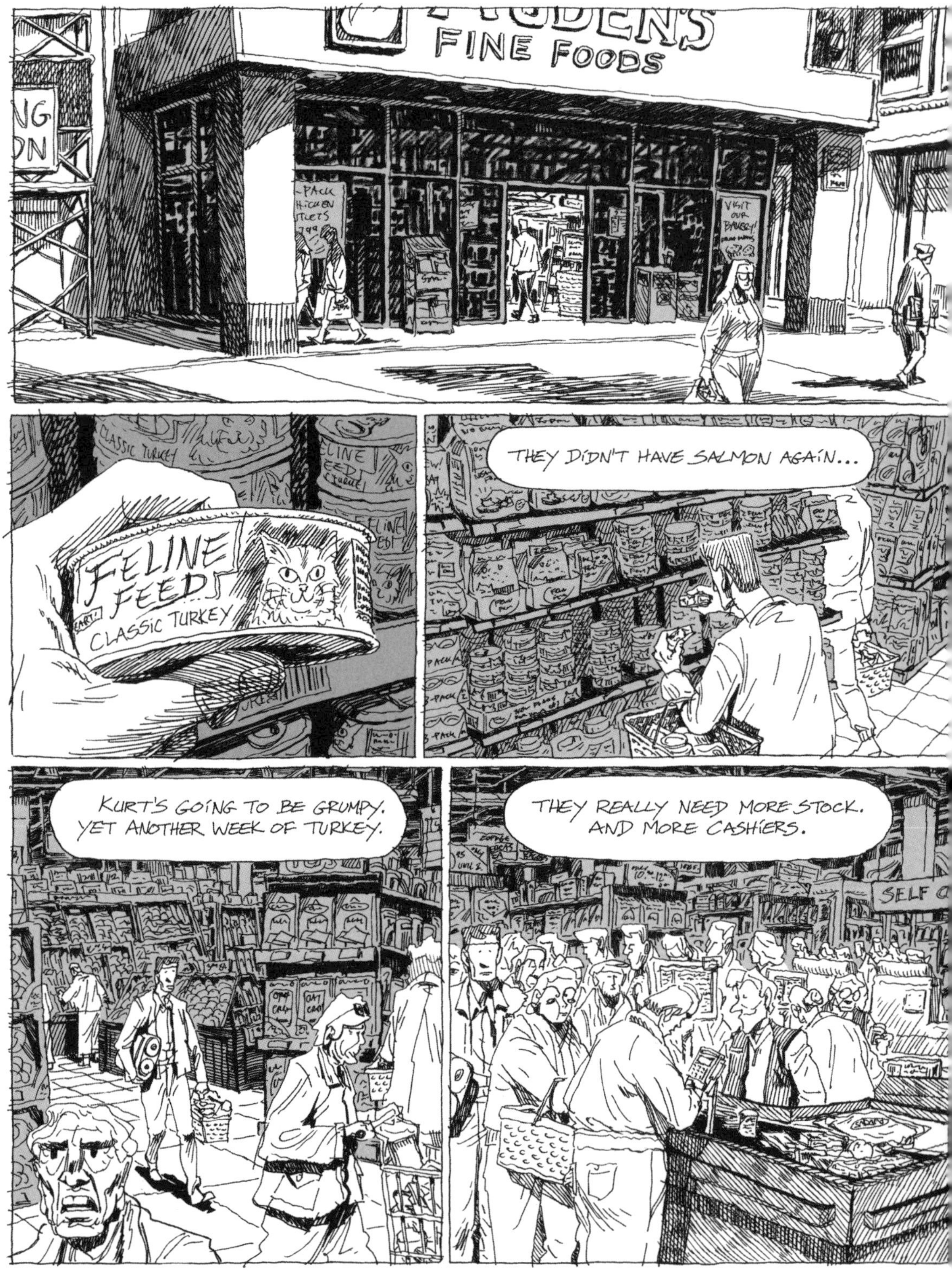
FINE FOODS
FELINE FEED
CLASSIC TURKEY
THEY DIDN'T HAVE SALMON AGAIN...
KURT'S GOING TO BE GRUMPY.
YET ANOTHER WEEK OF TURKEY.
THEY REALLY NEED MORE STOCK.
AND MORE CASHIERS.

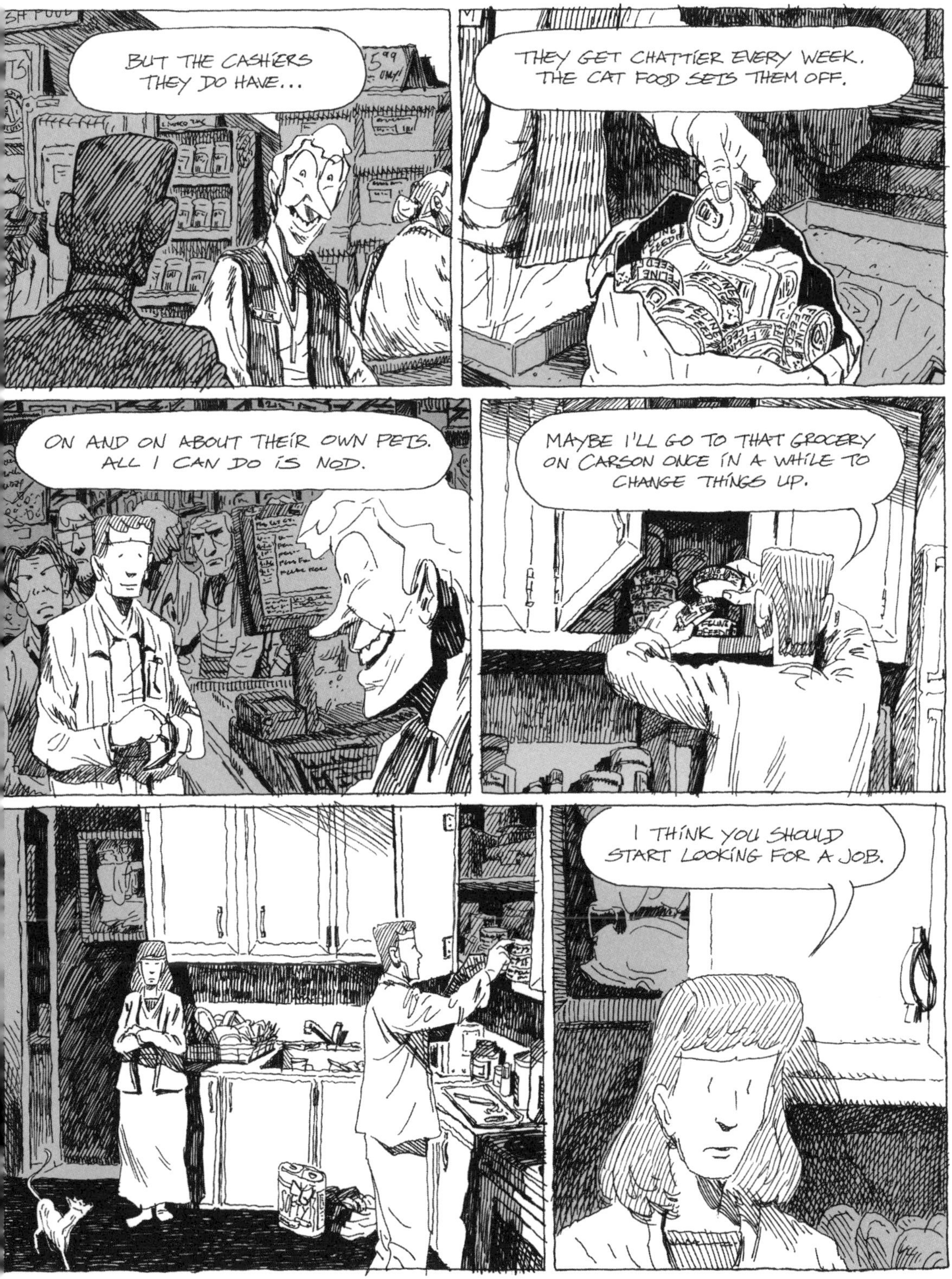
BUT THE CASHIERS THEY DO HAVE...
THEY GET CHATTIER EVERY WEEK. THE CAT FOOD SETS THEM OFF.
ON AND ON ABOUT THEIR OWN PETS. ALL I CAN DO IS NOD.
MAYBE I'LL GO TO THAT GROCERY ON CARSON ONCE IN A WHILE TO CHANGE THINGS UP.
I THINK YOU SHOULD START LOOKING FOR A JOB.

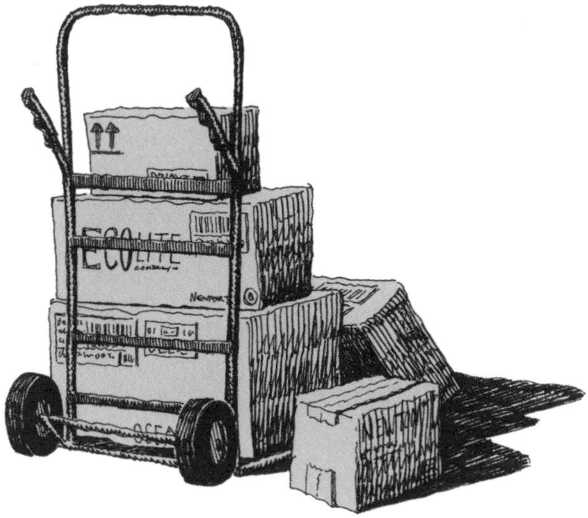
ECO LITE

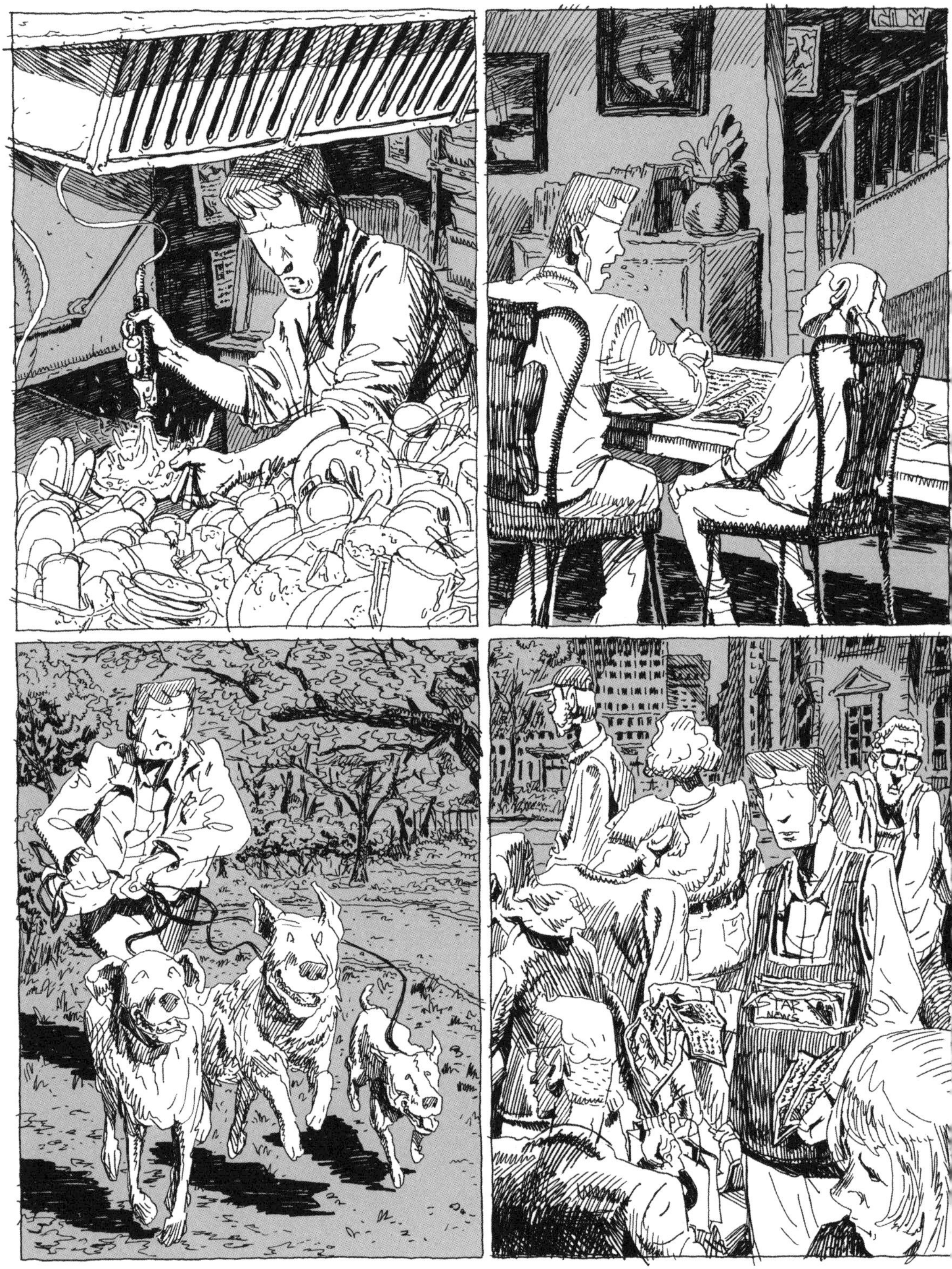
STAR NEWS

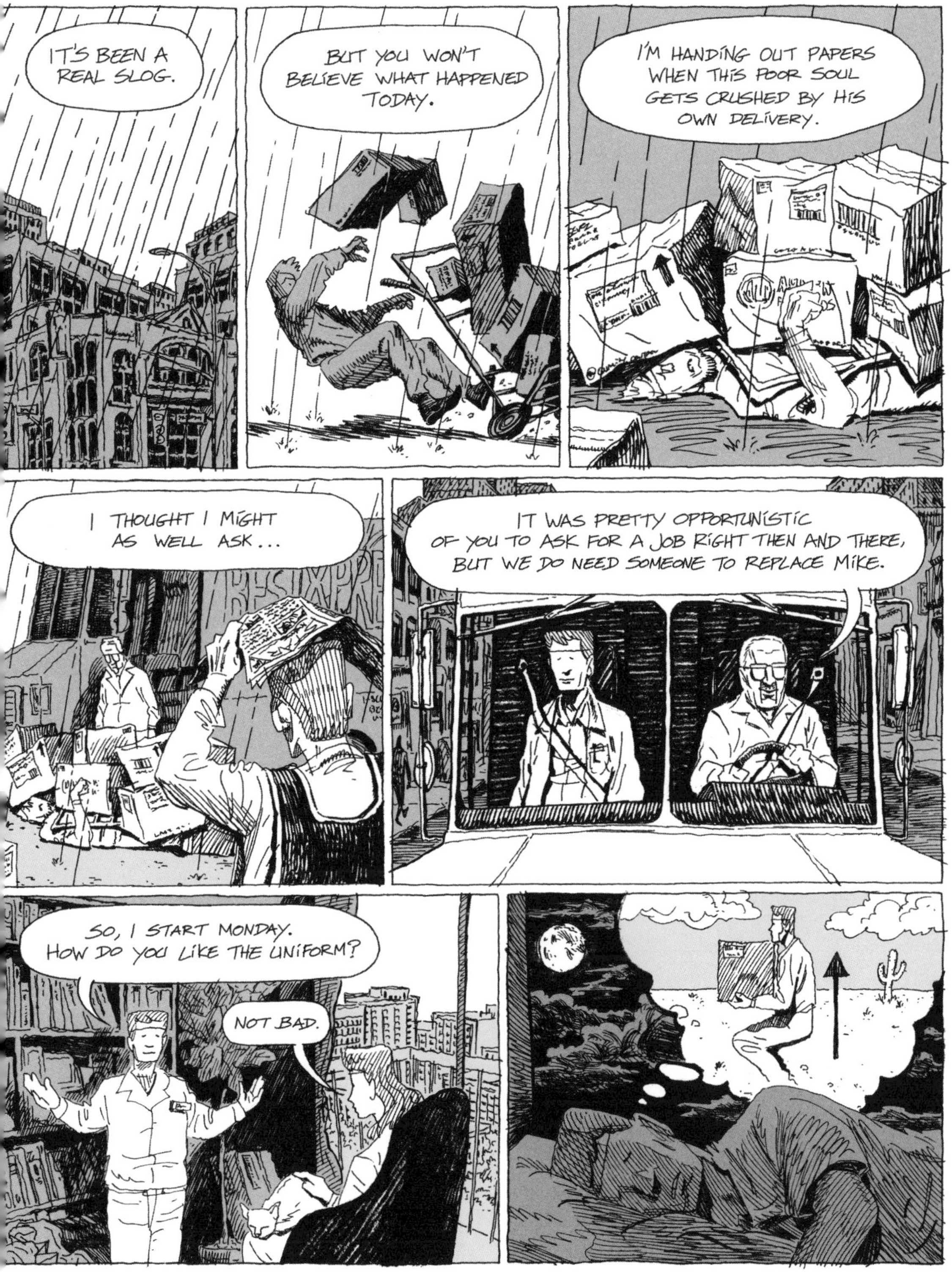
IT'S BEEN A REAL SLOG.
BUT YOU WON'T BELIEVE WHAT HAPPENED TODAY.
I'M HANDING OUT PAPERS WHEN THIS POOR SOUL GETS CRUSHED BY HIS OWN DELIVERY.
I THOUGHT I MIGHT AS WELL ASK...
IT WAS PRETTY OPPORTUNISTIC OF YOU TO ASK FOR A JOB RIGHT THEN AND THERE, BUT WE DO NEED SOMEONE TO REPLACE MIKE.
SO, I START MONDAY. HOW DO YOU LIKE THE UNIFORM?
NOT BAD.

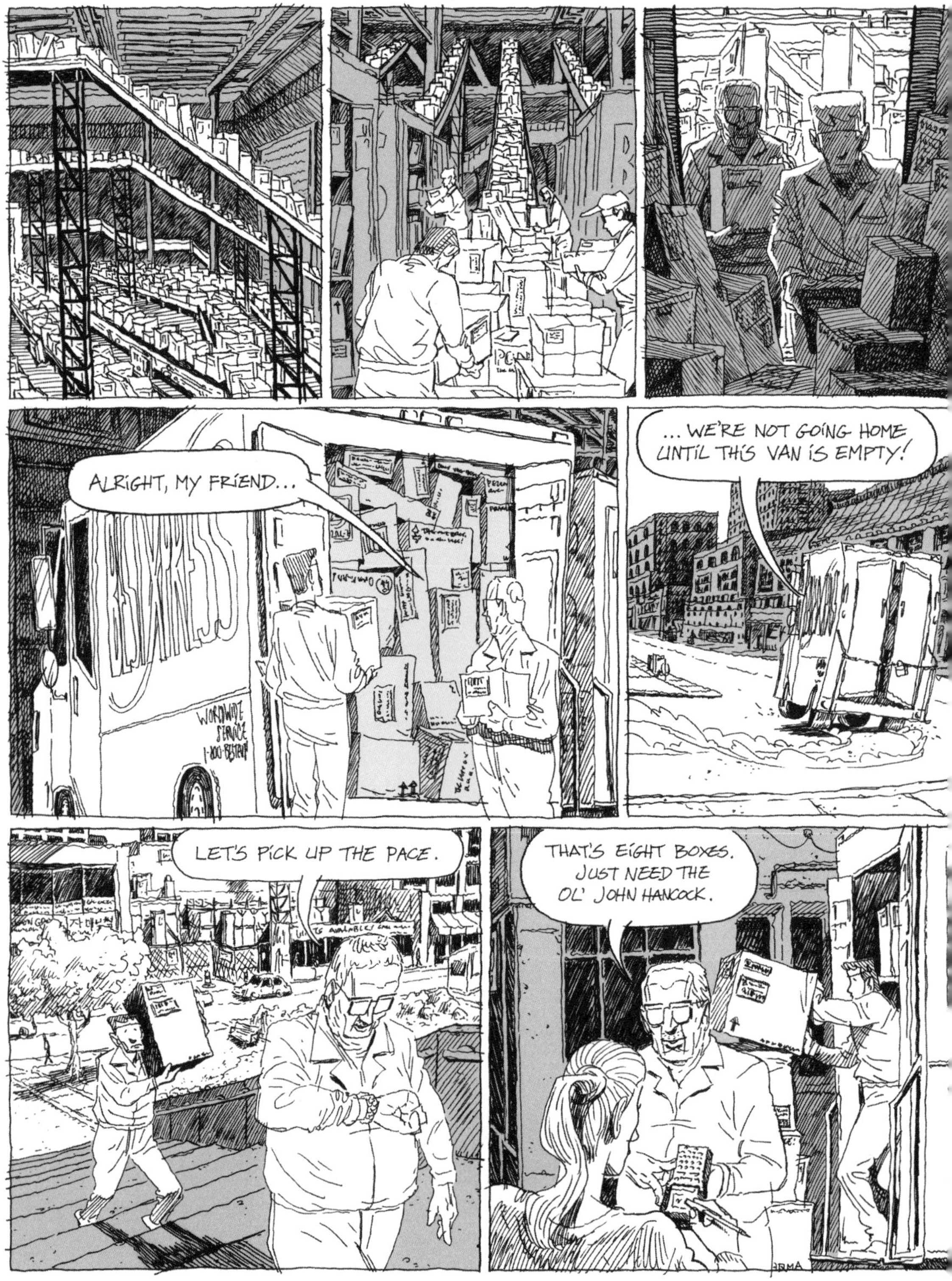
ALRIGHT, MY FRIEND...
... WE'RE NOT GOING HOME UNTIL THIS VAN IS EMPTY!
LET'S PICK UP THE PACE.
THAT'S EIGHT BOXES. JUST NEED THE OL' JOHN HANCOCK.

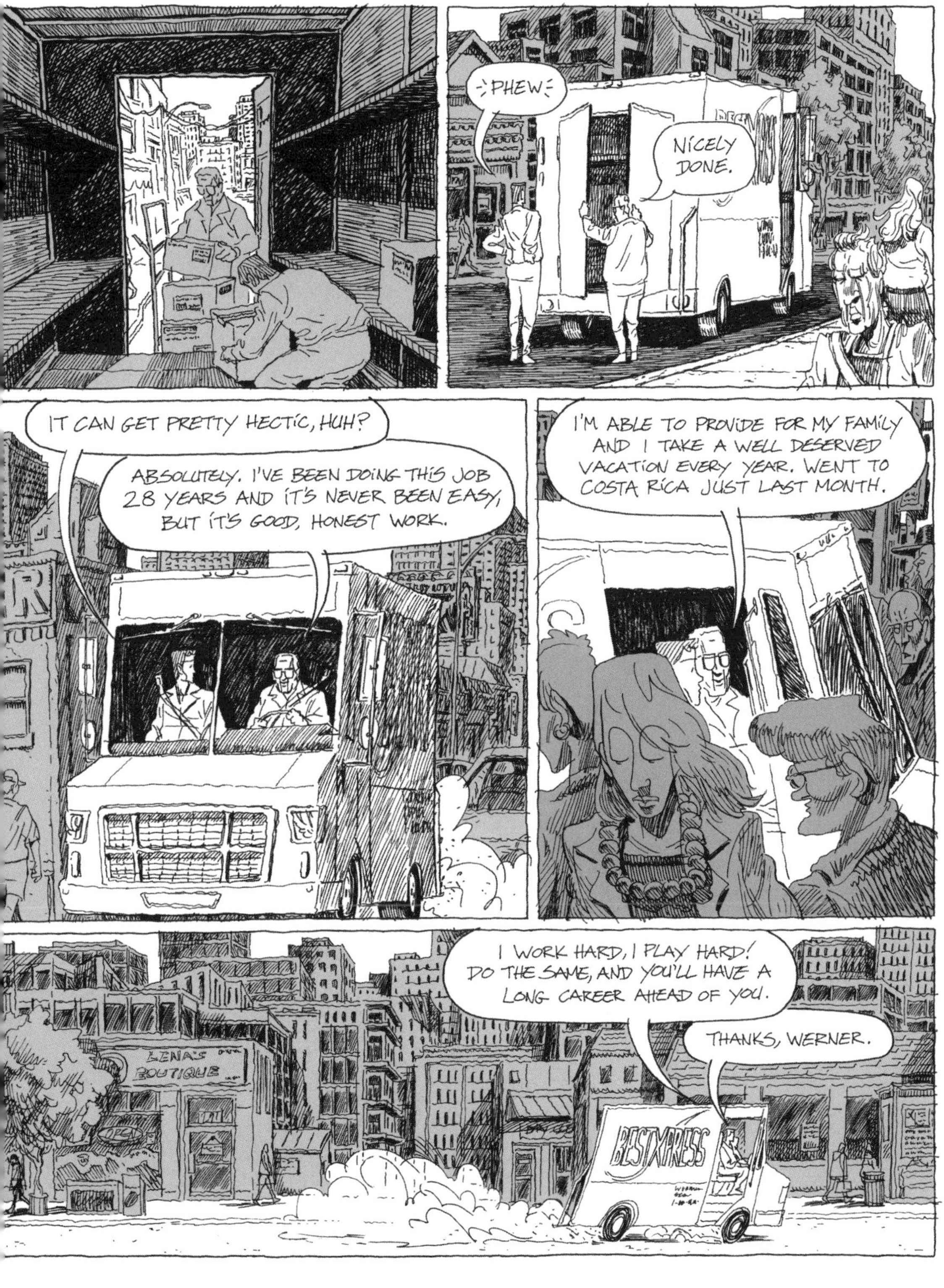
PHEW
NICELY DONE.
IT CAN GET PRETTY HECTIC, HUH?
ABSOLUTELY. I'VE BEEN DOING THIS JOB 28 YEARS AND IT'S NEVER BEEN EASY, BUT IT'S GOOD, HONEST WORK.
I'M ABLE TO PROVIDE FOR MY FAMILY AND I TAKE A WELL DESERVED VACATION EVERY YEAR. WENT TO COSTA RICA JUST LAST MONTH.
LENA'S BOUTIQUE
I WORK HARD, I PLAY HARD! DO THE SAME, AND YOU'LL HAVE A LONG CAREER AHEAD OF YOU.
THANKS, WERNER.
BESTXPRESS

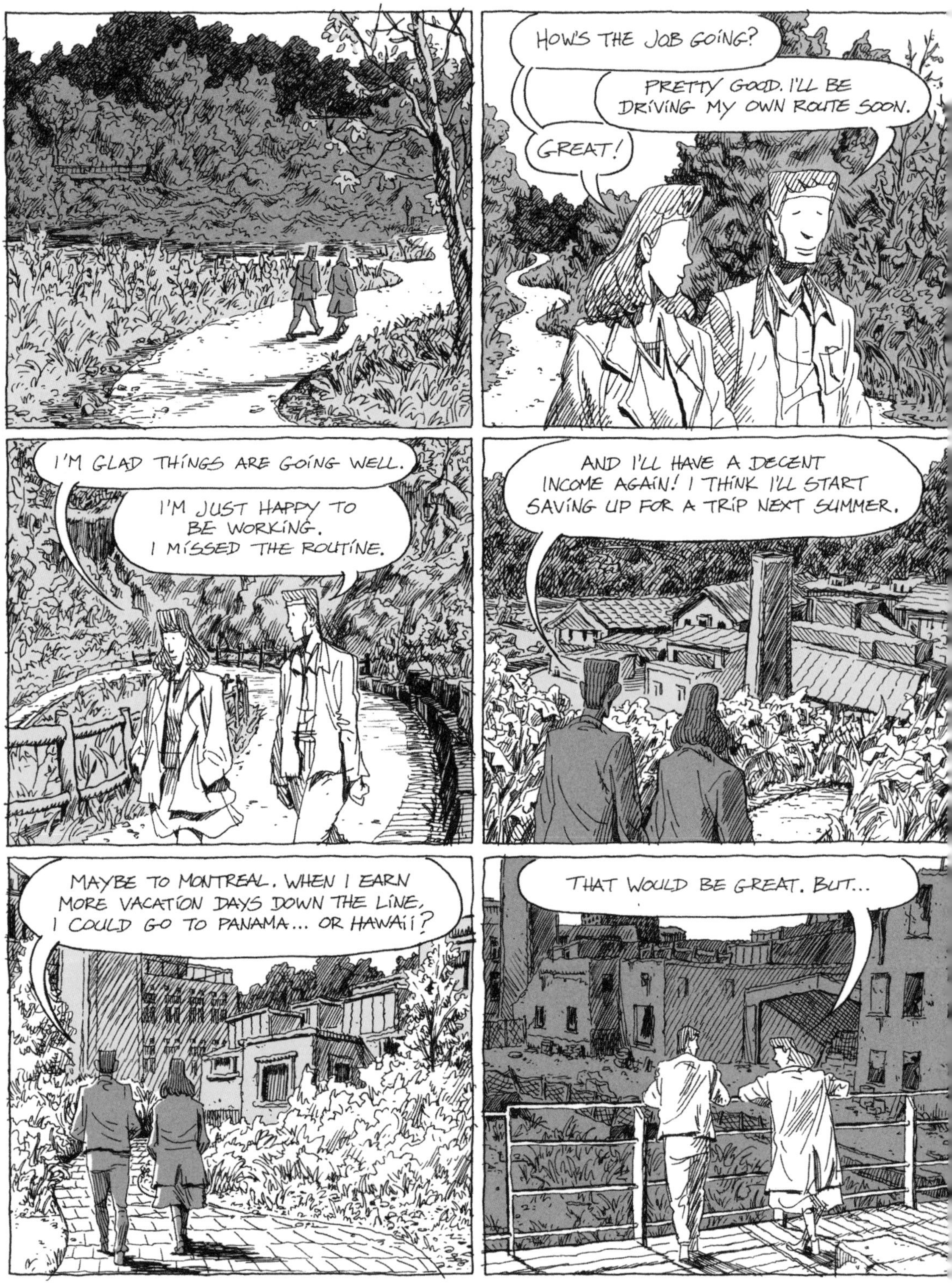
HOW'S THE JOB GOING?
PRETTY GOOD. I'LL BE DRIVING MY OWN ROUTE SOON.
GREAT!
I'M GLAD THINGS ARE GOING WELL.
I'M JUST HAPPY TO BE WORKING. I MISSED THE ROUTINE.
AND I'LL HAVE A DECENT INCOME AGAIN! I THINK I'LL START SAVING UP FOR A TRIP NEXT SUMMER.
MAYBE TO MONTREAL. WHEN I EARN MORE VACATION DAYS DOWN THE LINE, I COULD GO TO PANAMA... OR HAWAII?
THAT WOULD BE GREAT. BUT...

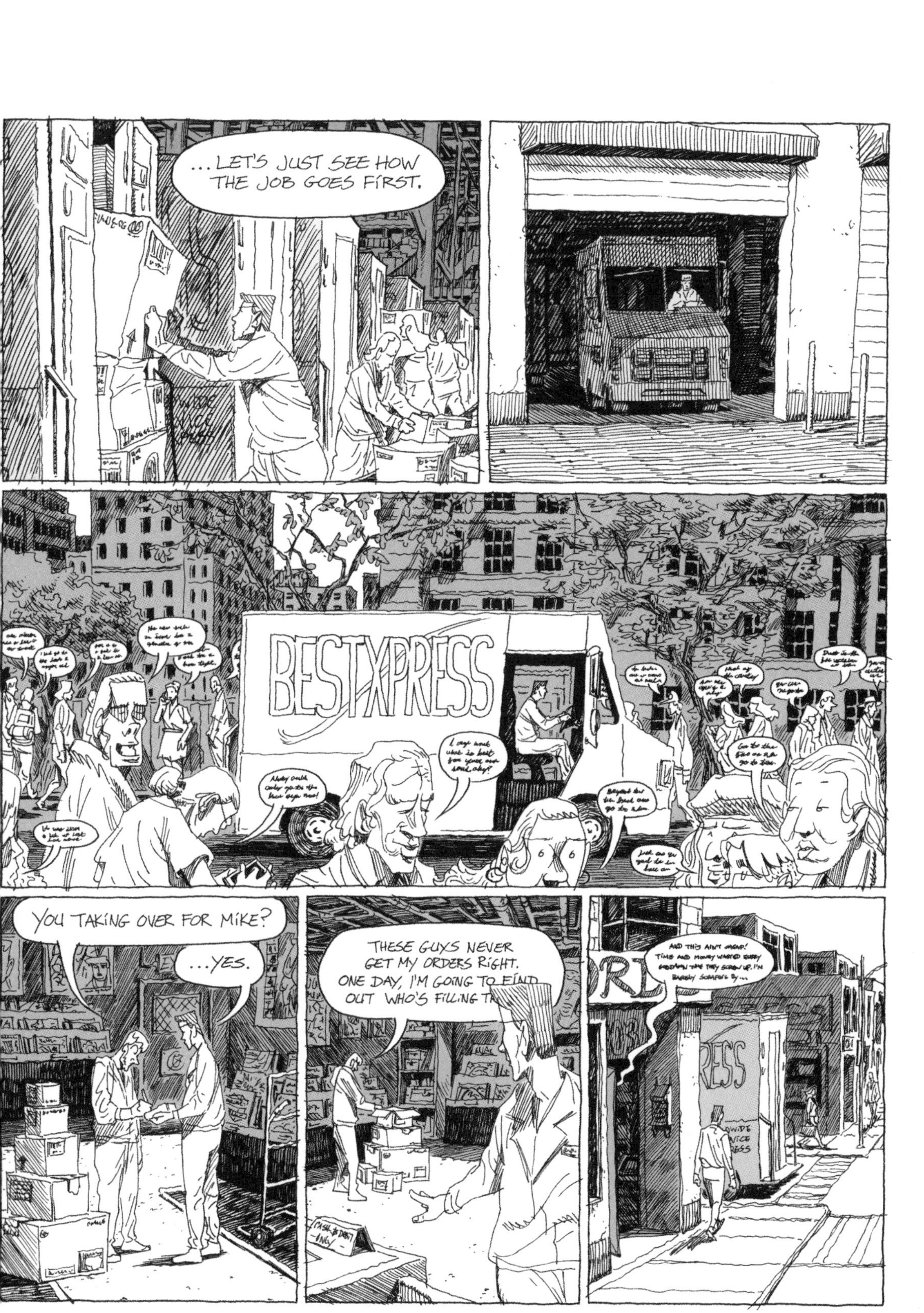
...LET'S JUST SEE HOW THE JOB GOES FIRST.
BESTXPRESS
YOU TAKING OVER FOR MIKE?
...YES.
THESE GUYS NEVER GET MY ORDERS RIGHT. ONE DAY, I'M GOING TO FIND OUT WHO'S FILLING T
AND THIS AIN'T CHEAP! TIME AND MONEY WASTED EVERY GODDAMN TIME THEY SCREW UP. I'M BARELY SCRAPING BY...

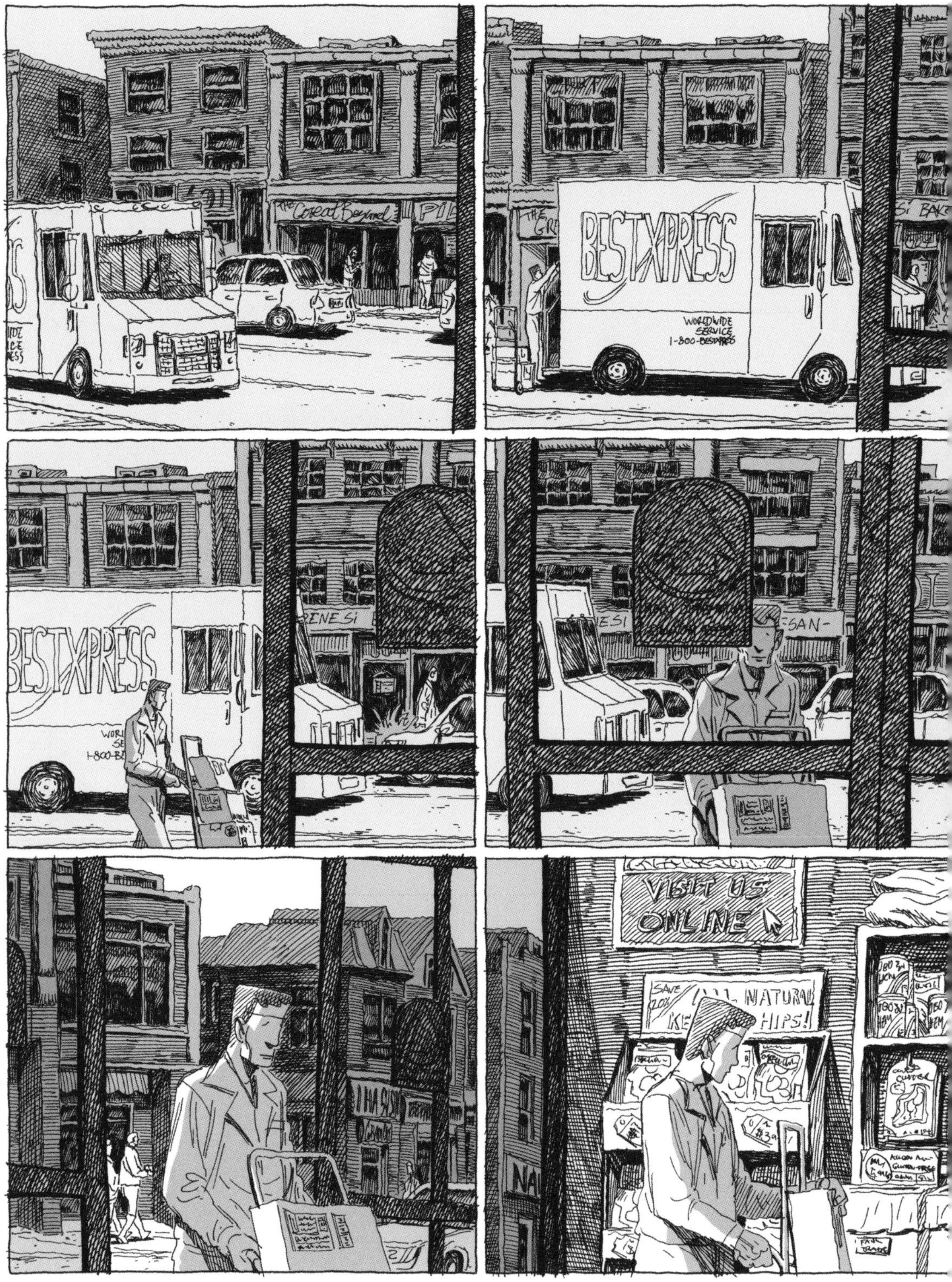
BESTXPRESS
WORLDWIDE SERVICE 1-800-BESTXPRESS
BESTXPRESS
VISIT US ONLINE
SAVE 20%
ALL NATURAL

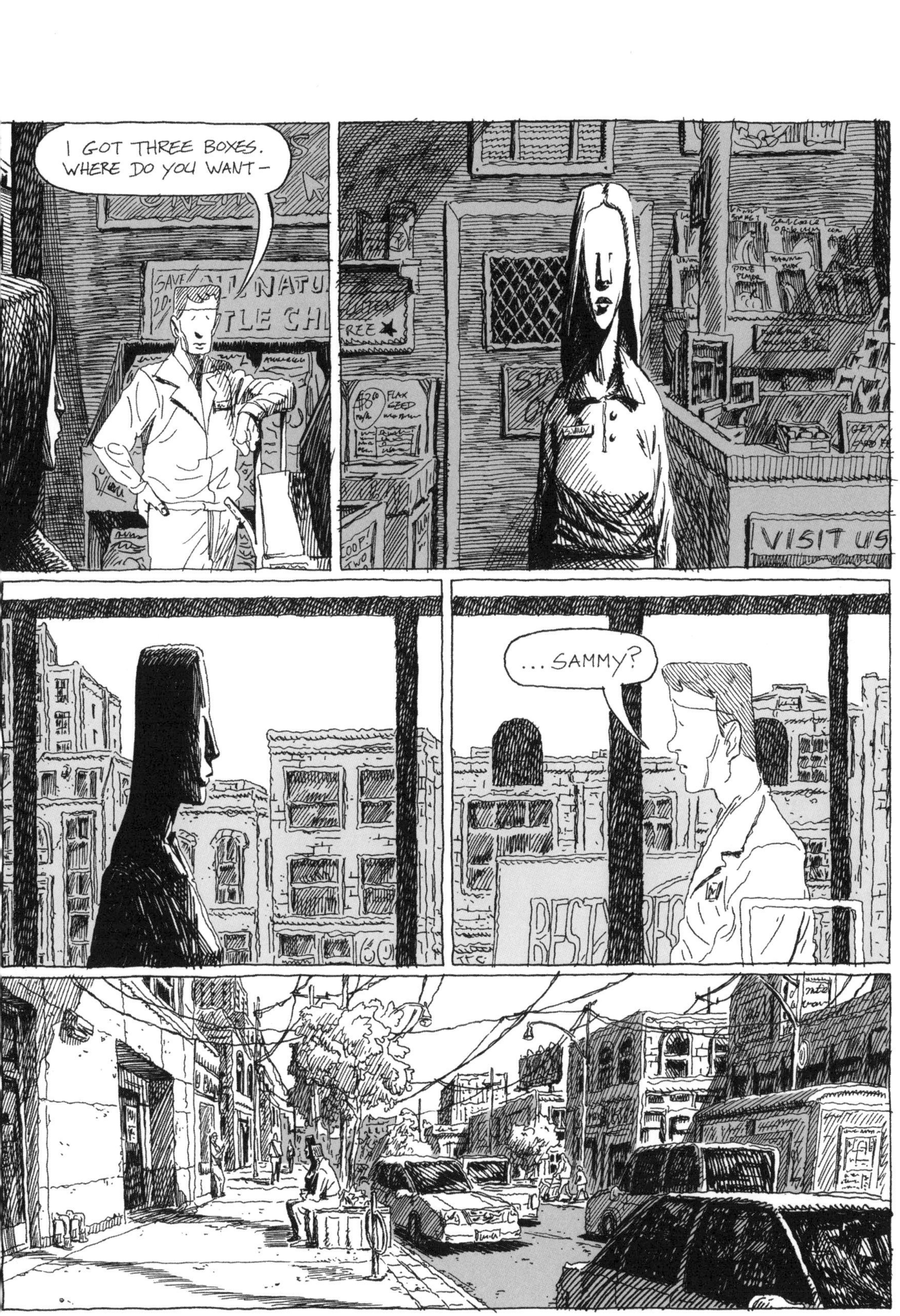
I GOT THREE BOXES. WHERE DO YOU WANT–
...SAMMY?

I COULDN'T BELIEVE MY EYES!

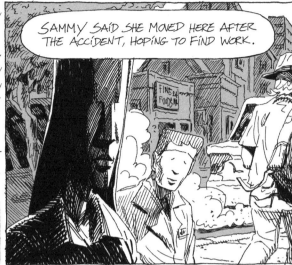

SAMMY SAID SHE MOVED HERE AFTER THE ACCIDENT, HOPING TO FIND WORK.

I ASKED HER WHAT HAPPENED TO EVERYONE AFTER THE TOWN WAS EVACUATED. IF THEY FOUND NEW HOMES, NEW JOBS...

BUT SHE HASN'T BEEN IN CONTACT WITH ANYONE SINCE THEN.

I TOLD HER WE SHOULD GRAB A DRINK SOMETIME AND CATCH UP. SHE SEEMED UP FOR IT.

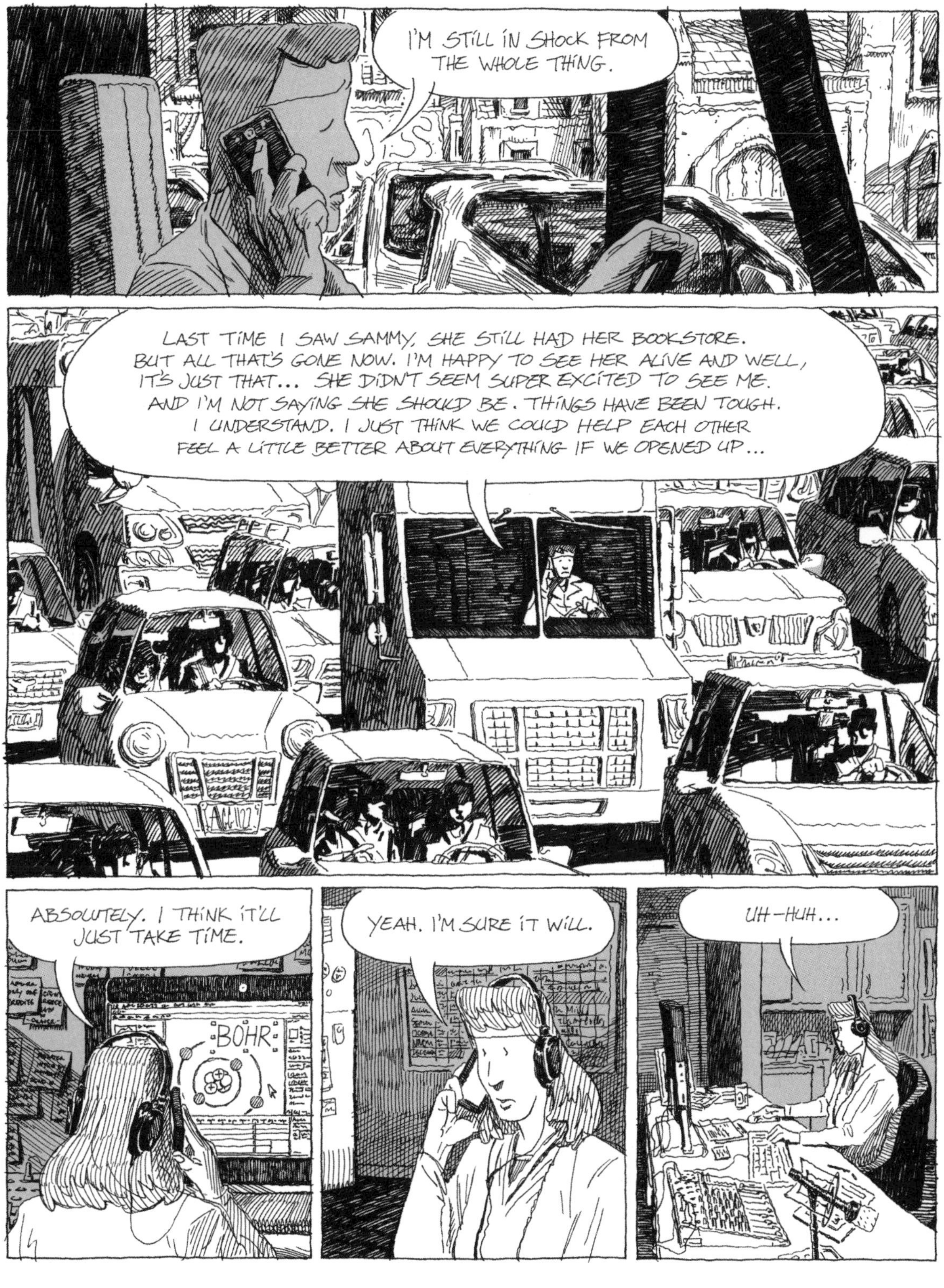
I'M STILL IN SHOCK FROM THE WHOLE THING.
LAST TIME I SAW SAMMY, SHE STILL HAD HER BOOKSTORE. BUT ALL THAT'S GONE NOW. I'M HAPPY TO SEE HER ALIVE AND WELL, IT'S JUST THAT... SHE DIDN'T SEEM SUPER EXCITED TO SEE ME. AND I'M NOT SAYING SHE SHOULD BE. THINGS HAVE BEEN TOUGH. I UNDERSTAND. I JUST THINK WE COULD HELP EACH OTHER FEEL A LITTLE BETTER ABOUT EVERYTHING IF WE OPENED UP...
ABSOLUTELY. I THINK IT'LL JUST TAKE TIME.
BOHR
YEAH. I'M SURE IT WILL.
UH-HUH...

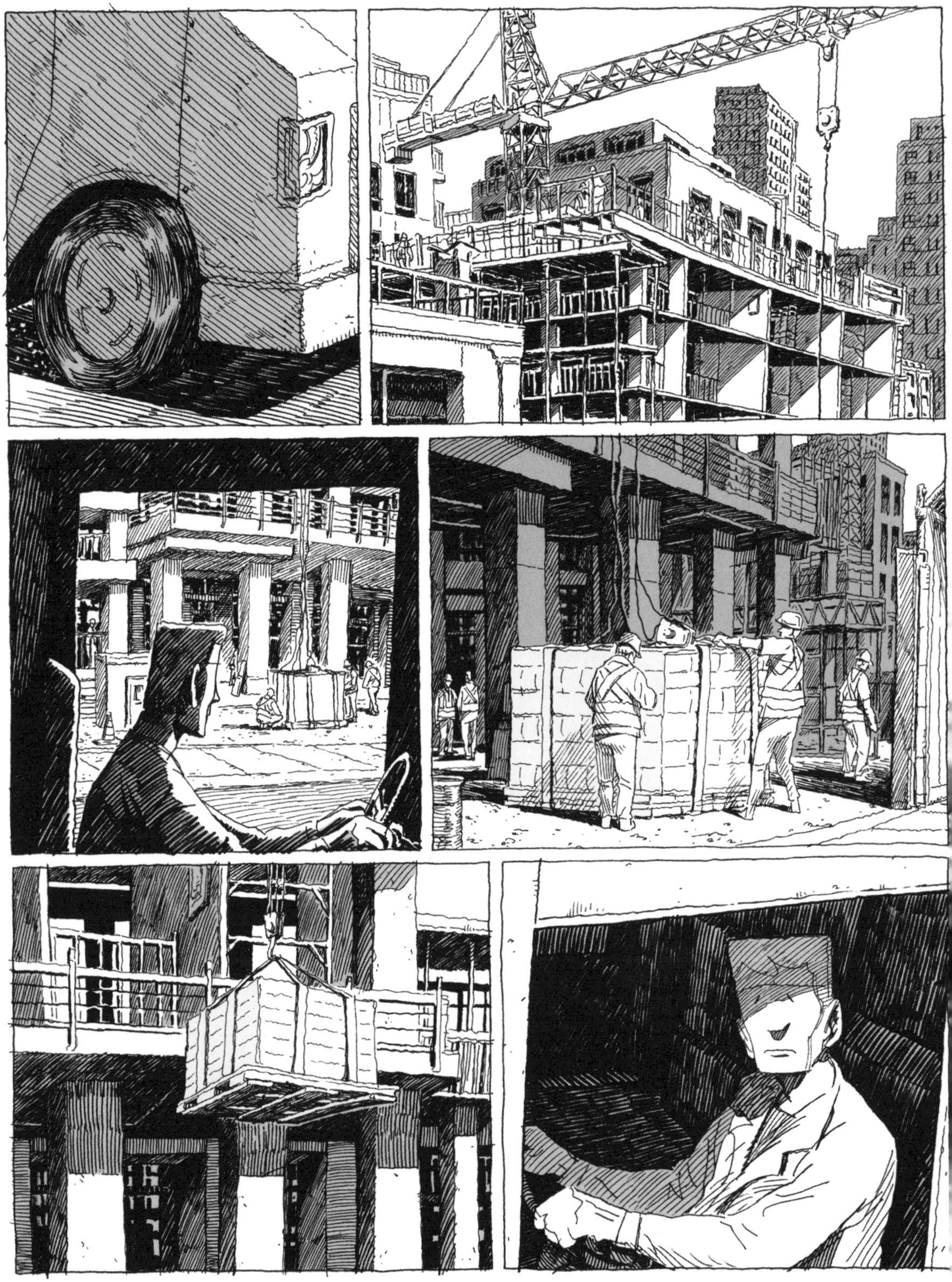

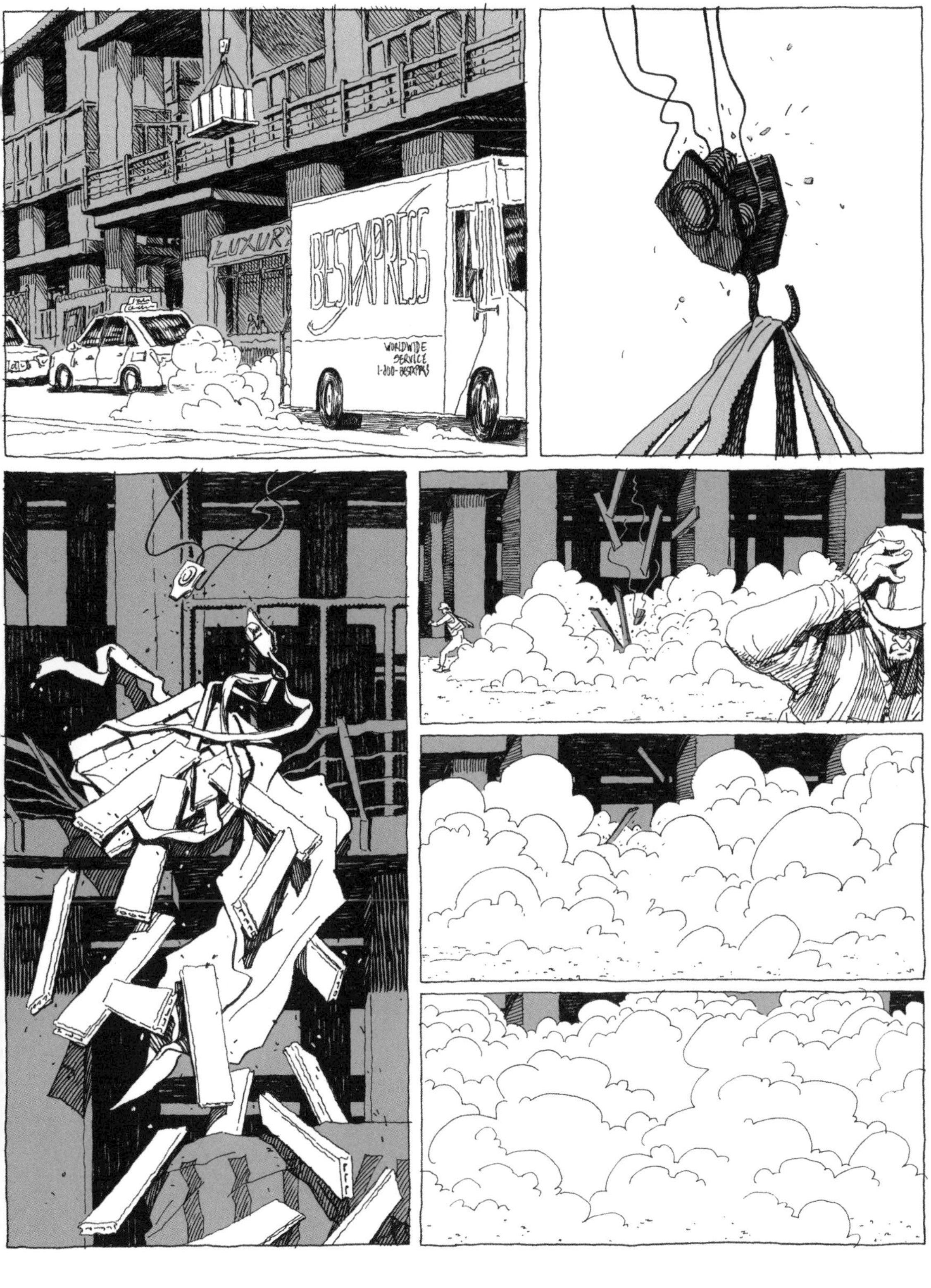
LUXURY
BESTXPRESS
WORLDWIDE SERVICE 1-800-BESTXPRS

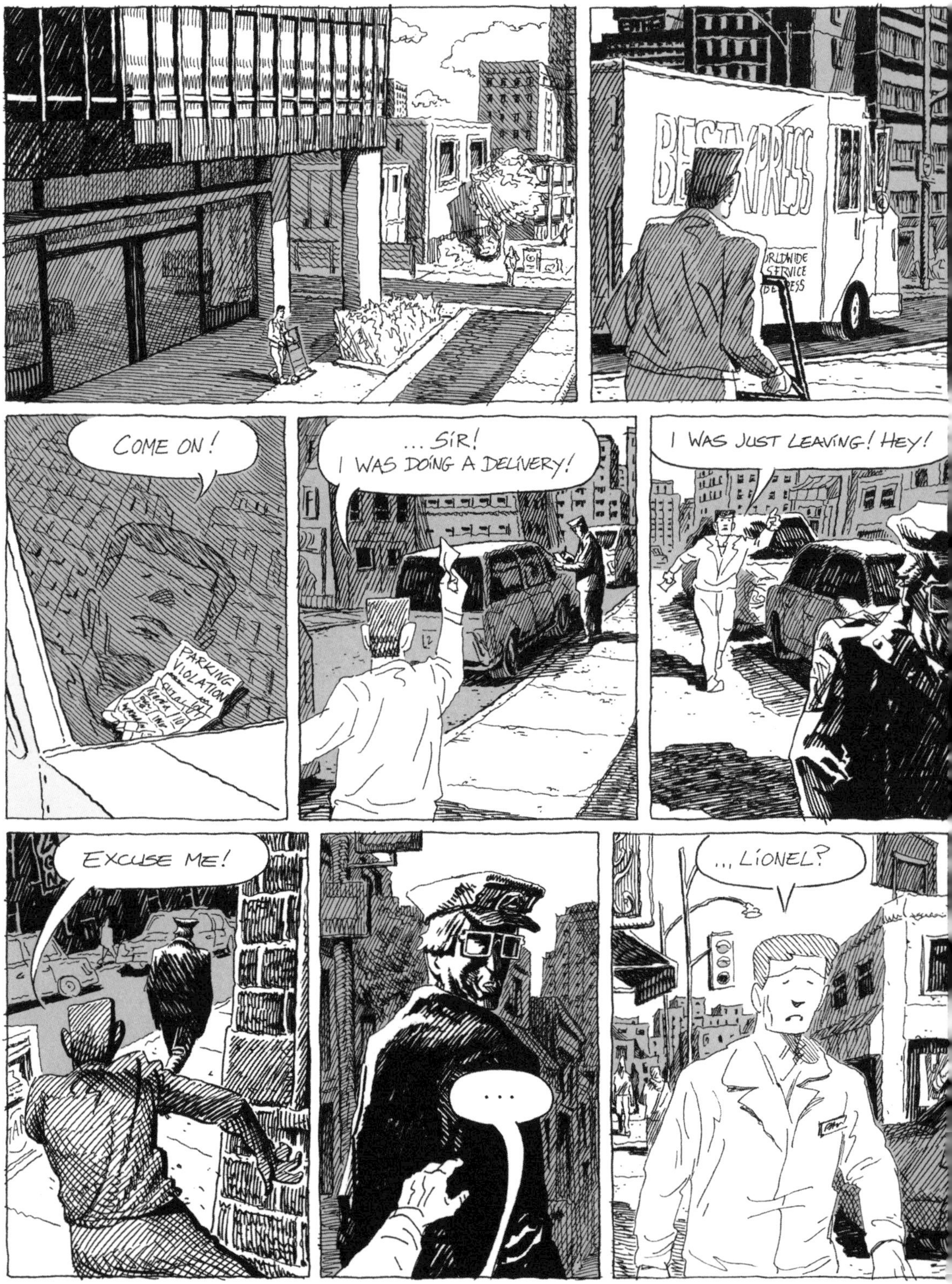
PARKING VIOLATION
COME ON!
... SIR!
I WAS DOING A DELIVERY!
I WAS JUST LEAVING! HEY!
EXCUSE ME!
...
... LIONEL?

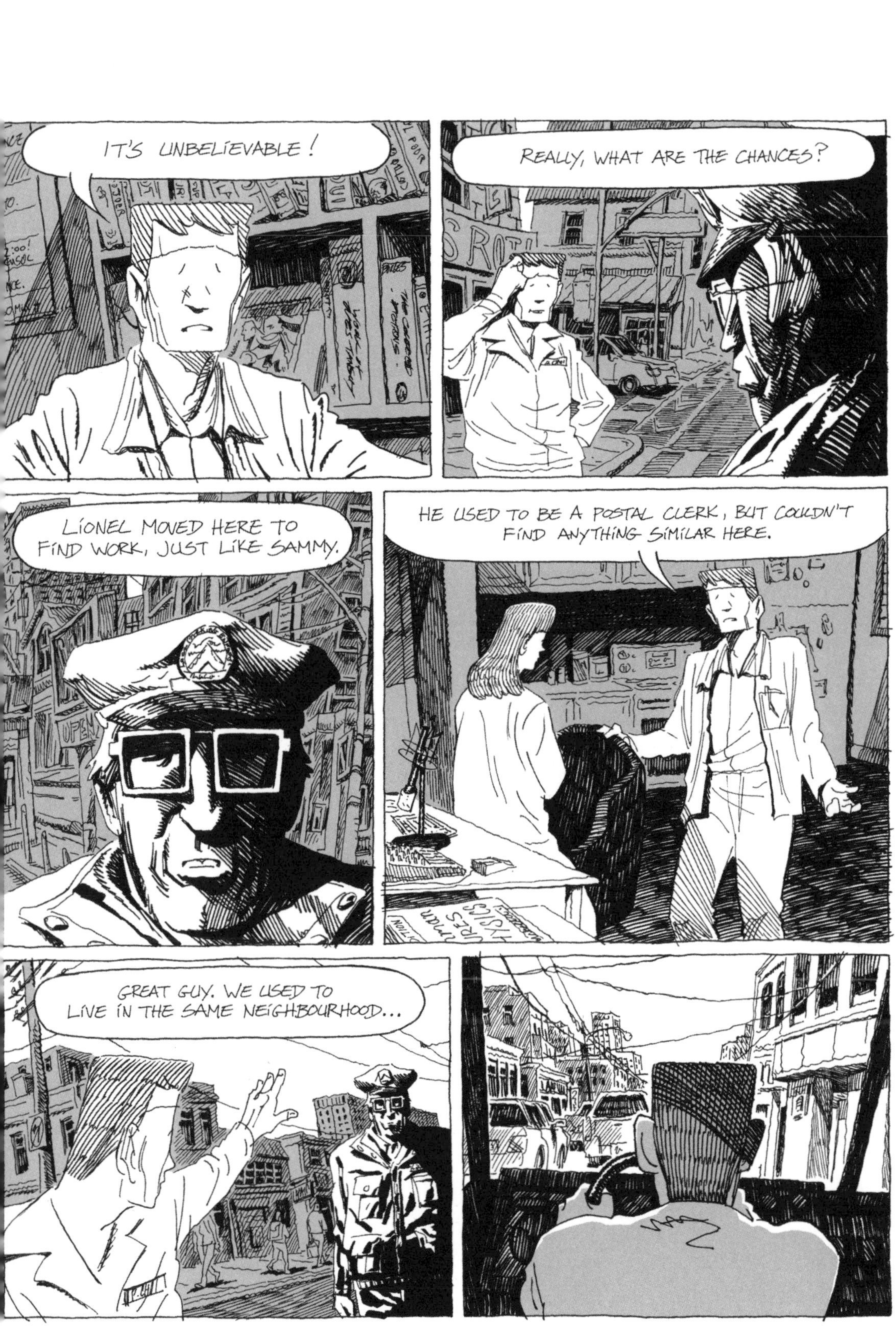
IT'S UNBELIEVABLE!
REALLY, WHAT ARE THE CHANCES?
LIONEL MOVED HERE TO FIND WORK, JUST LIKE SAMMY.
HE USED TO BE A POSTAL CLERK, BUT COULDN'T FIND ANYTHING SIMILAR HERE.
GREAT GUY. WE USED TO LIVE IN THE SAME NEIGHBOURHOOD...

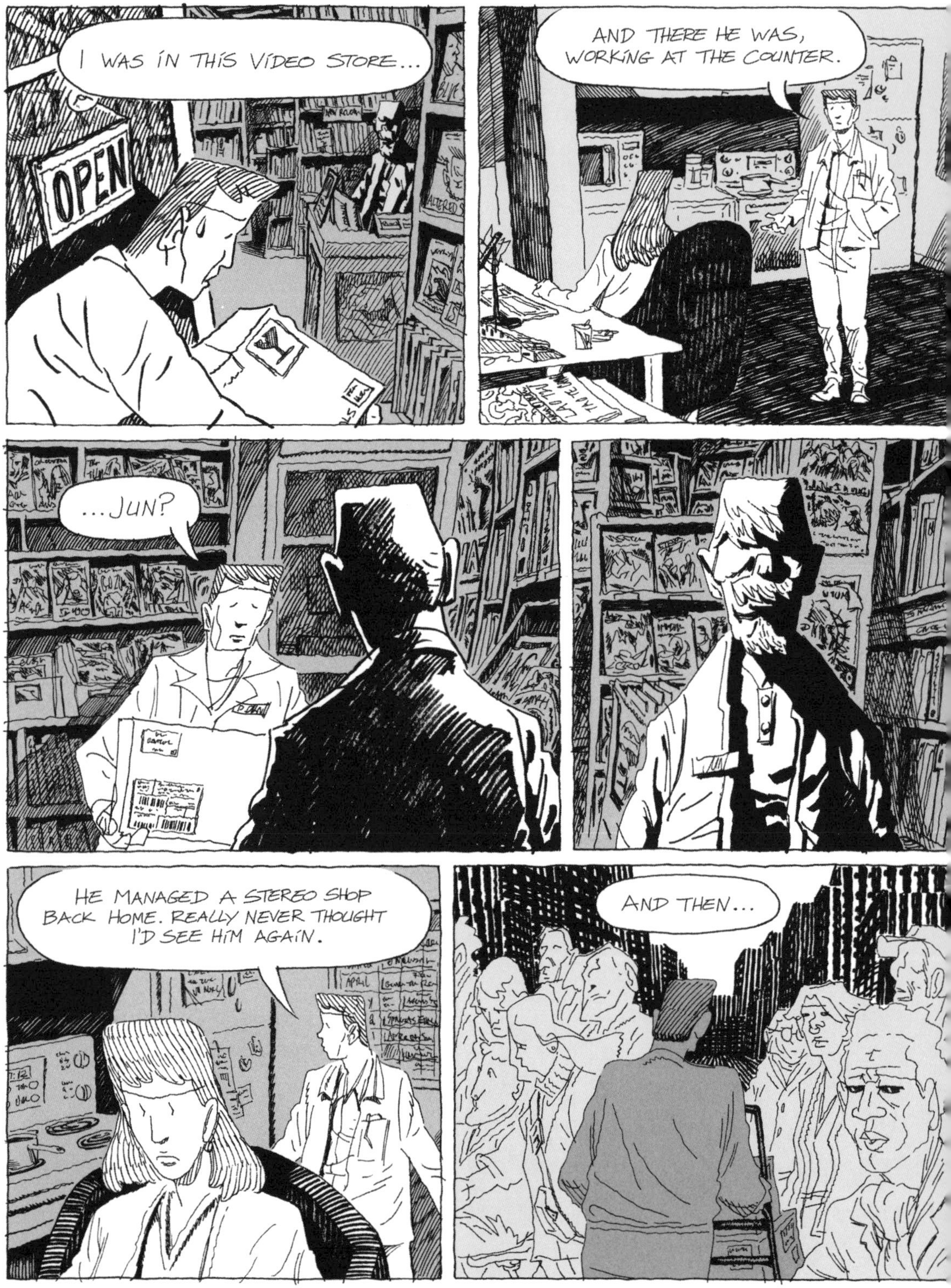
I WAS IN THIS VIDEO STORE...
OPEN
AND THERE HE WAS, WORKING AT THE COUNTER.
...JUN?
HE MANAGED A STEREO SHOP BACK HOME. REALLY NEVER THOUGHT I'D SEE HIM AGAIN.
AND THEN...

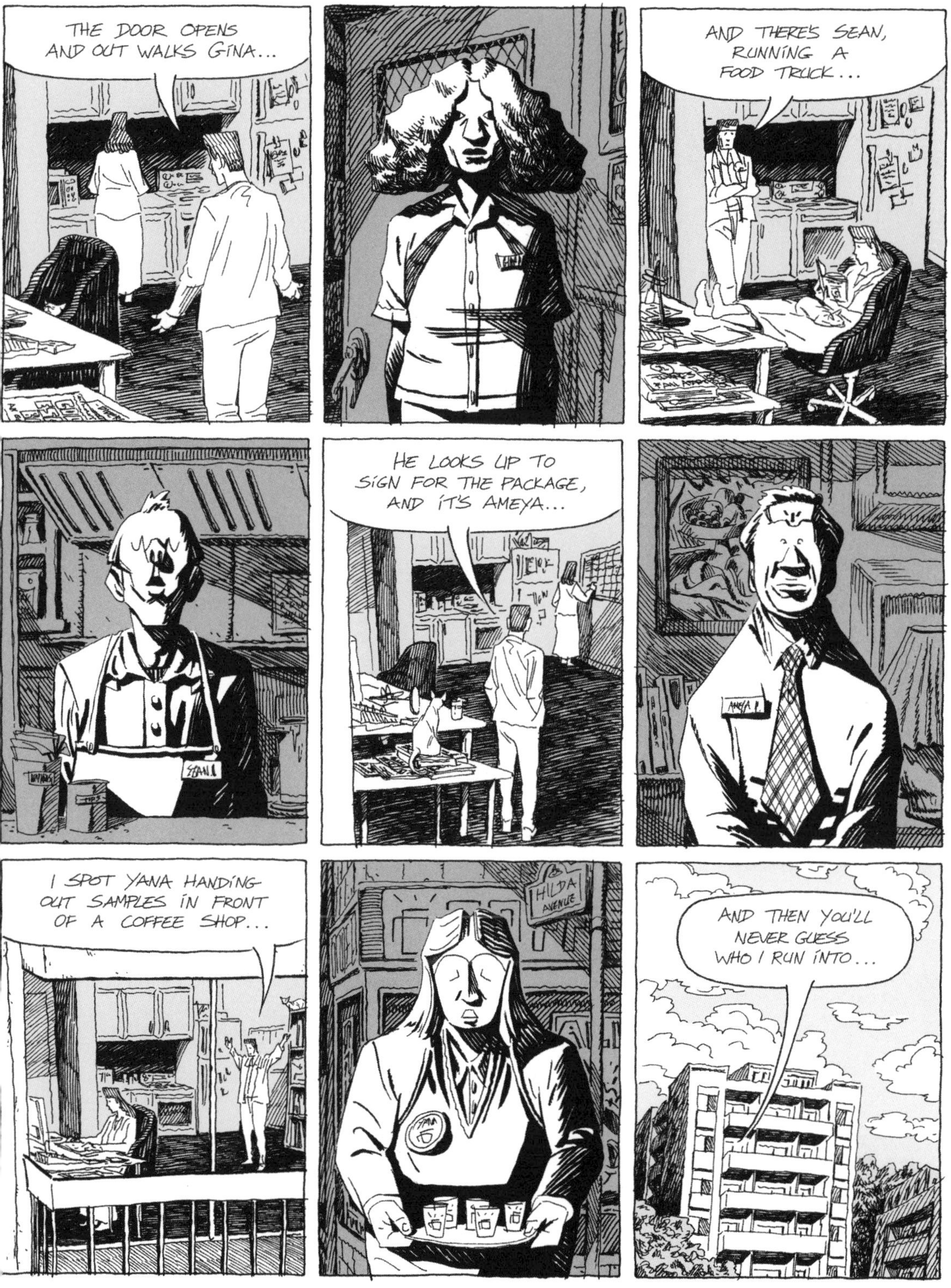
THE DOOR OPENS AND OUT WALKS GINA...
AND THERE'S SEAN, RUNNING A FOOD TRUCK...
HE LOOKS UP TO SIGN FOR THE PACKAGE, AND IT'S AMEYA...
I SPOT YANA HANDING OUT SAMPLES IN FRONT OF A COFFEE SHOP...
HILDA AVENUE
AND THEN YOU'LL NEVER GUESS WHO I RUN INTO...

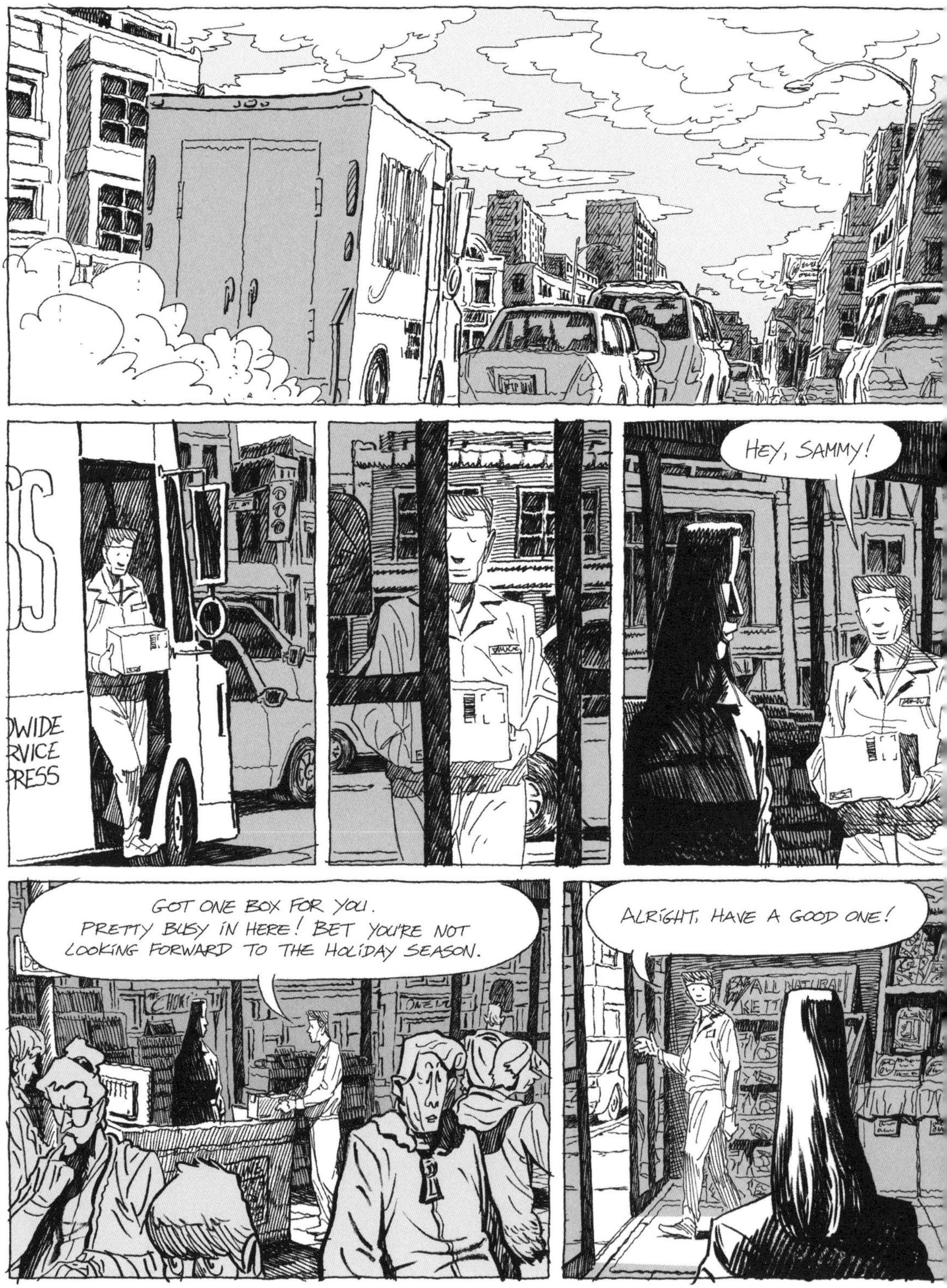

DWIDE
RVICE
PRESS
HEY, SAMMY!
GOT ONE BOX FOR YOU. PRETTY BUSY IN HERE! BET YOU'RE NOT LOOKING FORWARD TO THE HOLIDAY SEASON.
ALRIGHT, HAVE A GOOD ONE!

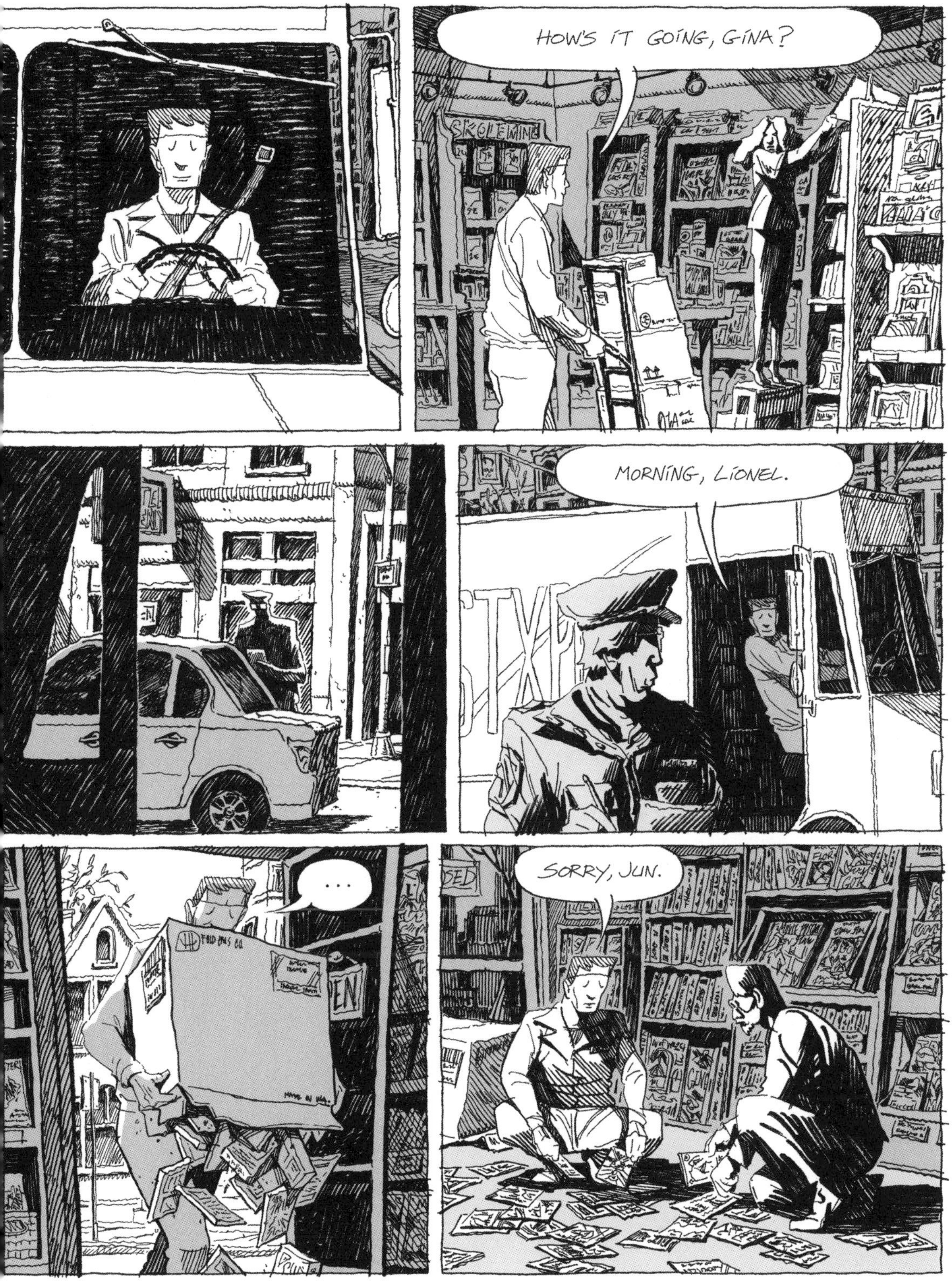
HOW'S IT GOING, GINA?
MORNING, LIONEL.
. . .
SORRY, JUN.

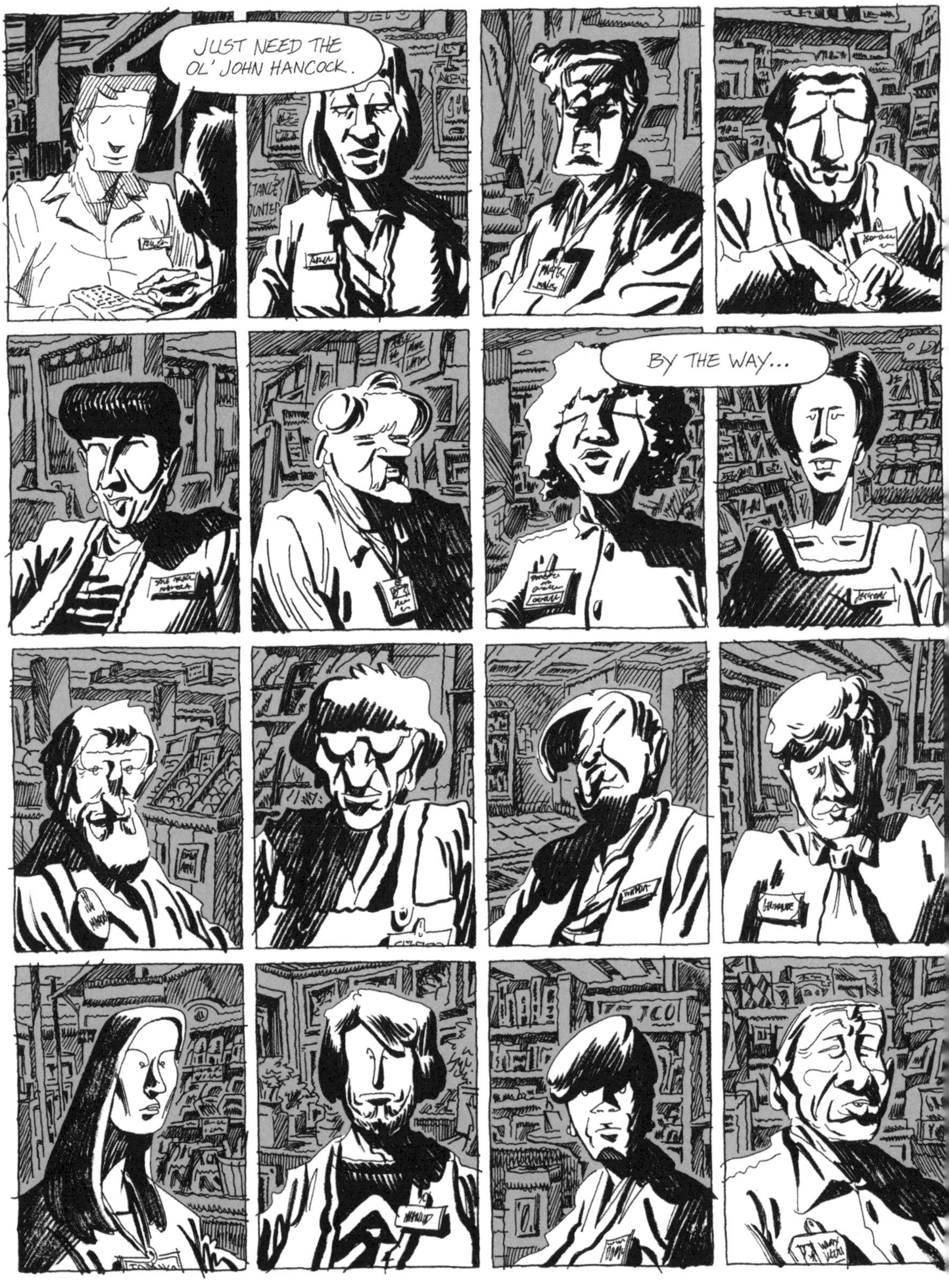
JUST NEED THE OL' JOHN HANCOCK.
BY THE WAY...

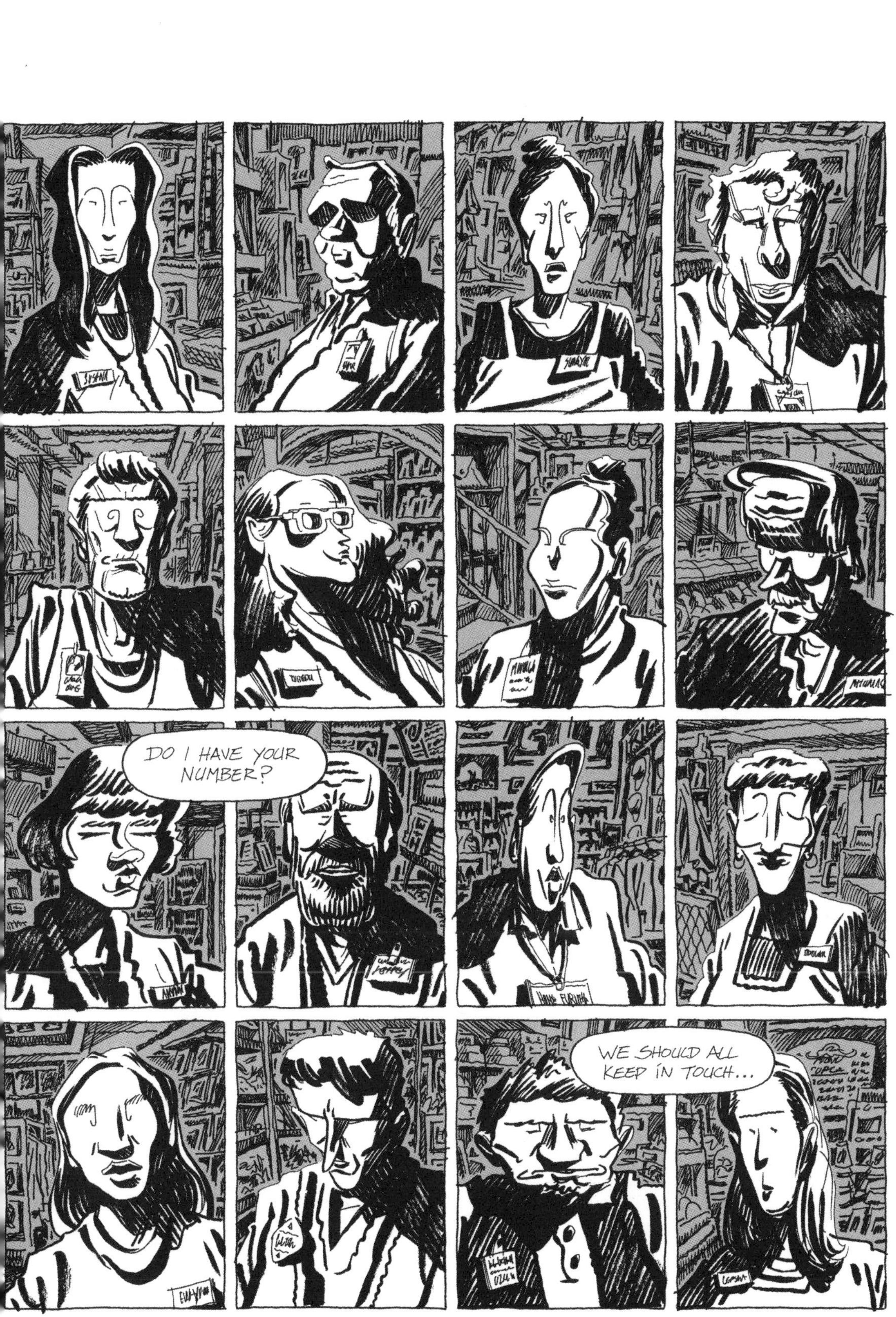
DO I HAVE YOUR NUMBER?
WE SHOULD ALL KEEP IN TOUCH...

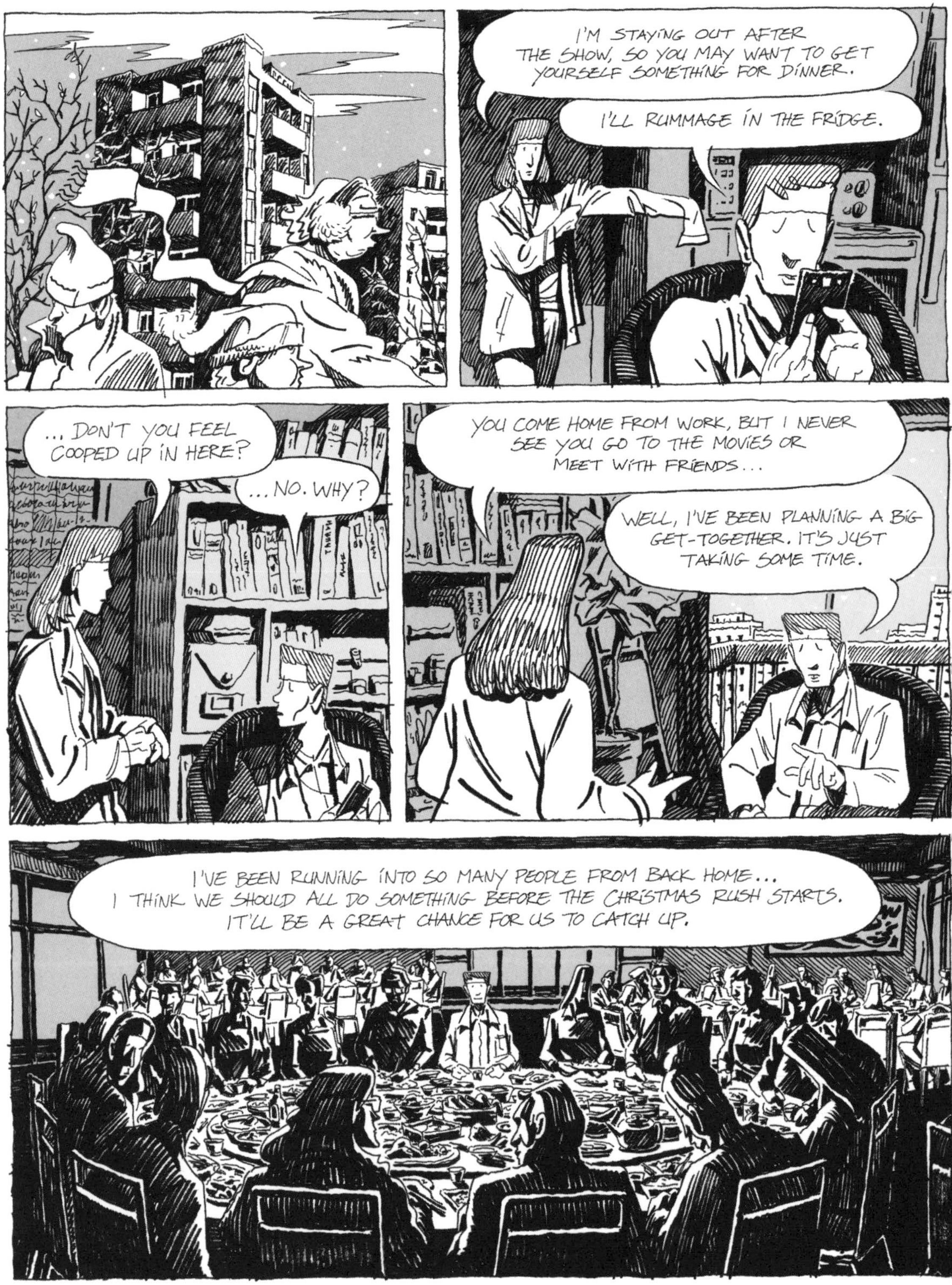
I'M STAYING OUT AFTER THE SHOW, SO YOU MAY WANT TO GET YOURSELF SOMETHING FOR DINNER.
I'LL RUMMAGE IN THE FRIDGE.
... DON'T YOU FEEL COOPED UP IN HERE?
... NO. WHY?
YOU COME HOME FROM WORK, BUT I NEVER SEE YOU GO TO THE MOVIES OR MEET WITH FRIENDS...
WELL, I'VE BEEN PLANNING A BIG GET-TOGETHER. IT'S JUST TAKING SOME TIME.
I'VE BEEN RUNNING INTO SO MANY PEOPLE FROM BACK HOME... I THINK WE SHOULD ALL DO SOMETHING BEFORE THE CHRISTMAS RUSH STARTS. IT'LL BE A GREAT CHANCE FOR US TO CATCH UP.

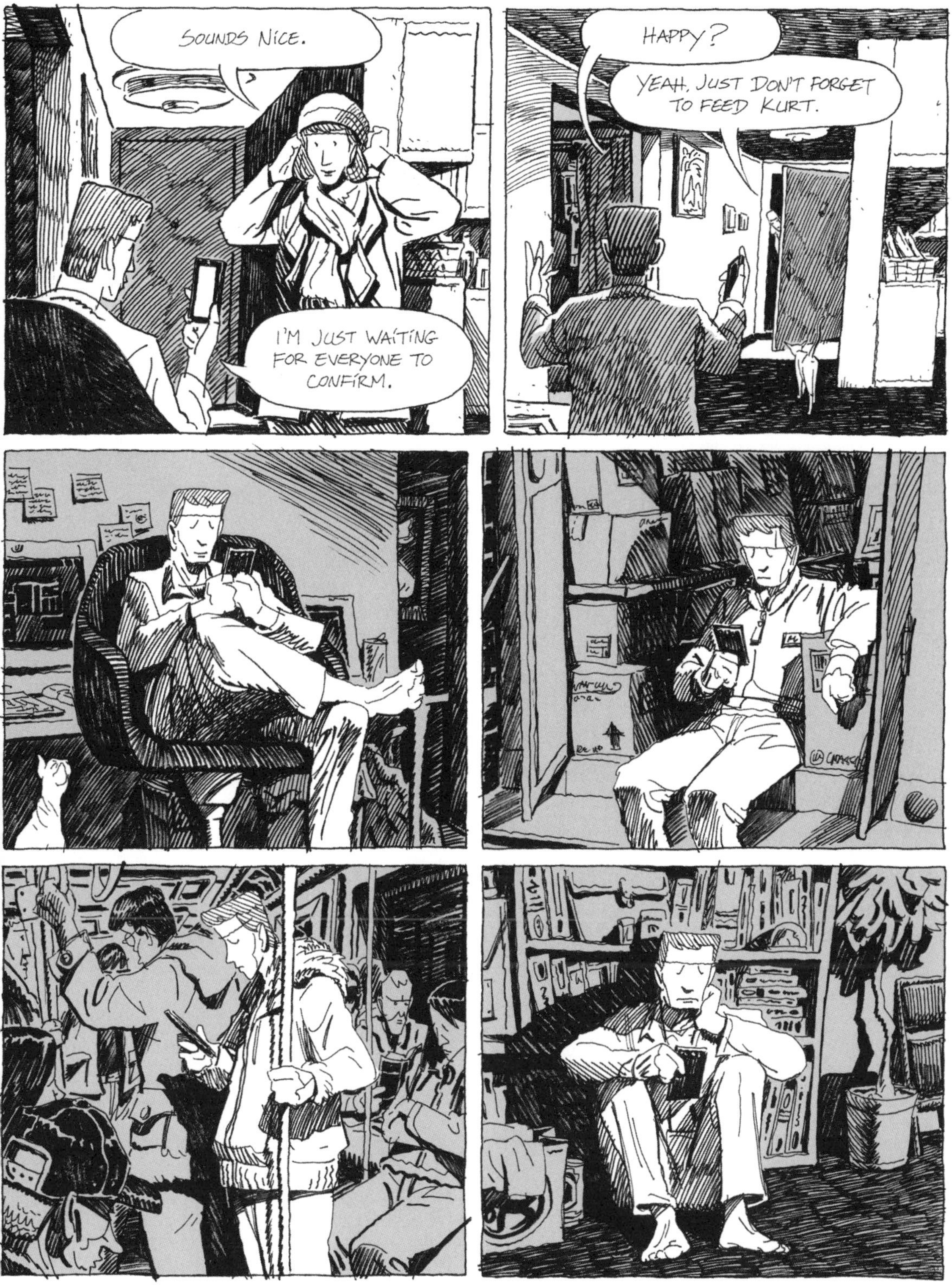
SOUNDS NICE.
I'M JUST WAITING FOR EVERYONE TO CONFIRM.
HAPPY?
YEAH, JUST DON'T FORGET TO FEED KURT.

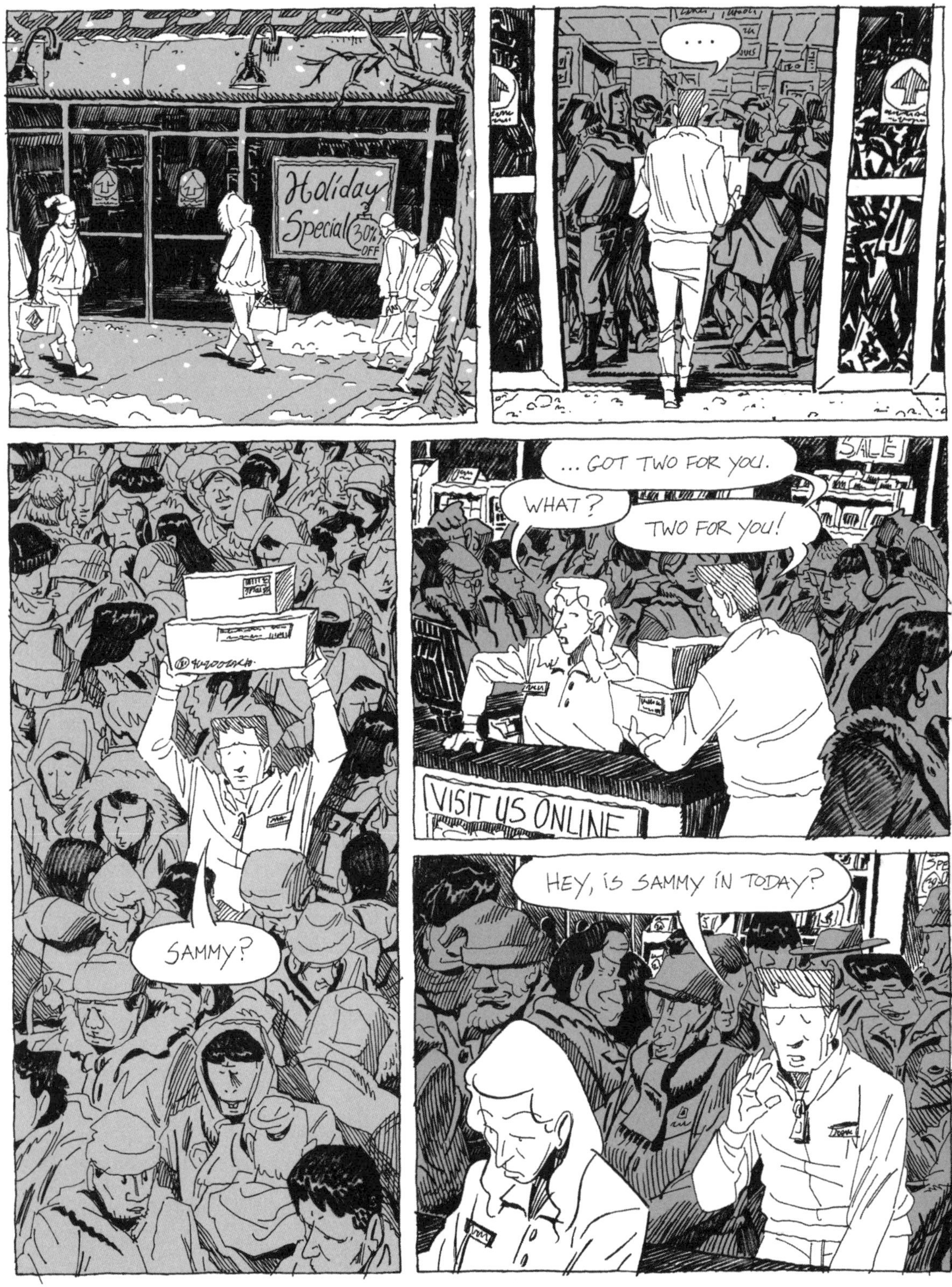
Holiday
Special
30% OFF
...
SAMMY?
SALE
... GOT TWO FOR YOU.
WHAT?
TWO FOR YOU!
VISIT US ONLINE
HEY, IS SAMMY IN TODAY?

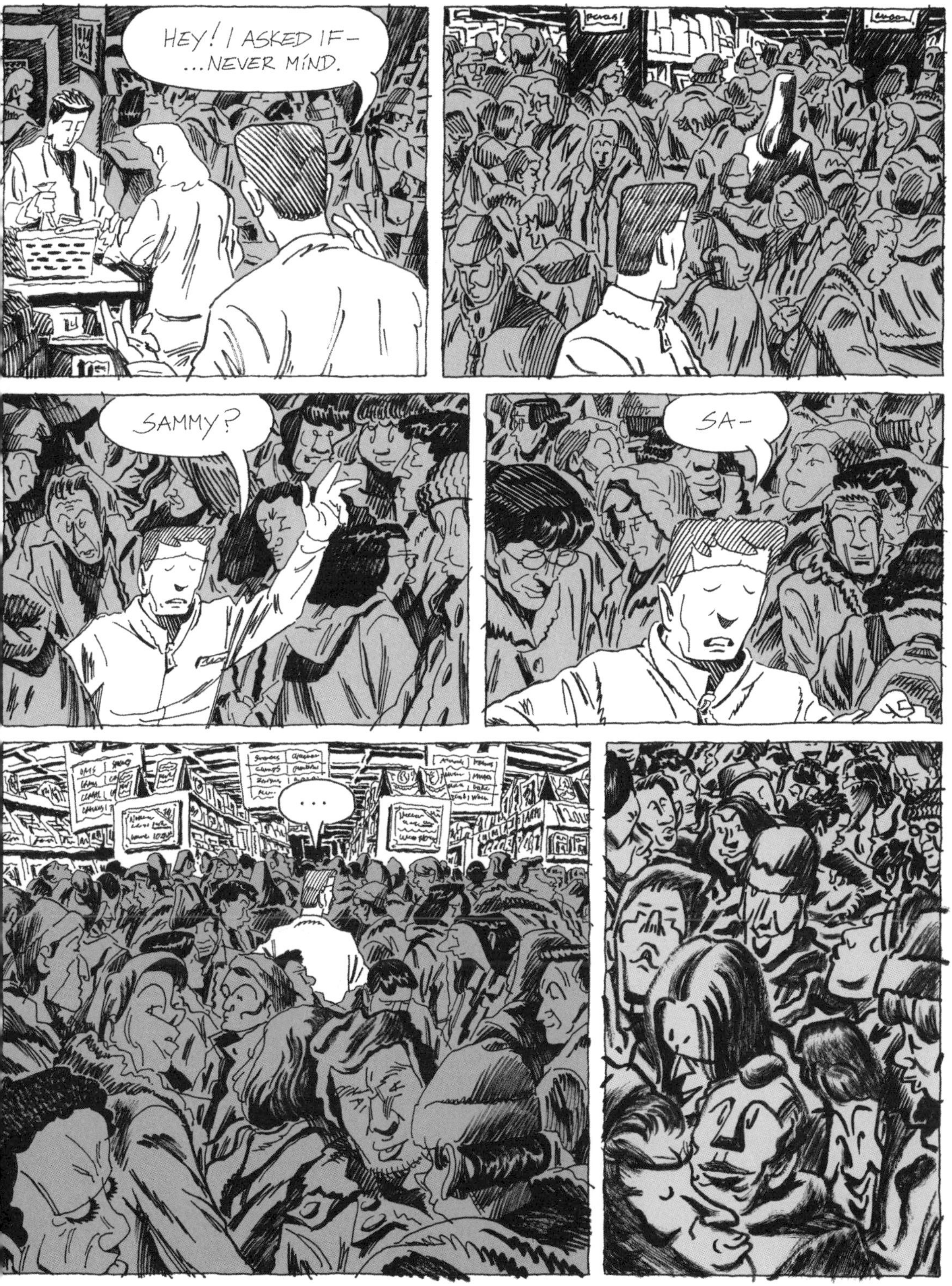
HEY! I ASKED IF—
...NEVER MIND.
SAMMY?
SA—
...

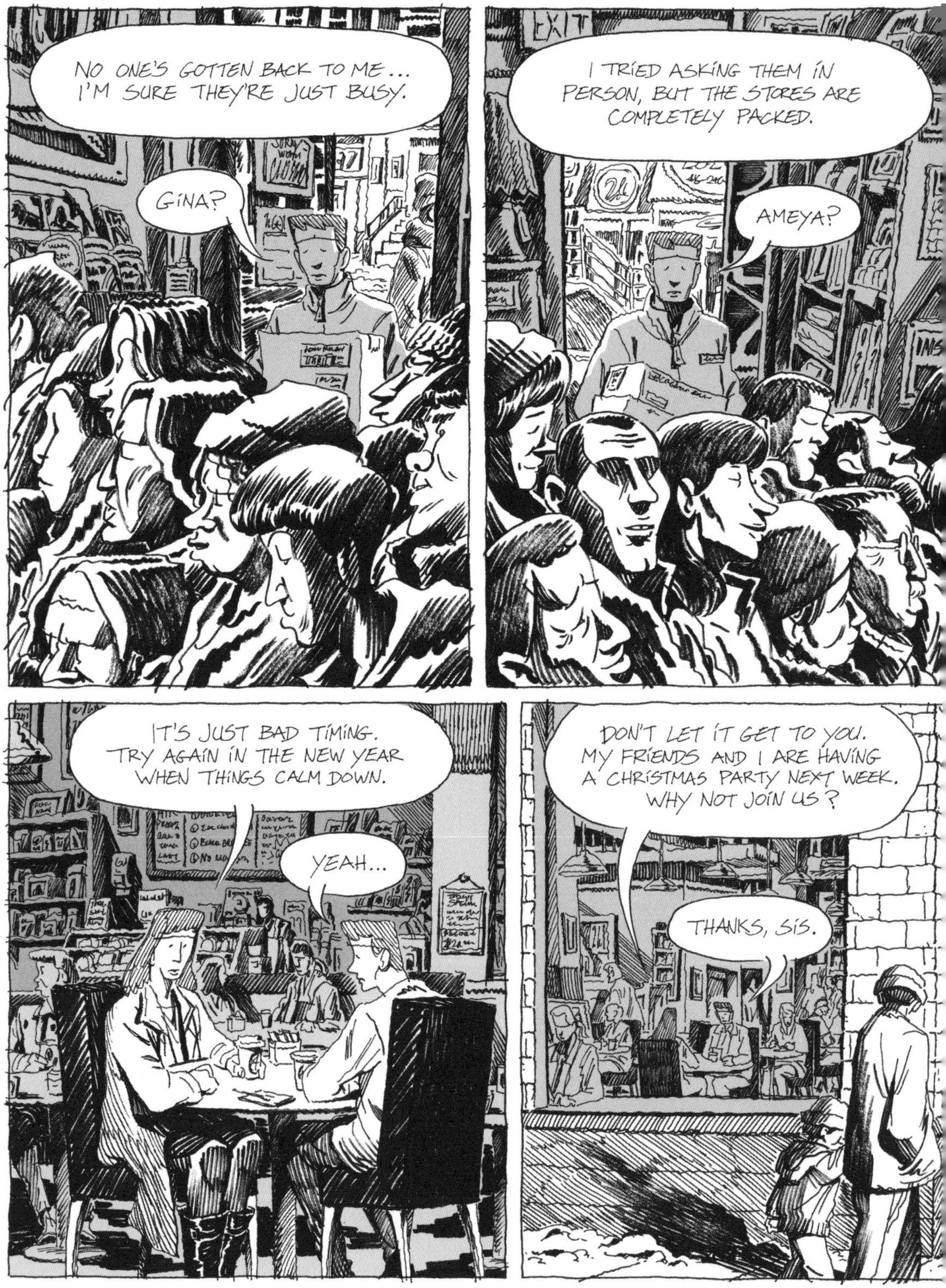
NO ONE'S GOTTEN BACK TO ME... I'M SURE THEY'RE JUST BUSY.
GINA?
I TRIED ASKING THEM IN PERSON, BUT THE STORES ARE COMPLETELY PACKED.
AMEYA?
IT'S JUST BAD TIMING. TRY AGAIN IN THE NEW YEAR WHEN THINGS CALM DOWN.
YEAH...
DON'T LET IT GET TO YOU. MY FRIENDS AND I ARE HAVING A CHRISTMAS PARTY NEXT WEEK. WHY NOT JOIN US?
THANKS, SIS.

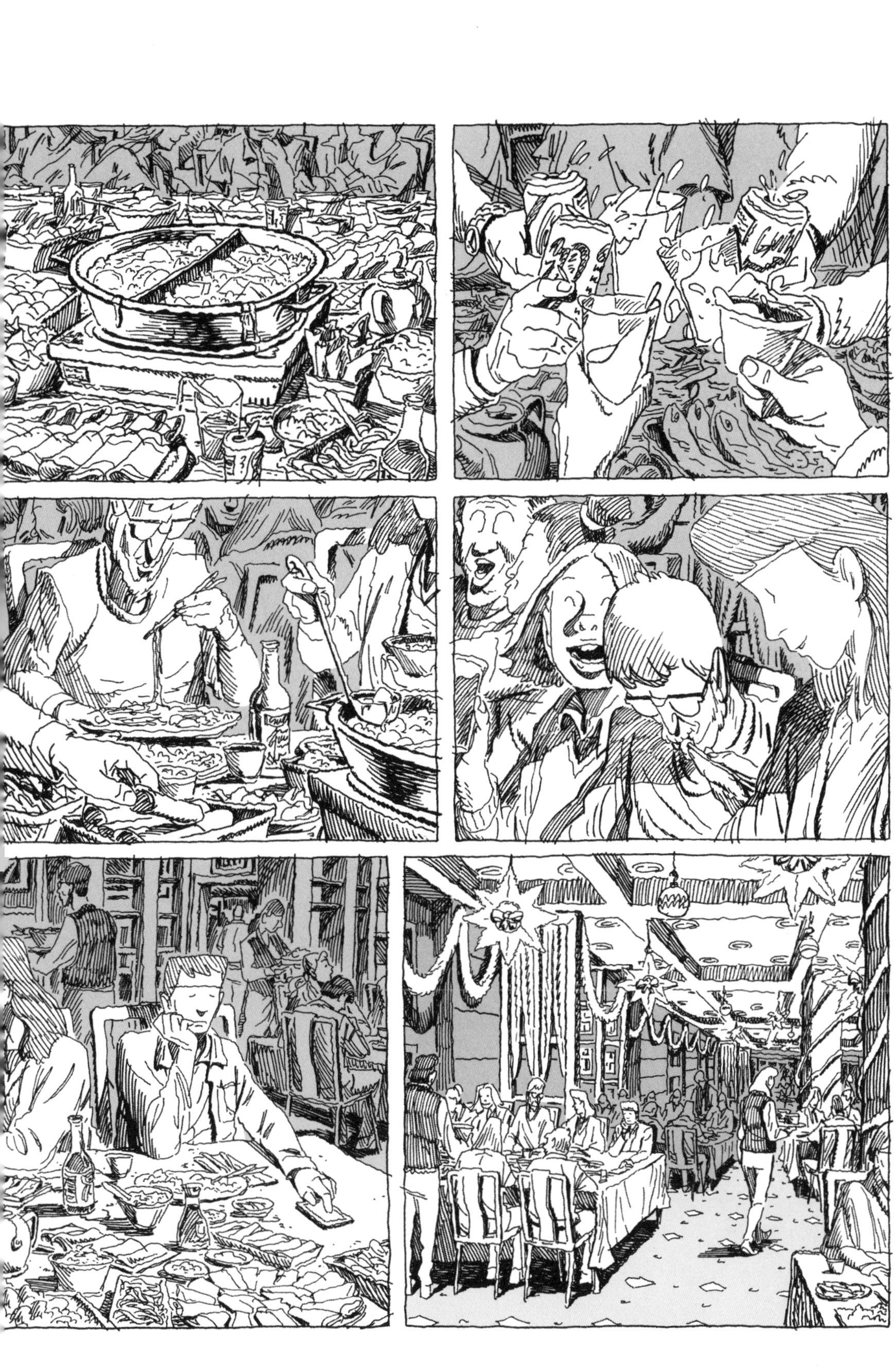

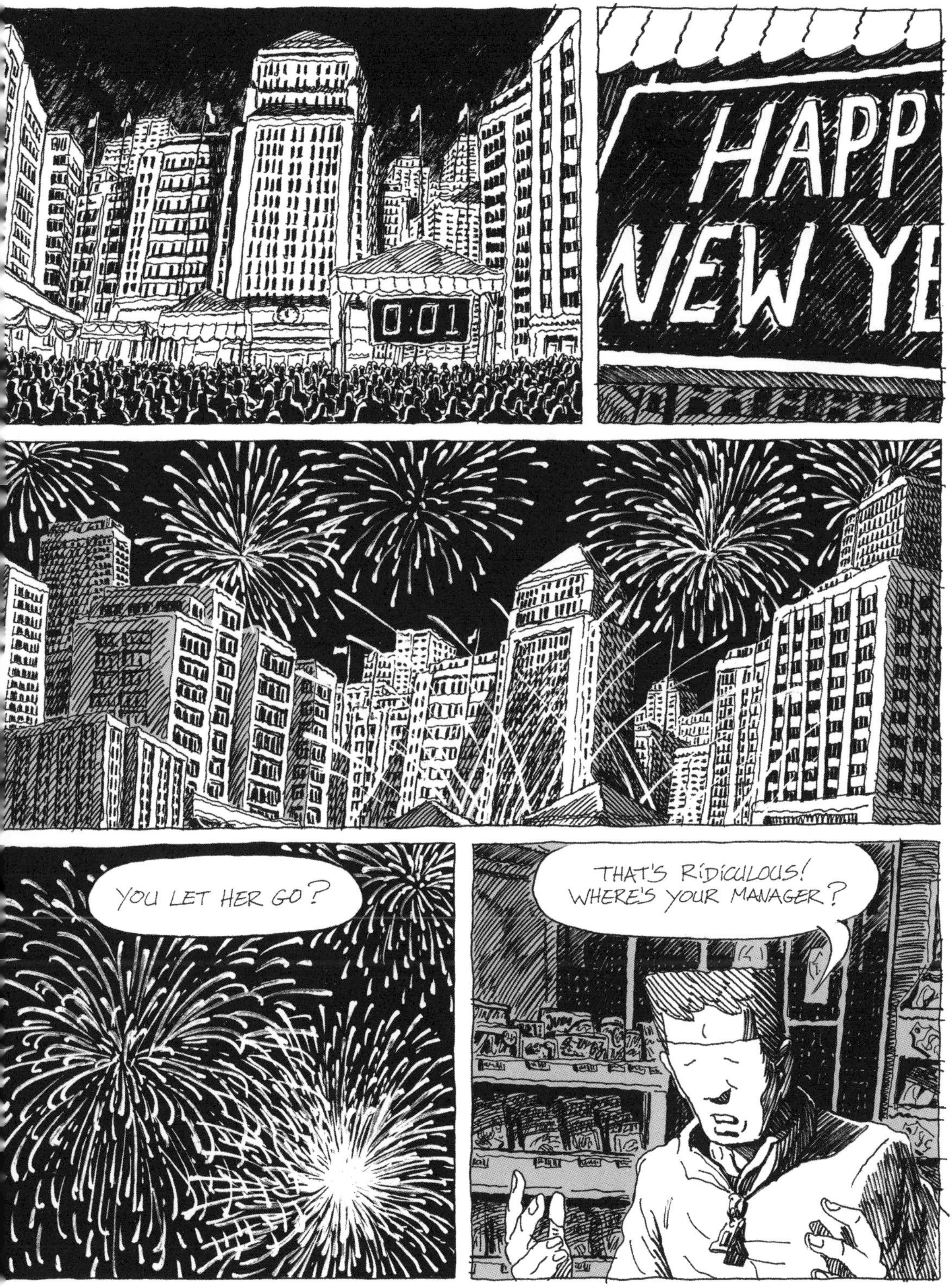
0:01
HAPP
NEW YE
YOU LET HER GO?
THAT'S RIDICULOUS!
WHERE'S YOUR MANAGER?

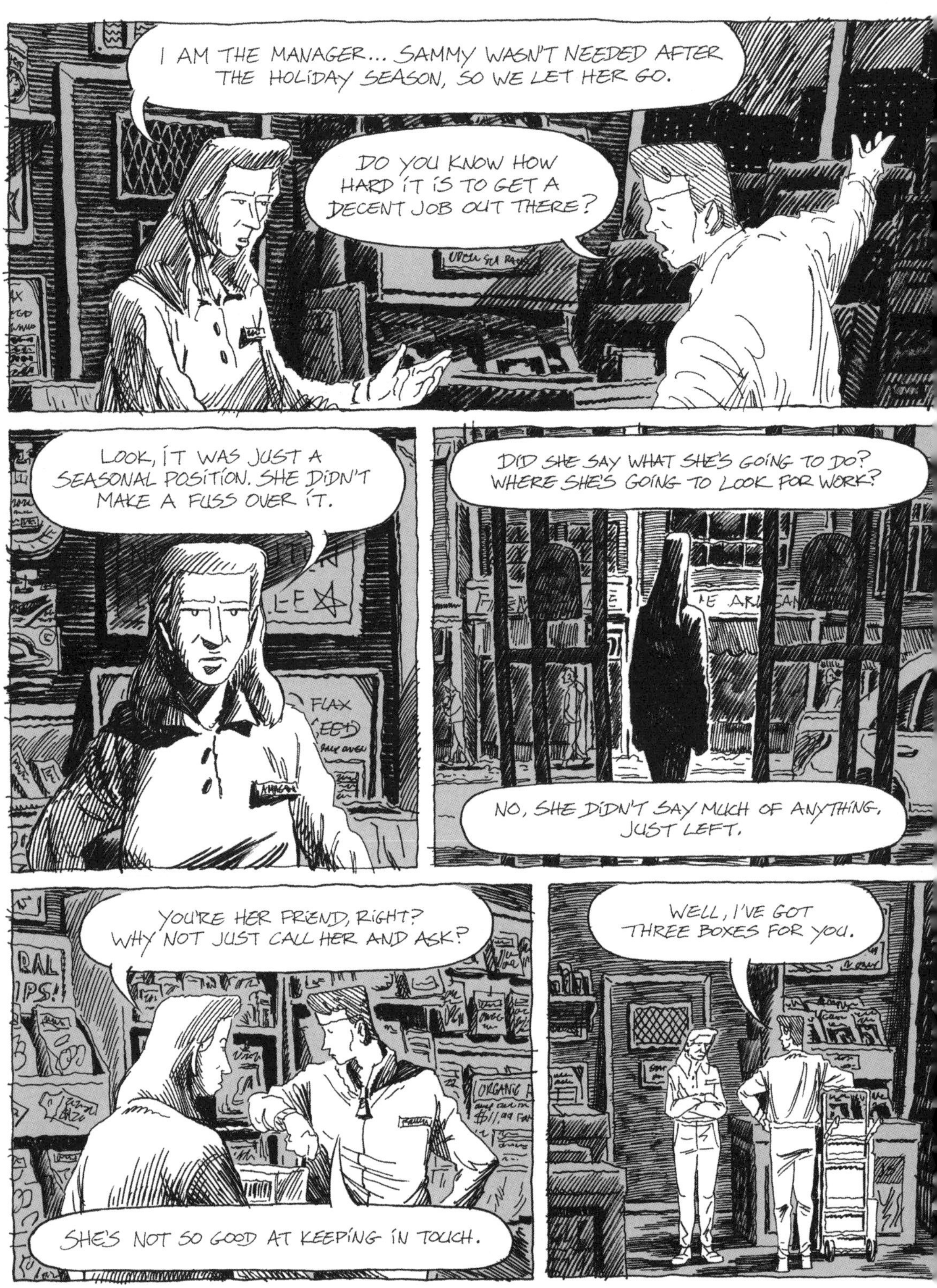
I AM THE MANAGER... SAMMY WASN'T NEEDED AFTER THE HOLIDAY SEASON, SO WE LET HER GO.
DO YOU KNOW HOW HARD IT IS TO GET A DECENT JOB OUT THERE?
LOOK, IT WAS JUST A SEASONAL POSITION. SHE DIDN'T MAKE A FUSS OVER IT.
DID SHE SAY WHAT SHE'S GOING TO DO? WHERE SHE'S GOING TO LOOK FOR WORK?
NO, SHE DIDN'T SAY MUCH OF ANYTHING, JUST LEFT.
YOU'RE HER FRIEND, RIGHT? WHY NOT JUST CALL HER AND ASK?
SHE'S NOT SO GOOD AT KEEPING IN TOUCH.
WELL, I'VE GOT THREE BOXES FOR YOU.

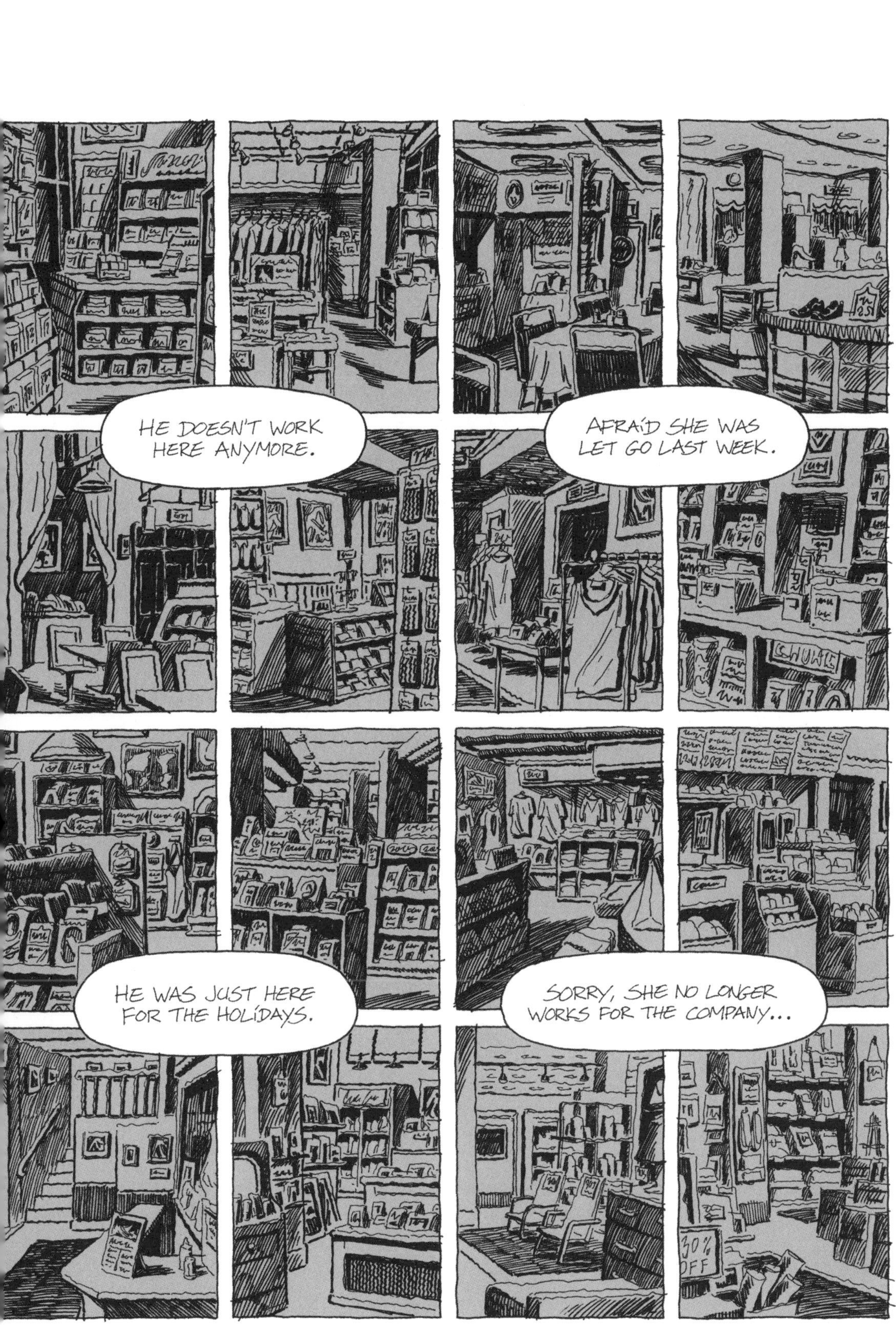
HE DOESN'T WORK HERE ANYMORE.
AFRAID SHE WAS LET GO LAST WEEK.
HE WAS JUST HERE FOR THE HOLIDAYS.
SORRY, SHE NO LONGER WORKS FOR THE COMPANY...

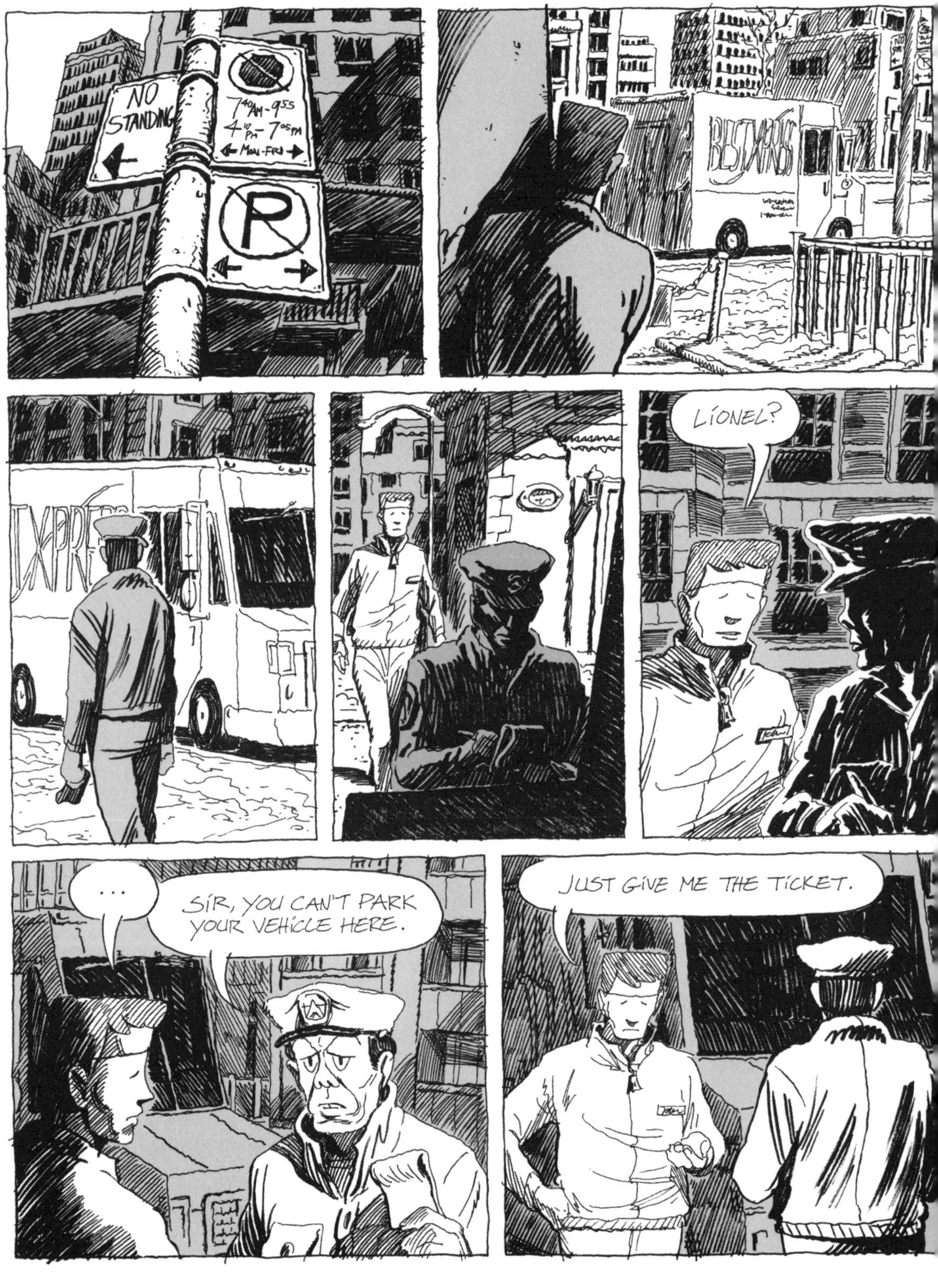
NO STANDING
7 40AM - 9 55
4 10PM - 7 05PM
MON-FRI
LIONEL?
...
SIR, YOU CAN'T PARK YOUR VEHICLE HERE.
JUST GIVE ME THE TICKET.

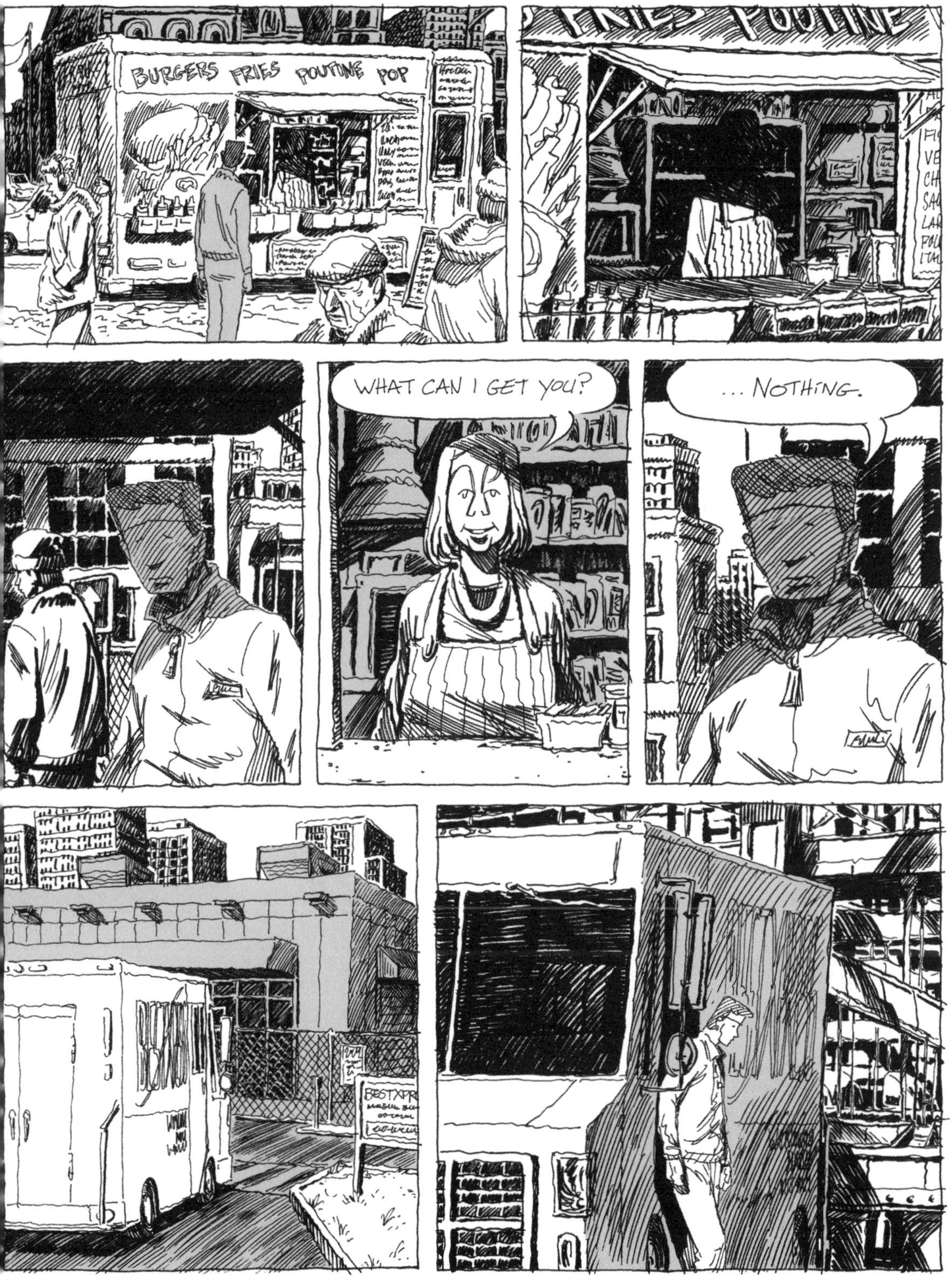
BURGERS FRIES POUTINE POP
FRIES POUTINE
WHAT CAN I GET YOU?
... NOTHING.

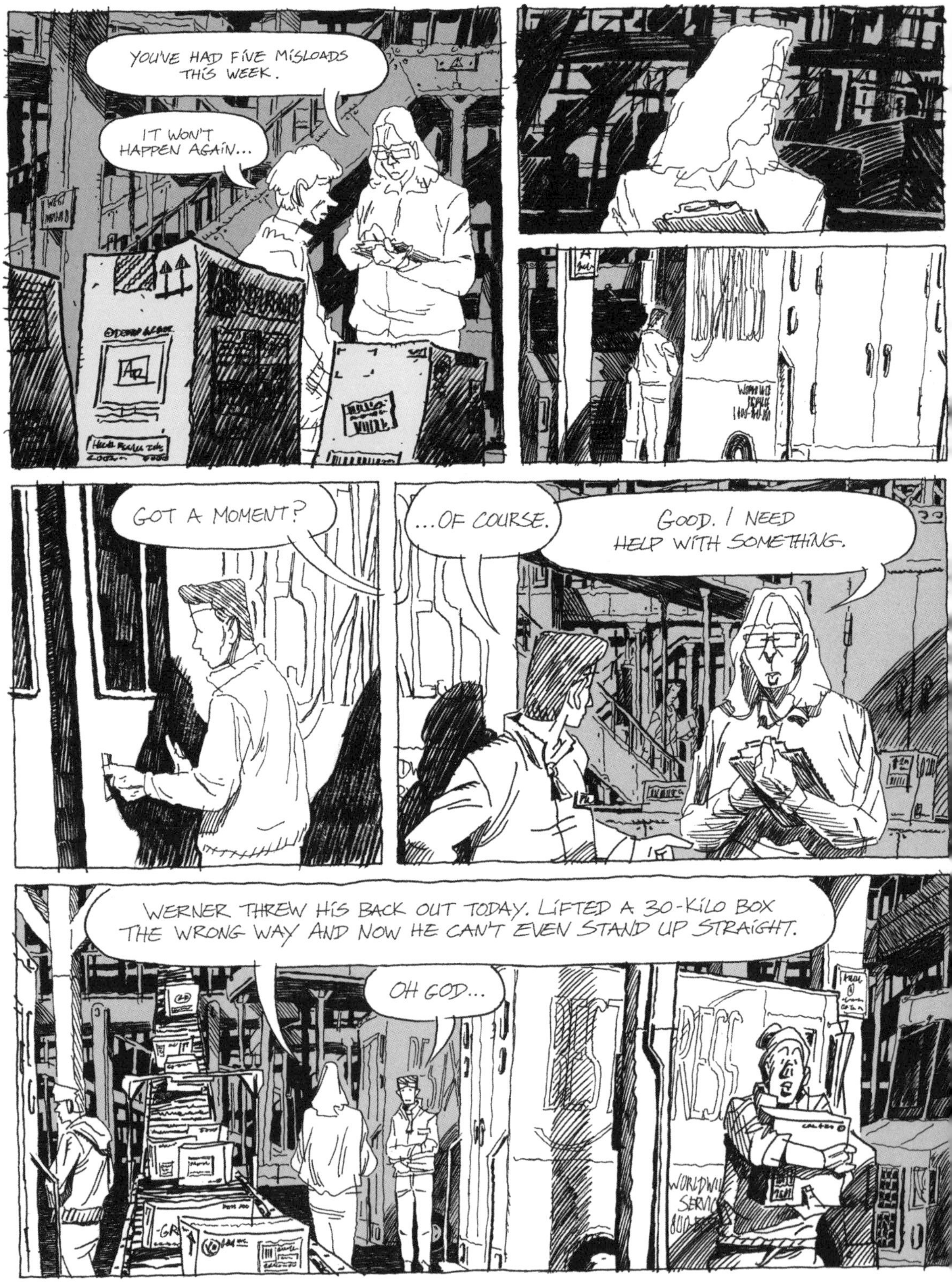
YOU'VE HAD FIVE MISLOADS THIS WEEK.
IT WON'T HAPPEN AGAIN...
GOT A MOMENT?
...OF COURSE.
GOOD. I NEED HELP WITH SOMETHING.
WERNER THREW HIS BACK OUT TODAY. LIFTED A 30-KILO BOX THE WRONG WAY AND NOW HE CAN'T EVEN STAND UP STRAIGHT.
OH GOD...

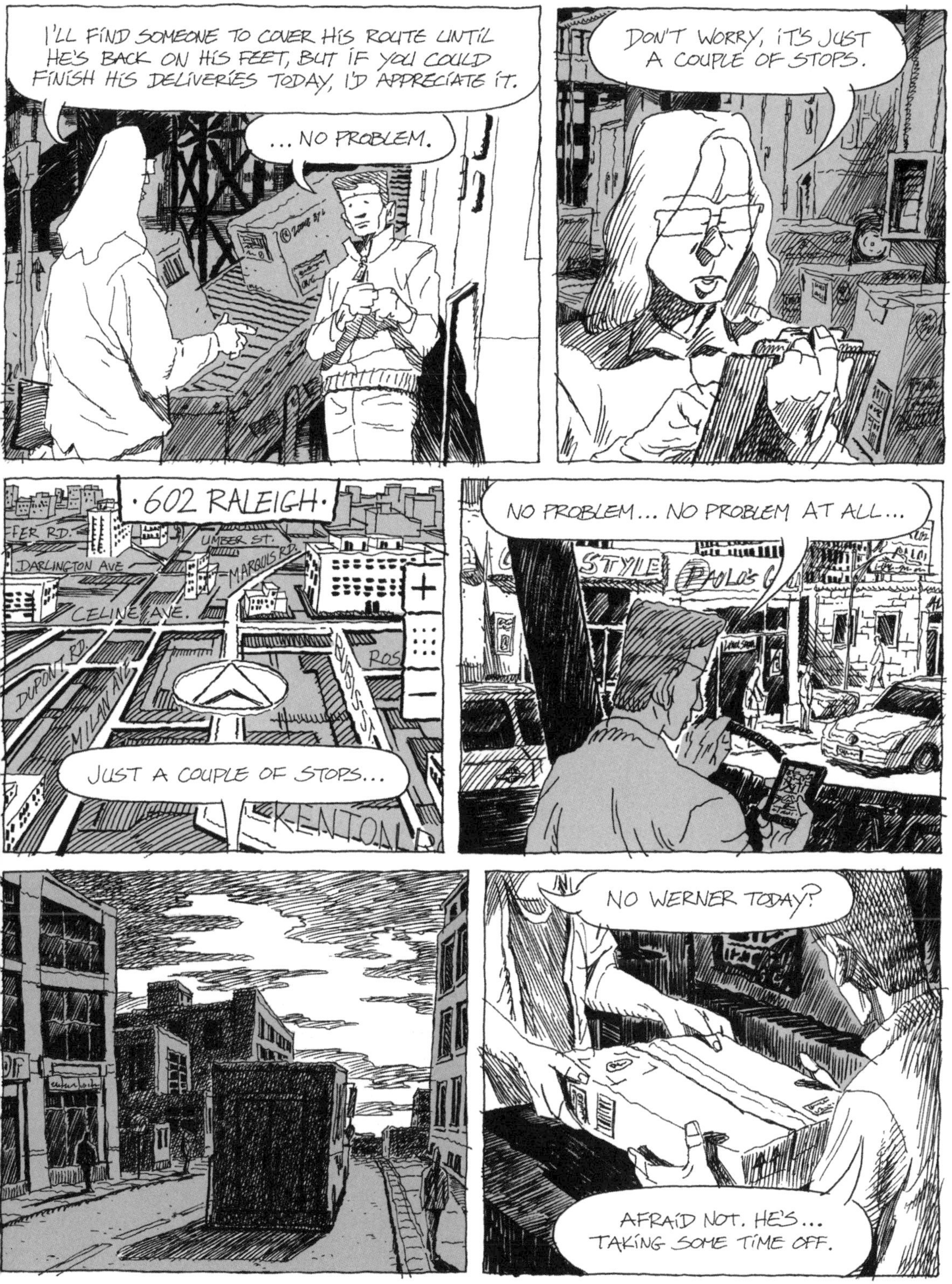
I'LL FIND SOMEONE TO COVER HIS ROUTE UNTIL HE'S BACK ON HIS FEET, BUT IF YOU COULD FINISH HIS DELIVERIES TODAY, I'D APPRECIATE IT.
... NO PROBLEM.
DON'T WORRY, IT'S JUST A COUPLE OF STOPS.
·602 RALEIGH·
UMBER ST.
DARLINGTON AVE
MARQUIS RD.
CELINE AVE.
DUPONT RD.
MILAN AVE
ROS
JUST A COUPLE OF STOPS...
KENTON
NO PROBLEM... NO PROBLEM AT ALL...
STYLE
PAULO'S
NO WERNER TODAY?
AFRAID NOT. HE'S... TAKING SOME TIME OFF.

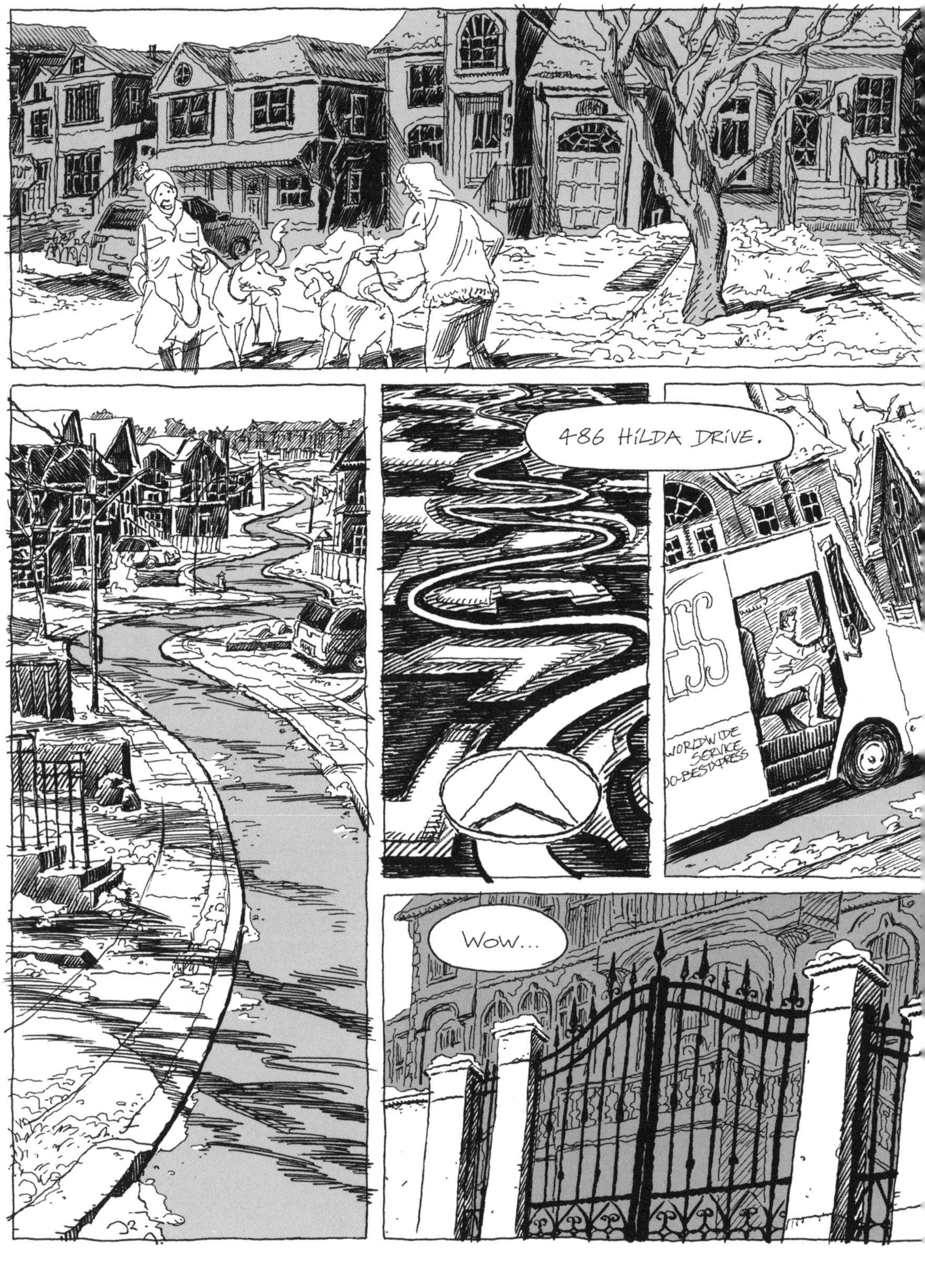
486 HILDA DRIVE.
WORLDWIDE SERVICE
Wow...

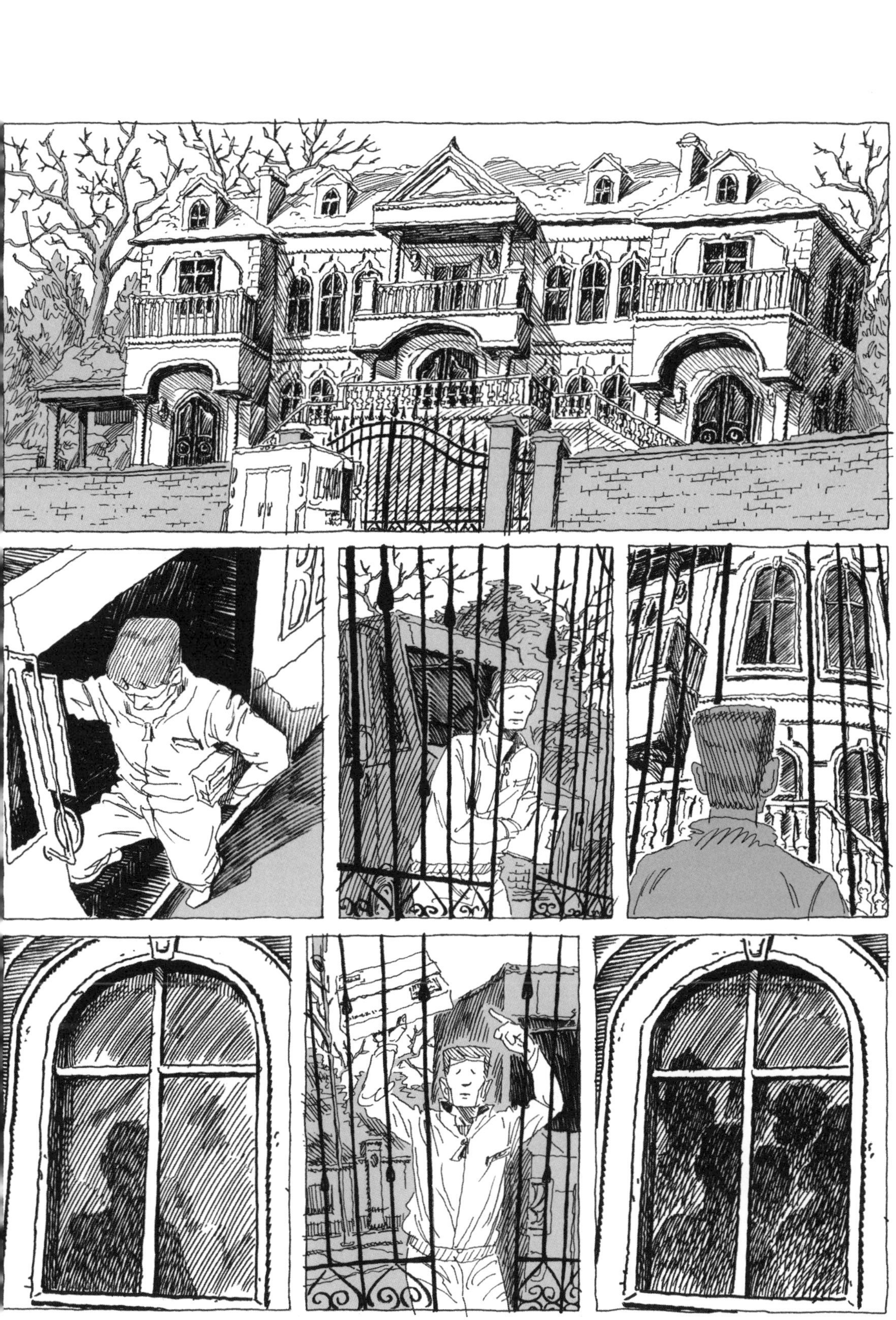

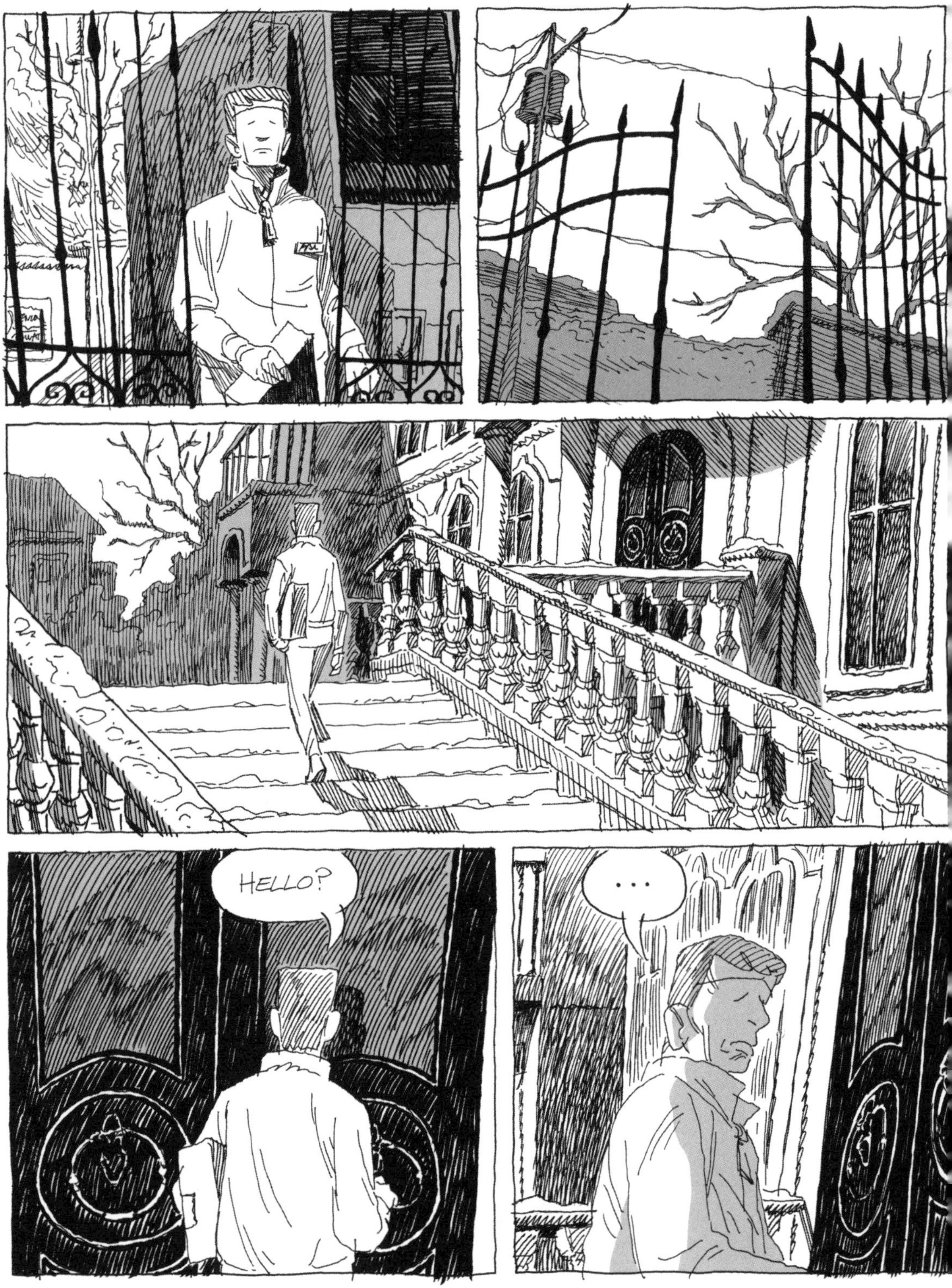
HELLO?
...

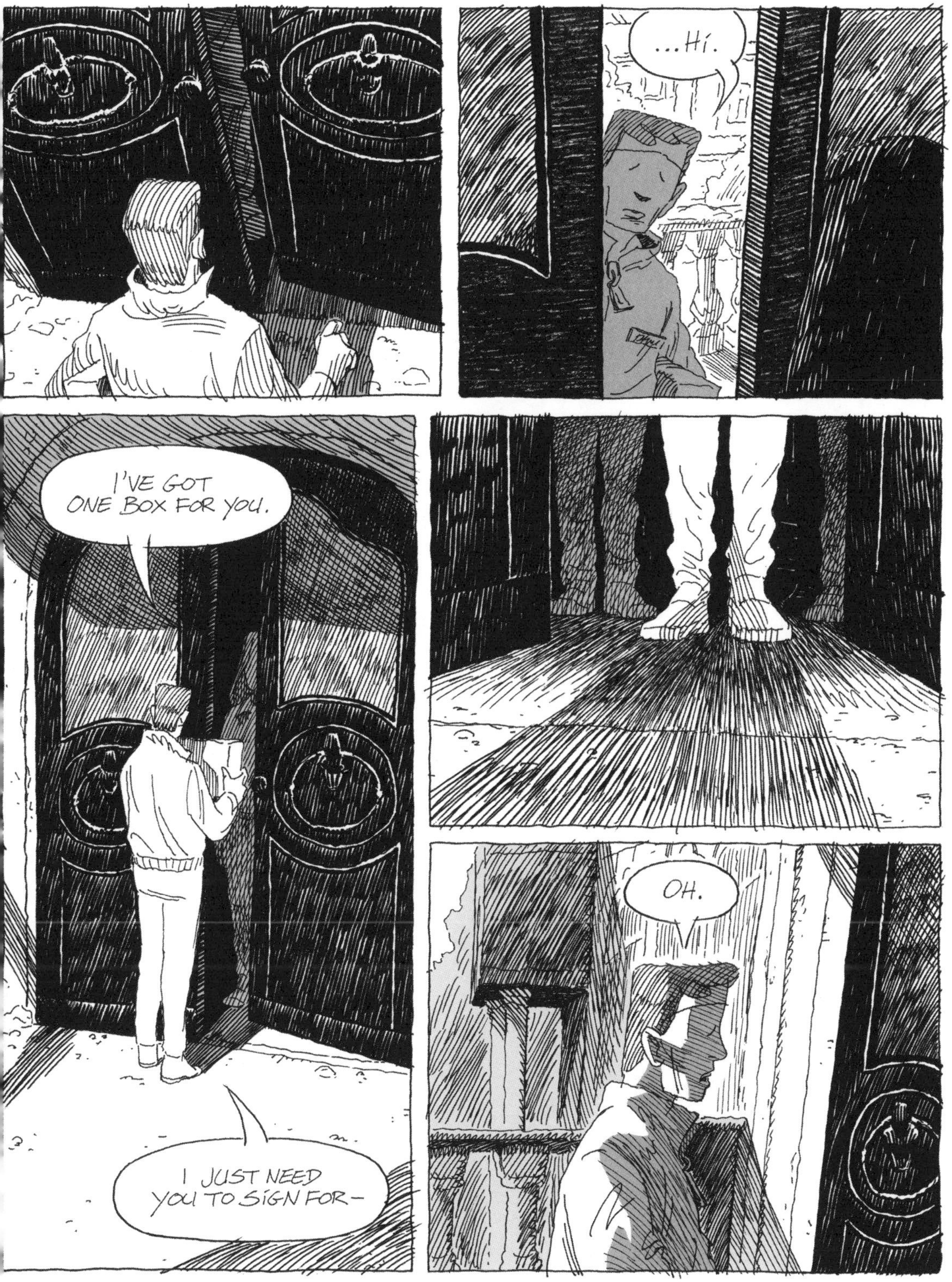
...Hi.
I'VE GOT ONE BOX FOR YOU.
I JUST NEED YOU TO SIGN FOR-
OH.

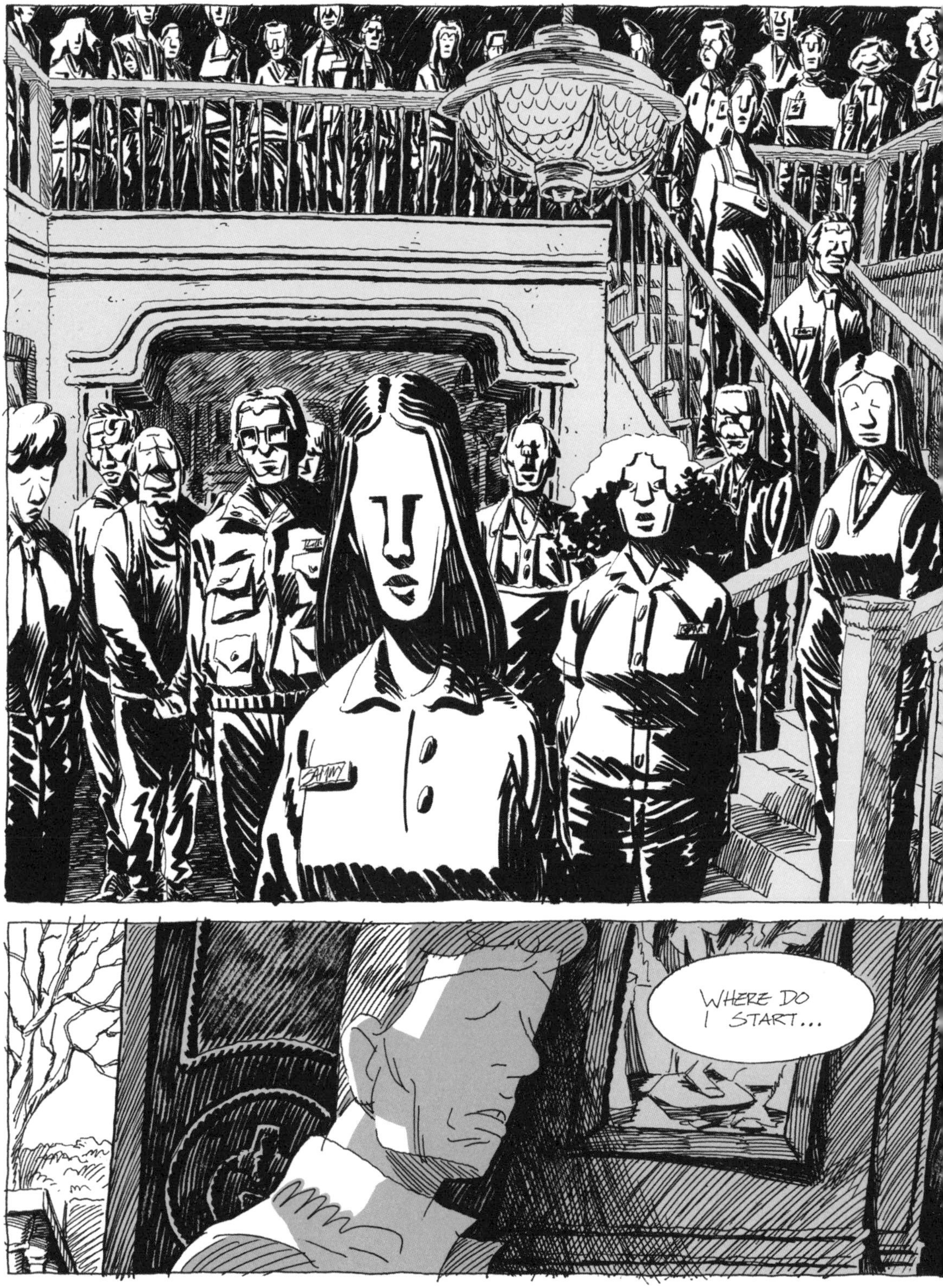
WHERE DO I START...

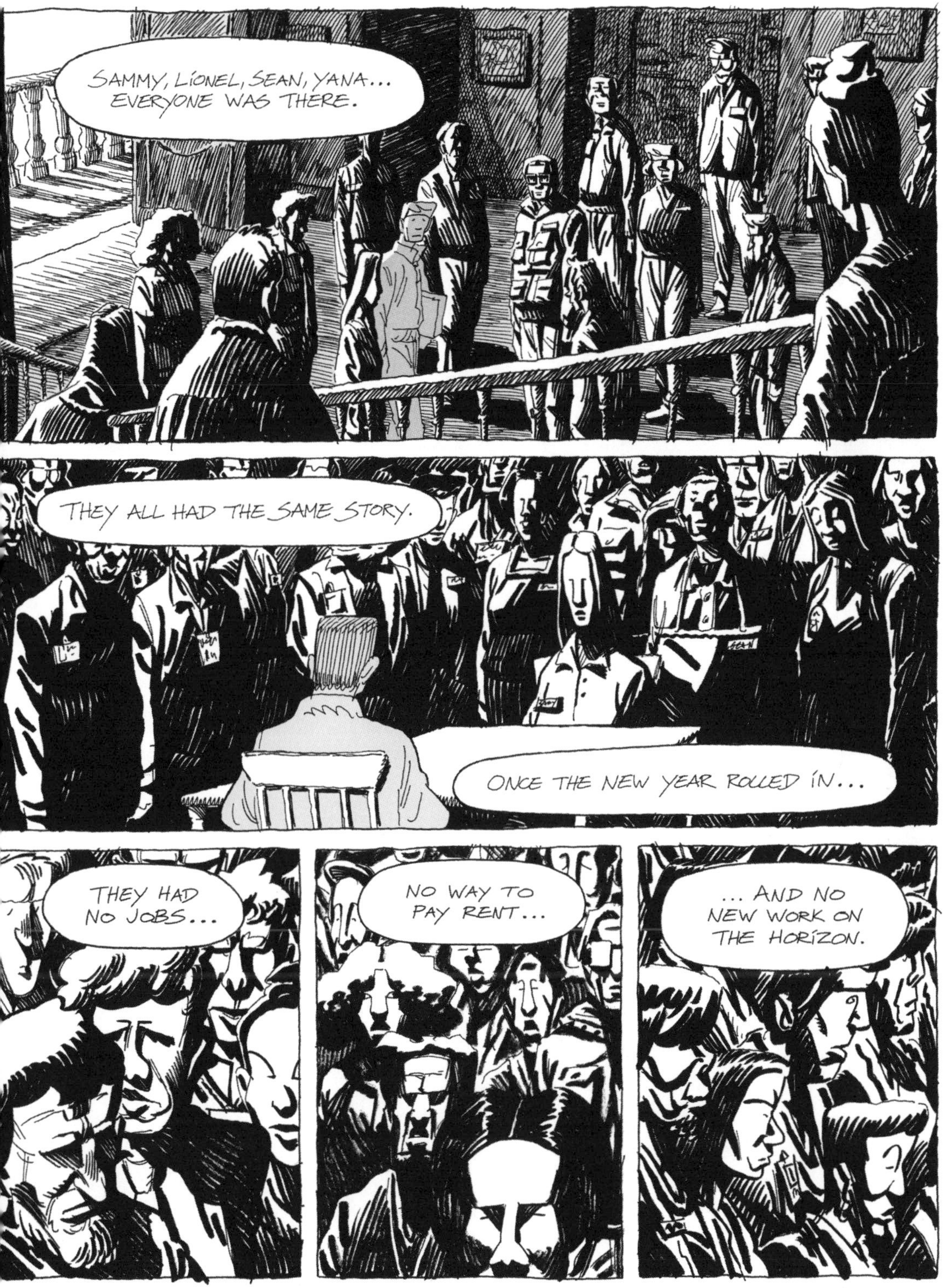
SAMMY, LIONEL, SEAN, YANA...
EVERYONE WAS THERE.
THEY ALL HAD THE SAME STORY.
ONCE THE NEW YEAR ROLLED IN...
THEY HAD NO JOBS...
NO WAY TO PAY RENT...
... AND NO NEW WORK ON THE HORIZON.

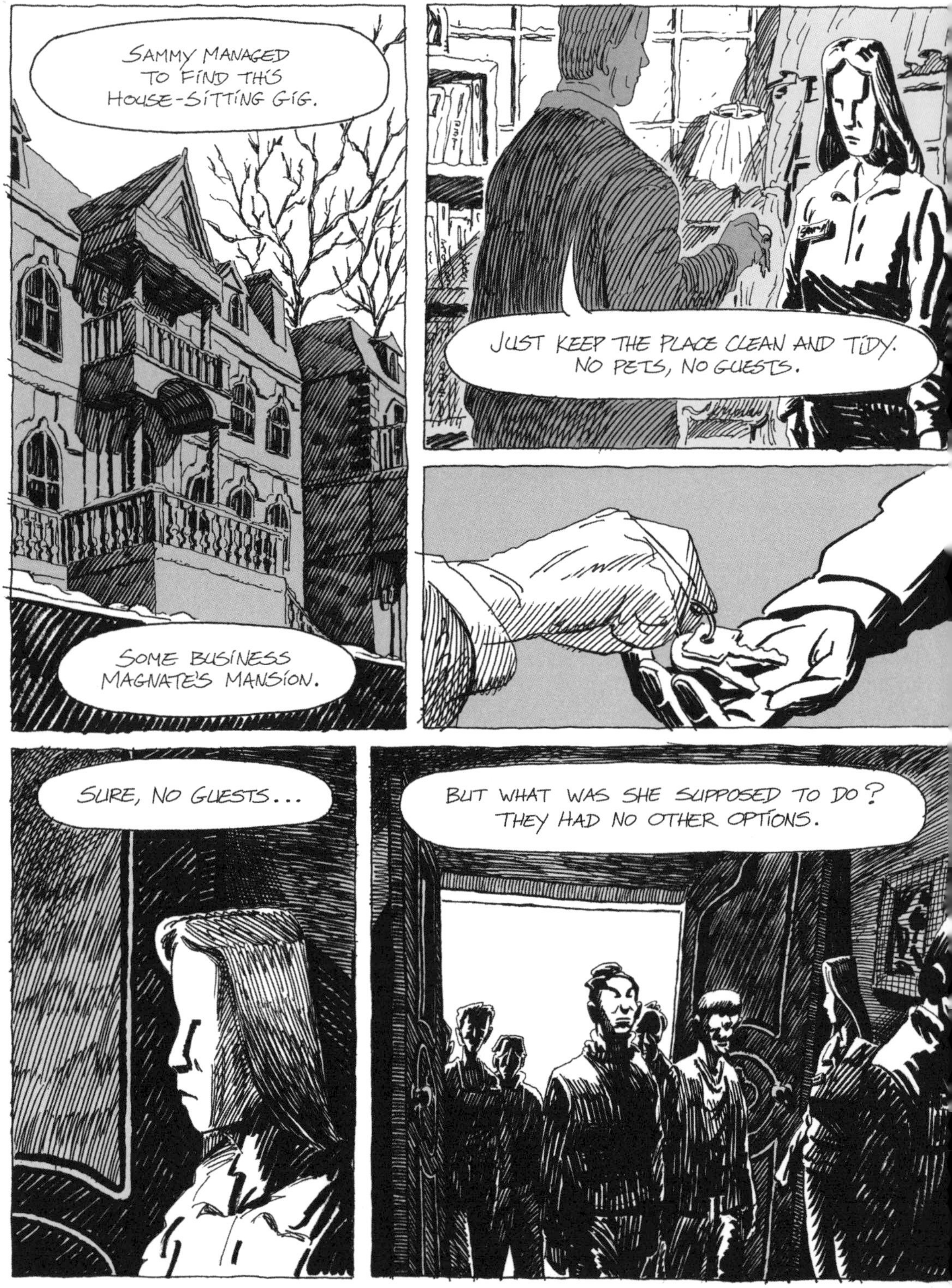
SAMMY MANAGED TO FIND THIS HOUSE-SITTING GIG.
SOME BUSINESS MAGNATE'S MANSION.
JUST KEEP THE PLACE CLEAN AND TIDY. NO PETS, NO GUESTS.
SURE, NO GUESTS...
BUT WHAT WAS SHE SUPPOSED TO DO? THEY HAD NO OTHER OPTIONS.

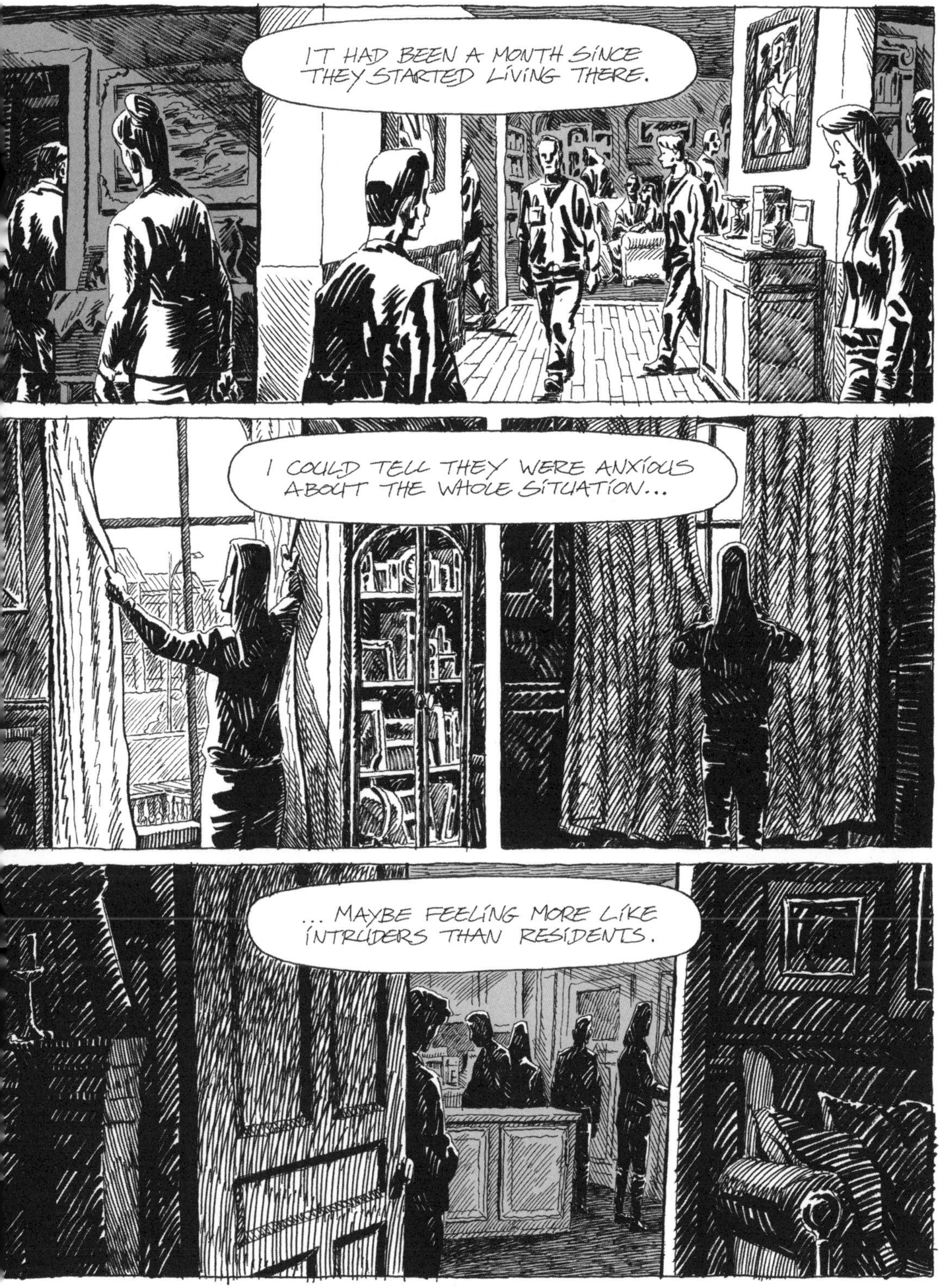
IT HAD BEEN A MONTH SINCE THEY STARTED LIVING THERE.
I COULD TELL THEY WERE ANXIOUS ABOUT THE WHOLE SITUATION...
... MAYBE FEELING MORE LIKE INTRUDERS THAN RESIDENTS.

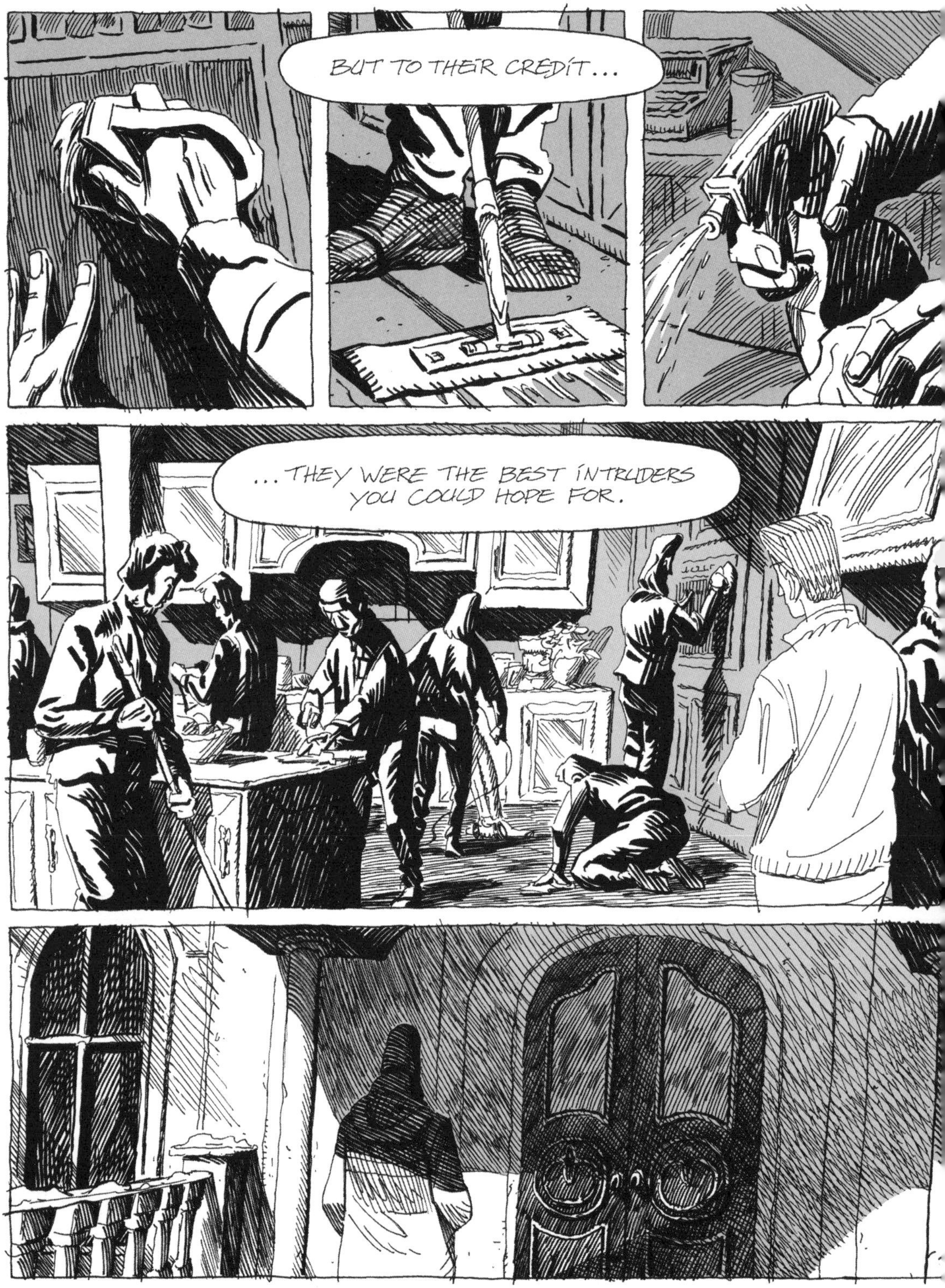
BUT TO THEIR CREDIT...
...THEY WERE THE BEST INTRUDERS YOU COULD HOPE FOR.

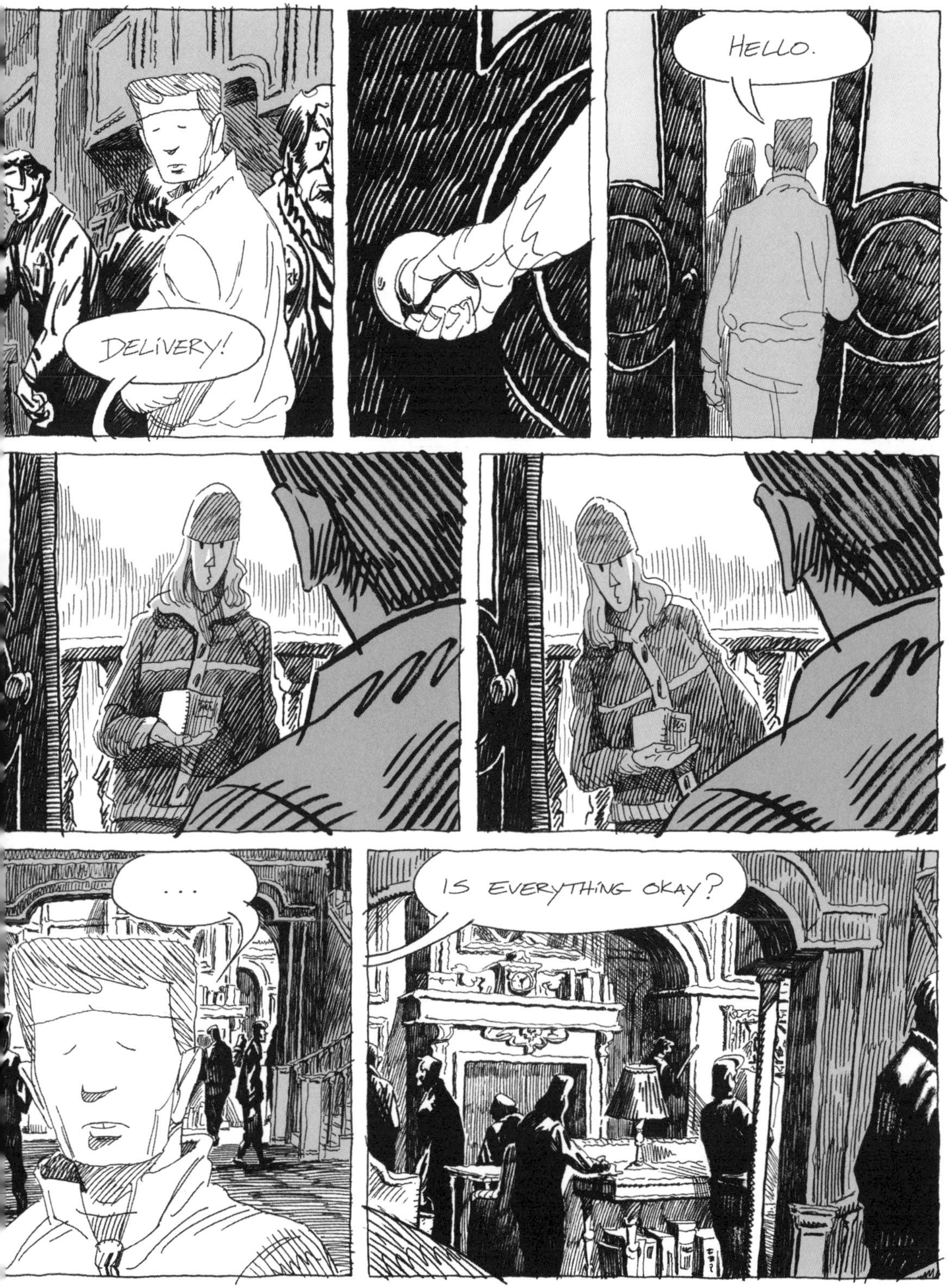
DELIVERY!
HELLO.
. . .
IS EVERYTHING OKAY?

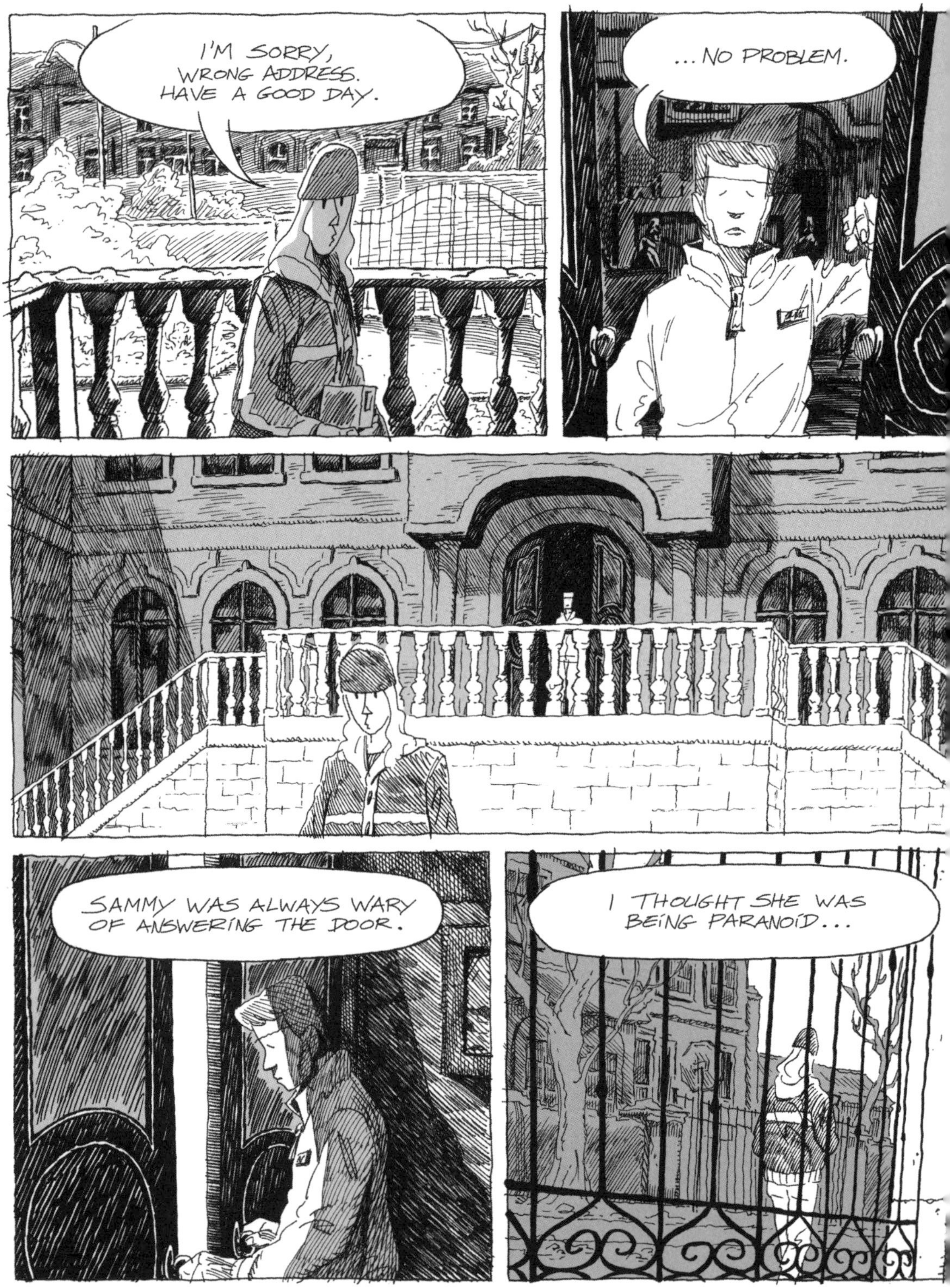
I'M SORRY, WRONG ADDRESS. HAVE A GOOD DAY.
... NO PROBLEM.
SAMMY WAS ALWAYS WARY OF ANSWERING THE DOOR.
I THOUGHT SHE WAS BEING PARANOID...

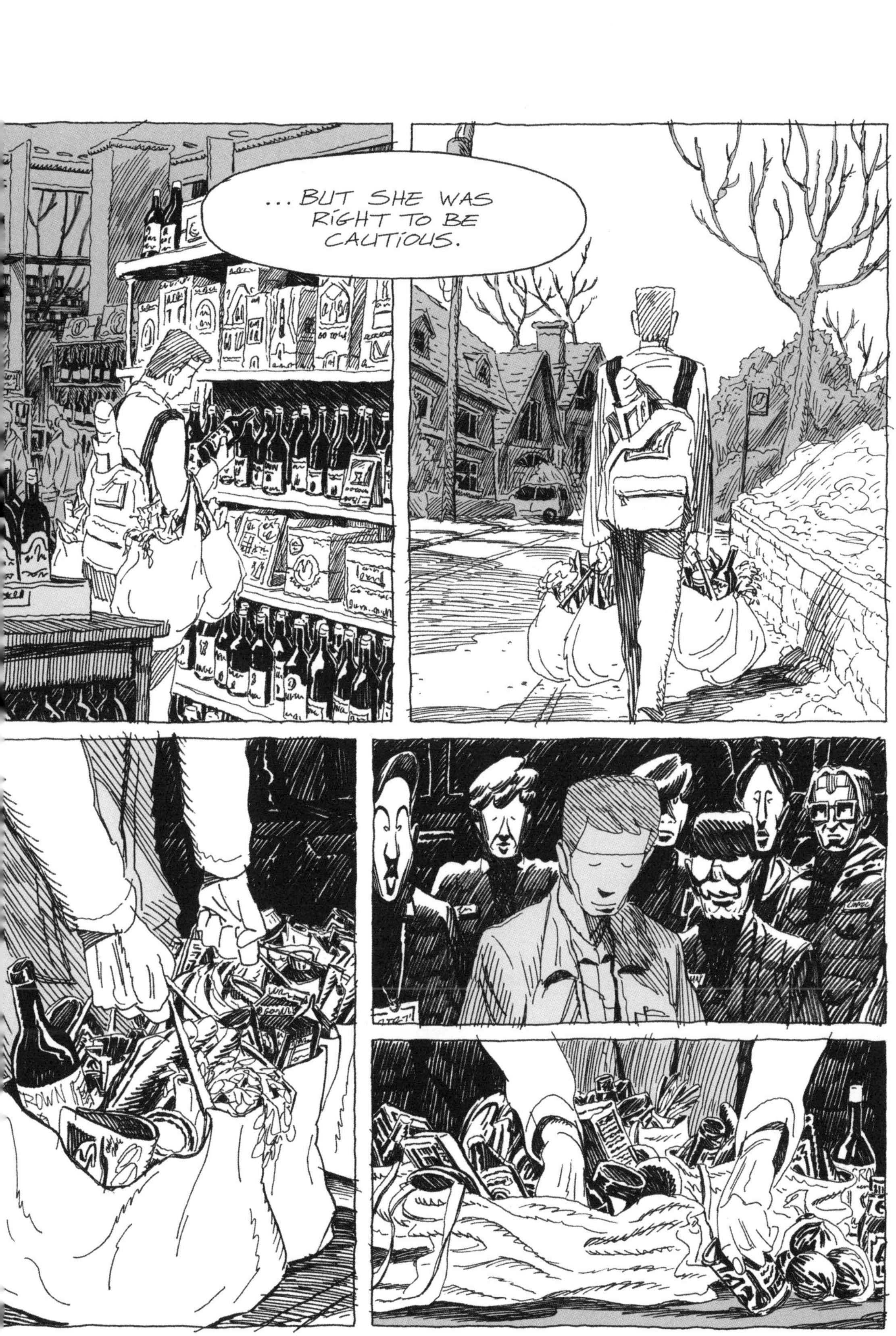
...BUT SHE WAS RIGHT TO BE CAUTIOUS.

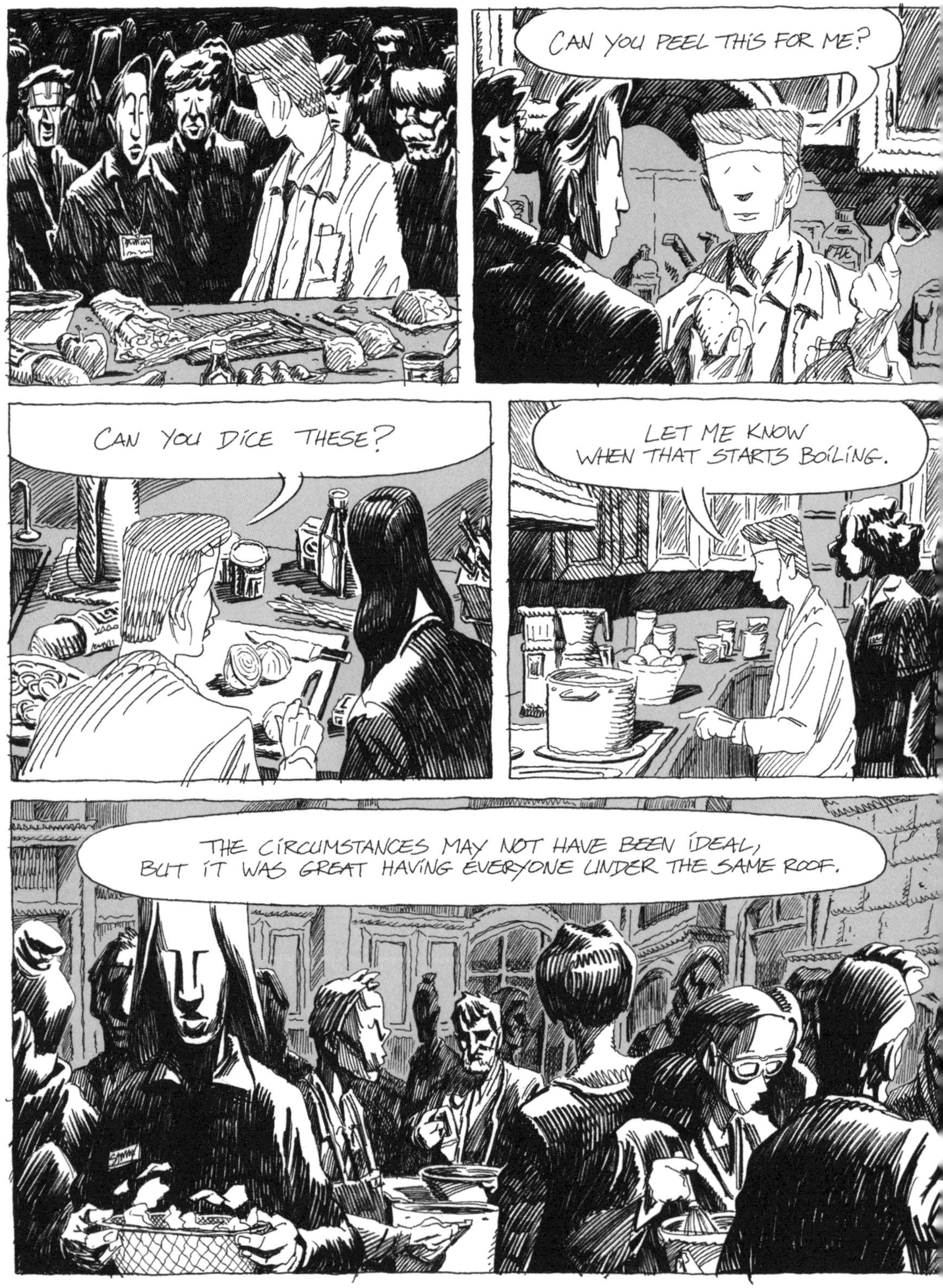
CAN YOU PEEL THIS FOR ME?
CAN YOU DICE THESE?
LET ME KNOW WHEN THAT STARTS BOILING.
THE CIRCUMSTANCES MAY NOT HAVE BEEN IDEAL, BUT IT WAS GREAT HAVING EVERYONE UNDER THE SAME ROOF.

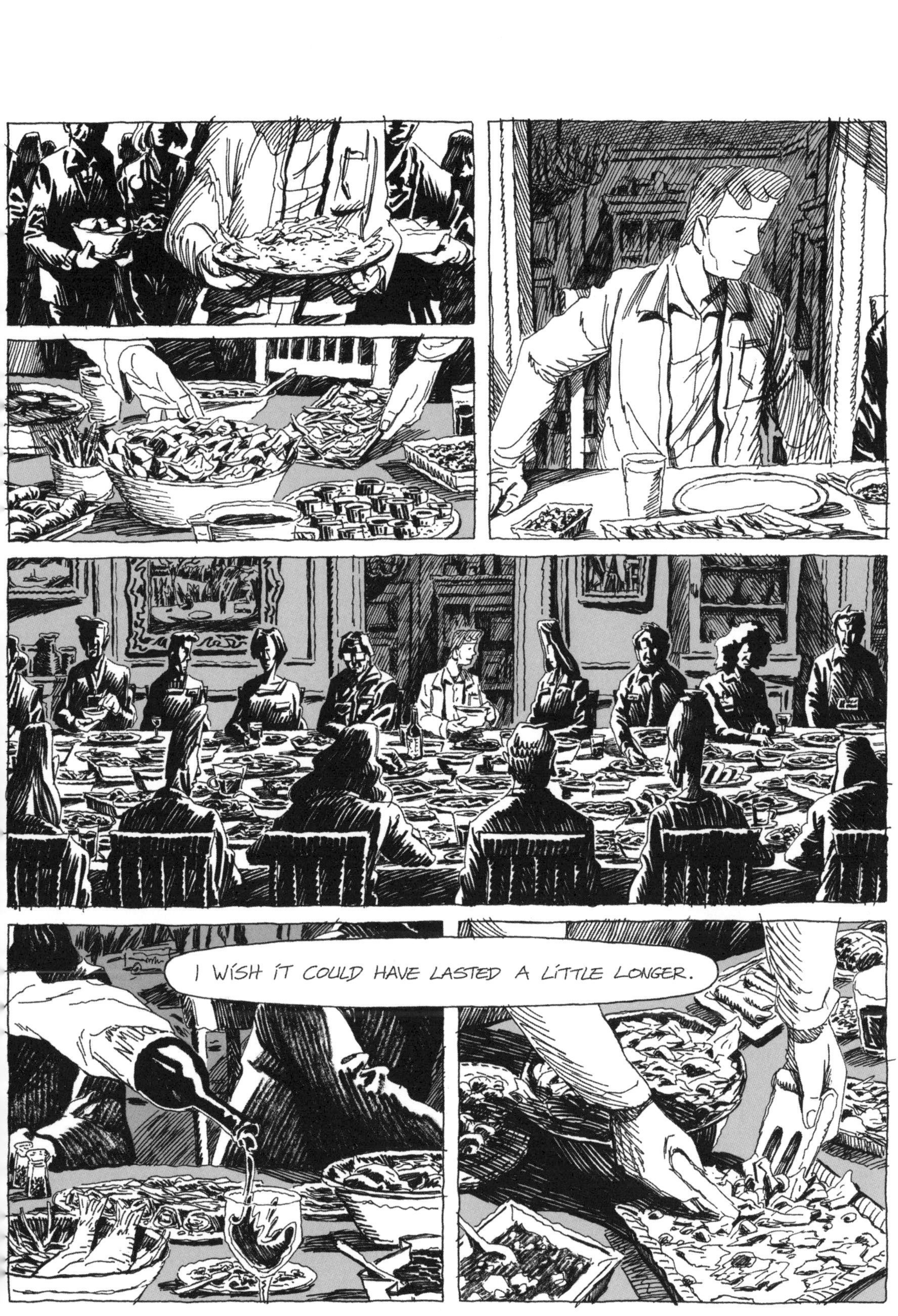
I WISH IT COULD HAVE LASTED A LITTLE LONGER.

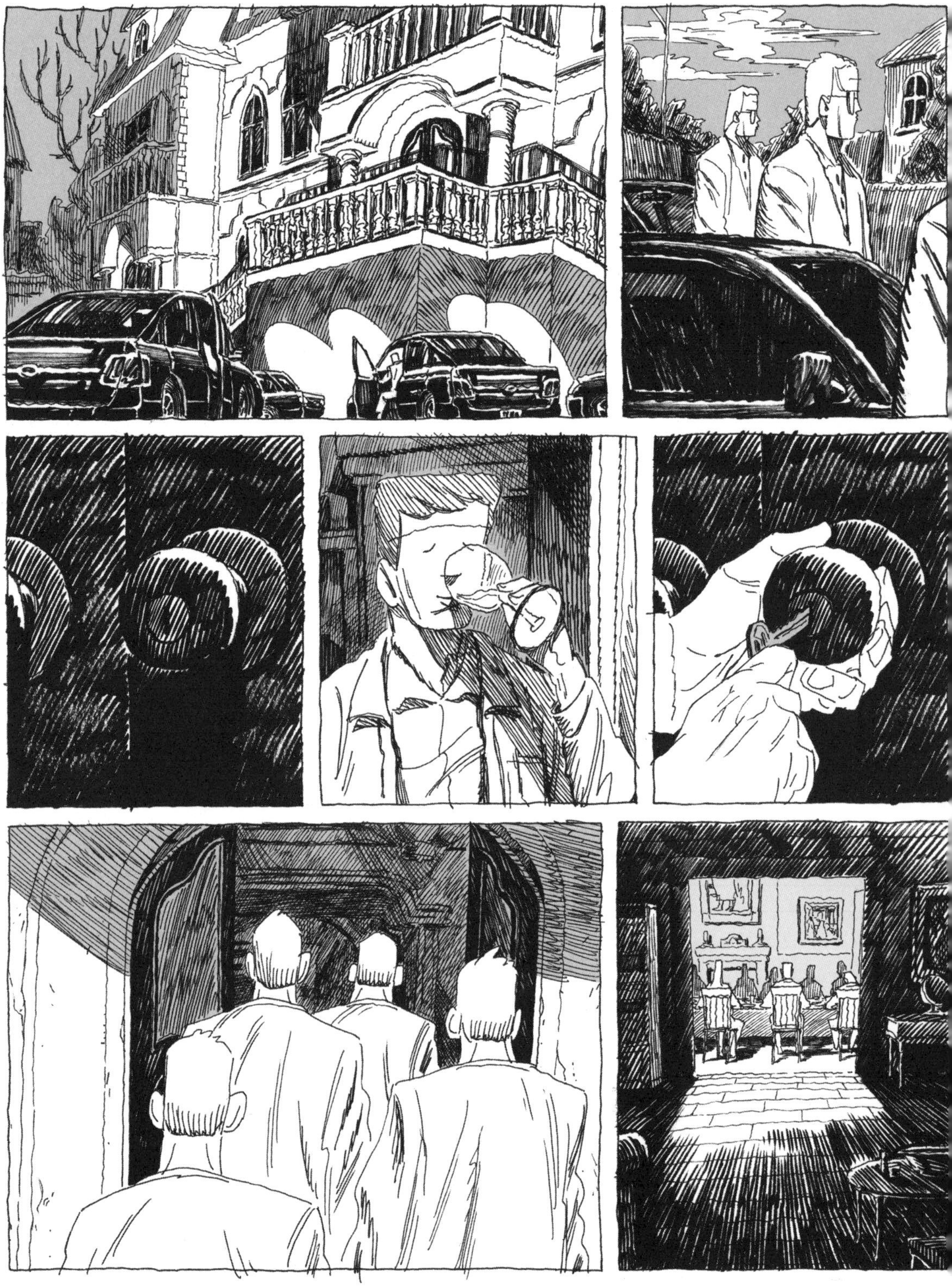

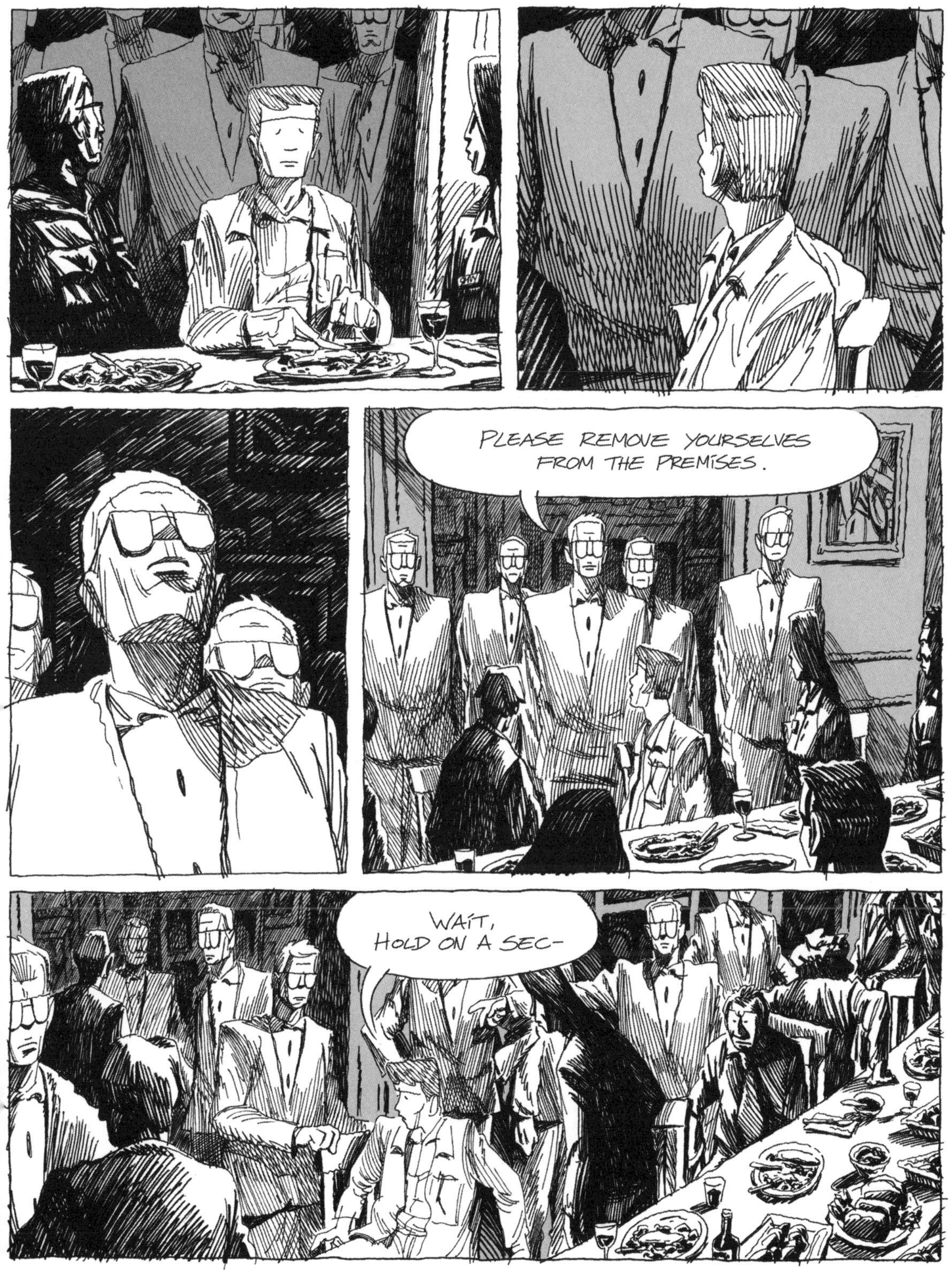
PLEASE REMOVE YOURSELVES FROM THE PREMISES.
WAIT, HOLD ON A SEC-

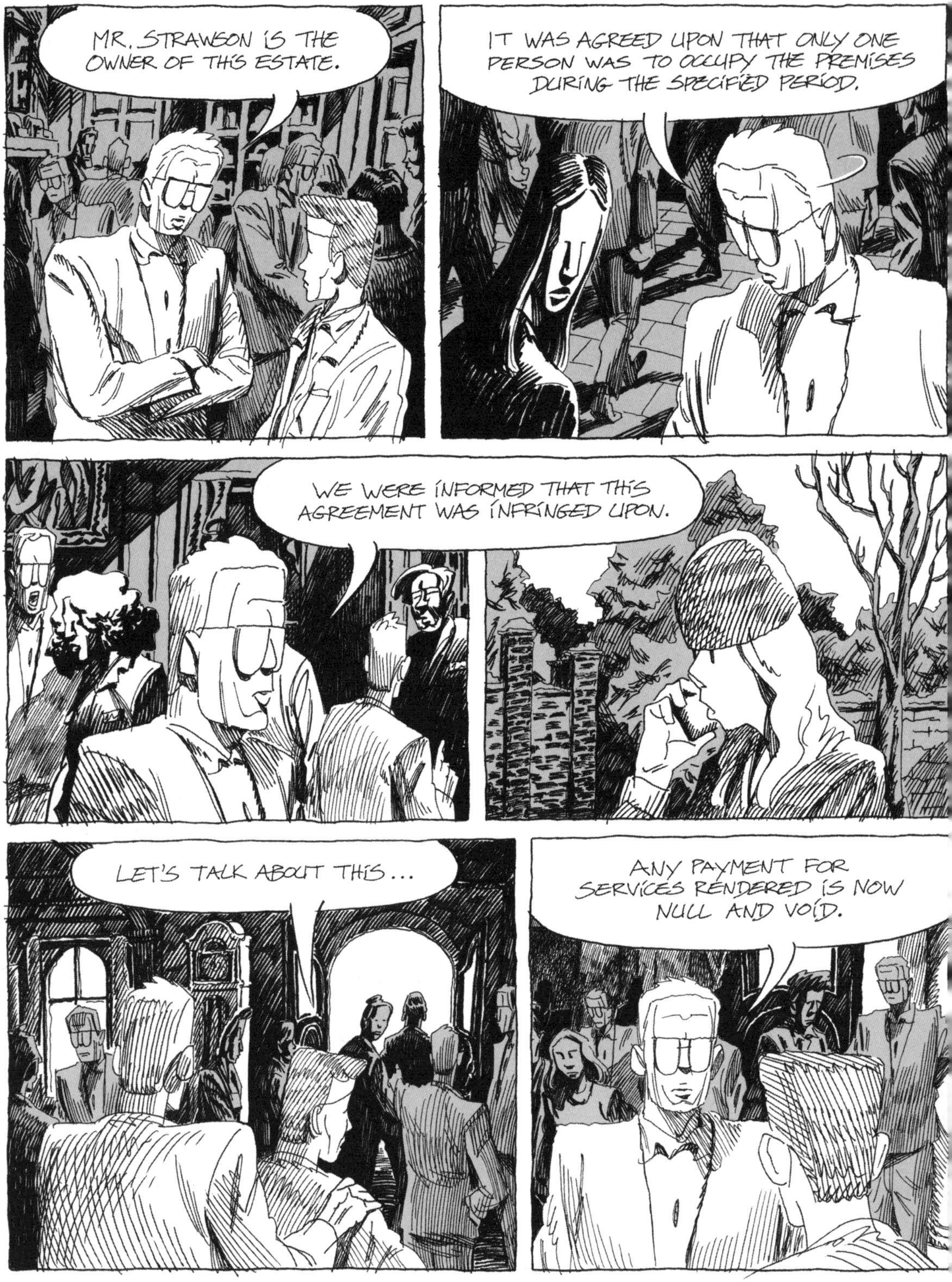
MR. STRAWSON IS THE OWNER OF THIS ESTATE.
IT WAS AGREED UPON THAT ONLY ONE PERSON WAS TO OCCUPY THE PREMISES DURING THE SPECIFIED PERIOD.
WE WERE INFORMED THAT THIS AGREEMENT WAS INFRINGED UPON.
LET'S TALK ABOUT THIS...
ANY PAYMENT FOR SERVICES RENDERED IS NOW NULL AND VOID.

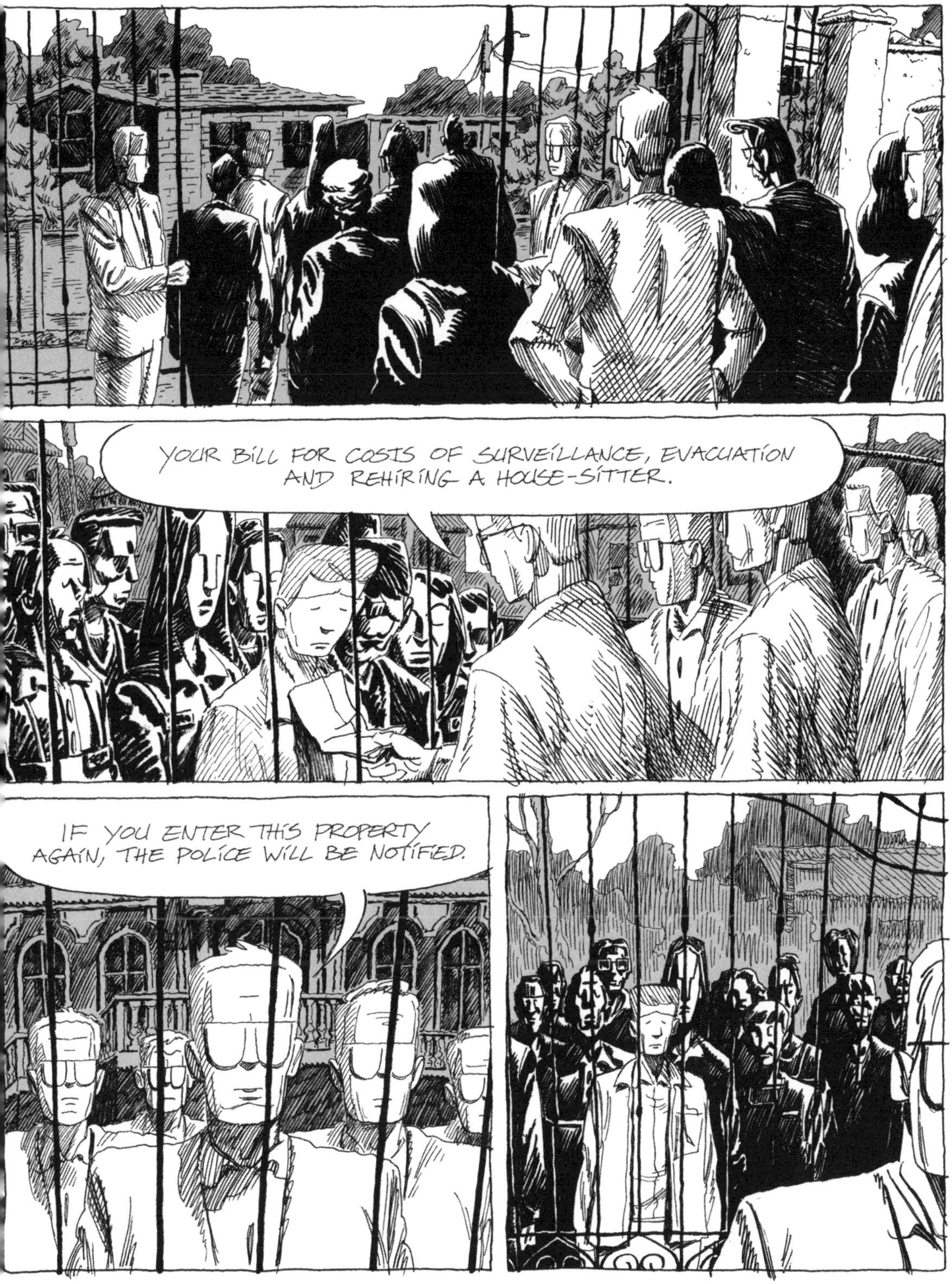
YOUR BILL FOR COSTS OF SURVEILLANCE, EVACUATION AND REHIRING A HOUSE-SITTER.
IF YOU ENTER THIS PROPERTY AGAIN, THE POLICE WILL BE NOTIFIED.

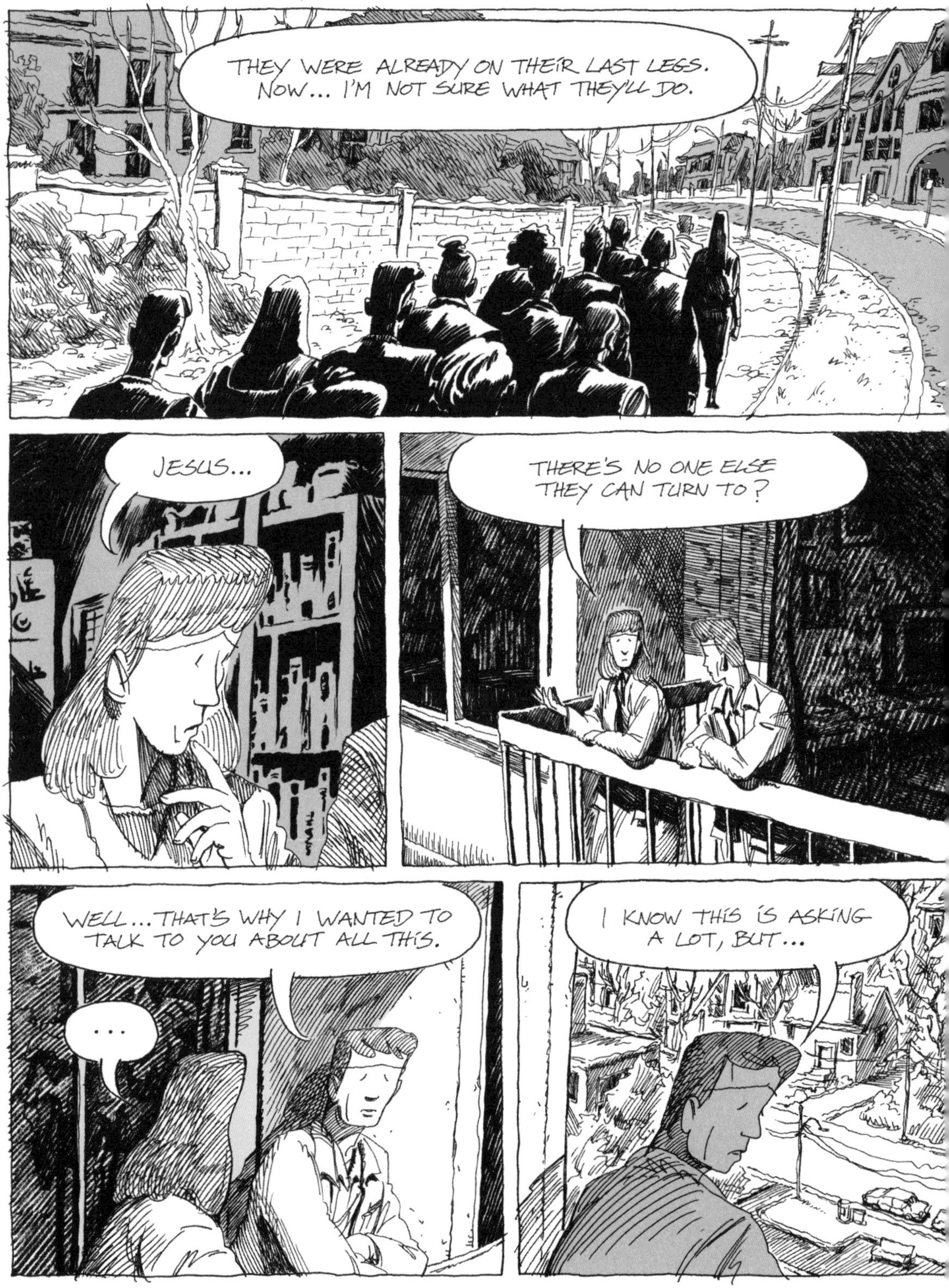
THEY WERE ALREADY ON THEIR LAST LEGS. NOW... I'M NOT SURE WHAT THEY'LL DO.
JESUS...
THERE'S NO ONE ELSE THEY CAN TURN TO?
WELL... THAT'S WHY I WANTED TO TALK TO YOU ABOUT ALL THIS.
...
I KNOW THIS IS ASKING A LOT, BUT...

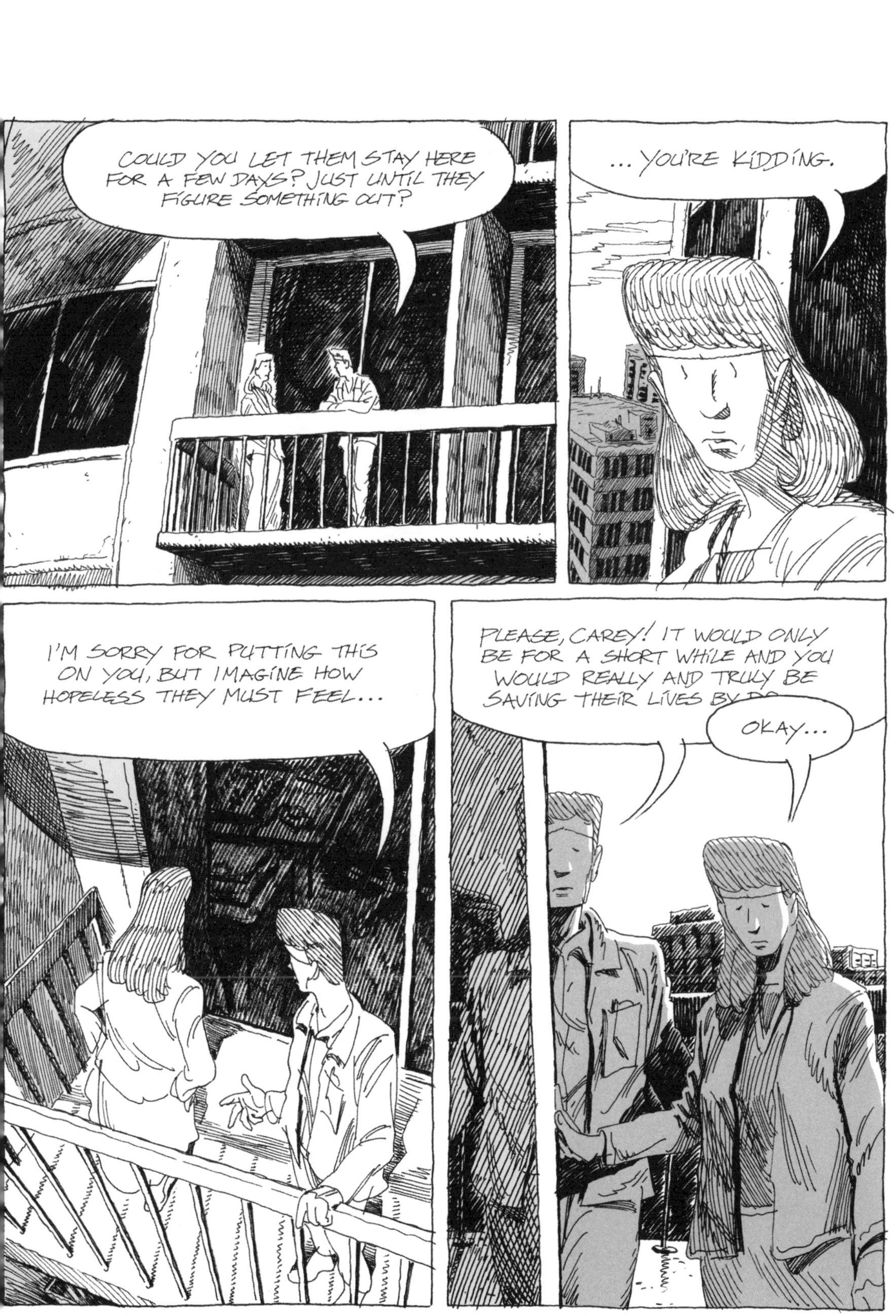
COULD YOU LET THEM STAY HERE FOR A FEW DAYS? JUST UNTIL THEY FIGURE SOMETHING OUT?
... YOU'RE KIDDING.
I'M SORRY FOR PUTTING THIS ON YOU, BUT IMAGINE HOW HOPELESS THEY MUST FEEL...
PLEASE, CAREY! IT WOULD ONLY BE FOR A SHORT WHILE AND YOU WOULD REALLY AND TRULY BE SAVING THEIR LIVES BY
OKAY...

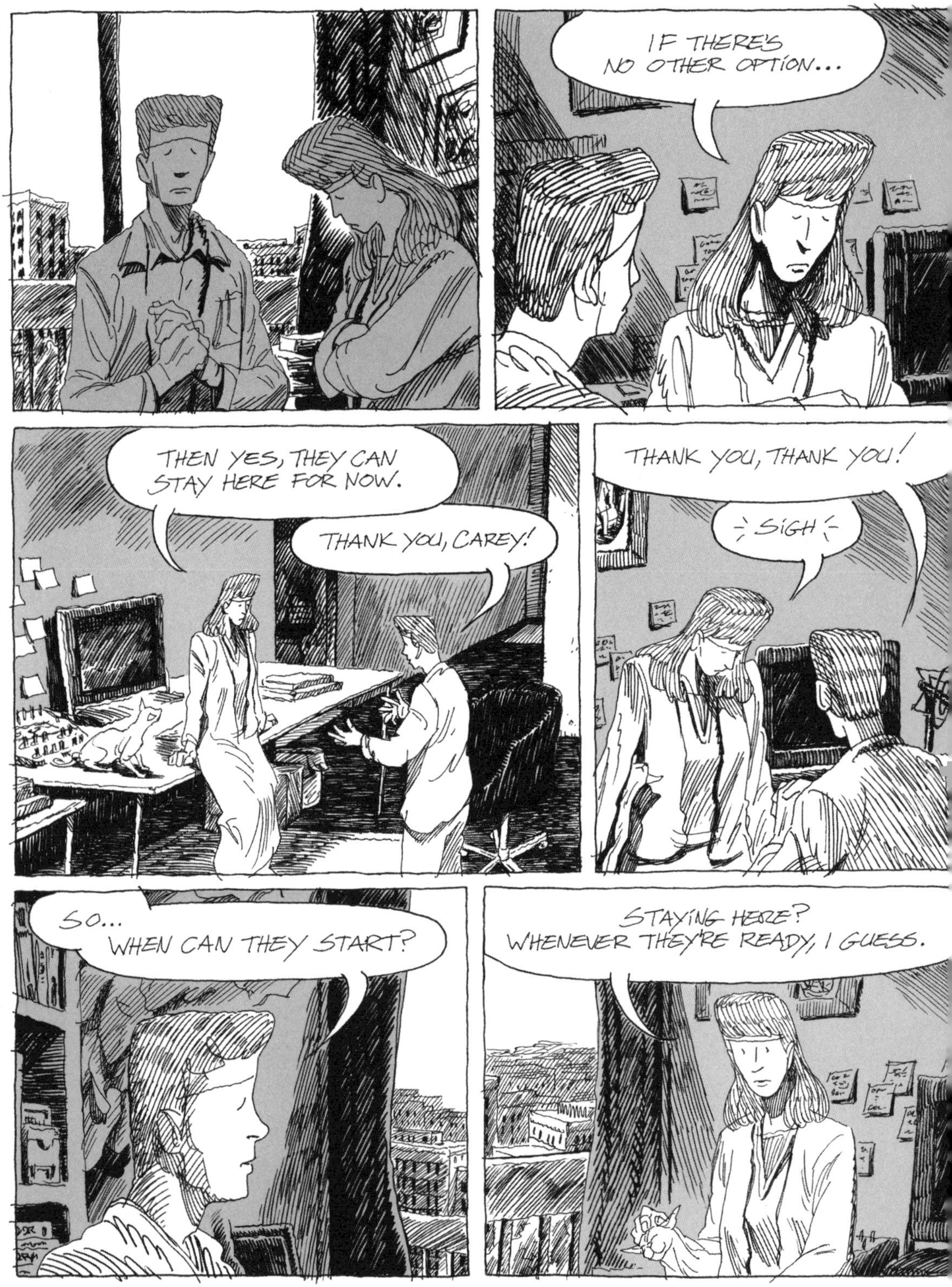
IF THERE'S NO OTHER OPTION...
THEN YES, THEY CAN STAY HERE FOR NOW.
THANK YOU, CAREY!
THANK YOU, THANK YOU!
SIGH
SO... WHEN CAN THEY START?
STAYING HERE? WHENEVER THEY'RE READY, I GUESS.

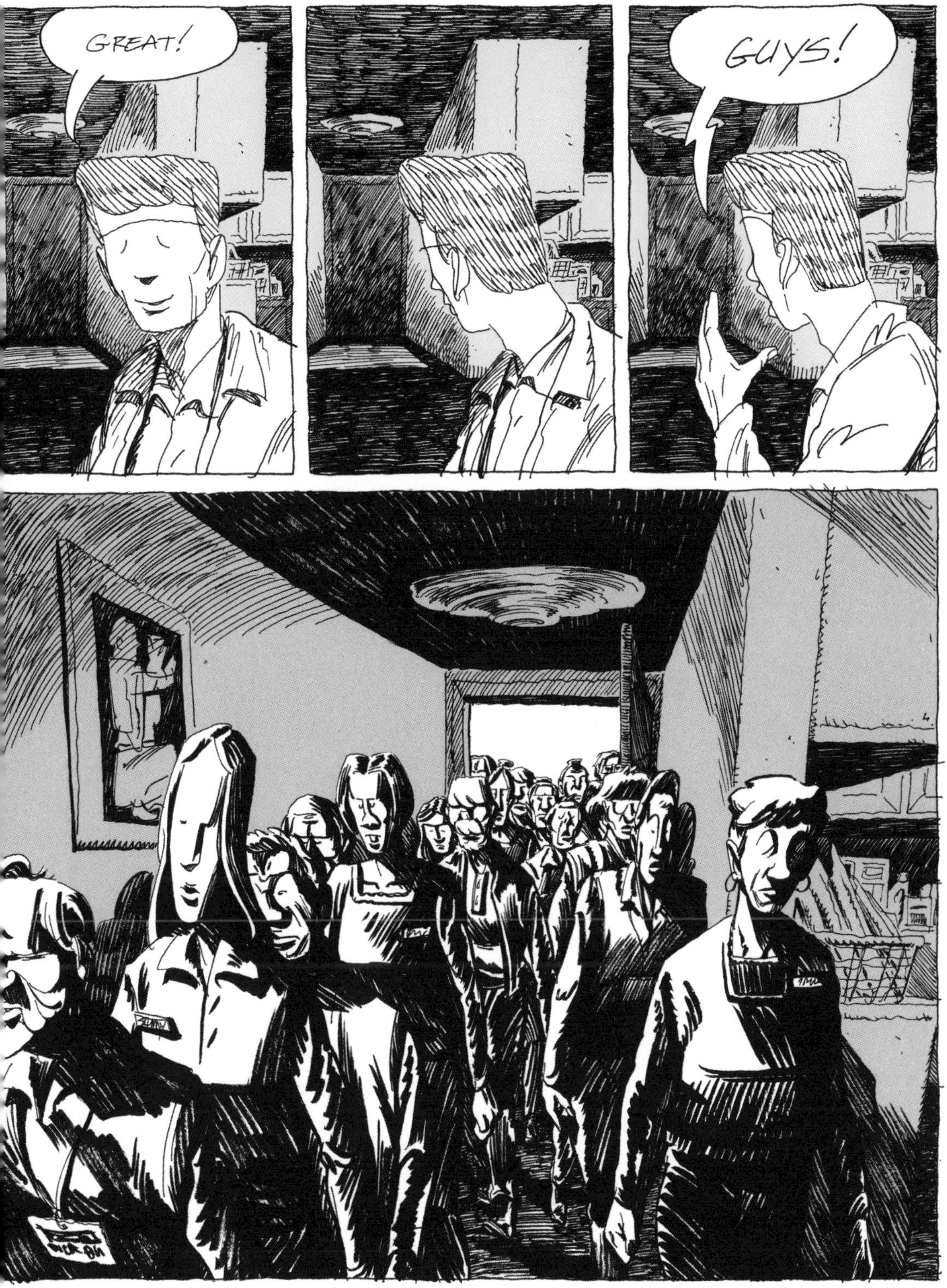
GREAT!
GUYS!

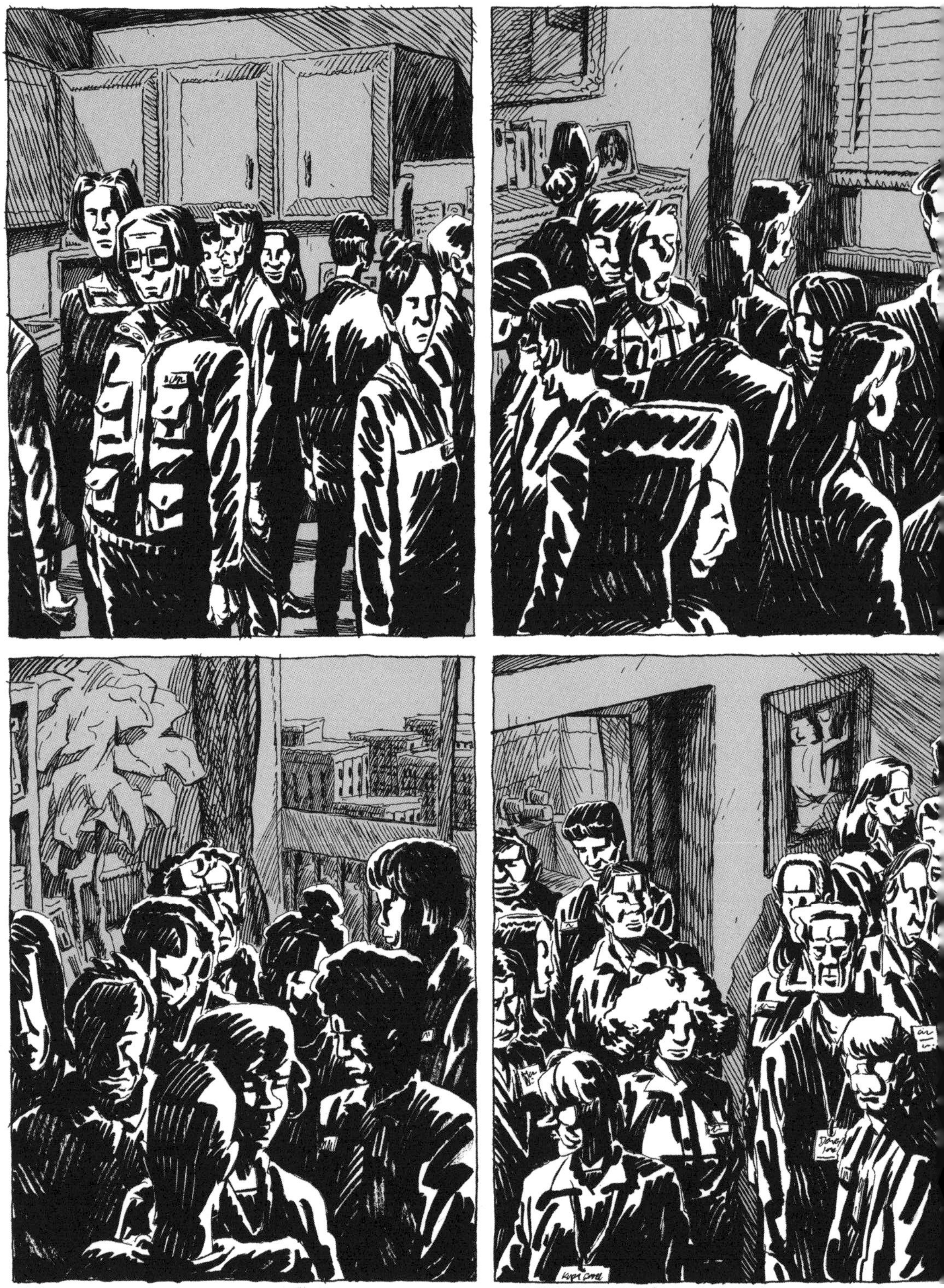

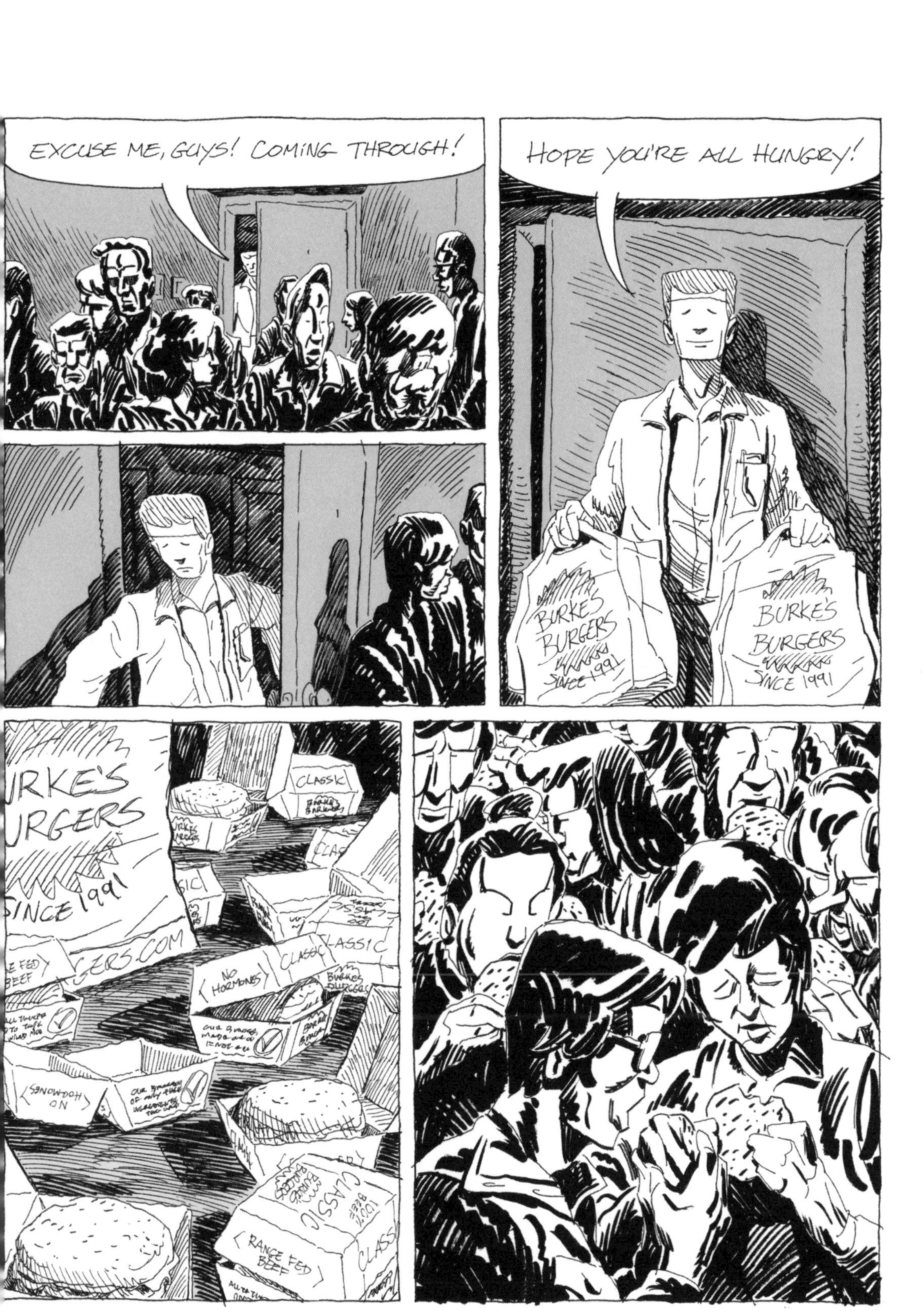

EXCUSE ME, GUYS! COMING THROUGH!
HOPE YOU'RE ALL HUNGRY!
BURKE'S BURGERS
SINCE 1991
BURKE'S BURGERS
SINCE 1991
URKE'S
URGERS
SINCE 1991
GERS.COM
CLASSIC
CLASSIC
CLASSIC
NO HORMONES
RANGE FED BEEF
CLASSIC

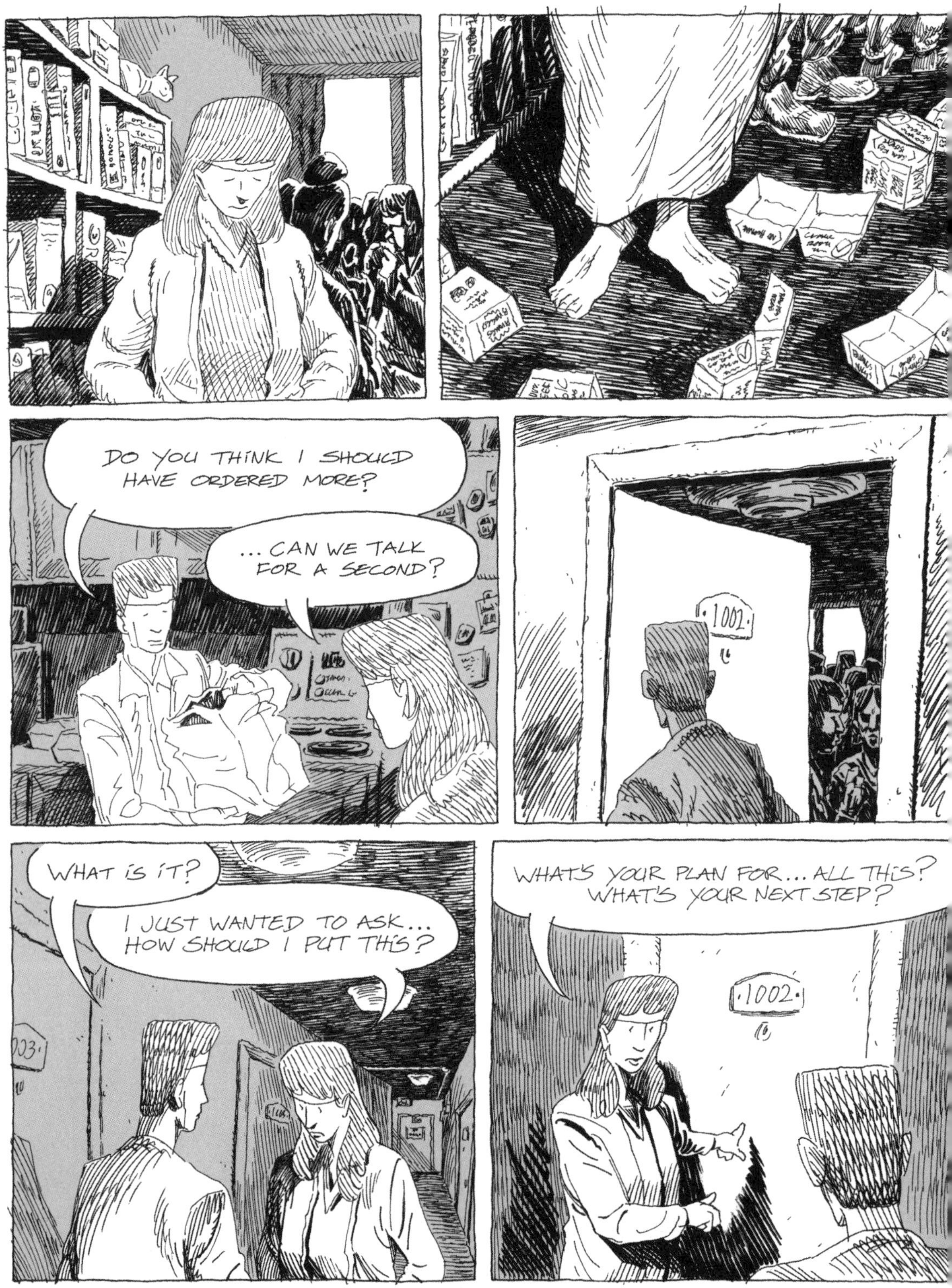
DO YOU THINK I SHOULD HAVE ORDERED MORE?
... CAN WE TALK FOR A SECOND?
·1002·
WHAT IS IT?
I JUST WANTED TO ASK... HOW SHOULD I PUT THIS?
WHAT'S YOUR PLAN FOR... ALL THIS? WHAT'S YOUR NEXT STEP?
·1002·

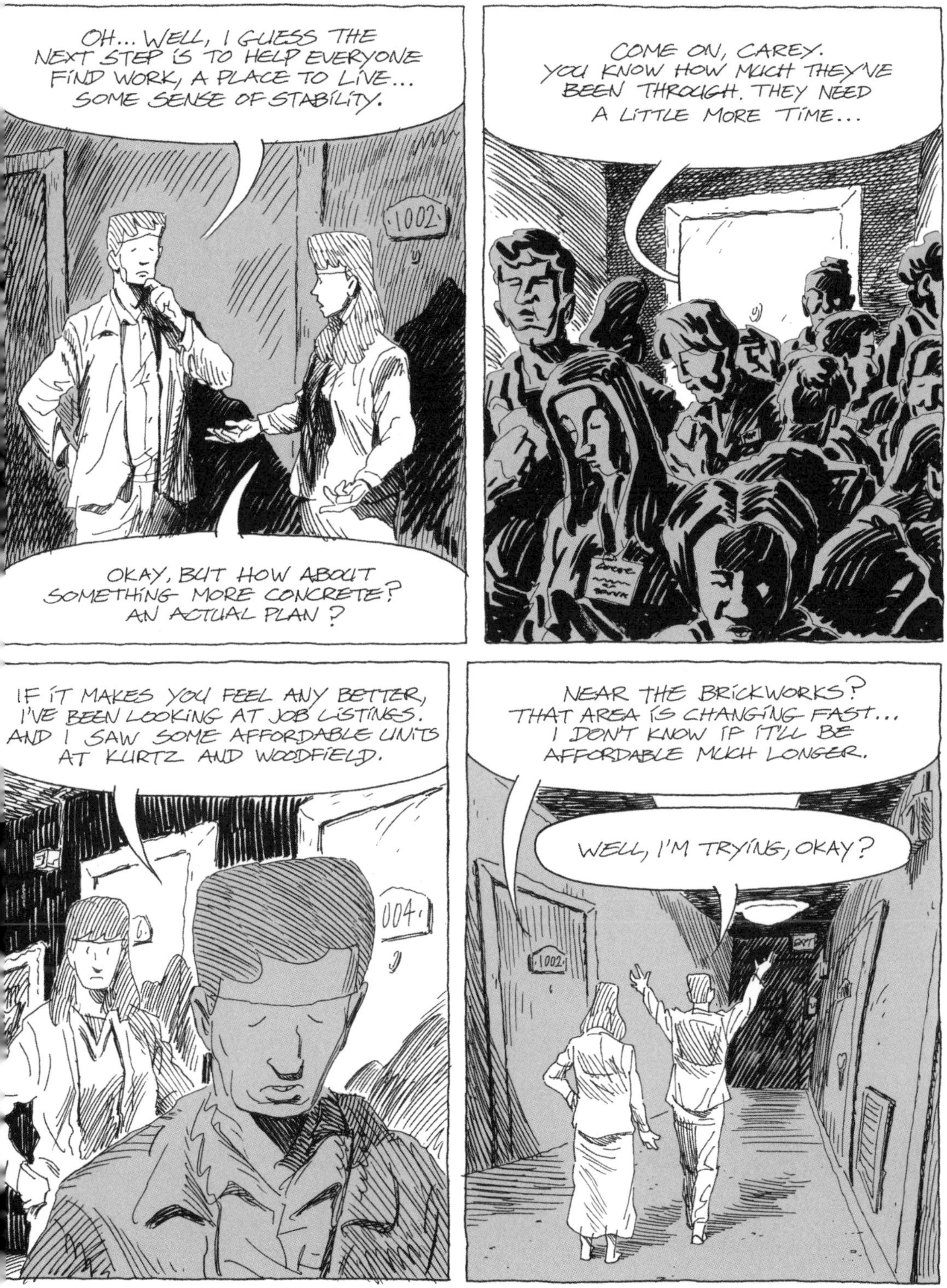
OH... WELL, I GUESS THE NEXT STEP IS TO HELP EVERYONE FIND WORK, A PLACE TO LIVE... SOME SENSE OF STABILITY.
OKAY, BUT HOW ABOUT SOMETHING MORE CONCRETE? AN ACTUAL PLAN?
1002
COME ON, CAREY. YOU KNOW HOW MUCH THEY'VE BEEN THROUGH. THEY NEED A LITTLE MORE TIME...
IF IT MAKES YOU FEEL ANY BETTER, I'VE BEEN LOOKING AT JOB LISTINGS. AND I SAW SOME AFFORDABLE UNITS AT KURTZ AND WOODFIELD.
NEAR THE BRICKWORKS? THAT AREA IS CHANGING FAST... I DON'T KNOW IF IT'LL BE AFFORDABLE MUCH LONGER.
WELL, I'M TRYING, OKAY?
1002
EXIT

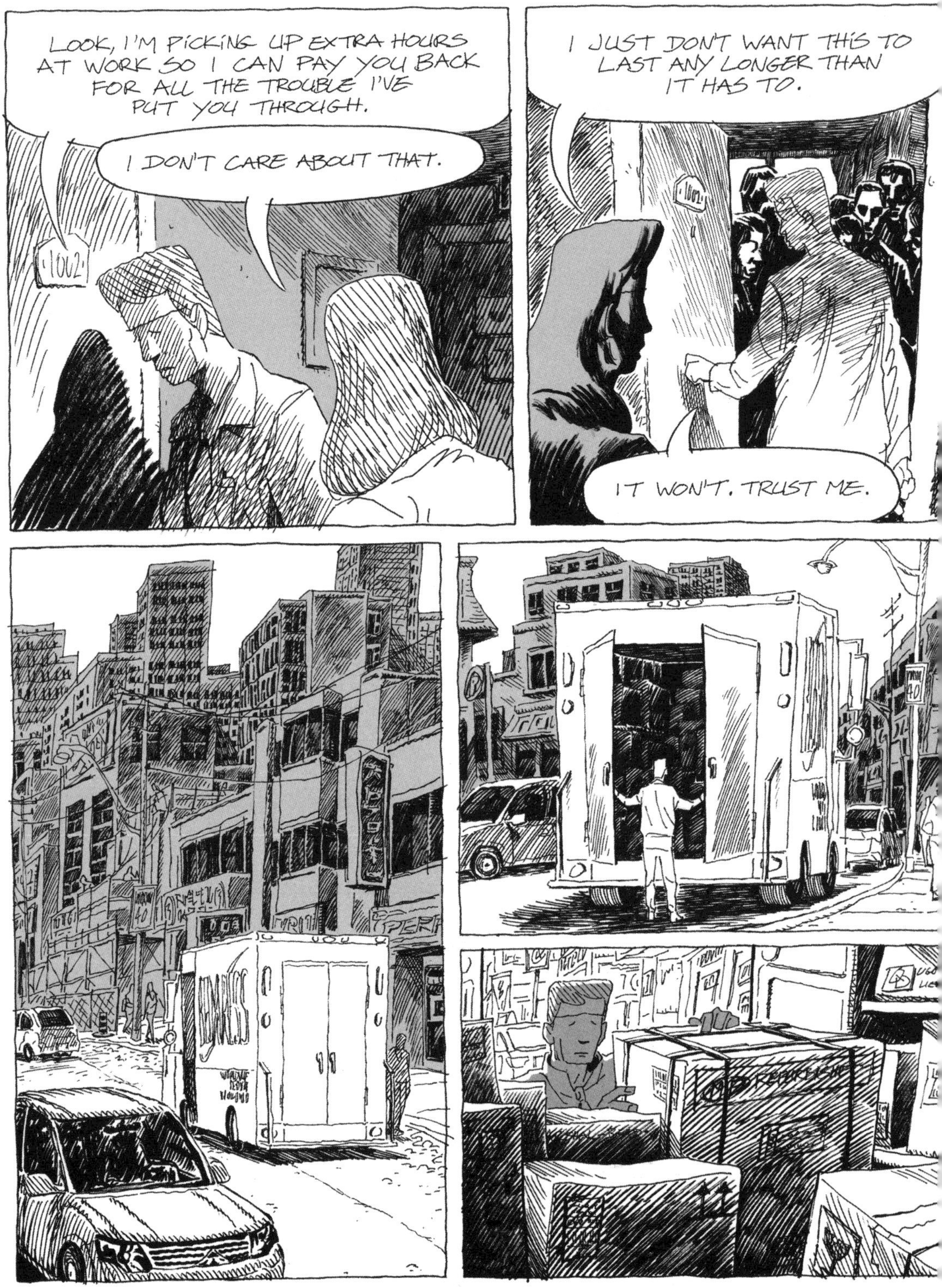
LOOK, I'M PICKING UP EXTRA HOURS AT WORK SO I CAN PAY YOU BACK FOR ALL THE TROUBLE I'VE PUT YOU THROUGH.
I DON'T CARE ABOUT THAT.
I JUST DON'T WANT THIS TO LAST ANY LONGER THAN IT HAS TO.
IT WON'T. TRUST ME.

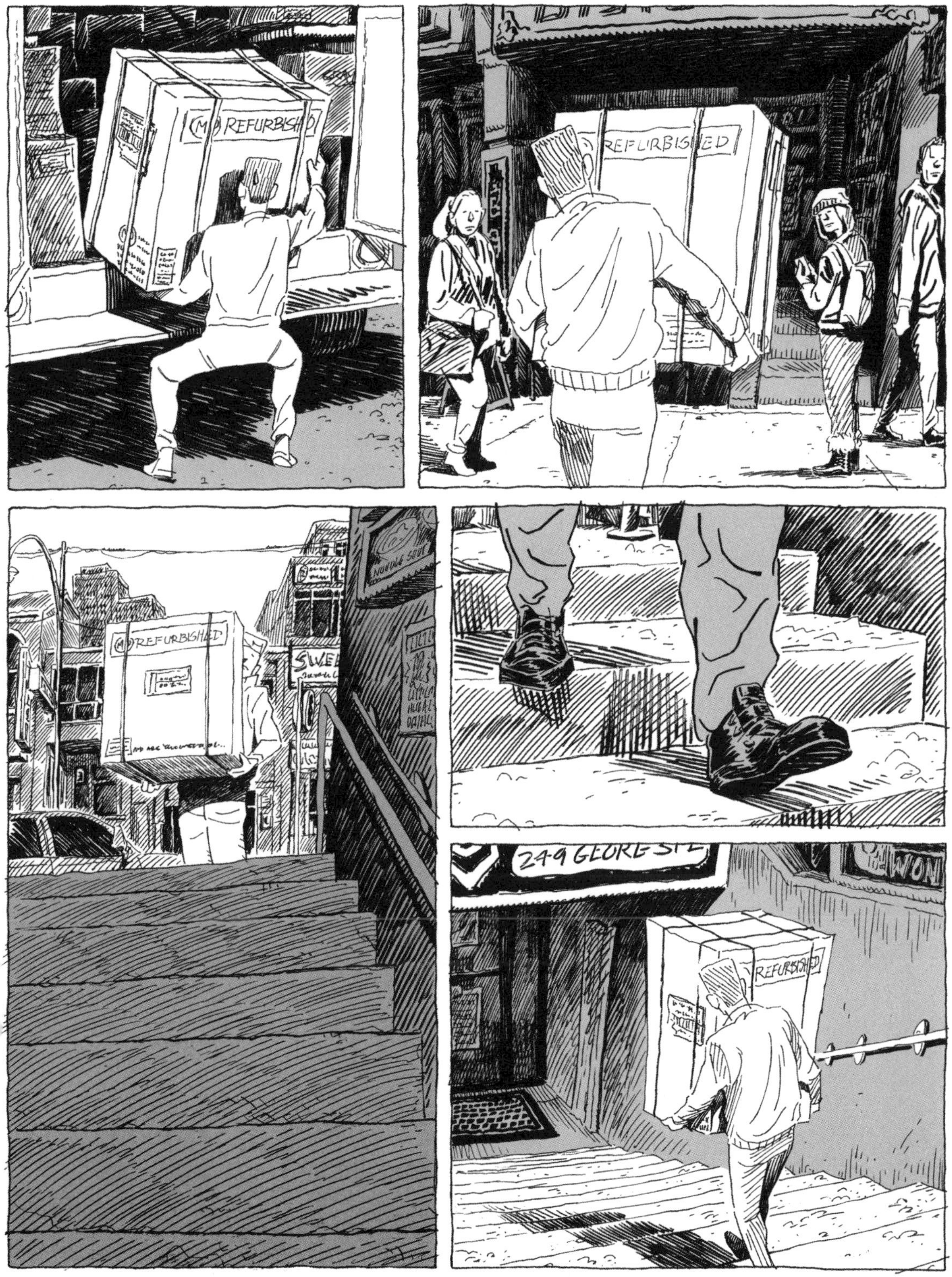
(M) REFURBISHED
REFURBISHED
(M) REFURBISHED
REFURBISHED
WON

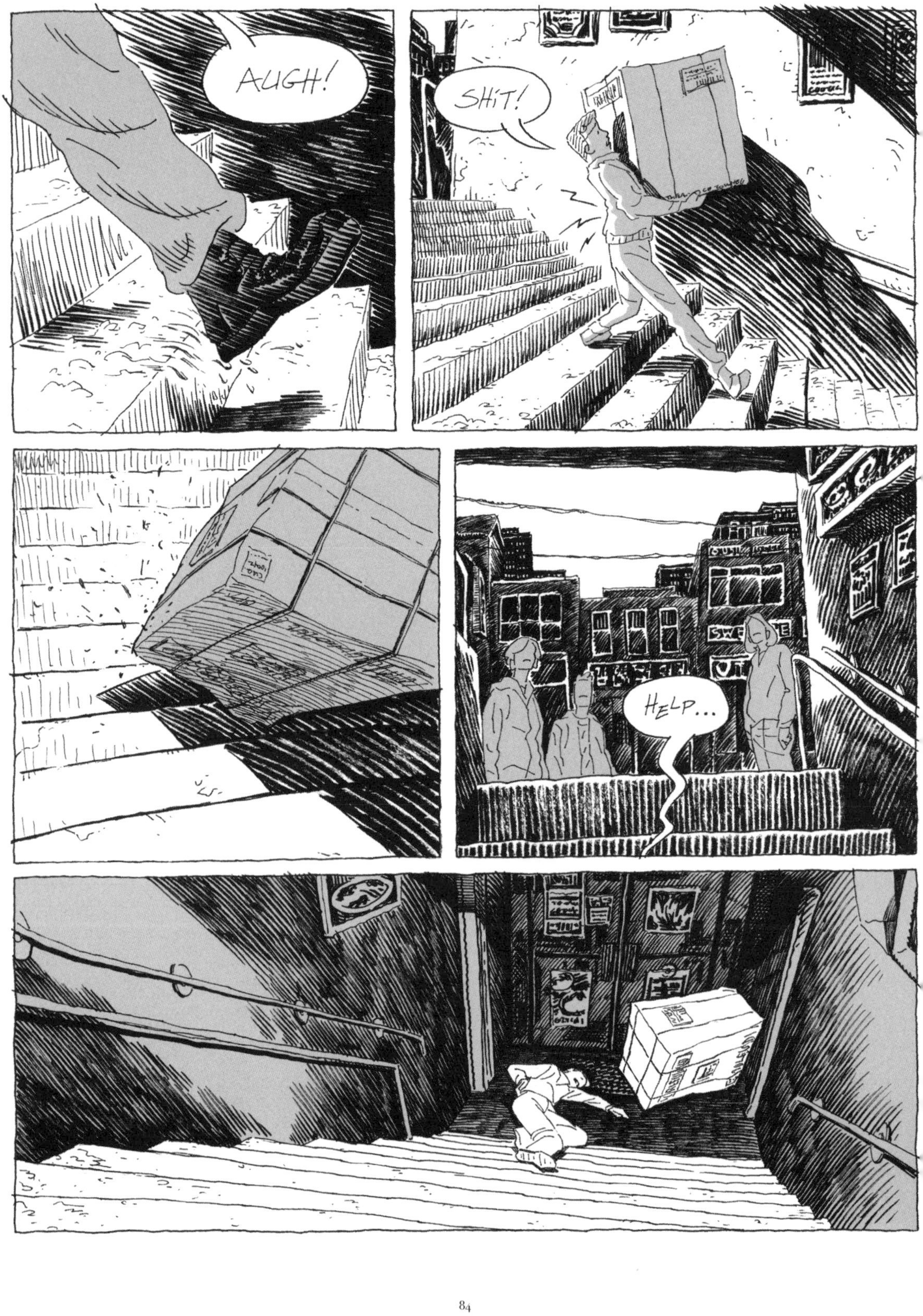
AUGH!
SHIT!
HELP...

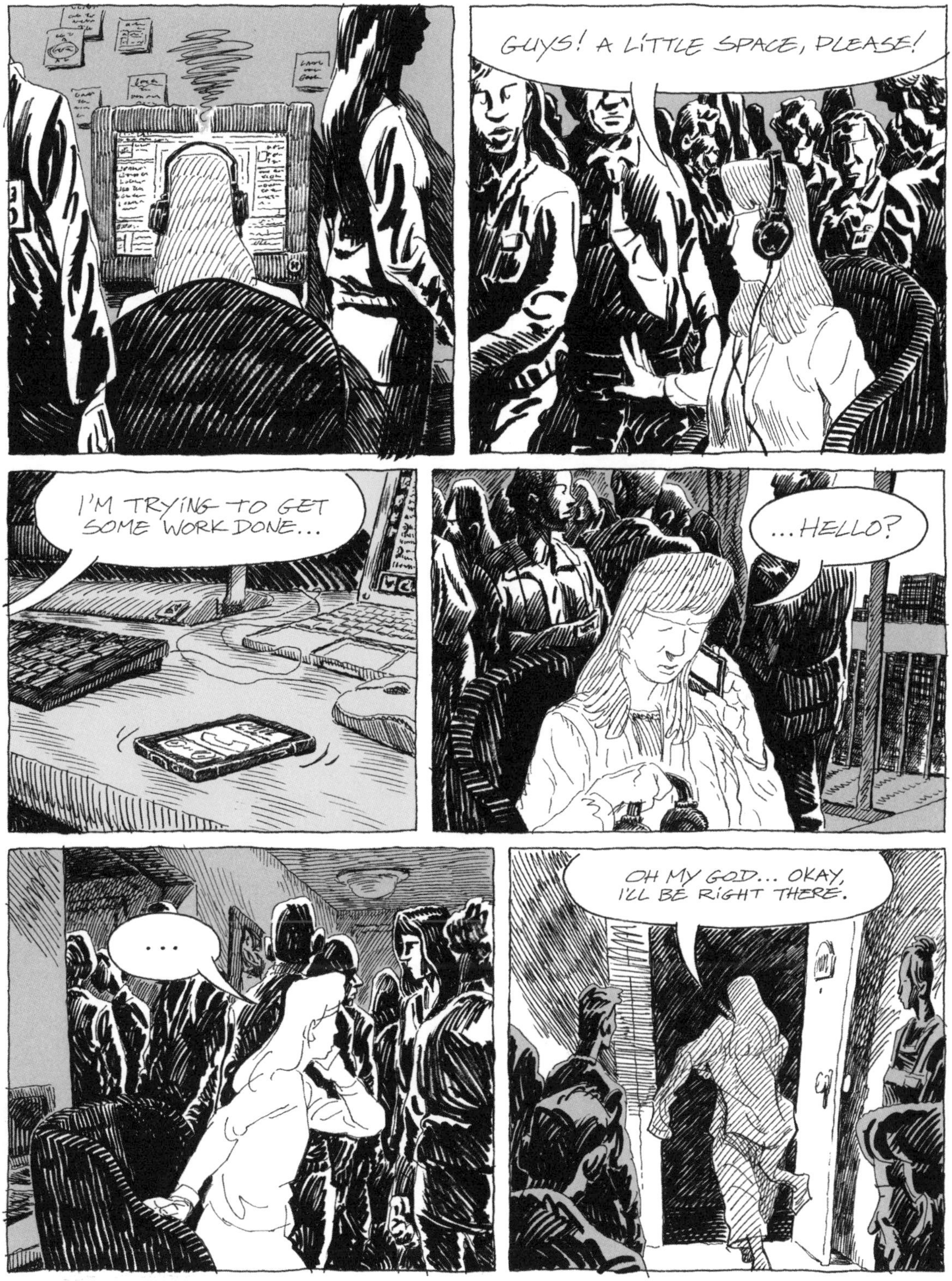
GUYS! A LITTLE SPACE, PLEASE!
I'M TRYING TO GET SOME WORK DONE...
...HELLO?
...
OH MY GOD... OKAY, I'LL BE RIGHT THERE.

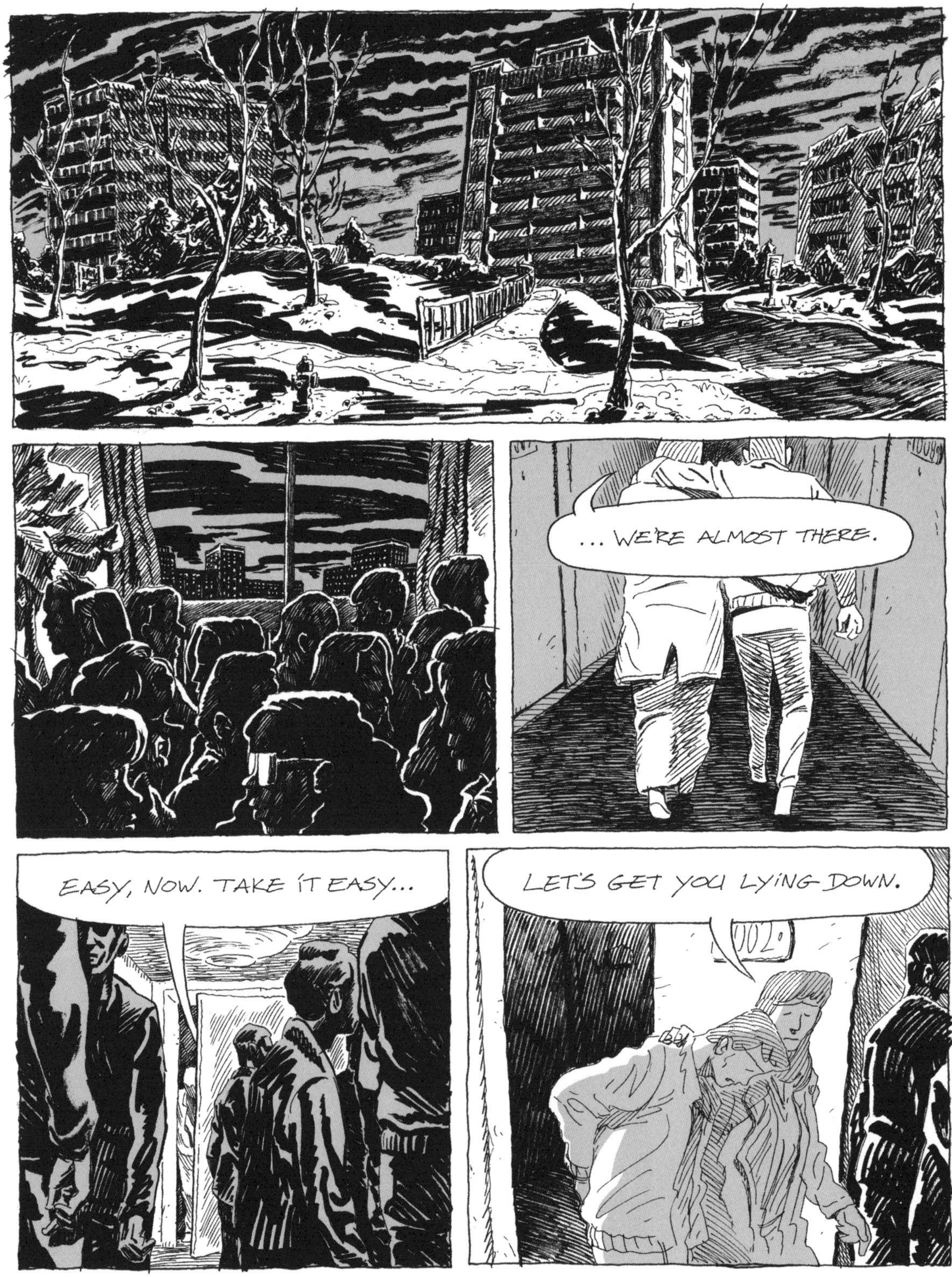
... WE'RE ALMOST THERE.
EASY, NOW. TAKE IT EASY...
LET'S GET YOU LYING DOWN.

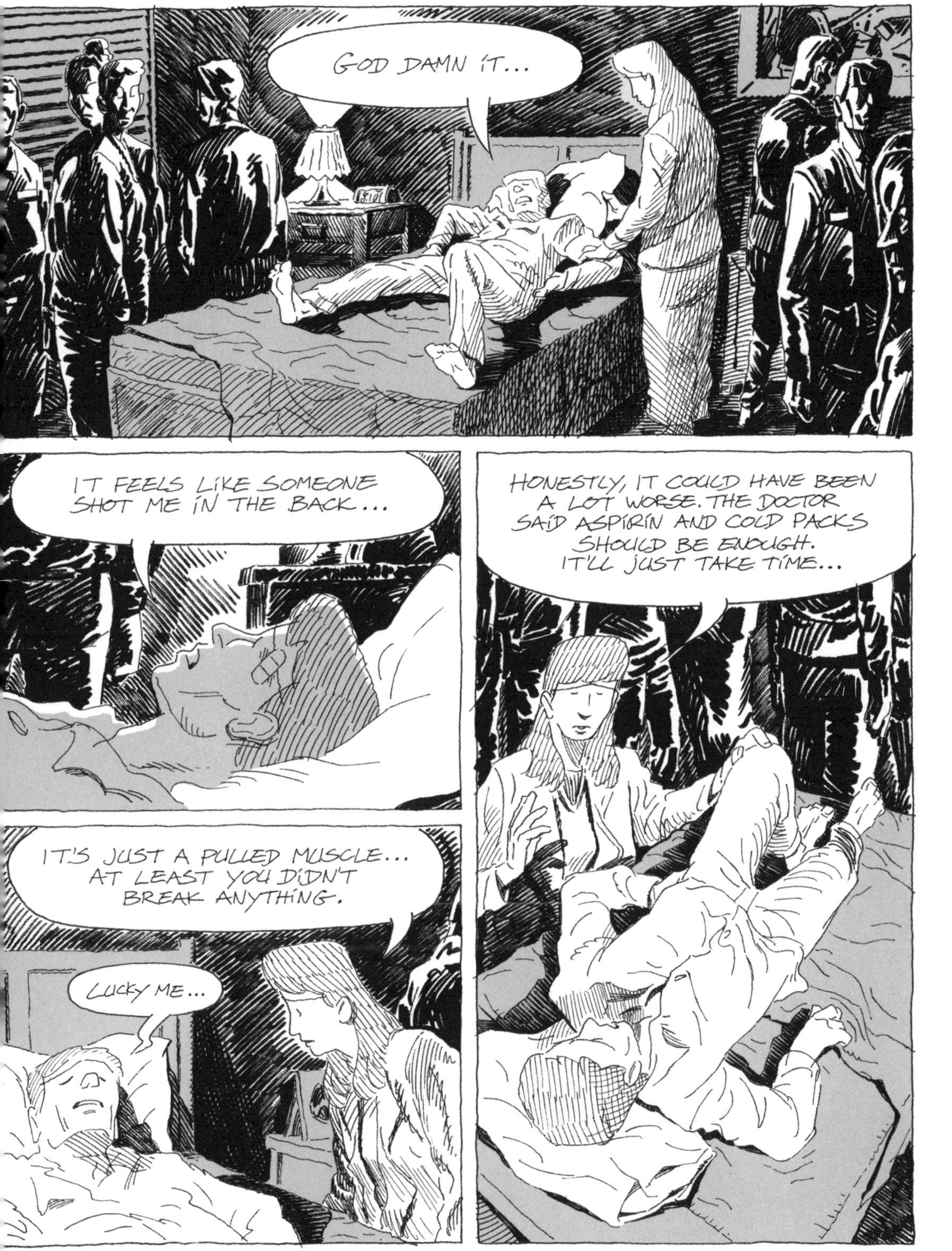
GOD DAMN IT...
IT FEELS LIKE SOMEONE SHOT ME IN THE BACK...
IT'S JUST A PULLED MUSCLE... AT LEAST YOU DIDN'T BREAK ANYTHING.
LUCKY ME...
HONESTLY, IT COULD HAVE BEEN A LOT WORSE. THE DOCTOR SAID ASPIRIN AND COLD PACKS SHOULD BE ENOUGH. IT'LL JUST TAKE TIME...

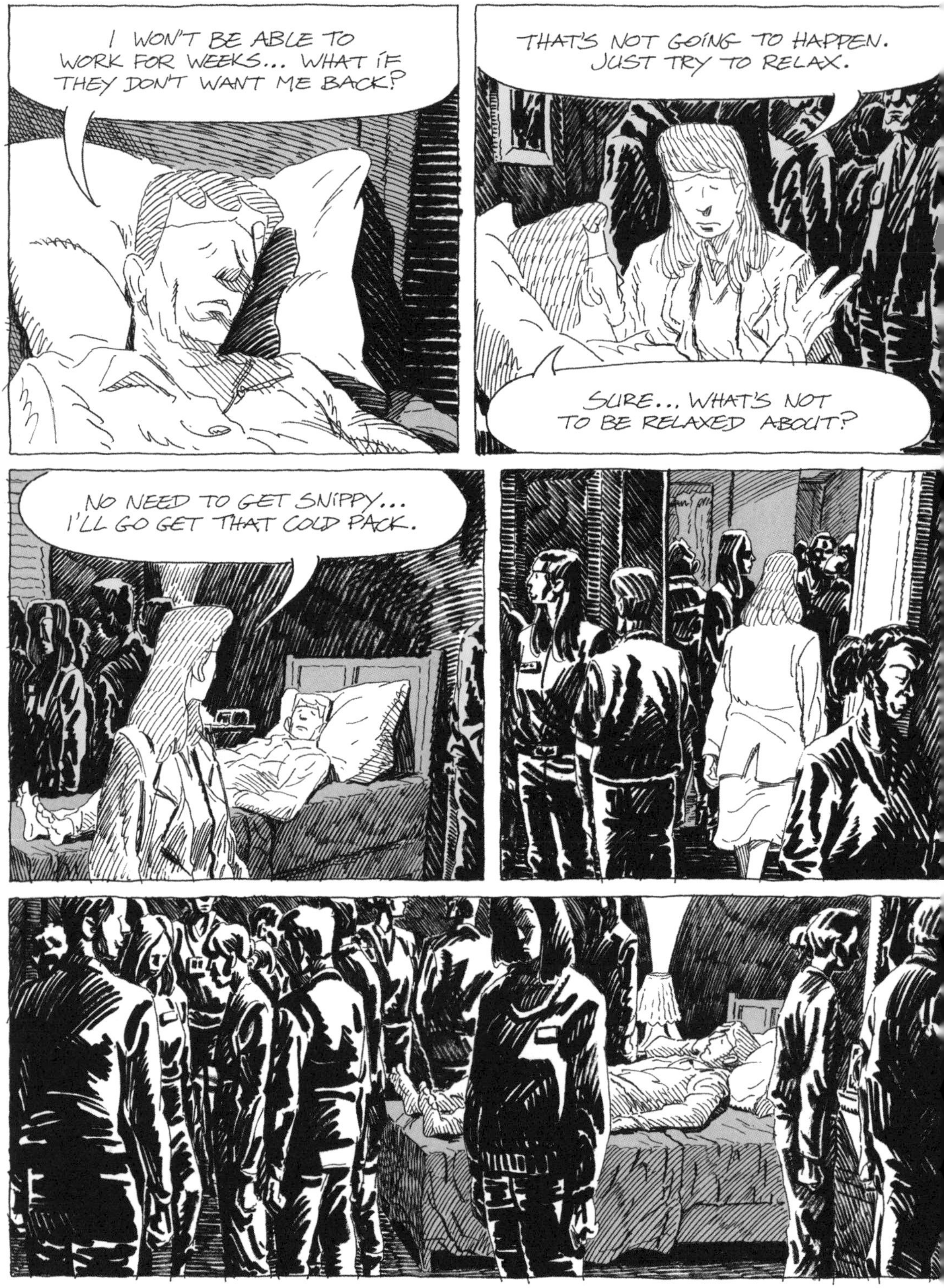
I WON'T BE ABLE TO WORK FOR WEEKS... WHAT IF THEY DON'T WANT ME BACK?
THAT'S NOT GOING TO HAPPEN. JUST TRY TO RELAX.
SURE... WHAT'S NOT TO BE RELAXED ABOUT?
NO NEED TO GET SNIPPY... I'LL GO GET THAT COLD PACK.

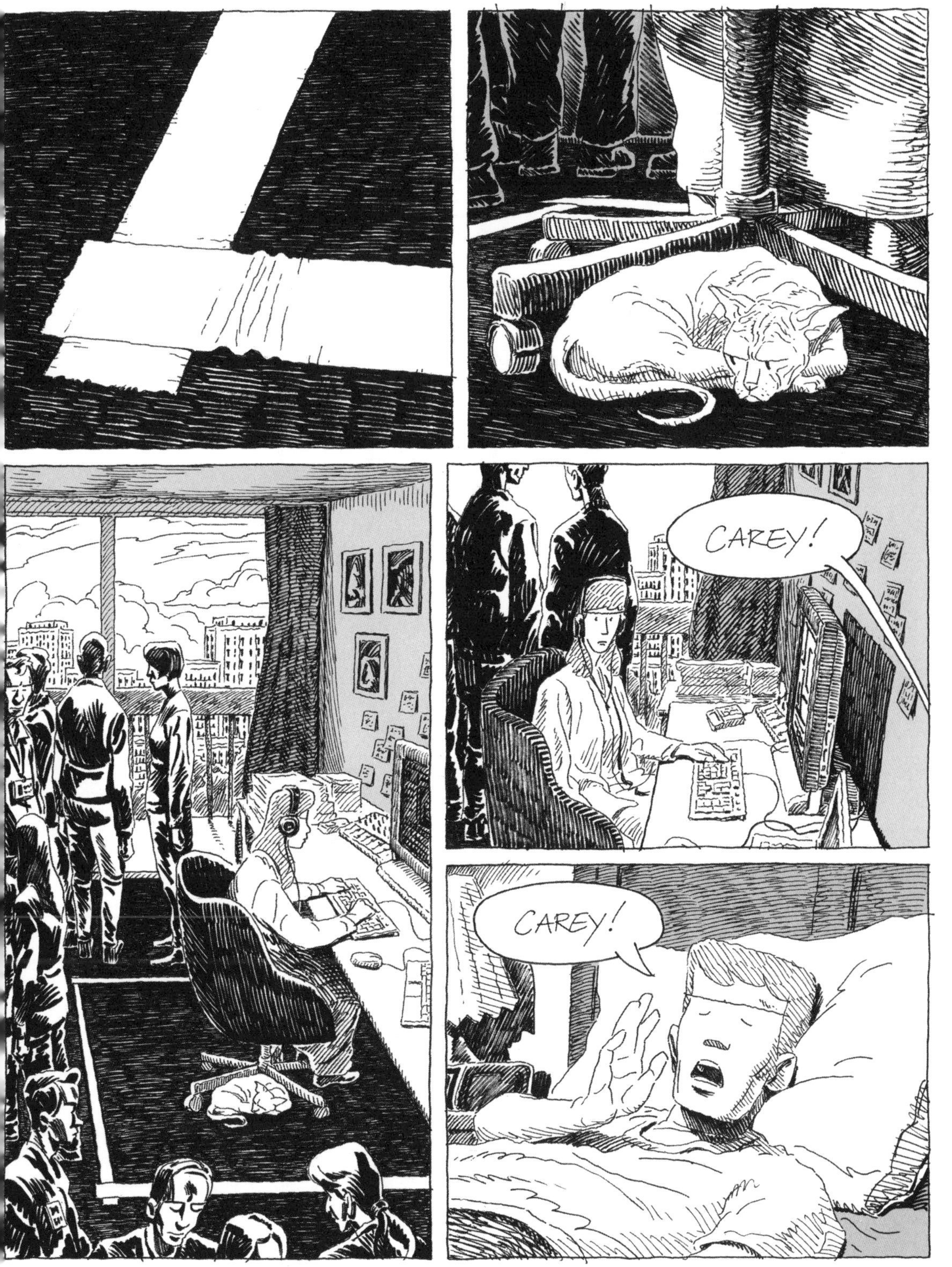
CAREY!
CAREY!

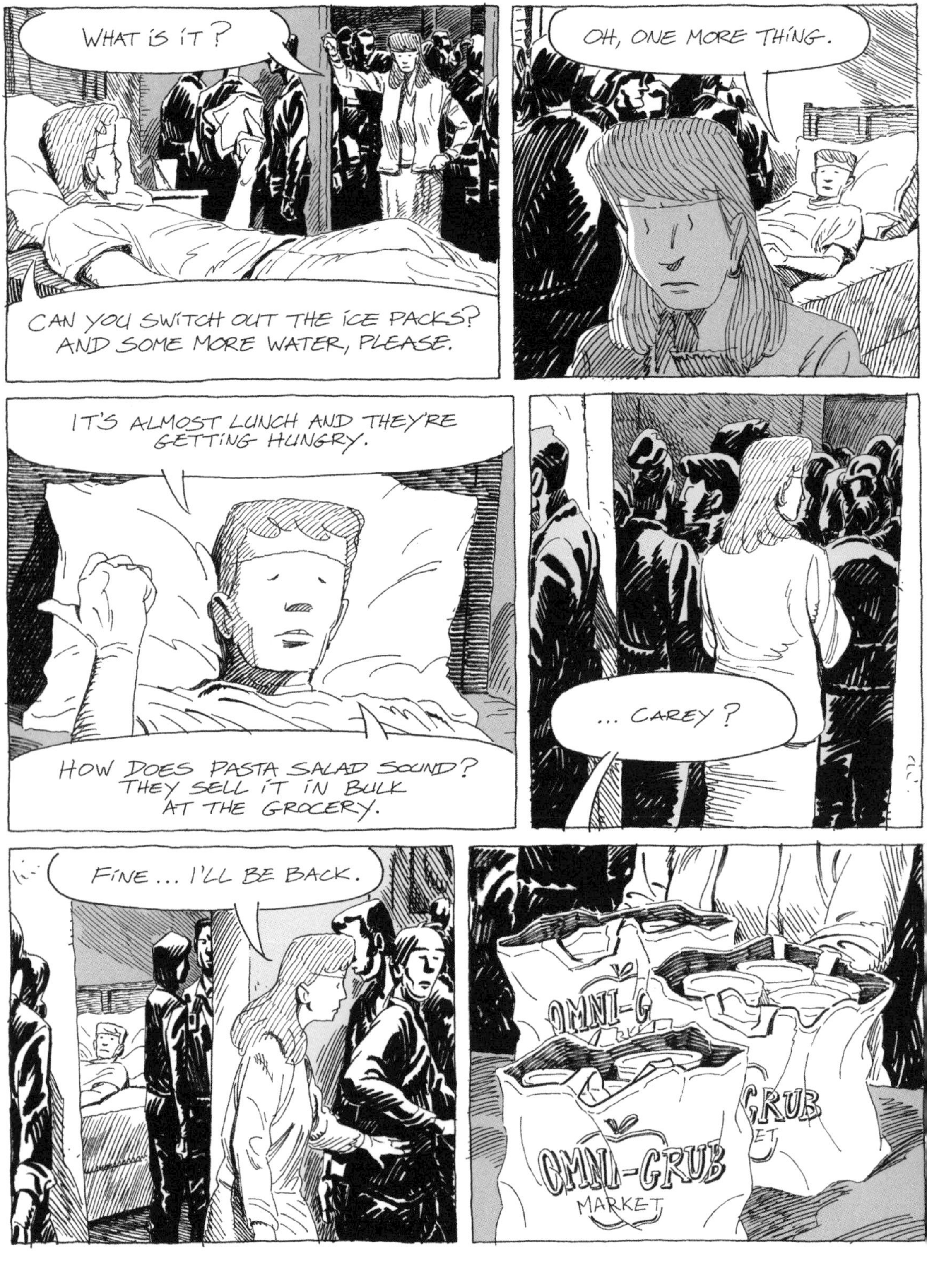
WHAT IS IT?
CAN YOU SWITCH OUT THE ICE PACKS? AND SOME MORE WATER, PLEASE.
OH, ONE MORE THING.
IT'S ALMOST LUNCH AND THEY'RE GETTING HUNGRY.
HOW DOES PASTA SALAD SOUND? THEY SELL IT IN BULK AT THE GROCERY.
... CAREY?
FINE... I'LL BE BACK.
OMNI-GRUB
MARKET

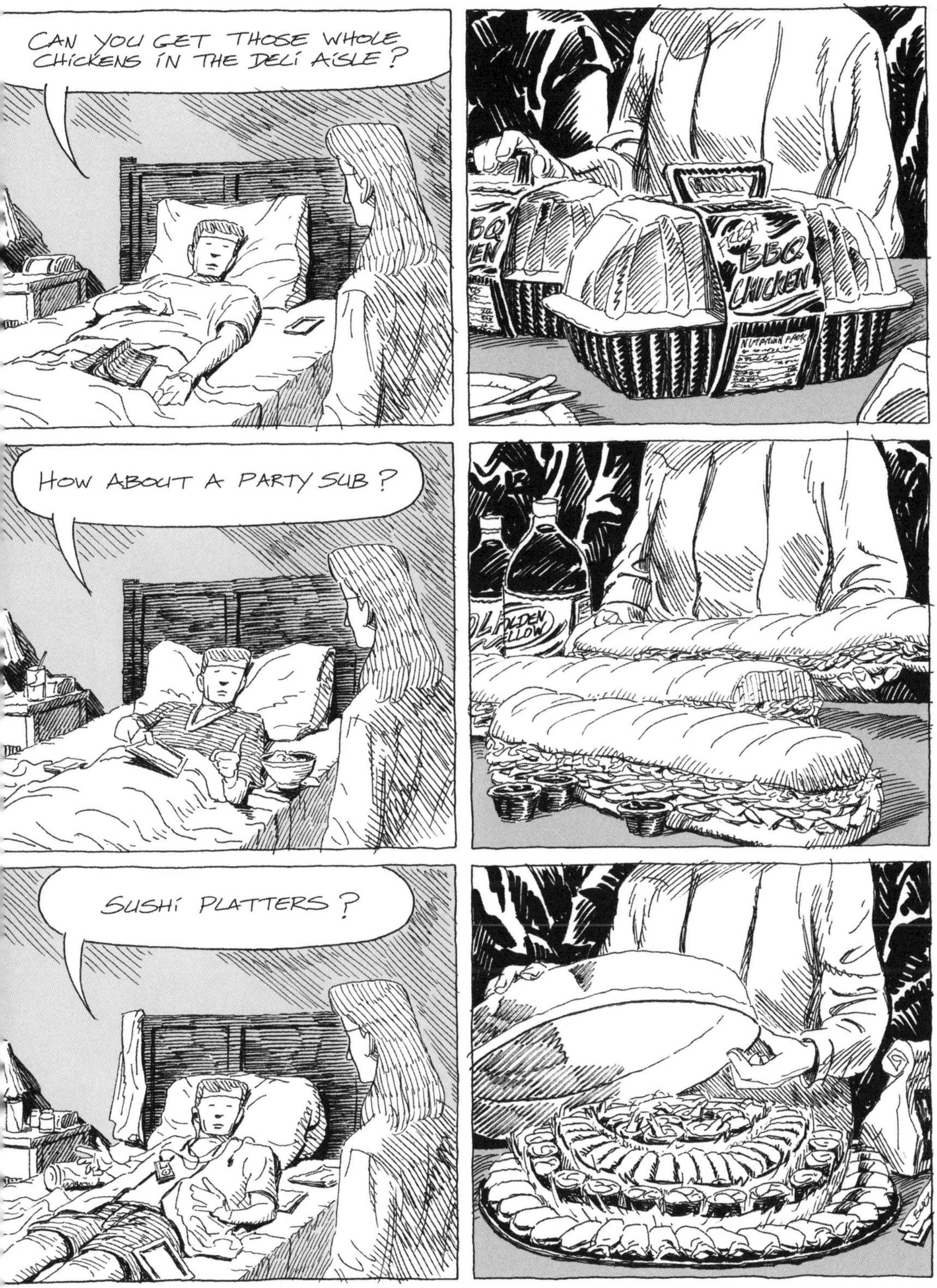
CAN YOU GET THOSE WHOLE CHICKENS IN THE DELI AISLE?
BBQ CHICKEN
HOW ABOUT A PARTY SUB?
SUSHI PLATTERS?

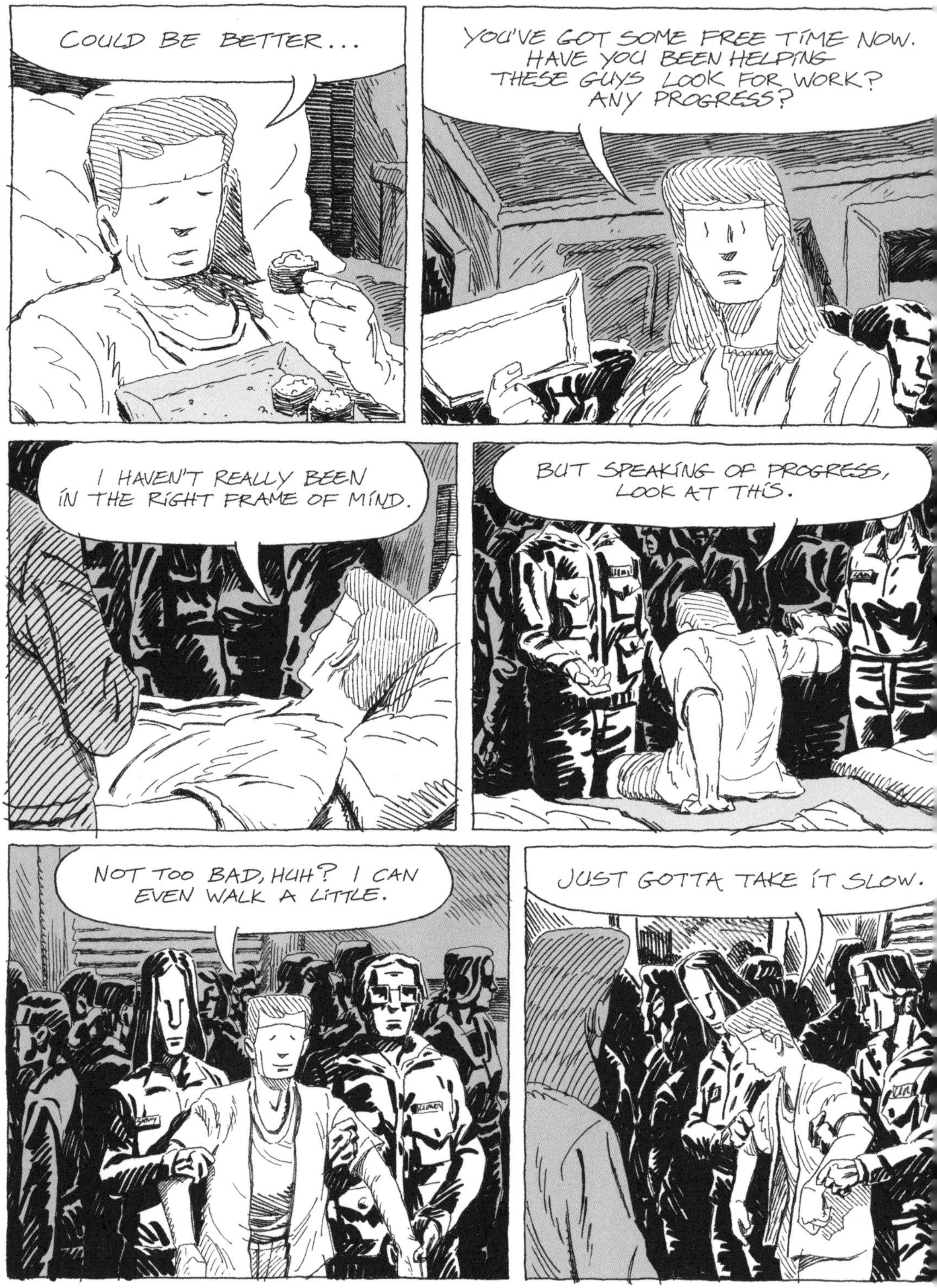
COULD BE BETTER...
YOU'VE GOT SOME FREE TIME NOW. HAVE YOU BEEN HELPING THESE GUYS LOOK FOR WORK? ANY PROGRESS?
I HAVEN'T REALLY BEEN IN THE RIGHT FRAME OF MIND.
BUT SPEAKING OF PROGRESS, LOOK AT THIS.
NOT TOO BAD, HUH? I CAN EVEN WALK A LITTLE.
JUST GOTTA TAKE IT SLOW.

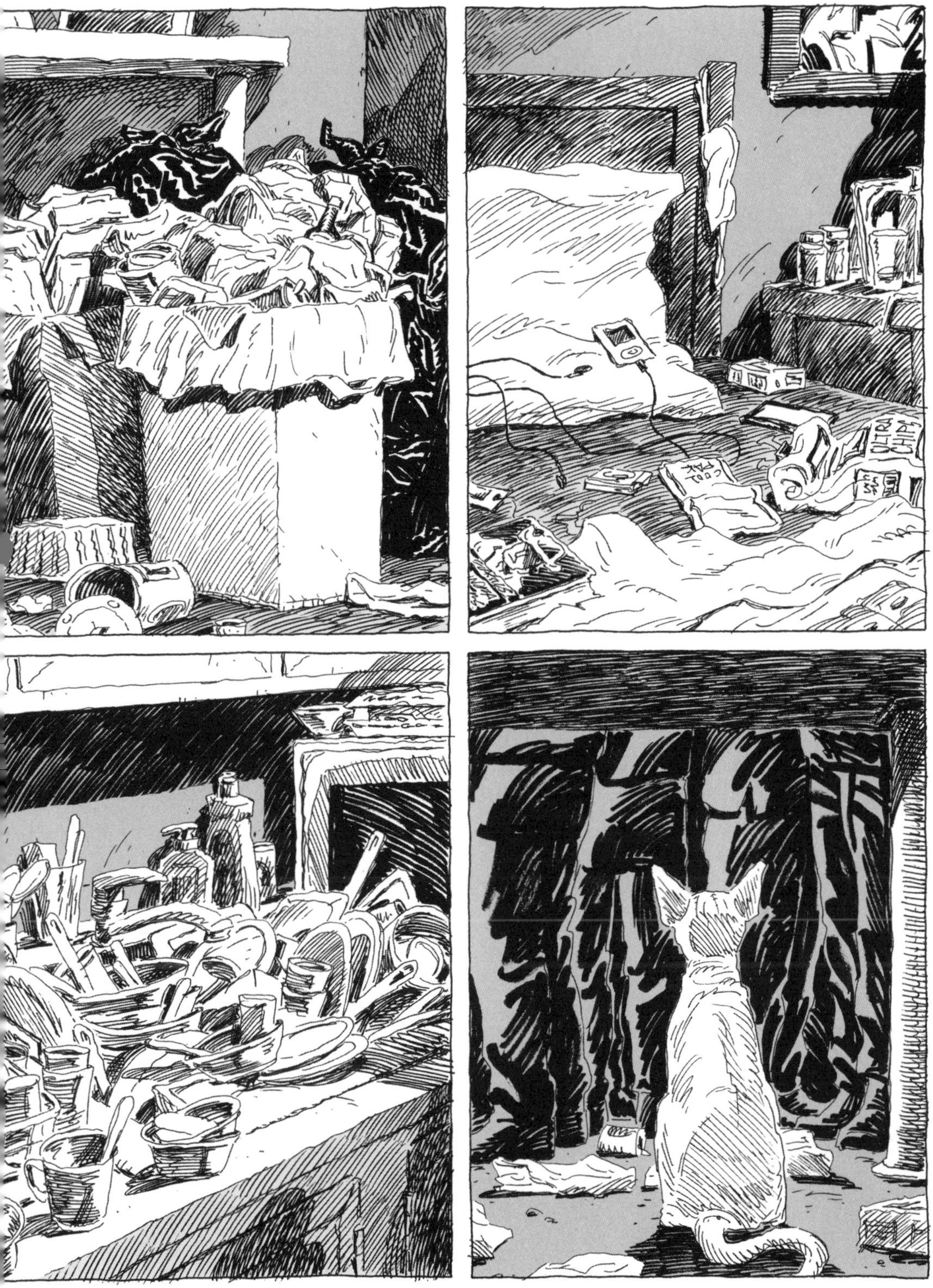
COOL PAK
ULTRA CHIPS

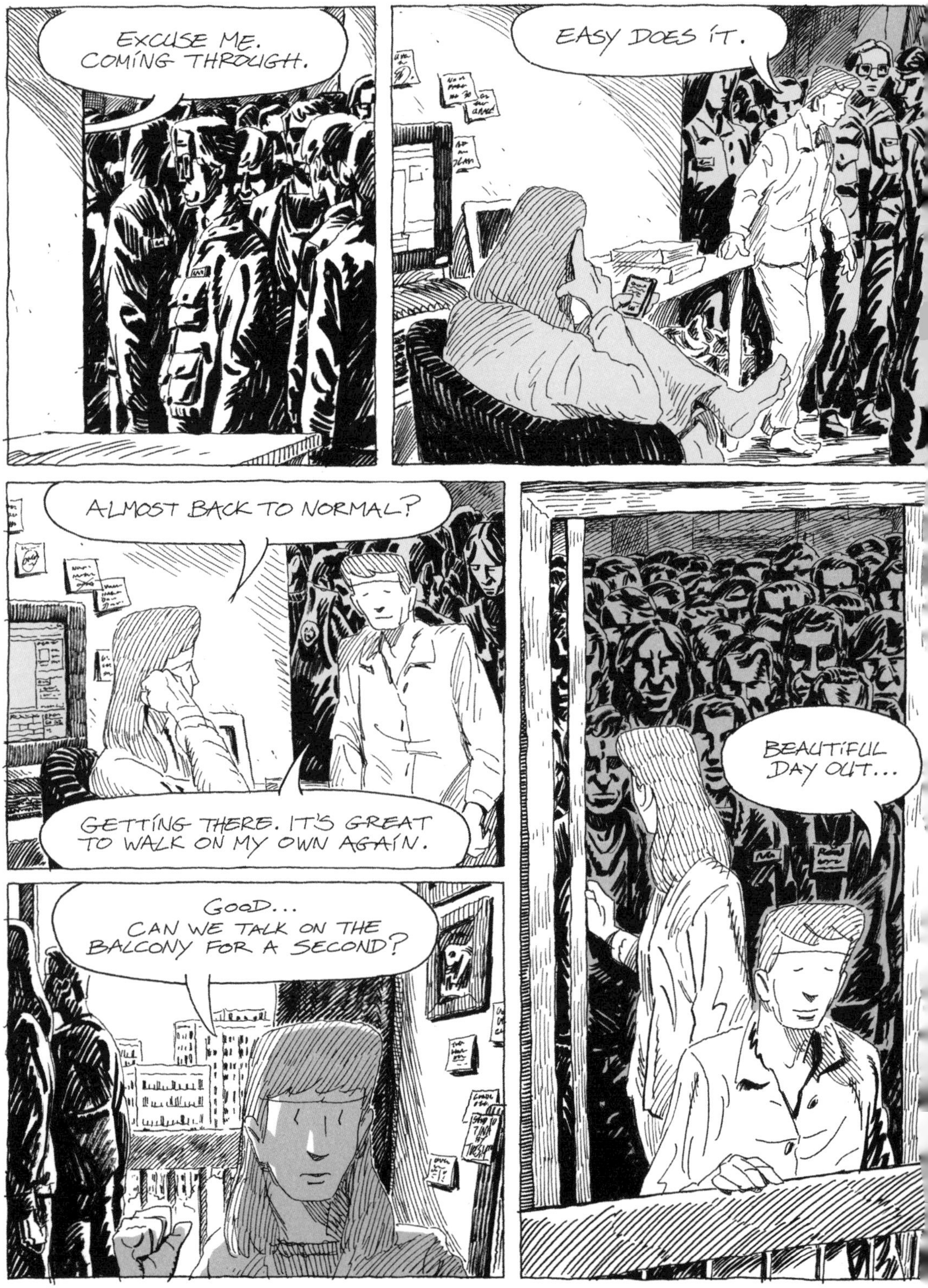
EXCUSE ME. COMING THROUGH.
EASY DOES IT.
ALMOST BACK TO NORMAL?
GETTING THERE. IT'S GREAT TO WALK ON MY OWN AGAIN.
GOOD... CAN WE TALK ON THE BALCONY FOR A SECOND?
BEAUTIFUL DAY OUT...

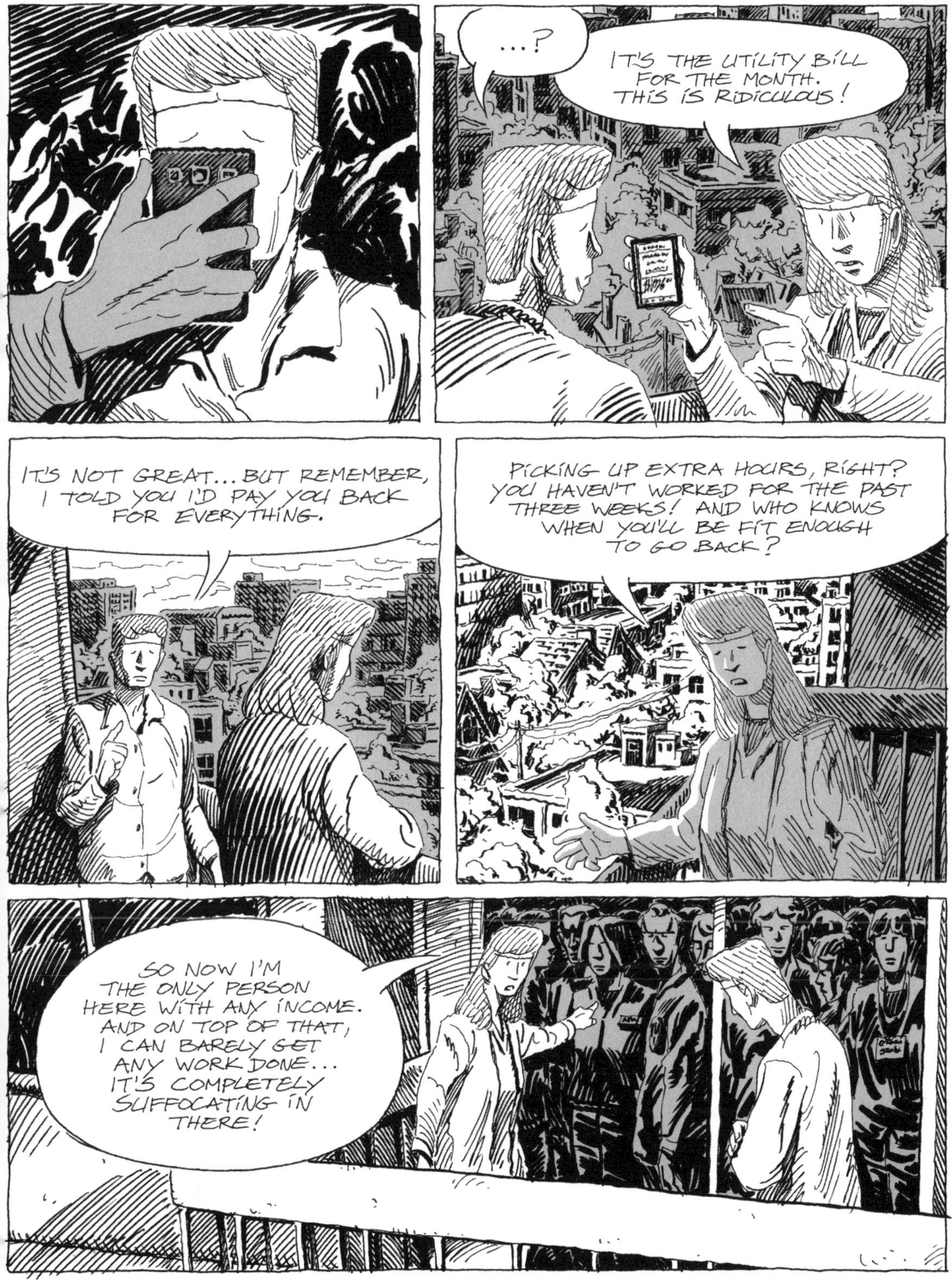
...?
IT'S THE UTILITY BILL FOR THE MONTH. THIS IS RIDICULOUS!
IT'S NOT GREAT... BUT REMEMBER, I TOLD YOU I'D PAY YOU BACK FOR EVERYTHING.
PICKING UP EXTRA HOURS, RIGHT? YOU HAVEN'T WORKED FOR THE PAST THREE WEEKS! AND WHO KNOWS WHEN YOU'LL BE FIT ENOUGH TO GO BACK?
SO NOW I'M THE ONLY PERSON HERE WITH ANY INCOME. AND ON TOP OF THAT, I CAN BARELY GET ANY WORK DONE... IT'S COMPLETELY SUFFOCATING IN THERE!

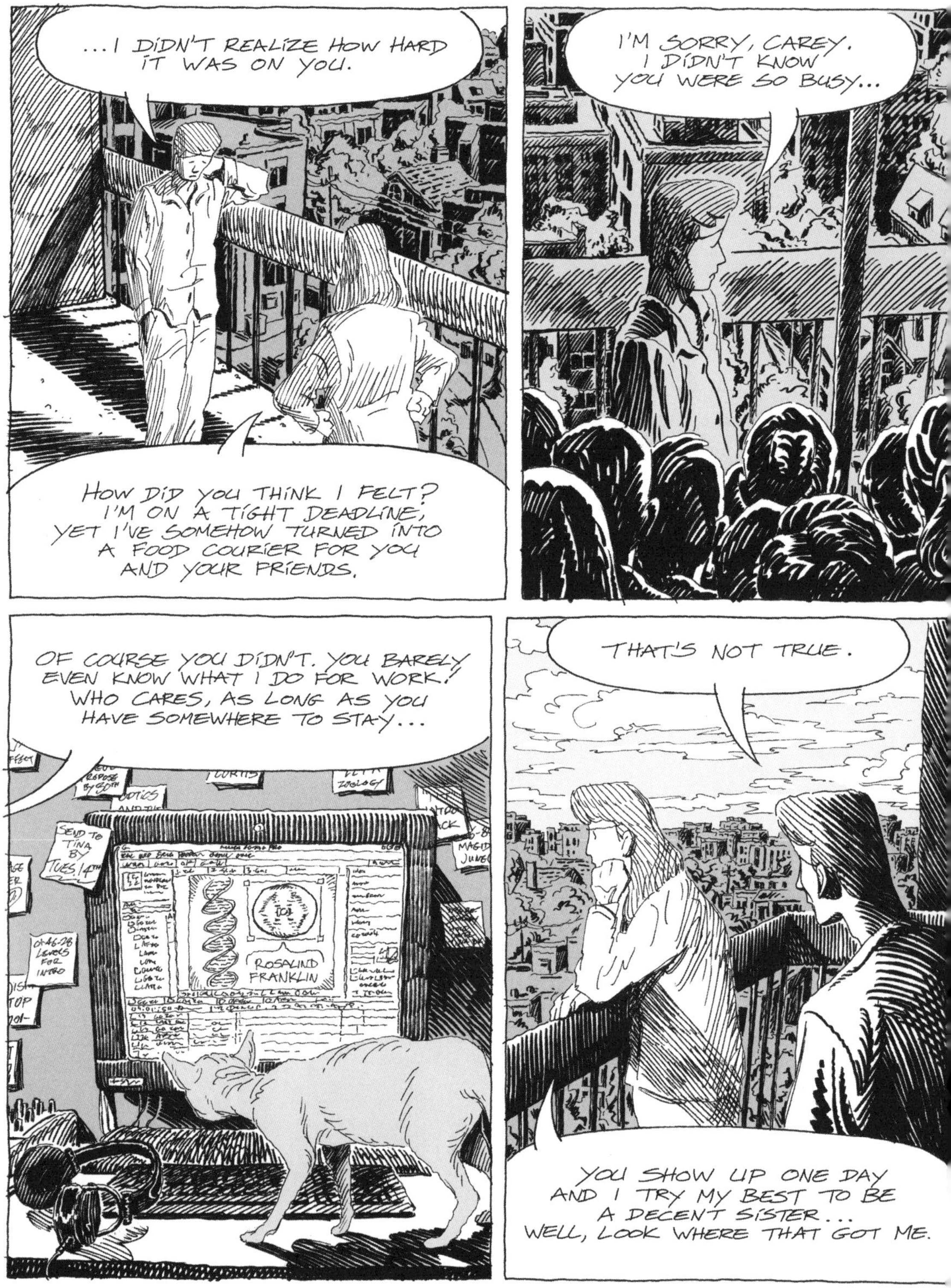
...I DIDN'T REALIZE HOW HARD IT WAS ON YOU.
HOW DID YOU THINK I FELT? I'M ON A TIGHT DEADLINE, YET I'VE SOMEHOW TURNED INTO A FOOD COURIER FOR YOU AND YOUR FRIENDS.
I'M SORRY, CAREY. I DIDN'T KNOW YOU WERE SO BUSY...
OF COURSE YOU DIDN'T. YOU BARELY EVEN KNOW WHAT I DO FOR WORK. WHO CARES, AS LONG AS YOU HAVE SOMEWHERE TO STAY...
SEND TO TINA BY TUES 14TH
ZOOLOGY
ROSALIND FRANKLIN
THAT'S NOT TRUE.
YOU SHOW UP ONE DAY AND I TRY MY BEST TO BE A DECENT SISTER... WELL, LOOK WHERE THAT GOT ME.

...

THE PAST FEW YEARS HAVE FELT LIKE ONE DEAD-END AFTER ANOTHER. AND NOW I FIND MY FRIENDS STRUGGLING TO SURVIVE...

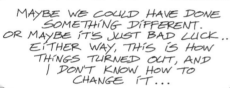

MAYBE WE COULD HAVE DONE SOMETHING DIFFERENT. OR MAYBE IT'S JUST BAD LUCK... EITHER WAY, THIS IS HOW THINGS TURNED OUT, AND I DON'T KNOW HOW TO CHANGE IT...

LOOK, I KNOW IT HASN'T BEEN EASY FOR YOU. I JUST NEED TO SEE YOU GUYS MAKE AN EFFORT TO MOVE ON WITH YOUR LIVES.

SOMEWHERE... AWAY FROM MY APARTMENT.

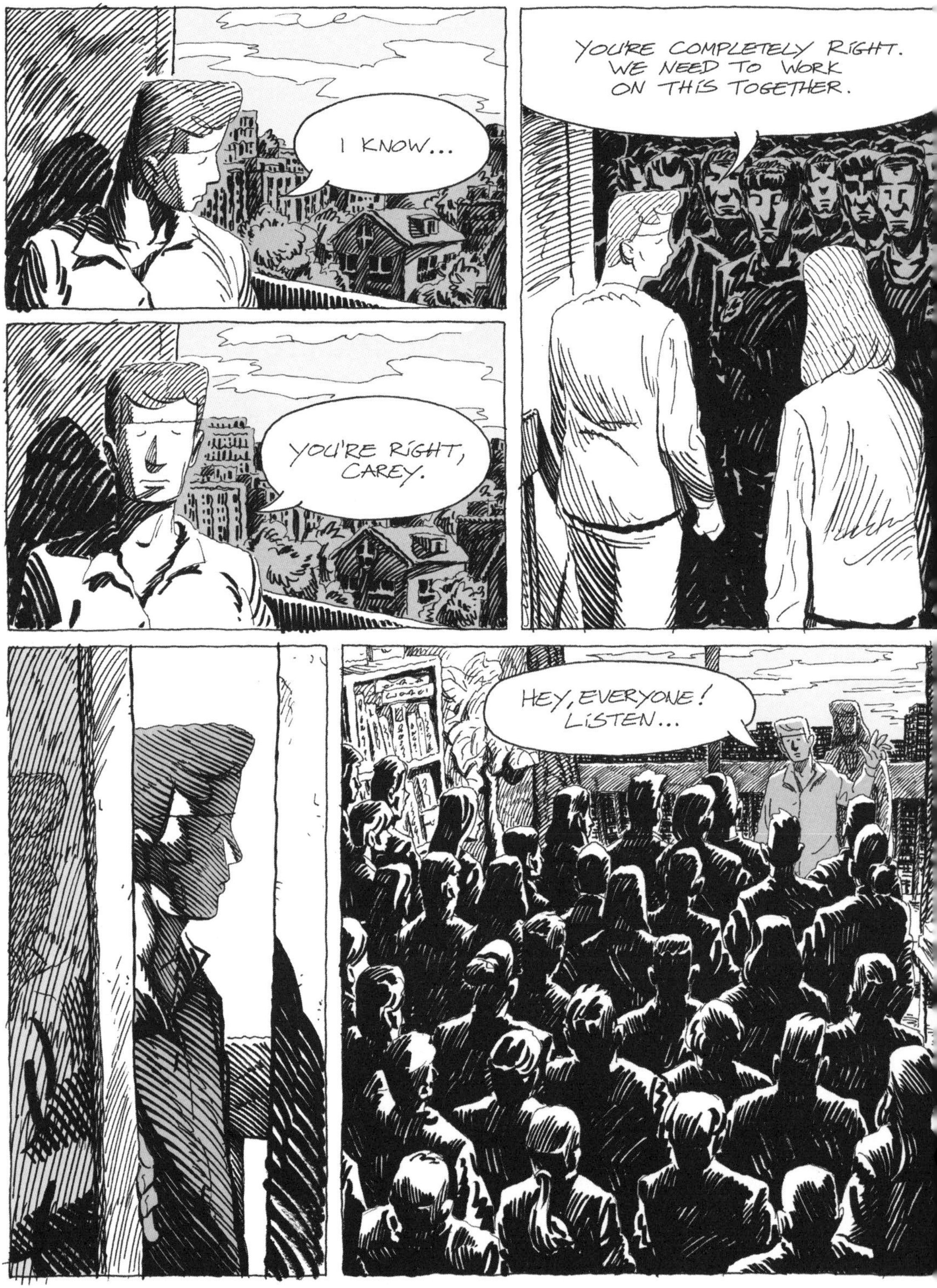
I KNOW...
YOU'RE COMPLETELY RIGHT. WE NEED TO WORK ON THIS TOGETHER.
YOU'RE RIGHT, CAREY.
HEY, EVERYONE! LISTEN...

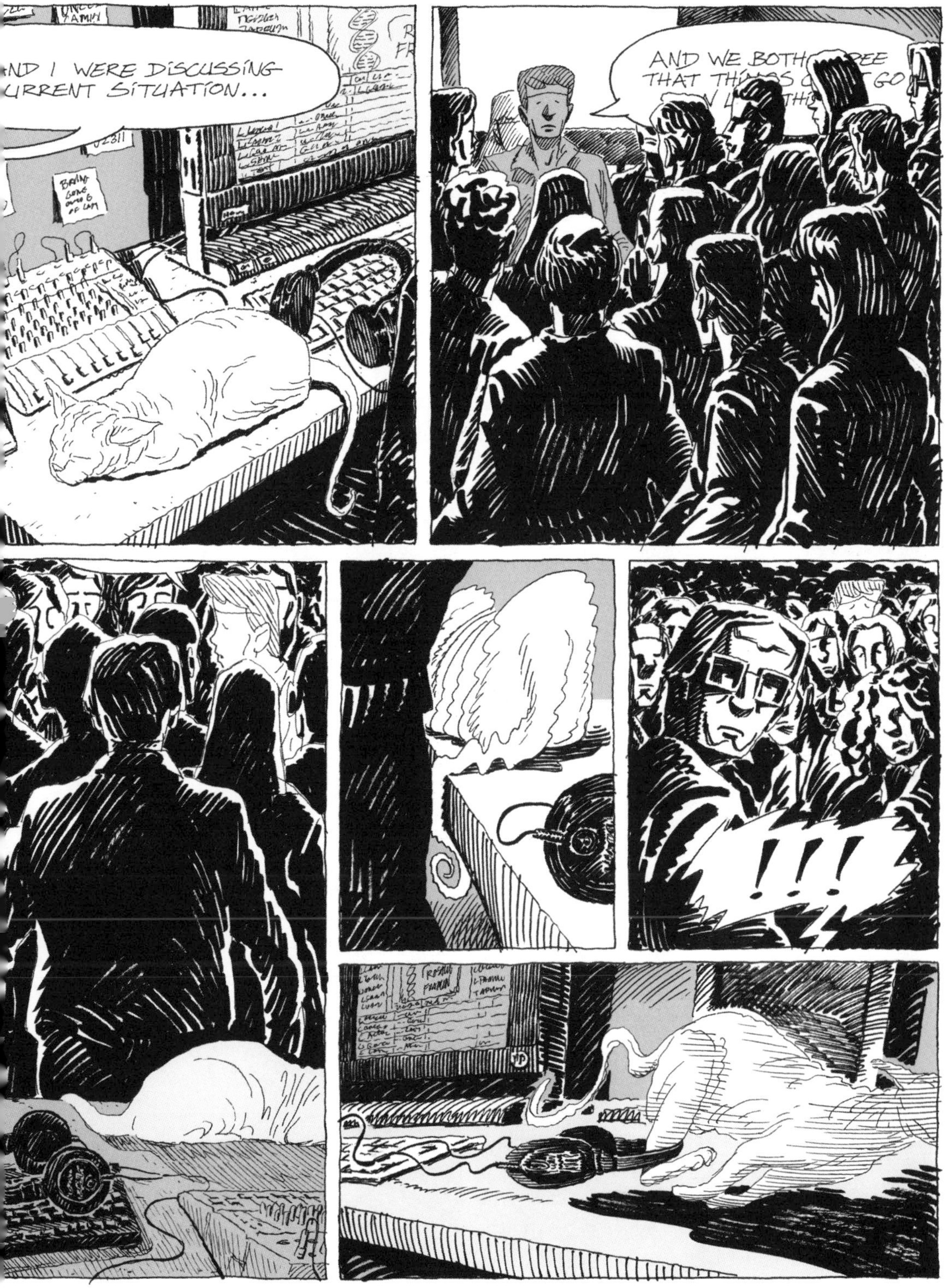
ND I WERE DISCUSSING
URRENT SITUATION...
AND WE BOTH
THAT TH
GO
!!!

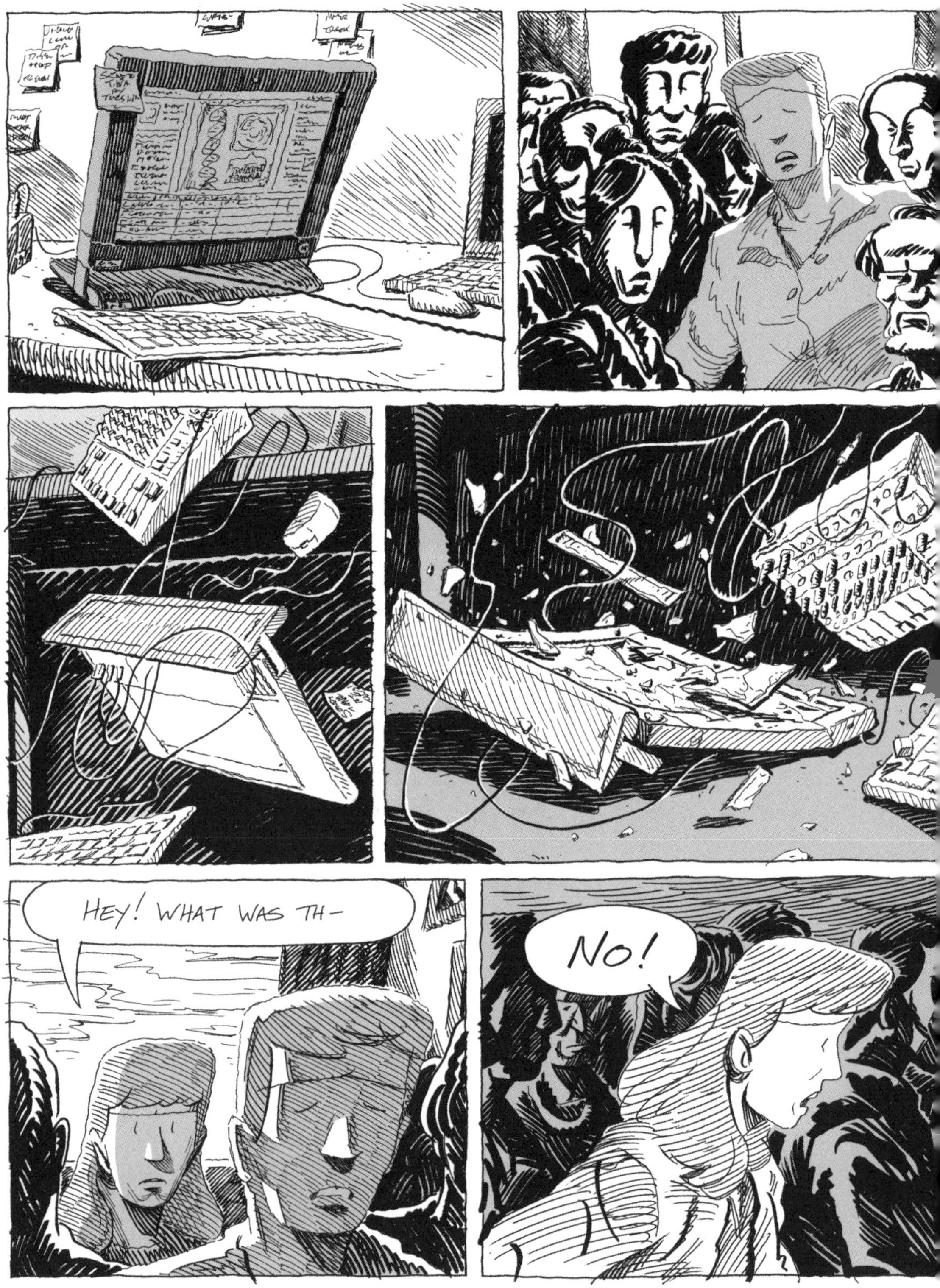
HEY! WHAT WAS TH-
NO!

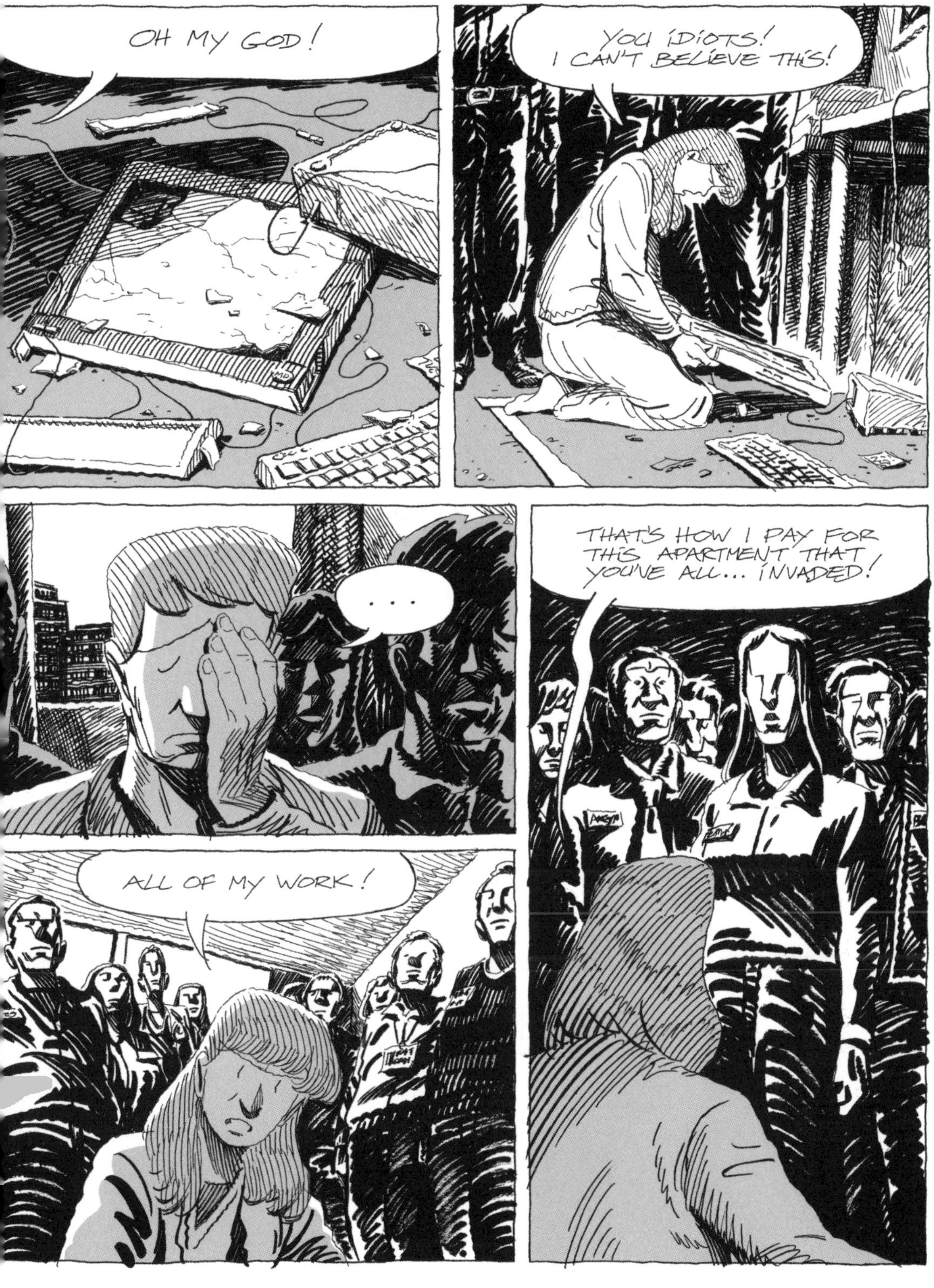
OH MY GOD!
YOU IDIOTS! I CAN'T BELIEVE THIS!
. . .
ALL OF MY WORK!
THAT'S HOW I PAY FOR THIS APARTMENT THAT YOU'VE ALL... INVADED!

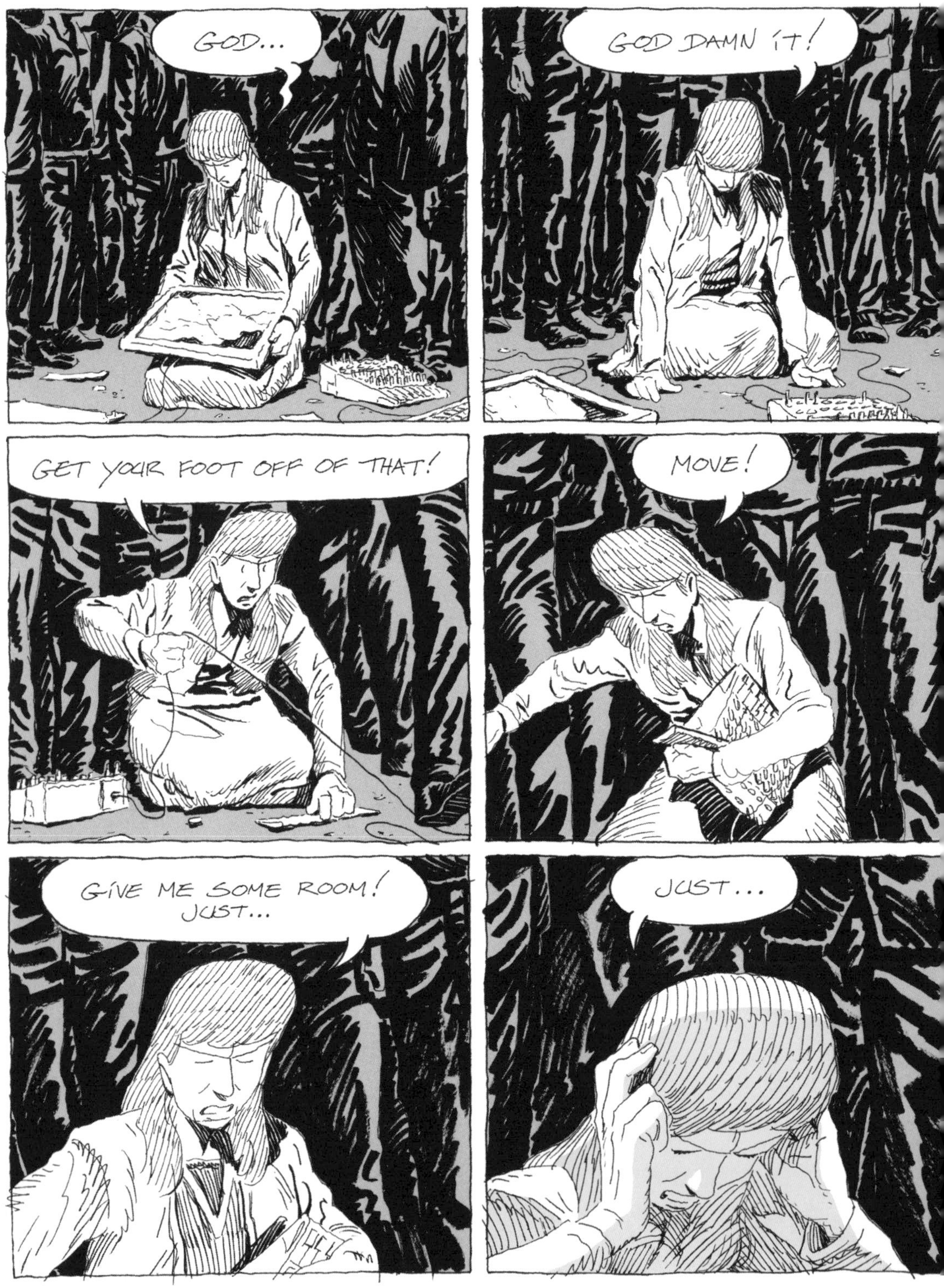
GOD...
GOD DAMN IT!
GET YOUR FOOT OFF OF THAT!
MOVE!
GIVE ME SOME ROOM! JUST...
JUST...

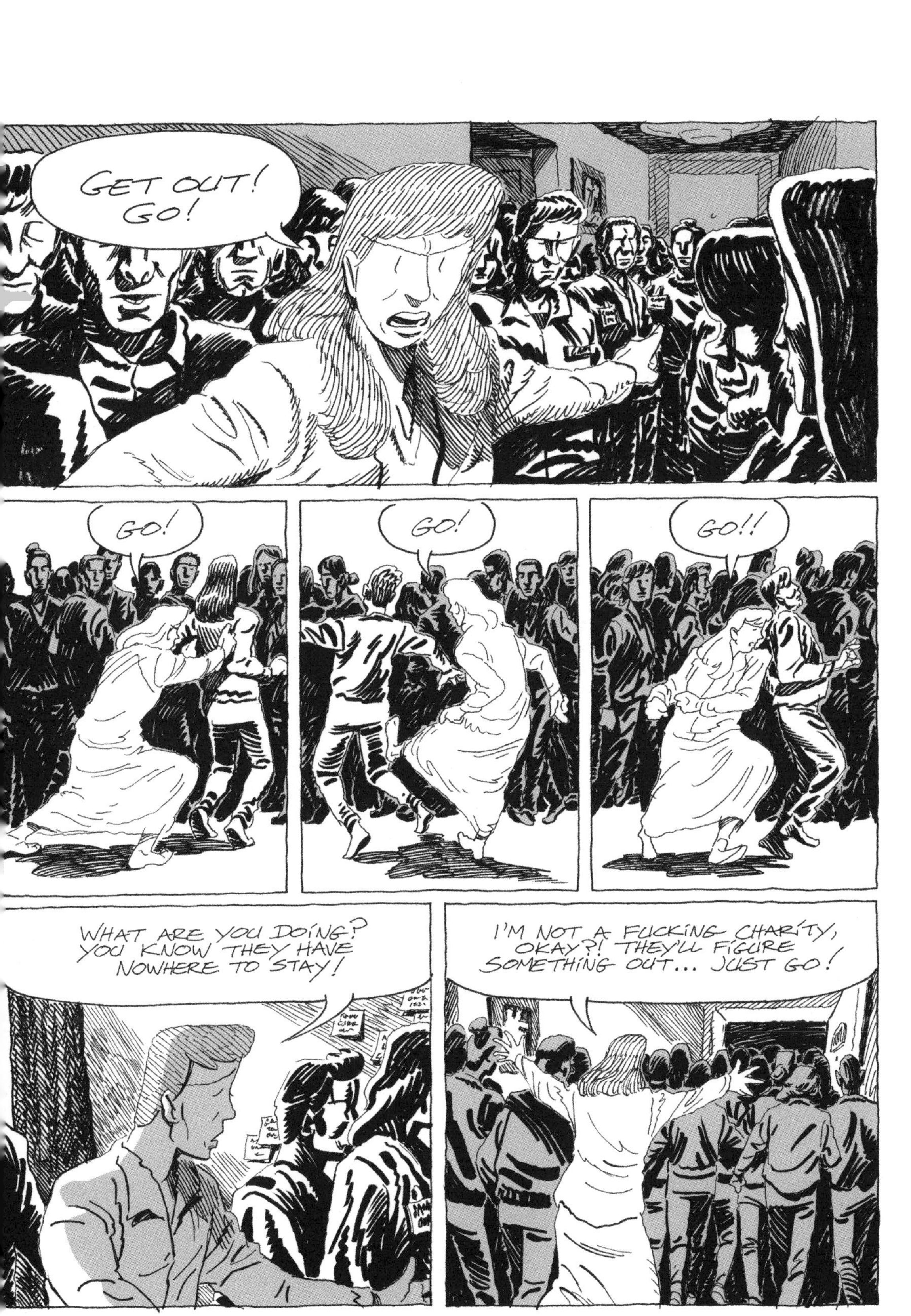
GET OUT! GO!
GO!
GO!
GO!!
WHAT ARE YOU DOING? YOU KNOW THEY HAVE NOWHERE TO STAY!
I'M NOT A FUCKING CHARITY, OKAY?! THEY'LL FIGURE SOMETHING OUT... JUST GO!

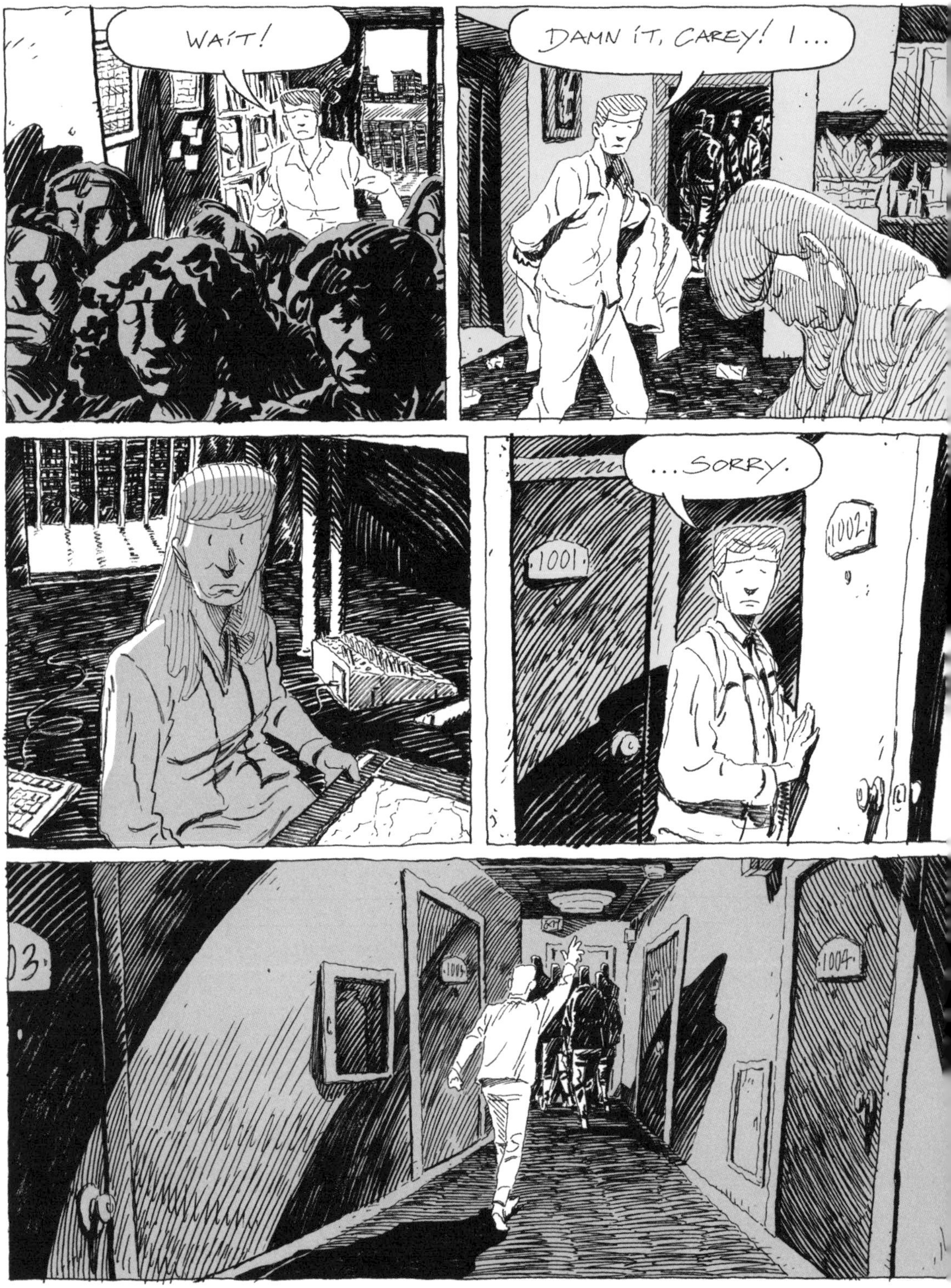
WAIT!
DAMN IT, CAREY! I...
...SORRY.
1001
1002
1004

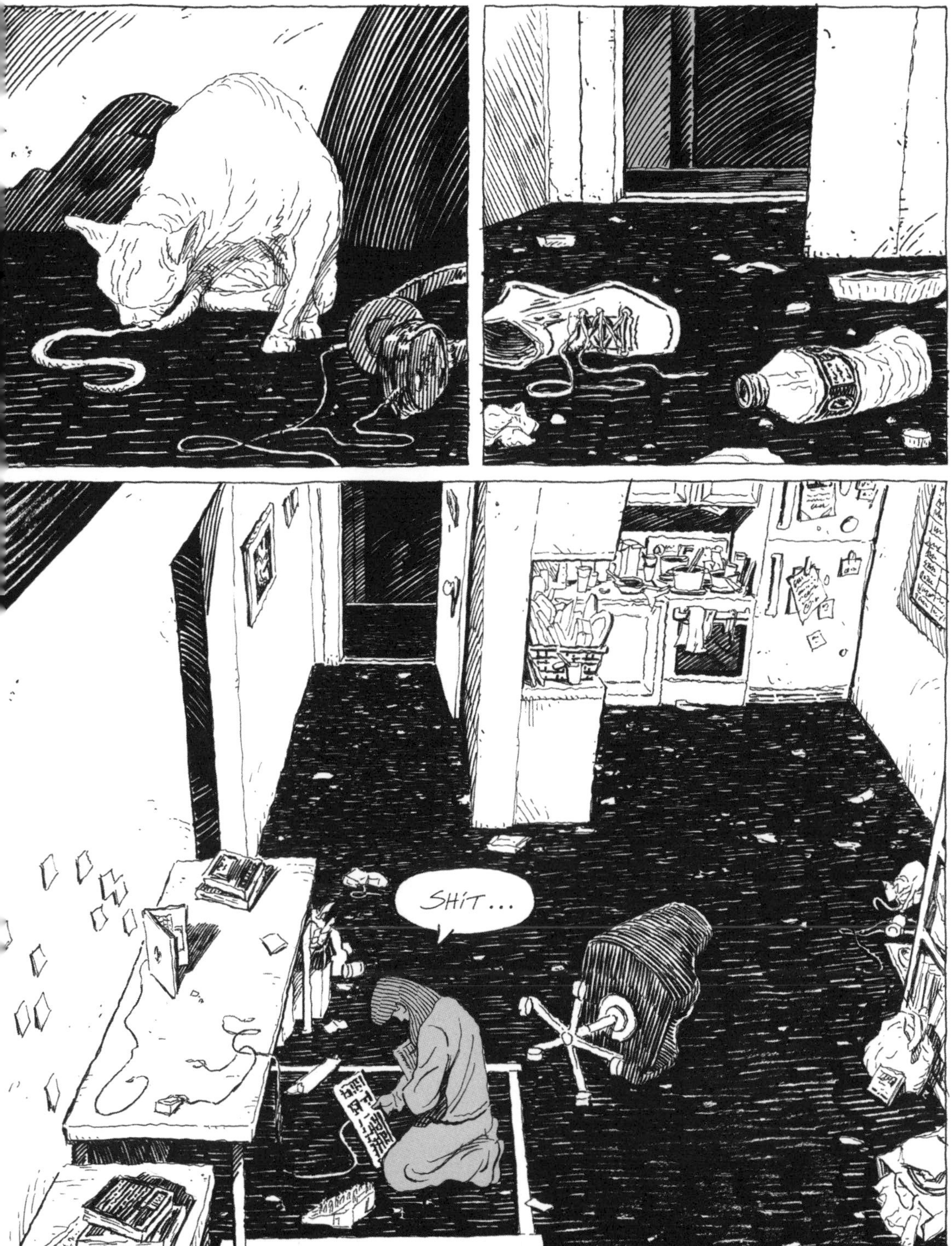
SHIT...

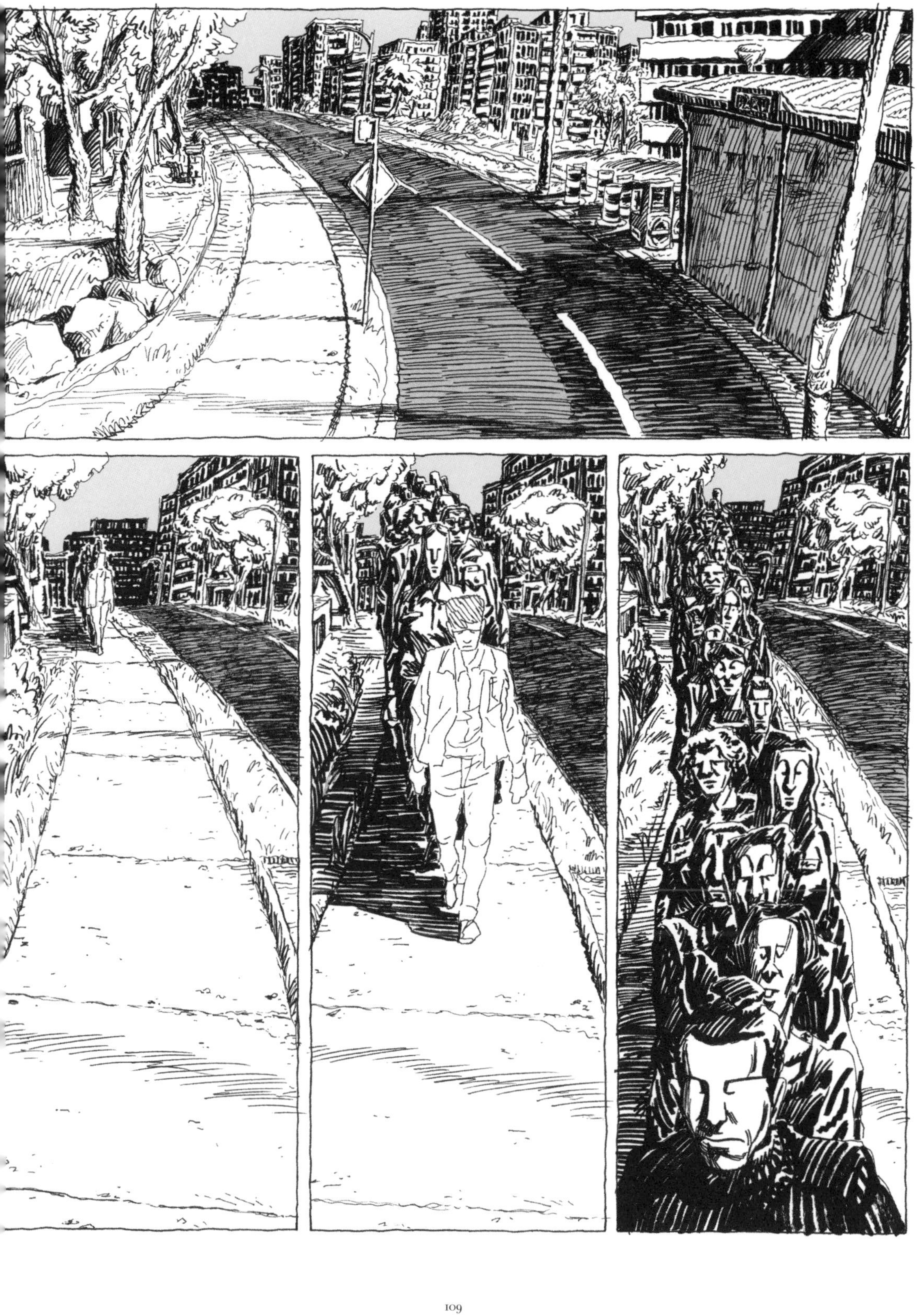

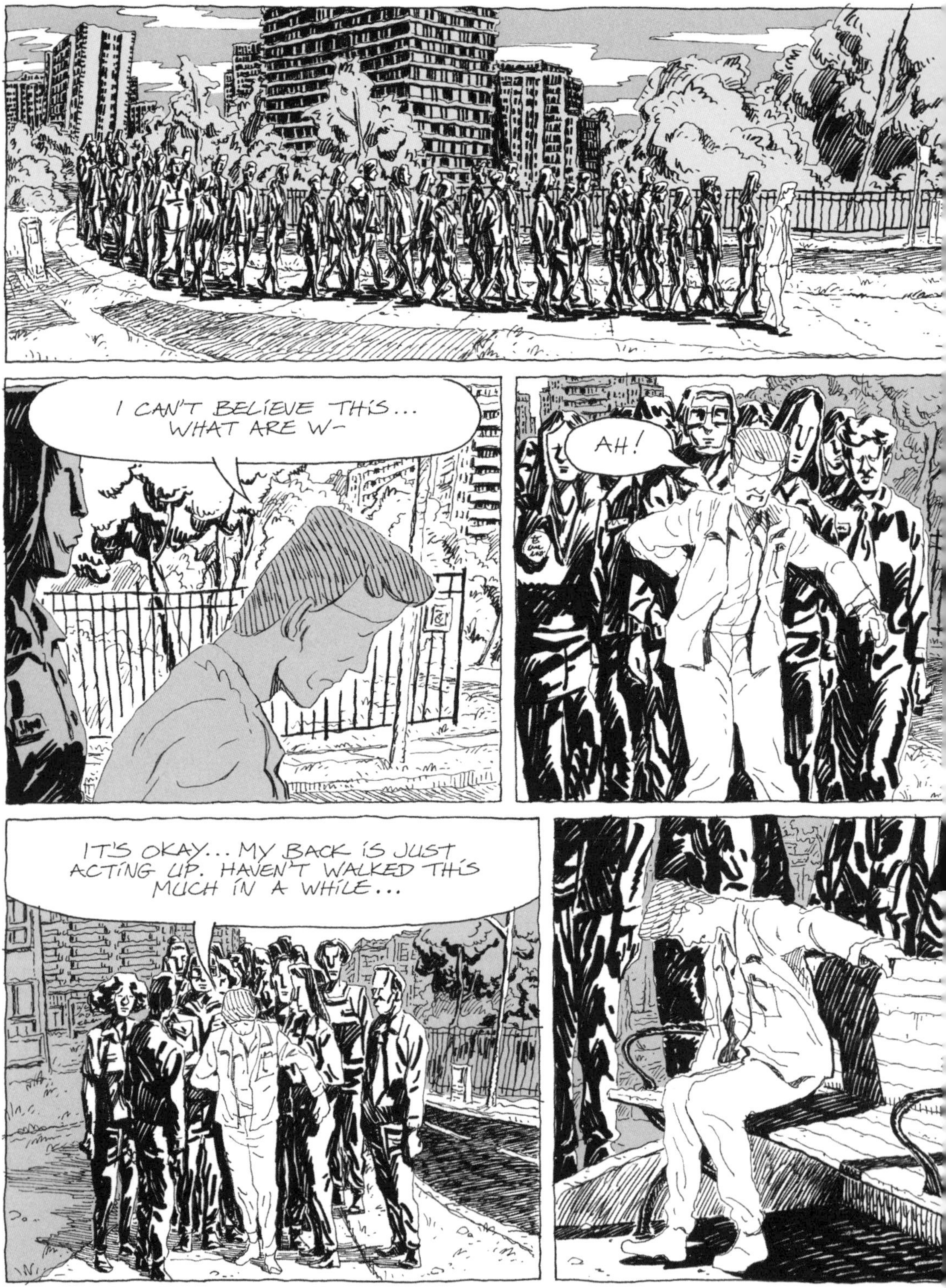
I CAN'T BELIEVE THIS...
WHAT ARE W-
AH!
IT'S OKAY... MY BACK IS JUST ACTING UP. HAVEN'T WALKED THIS MUCH IN A WHILE...

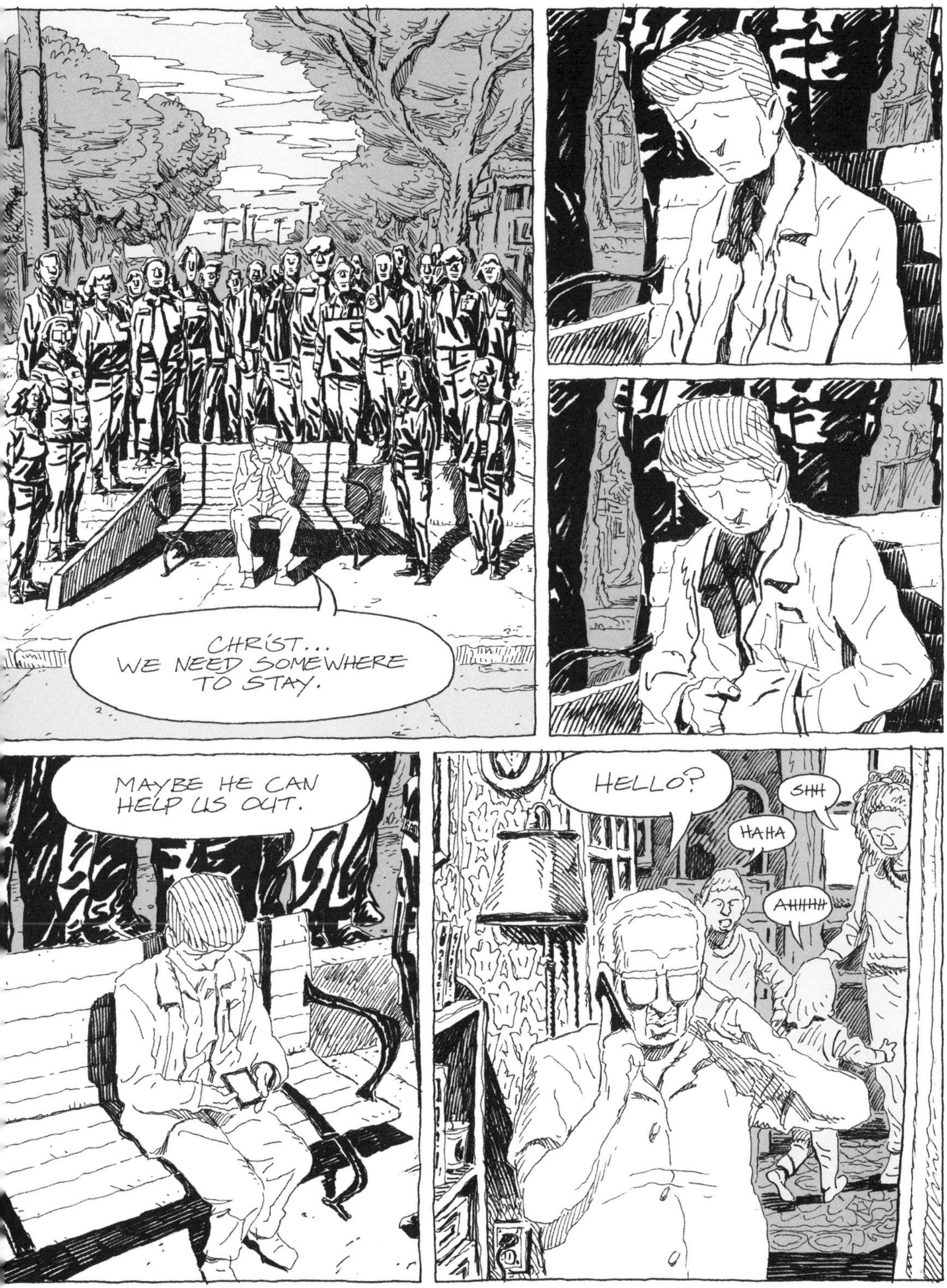
CHRIST...
WE NEED SOMEWHERE TO STAY.
MAYBE HE CAN HELP US OUT.
HELLO?
SHH
HAHA
AHHHH

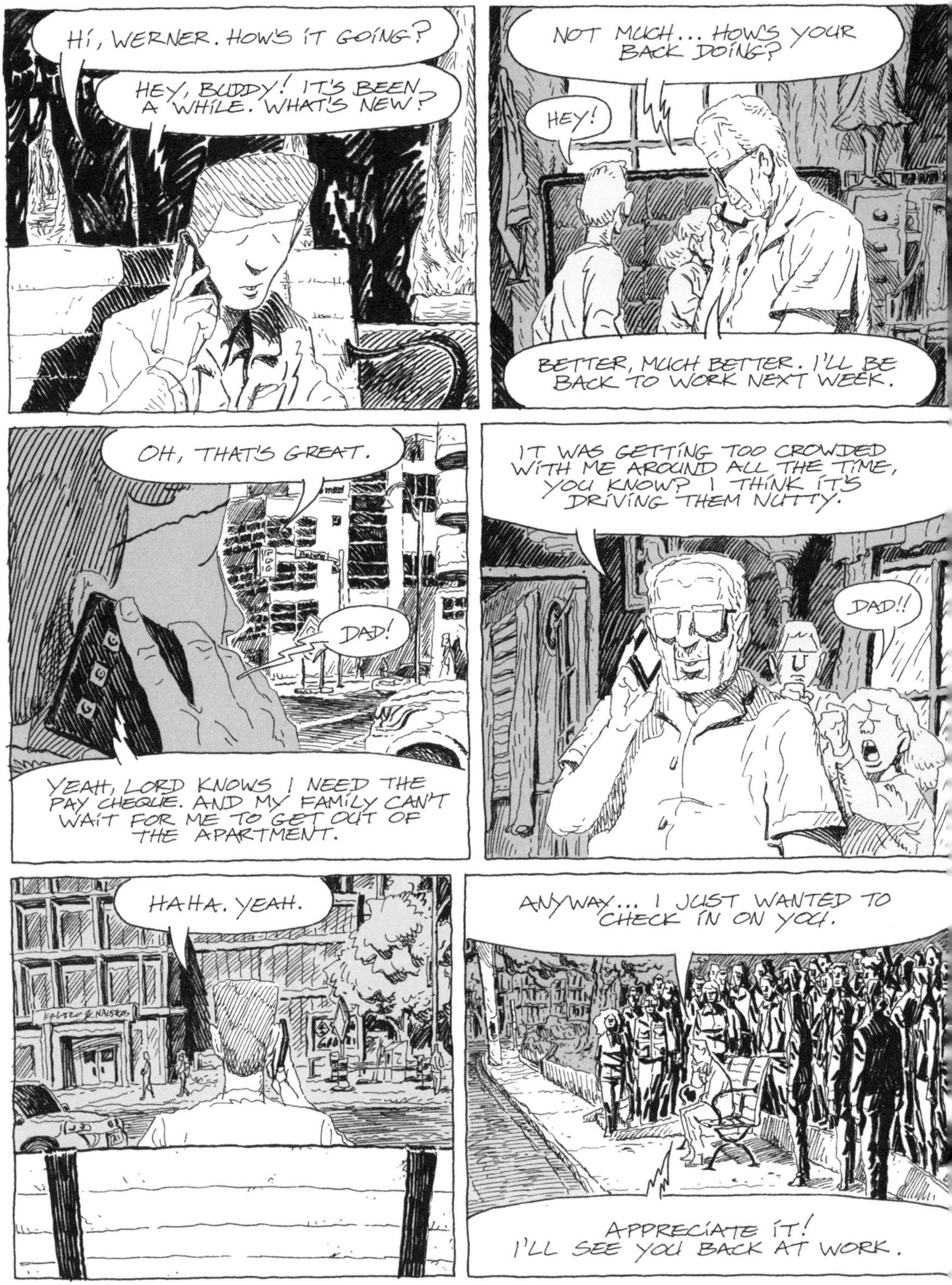
HI, WERNER. HOW'S IT GOING?
HEY, BUDDY! IT'S BEEN A WHILE. WHAT'S NEW?
NOT MUCH... HOW'S YOUR BACK DOING?
HEY!
BETTER, MUCH BETTER. I'LL BE BACK TO WORK NEXT WEEK.
OH, THAT'S GREAT.
DAD!
YEAH, LORD KNOWS I NEED THE PAY CHEQUE. AND MY FAMILY CAN'T WAIT FOR ME TO GET OUT OF THE APARTMENT.
IT WAS GETTING TOO CROWDED WITH ME AROUND ALL THE TIME, YOU KNOW? I THINK IT'S DRIVING THEM NUTTY.
DAD!!
HAHA. YEAH.
ANYWAY... I JUST WANTED TO CHECK IN ON YOU.
APPRECIATE IT! I'LL SEE YOU BACK AT WORK.

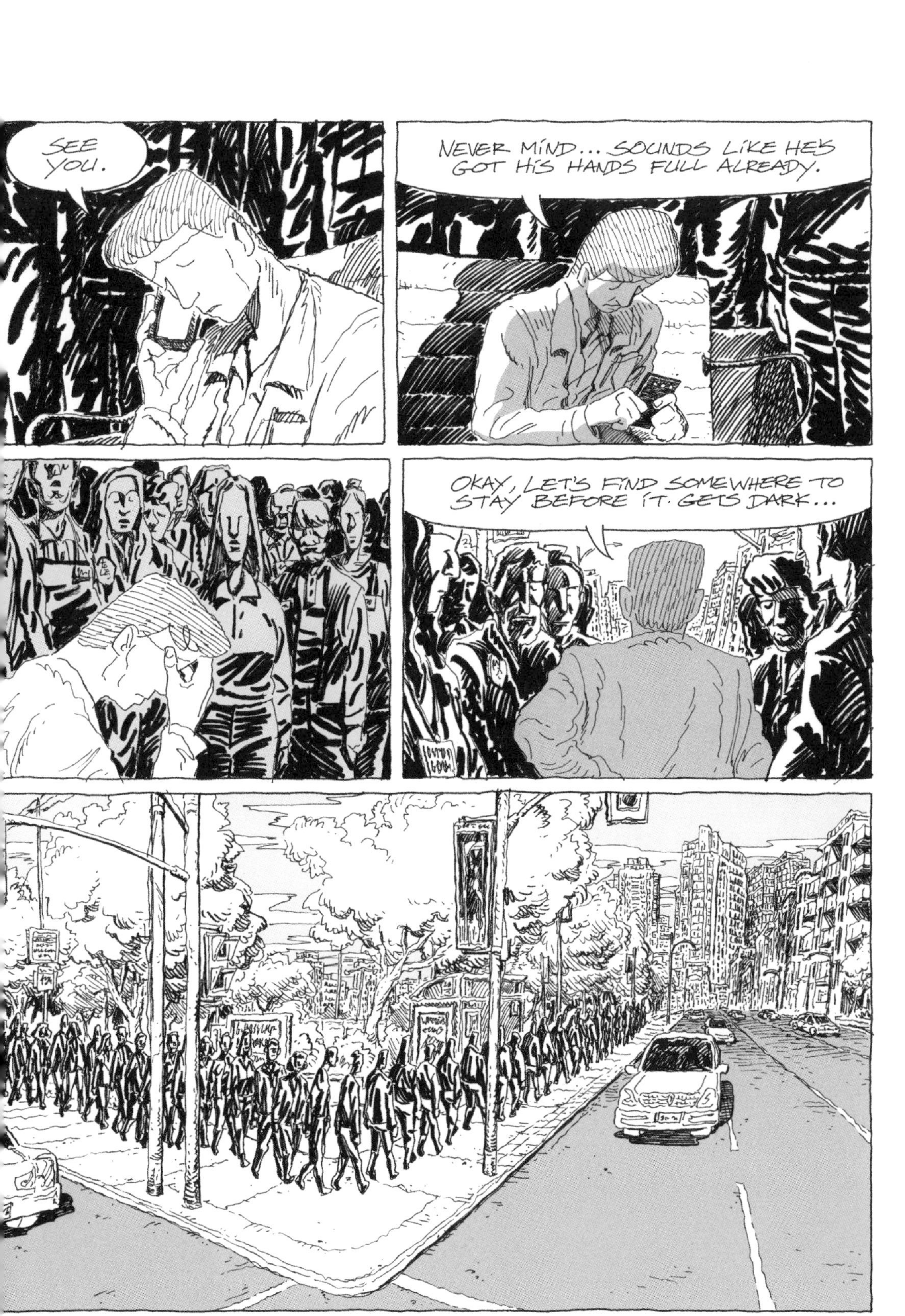
SEE YOU.
NEVER MIND... SOUNDS LIKE HE'S GOT HIS HANDS FULL ALREADY.
OKAY, LET'S FIND SOMEWHERE TO STAY BEFORE IT GETS DARK...

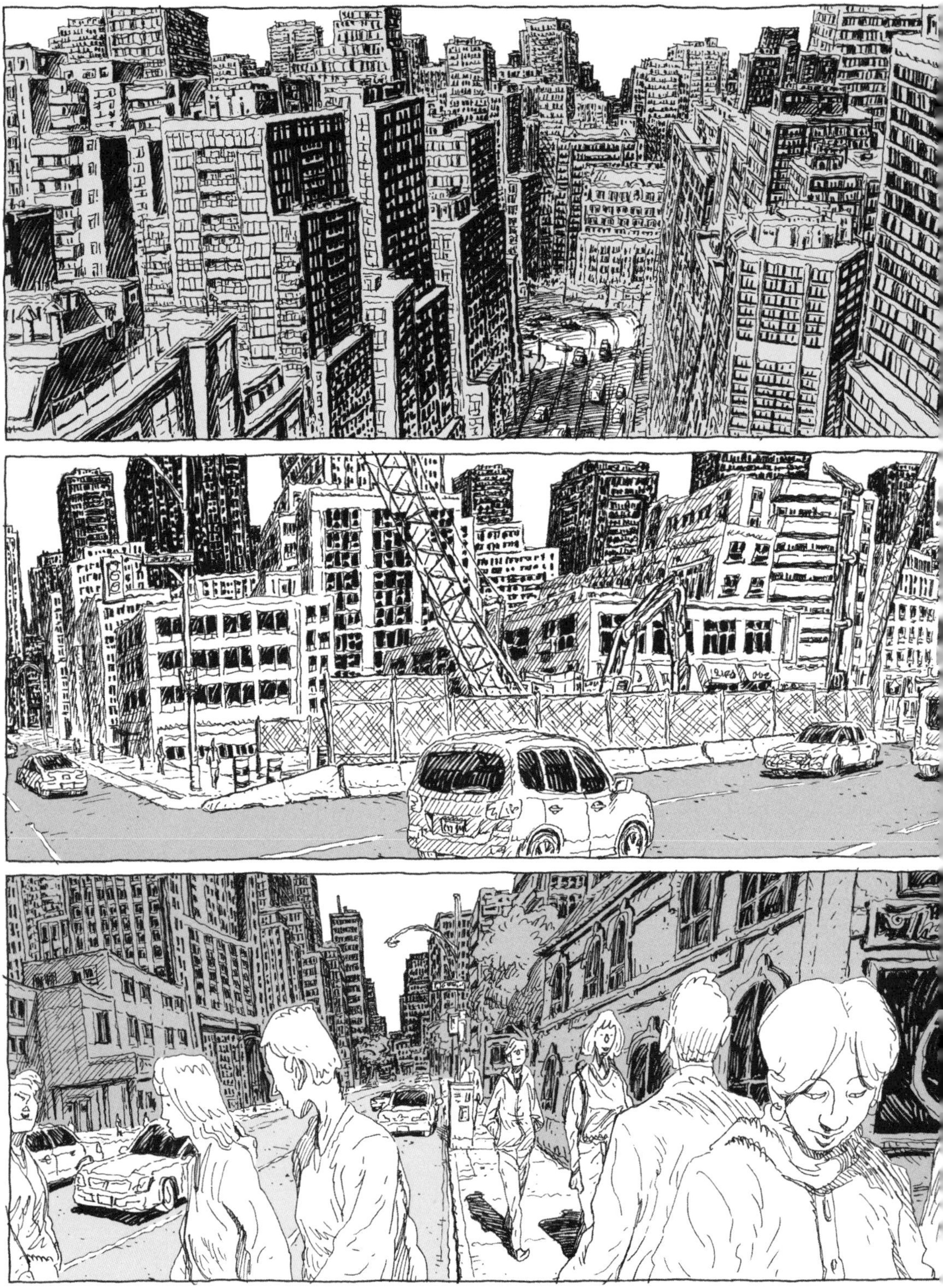

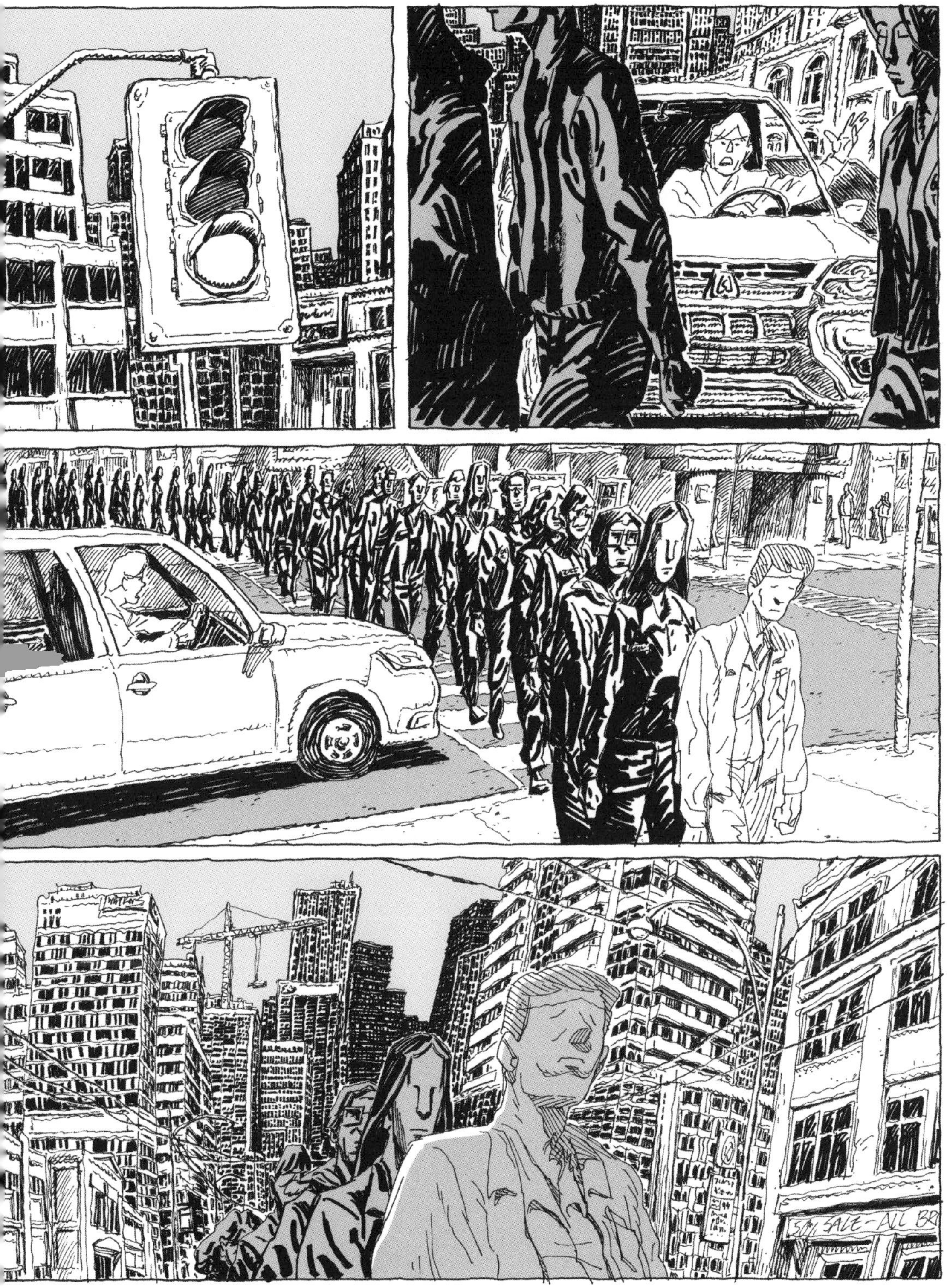
50% SALE-ALL BR

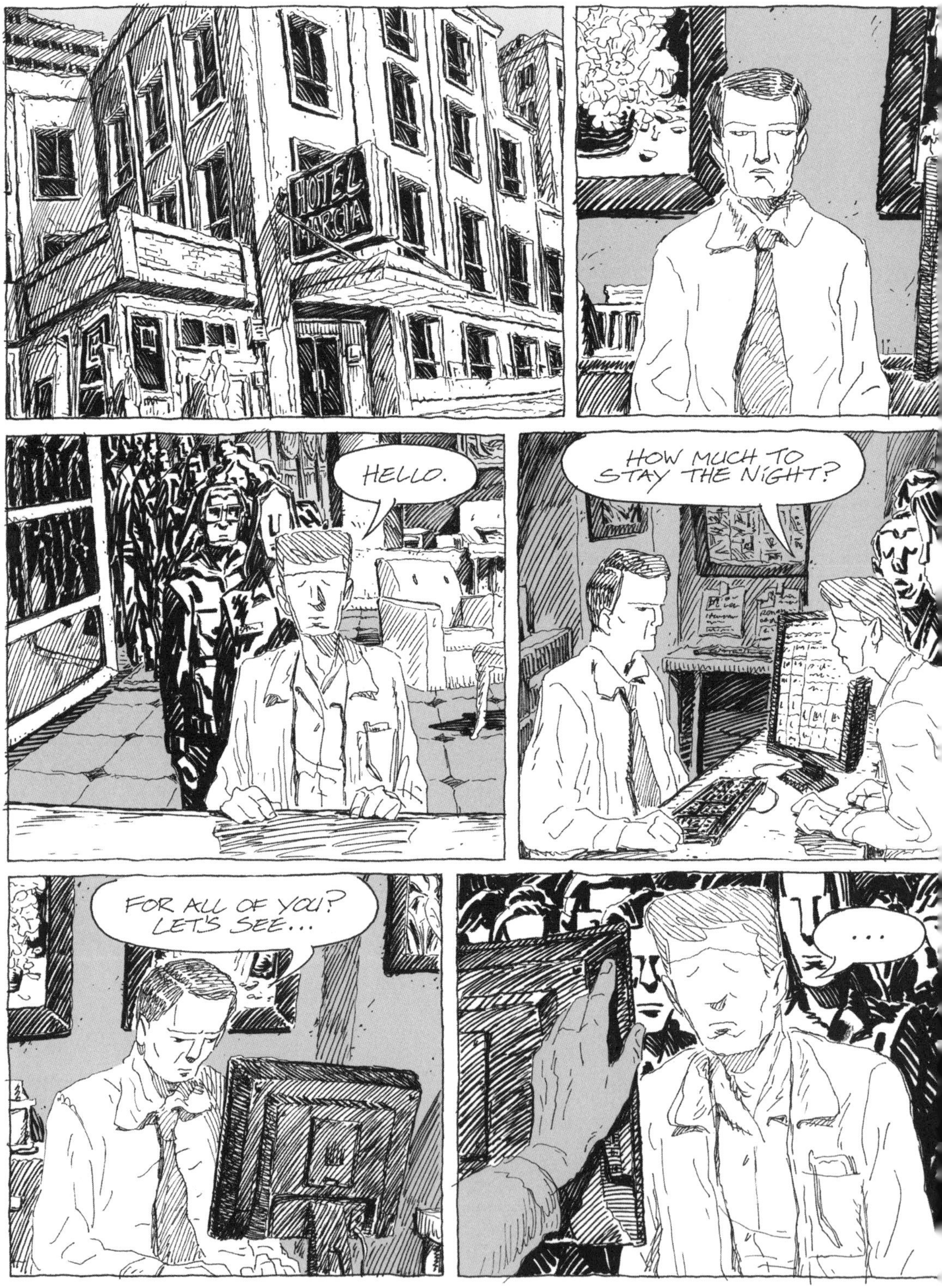
HOTEL MARCIA
HELLO.
HOW MUCH TO STAY THE NIGHT?
FOR ALL OF YOU? LET'S SEE...
...

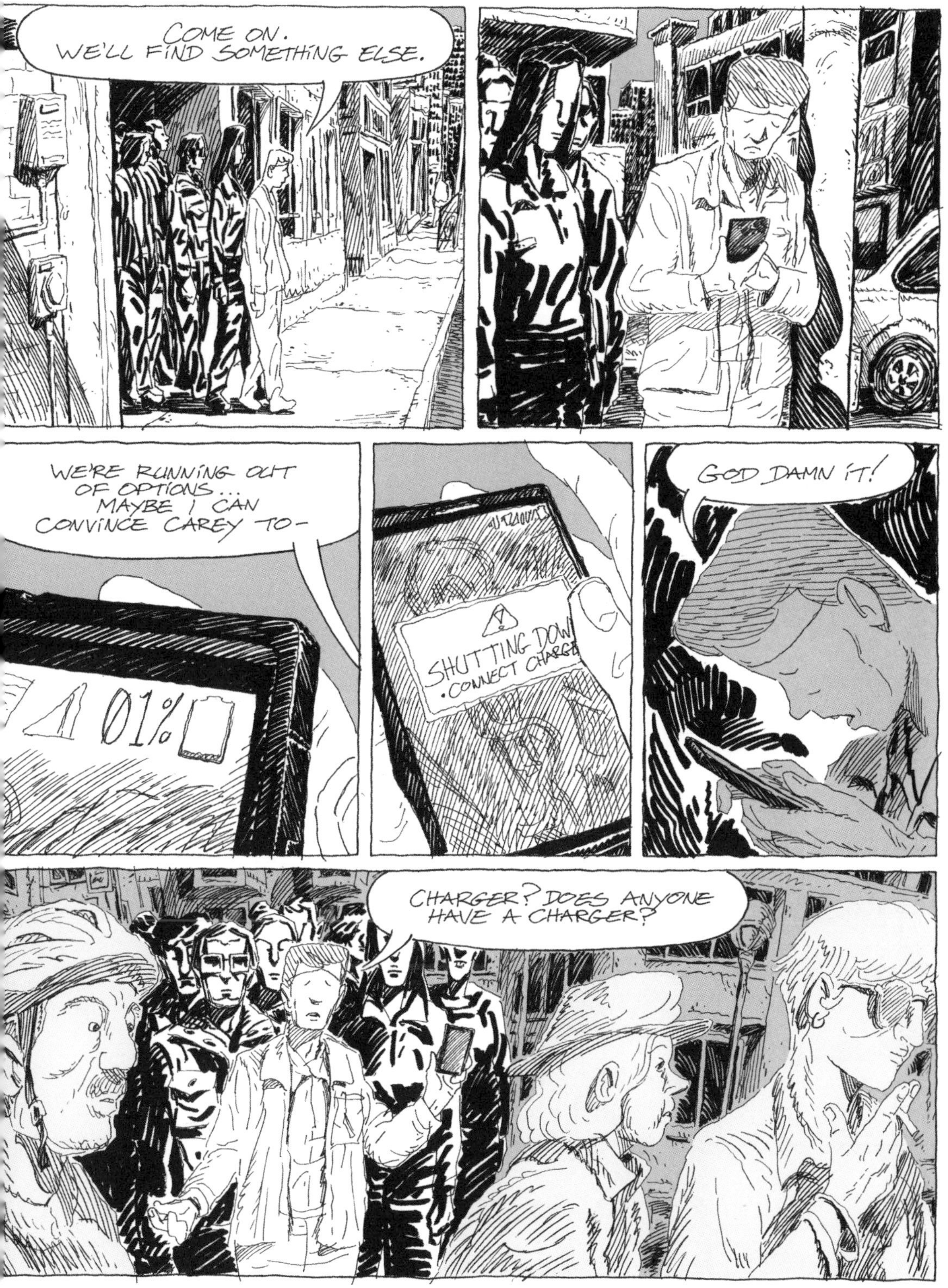
COME ON.
WE'LL FIND SOMETHING ELSE.
WE'RE RUNNING OUT OF OPTIONS...
MAYBE I CAN
CONVINCE CAREY TO-
01%
SHUTTING DOW
GOD DAMN IT!
CHARGER? DOES ANYONE
HAVE A CHARGER?

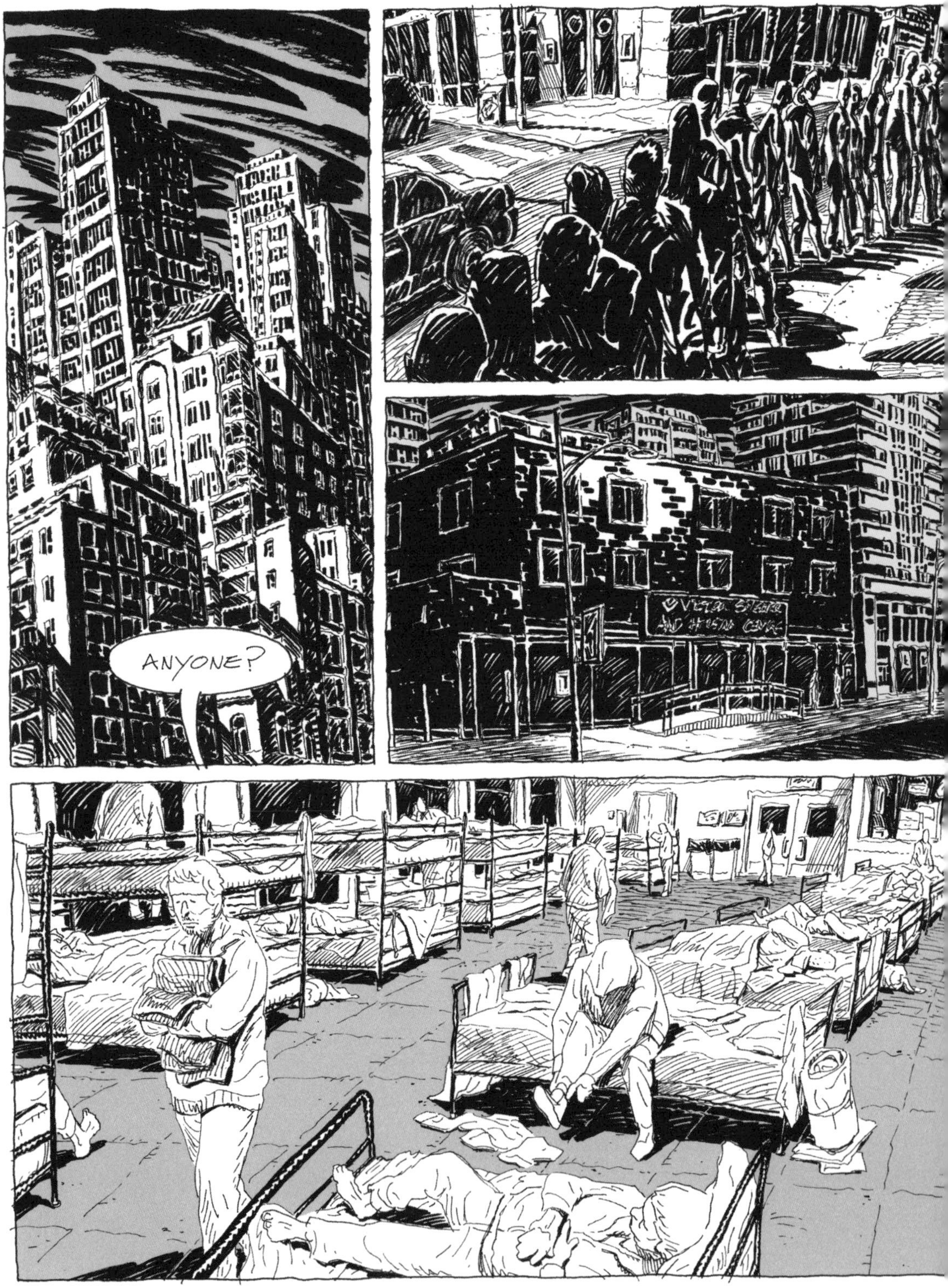
ANYONE?

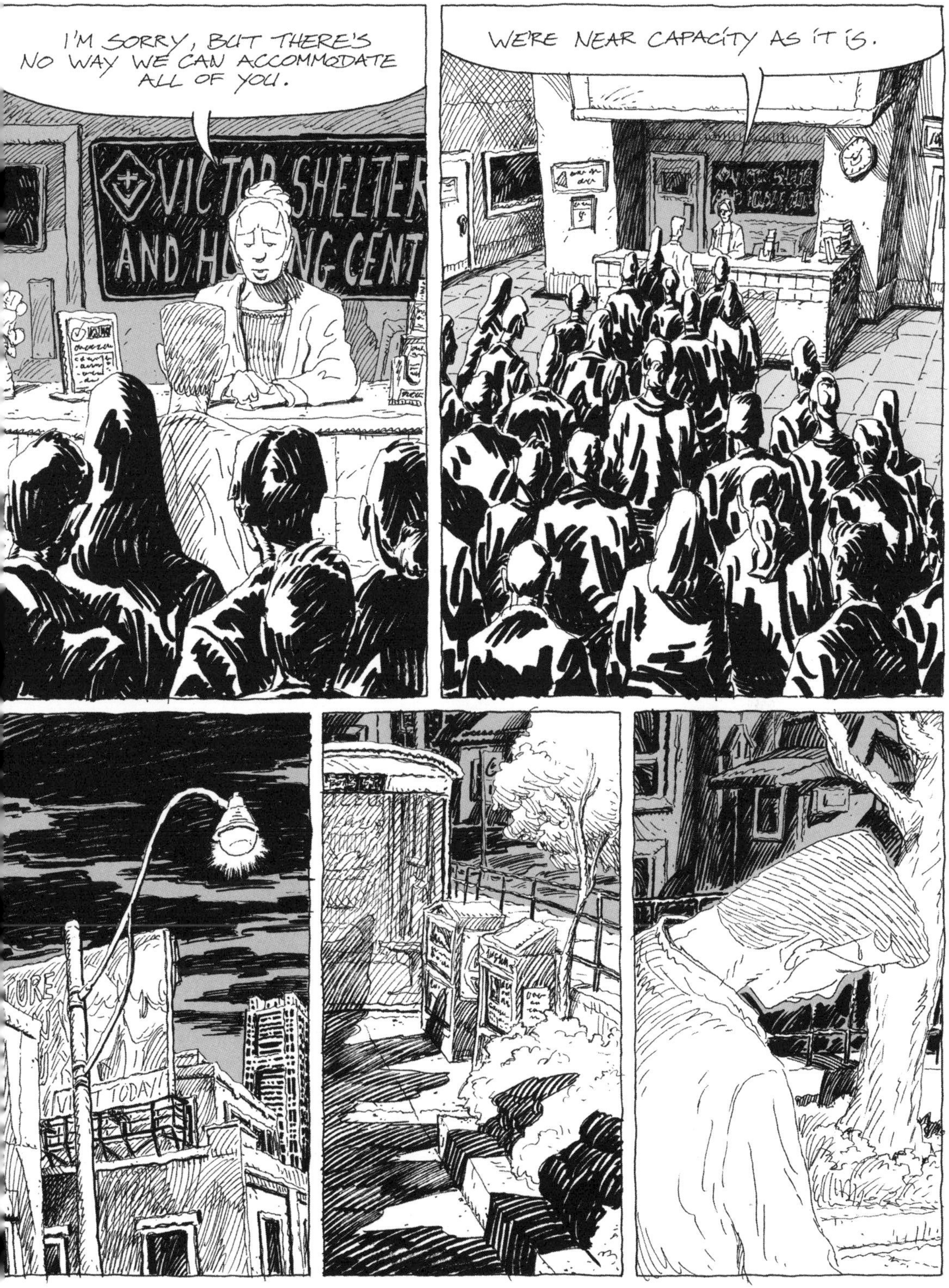
I'M SORRY, BUT THERE'S NO WAY WE CAN ACCOMMODATE ALL OF YOU.
WE'RE NEAR CAPACITY AS IT IS.

JUST GIVE ME A MINUTE...
I'LL BE FINE.

EVERYTHING WILL BE FINE.

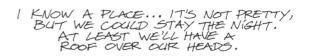

I KNOW A PLACE... IT'S NOT PRETTY,
BUT WE COULD STAY THE NIGHT.
AT LEAST WE'LL HAVE A
ROOF OVER OUR HEADS.

OKAY.

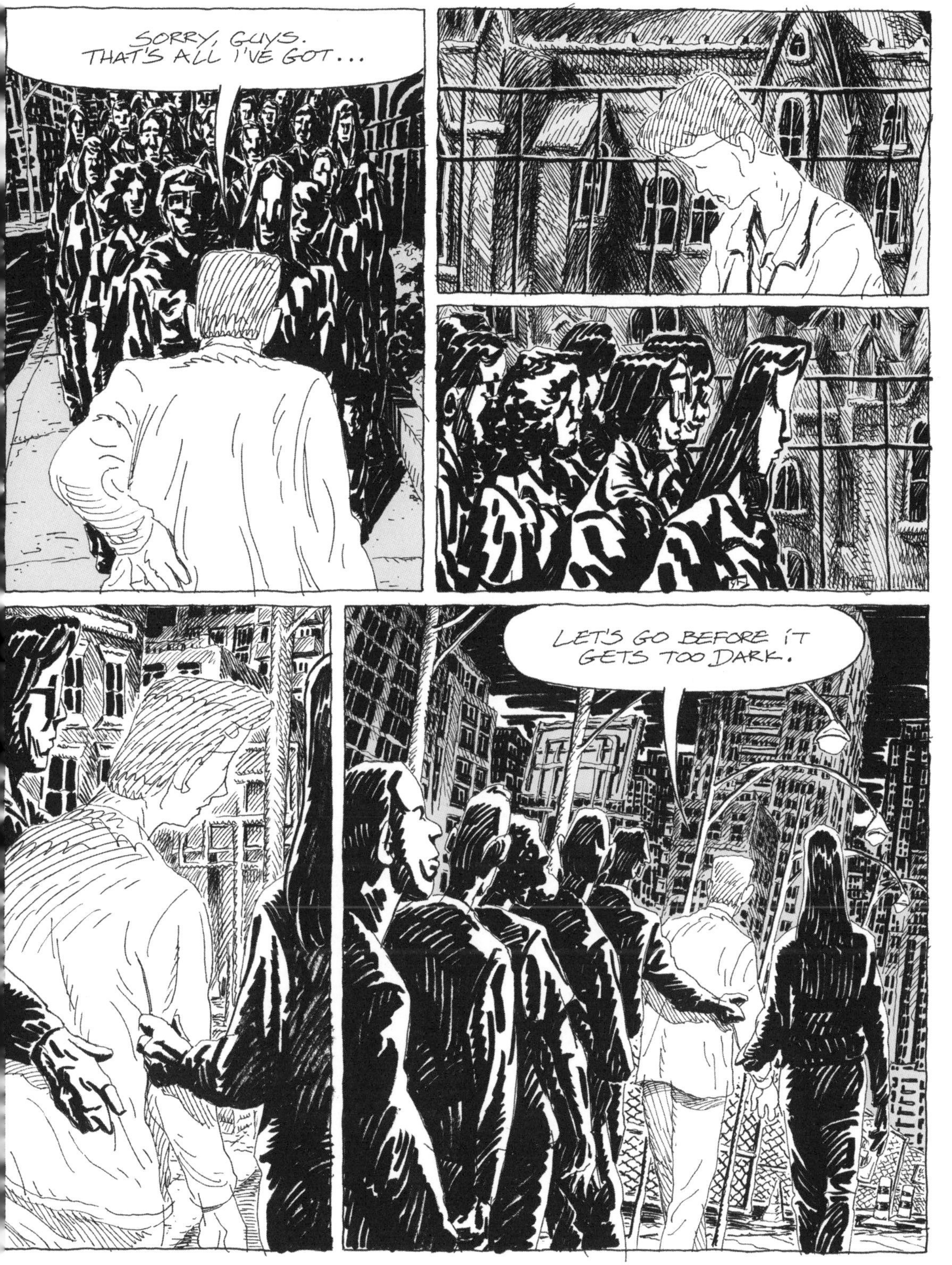
SORRY, GUYS. THAT'S ALL I'VE GOT...
LET'S GO BEFORE IT GETS TOO DARK.

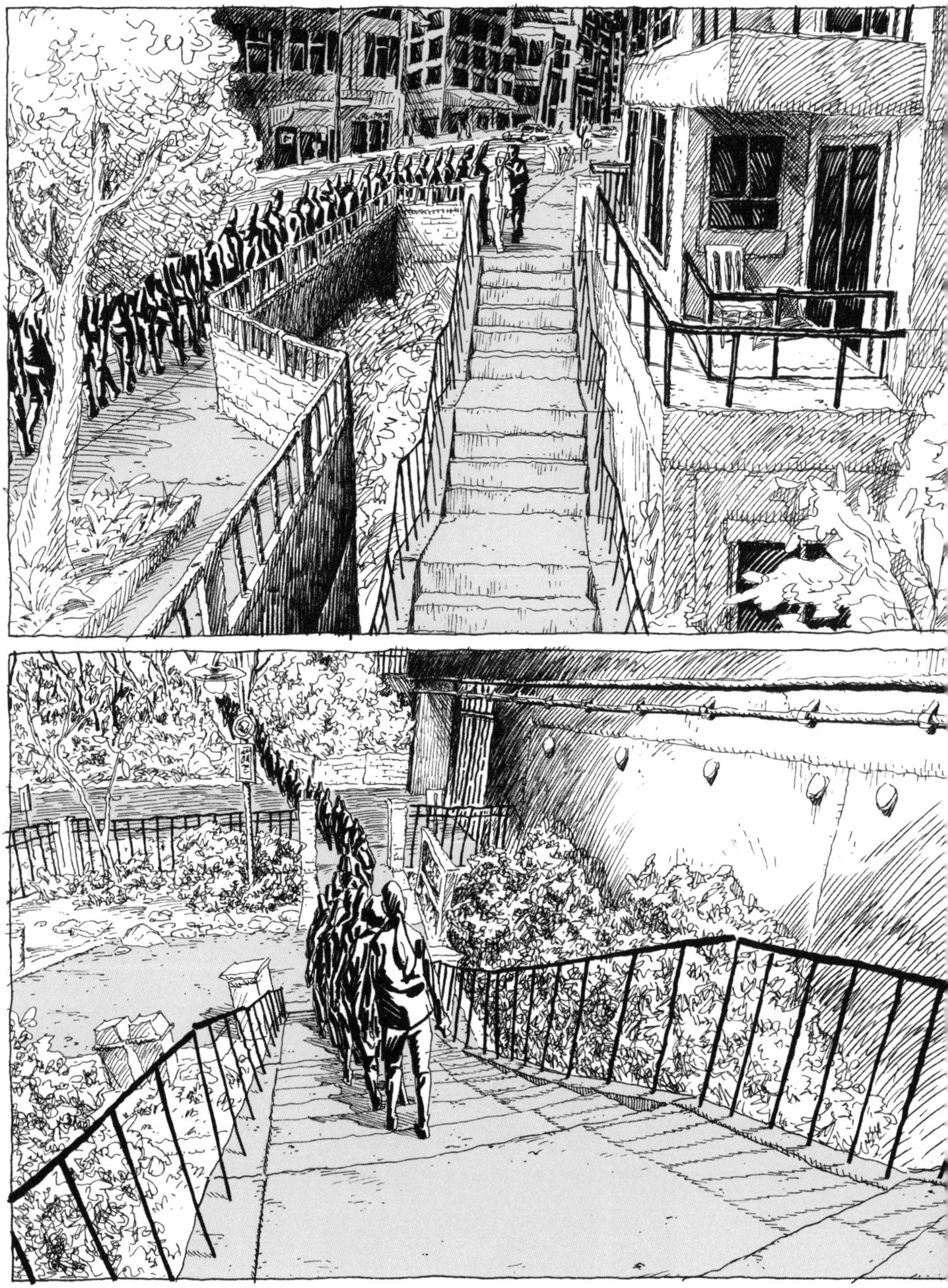

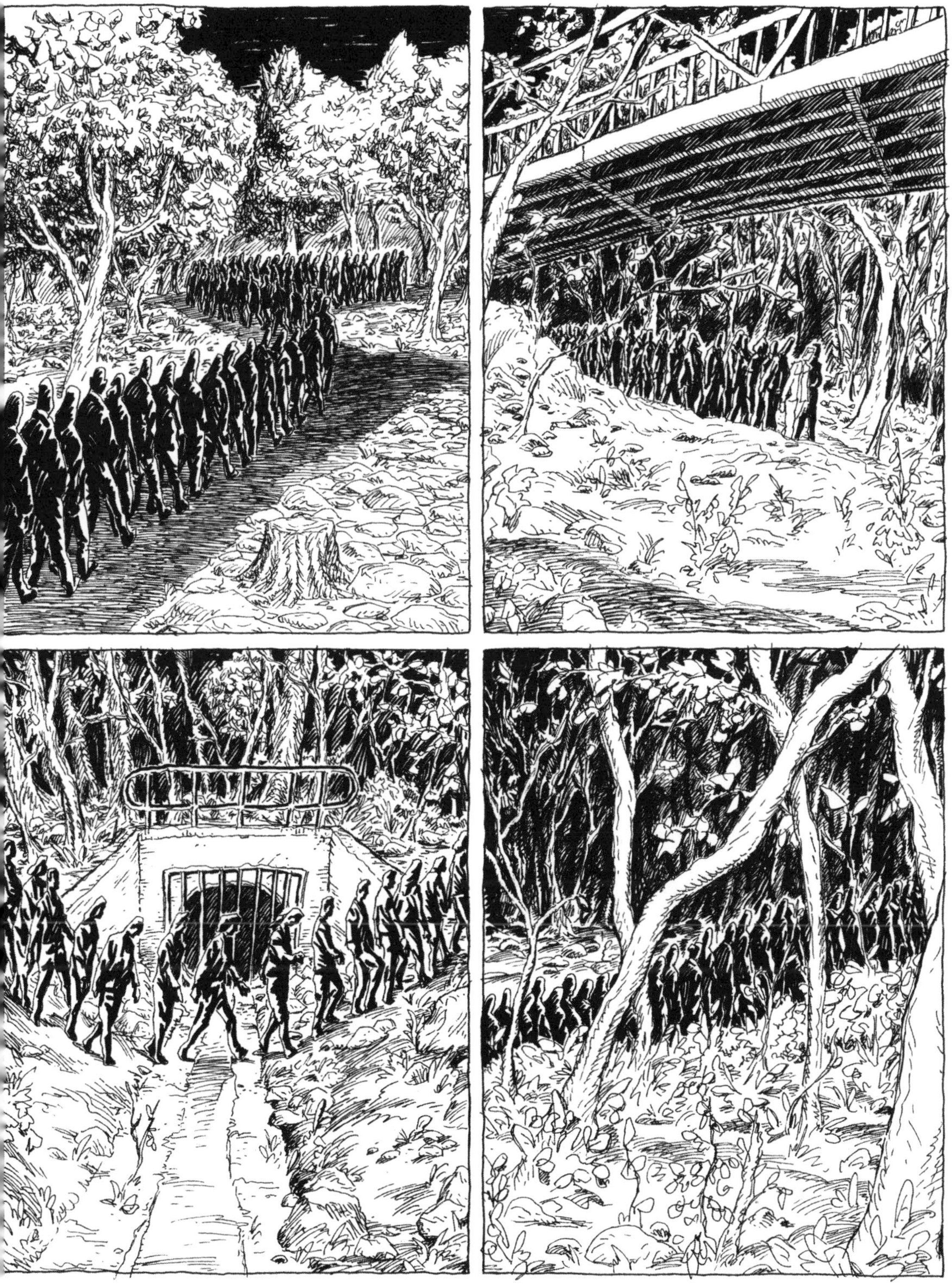

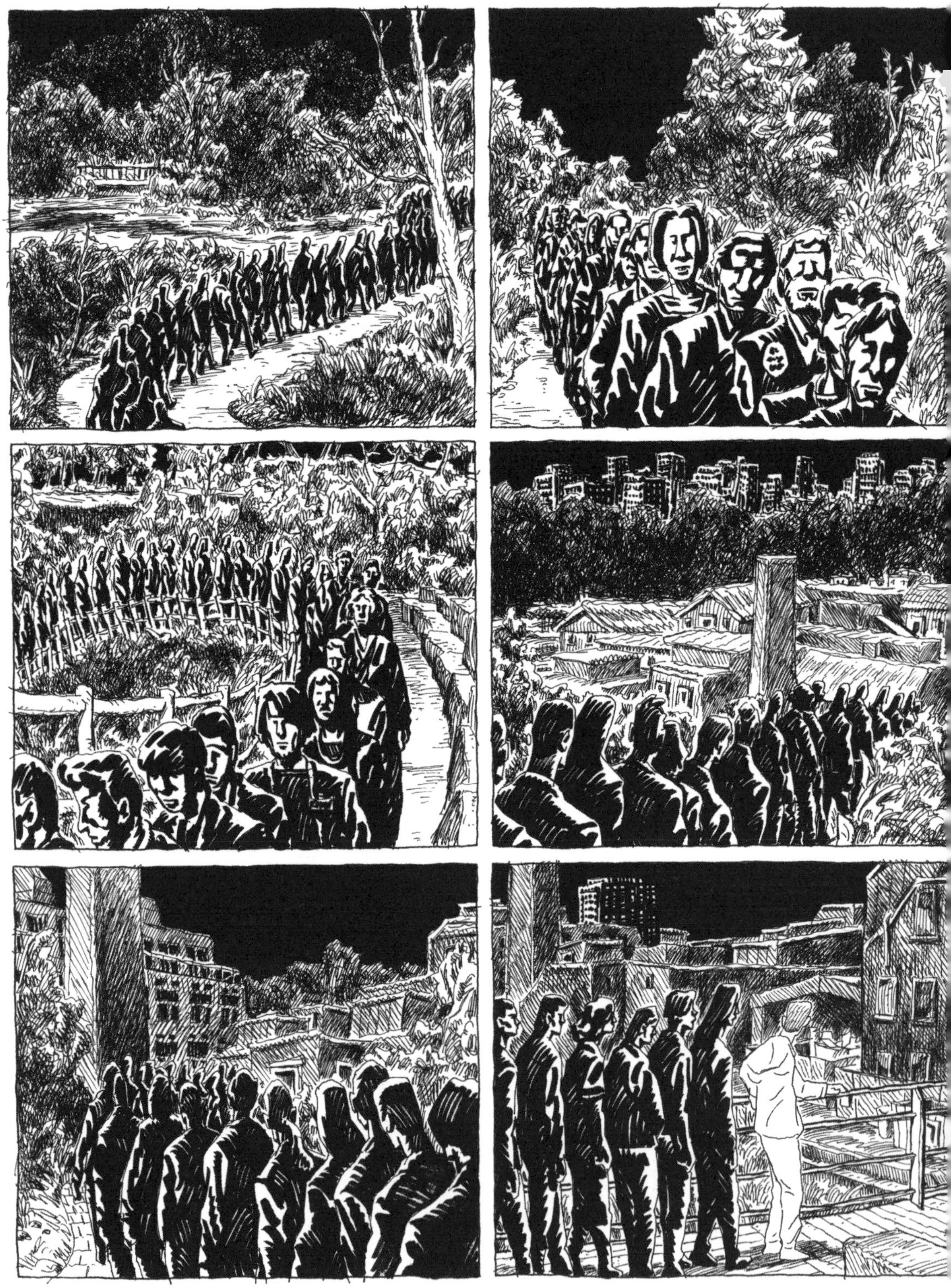

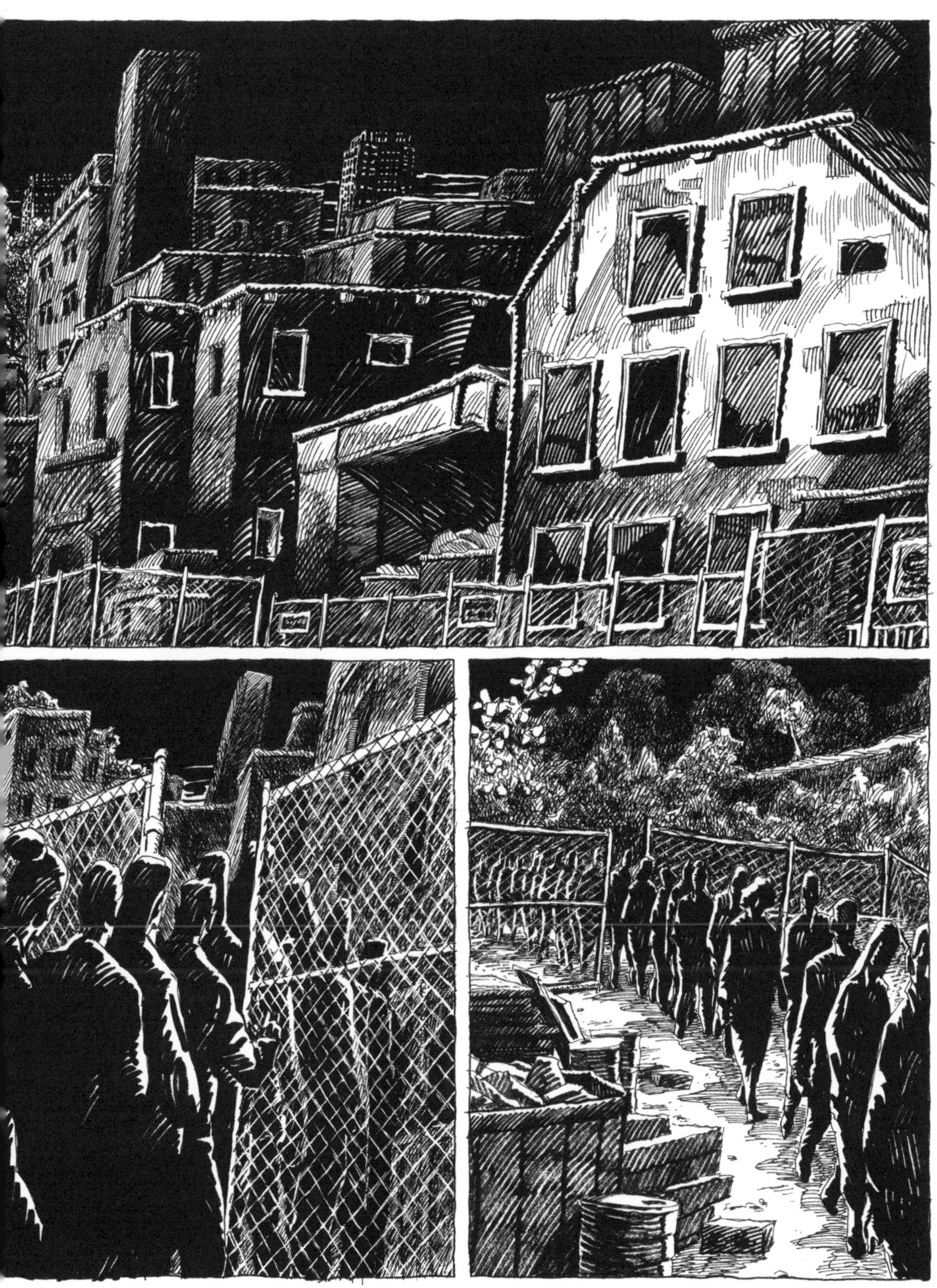

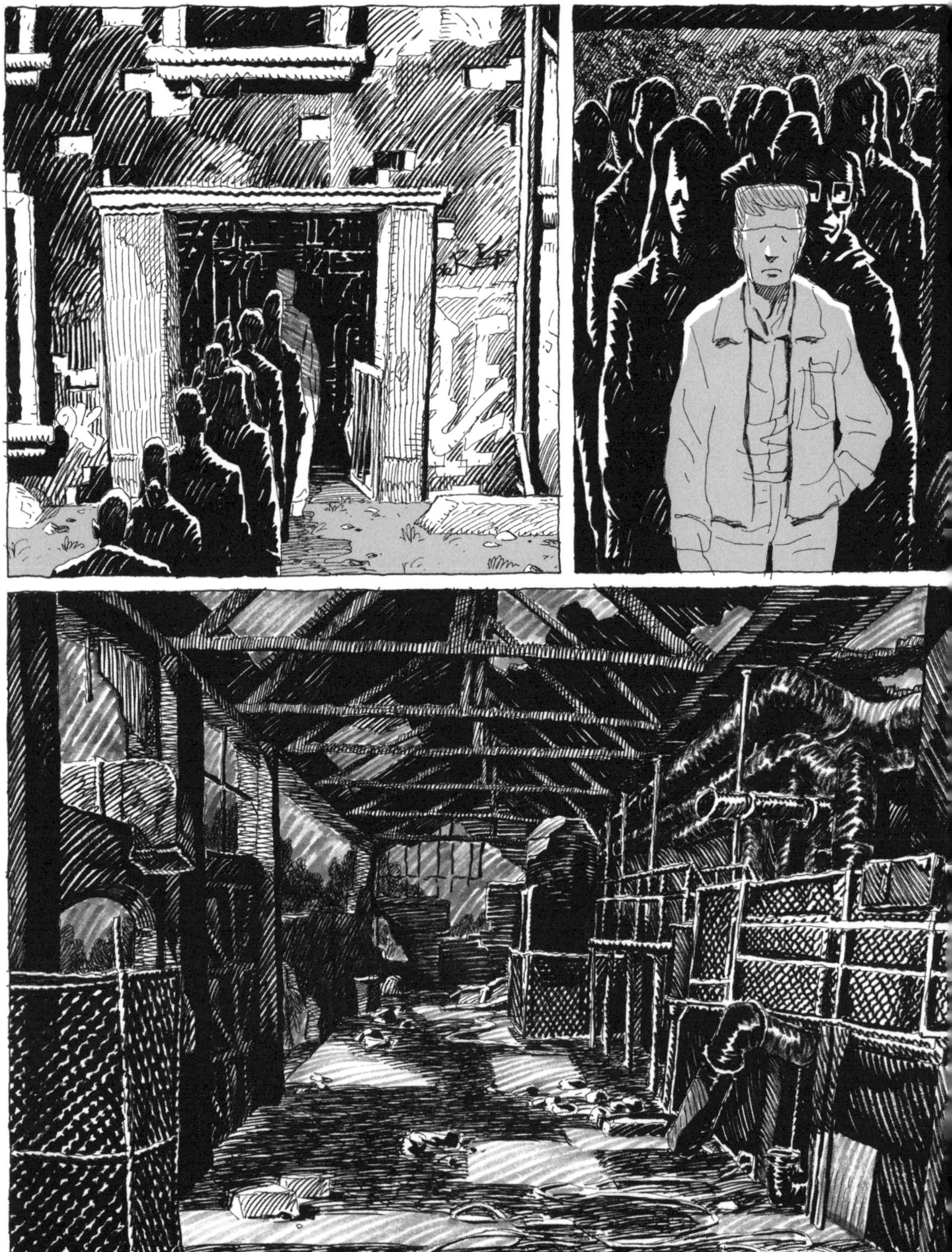

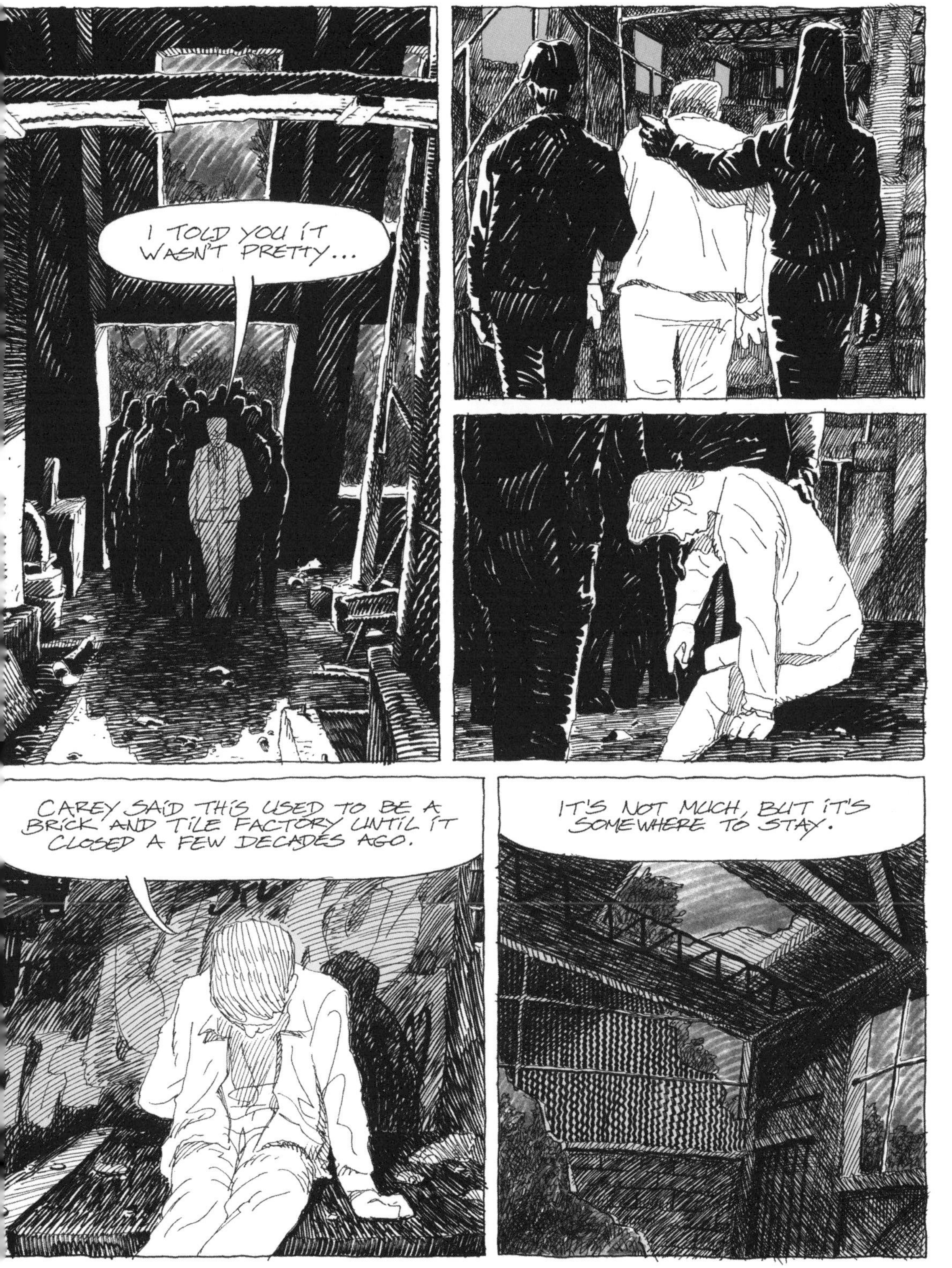
I TOLD YOU IT WASN'T PRETTY...
CAREY SAID THIS USED TO BE A BRICK AND TILE FACTORY UNTIL IT CLOSED A FEW DECADES AGO.
IT'S NOT MUCH, BUT IT'S SOMEWHERE TO STAY.

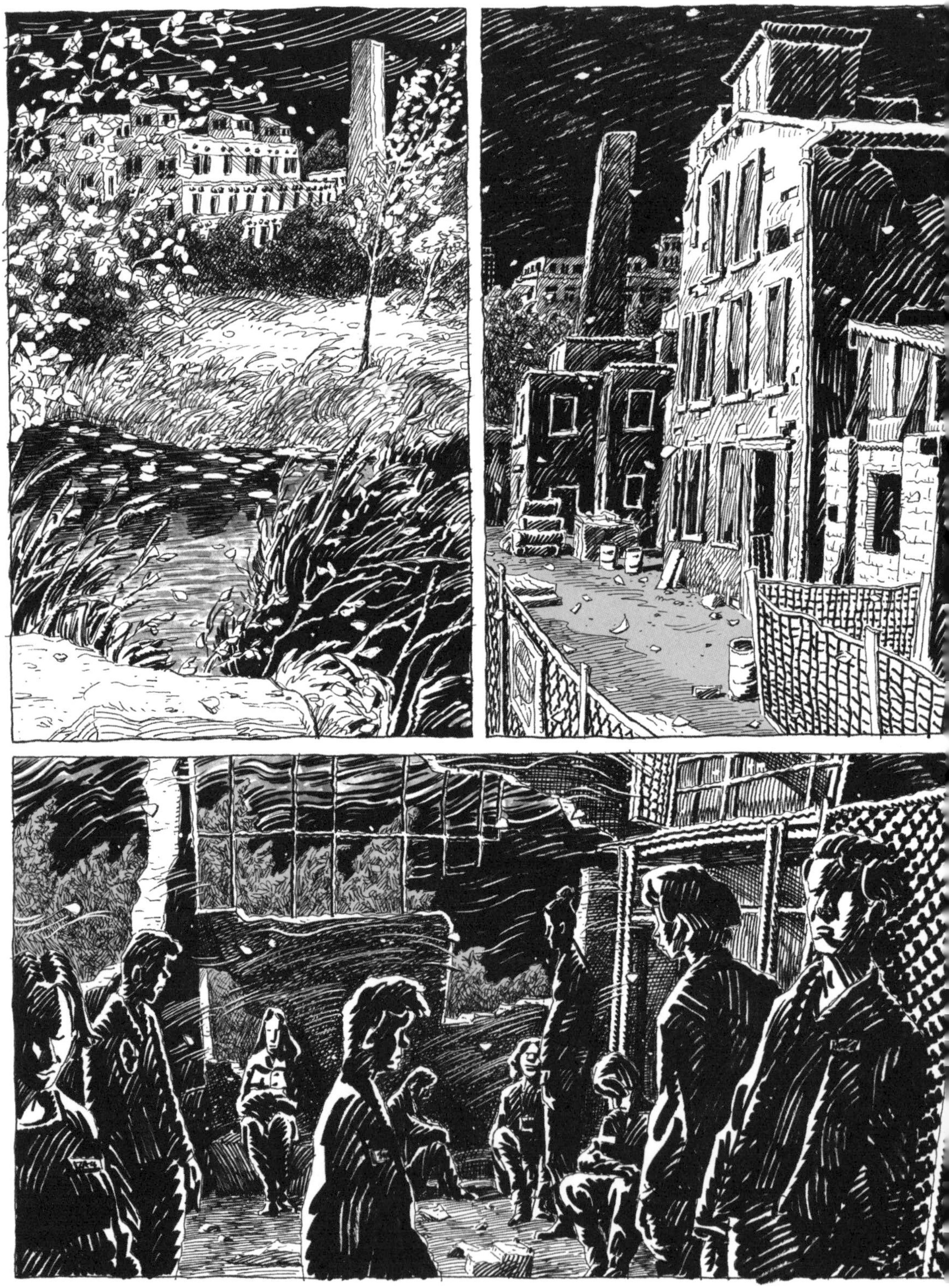

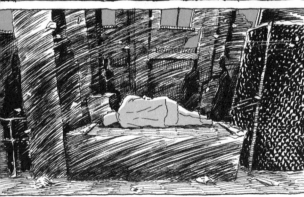

WE'RE GOING TO FREEZE IN HERE.

I CAN'T TAKE THIS...

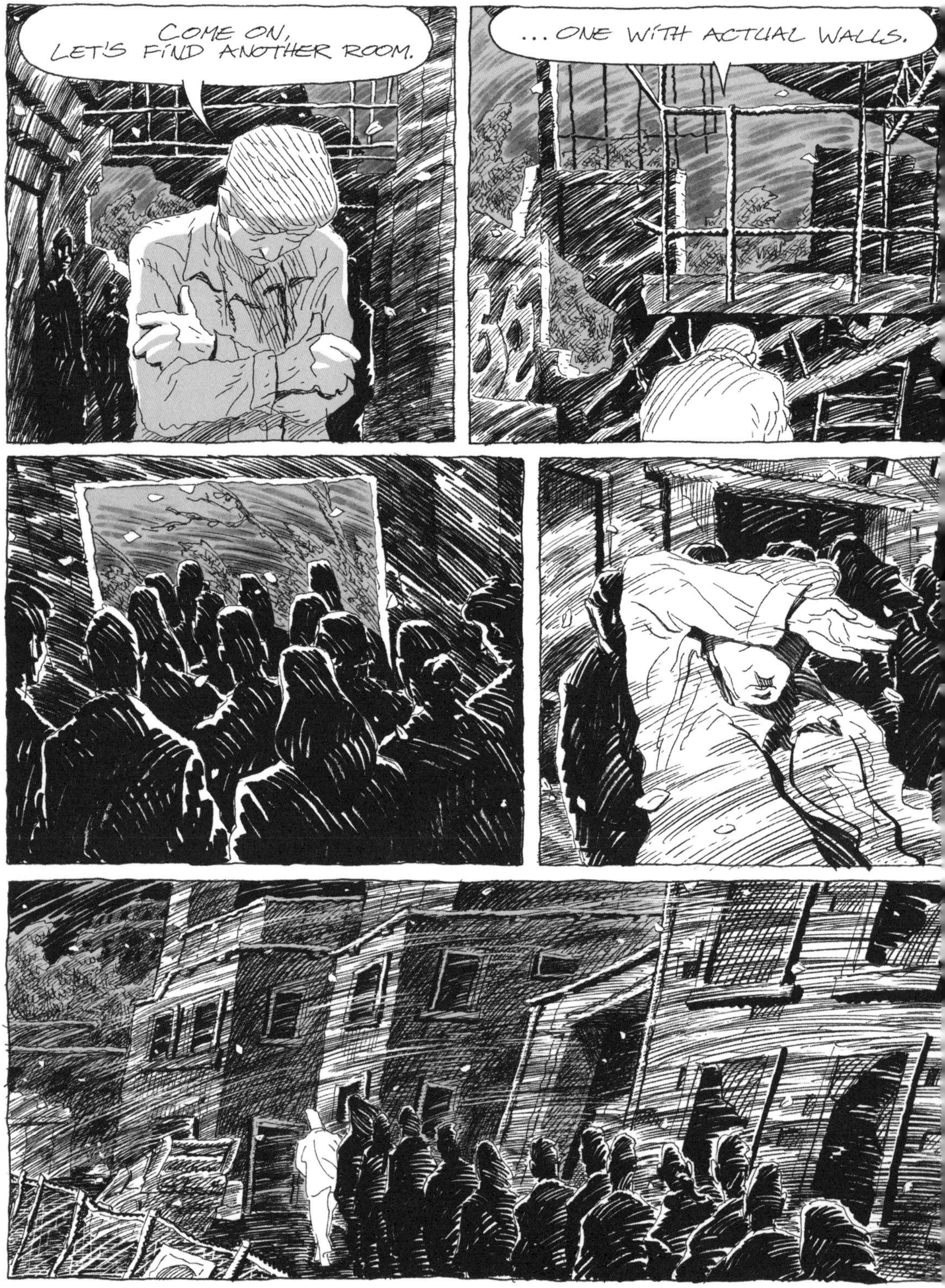
COME ON, LET'S FIND ANOTHER ROOM.
... ONE WITH ACTUAL WALLS.

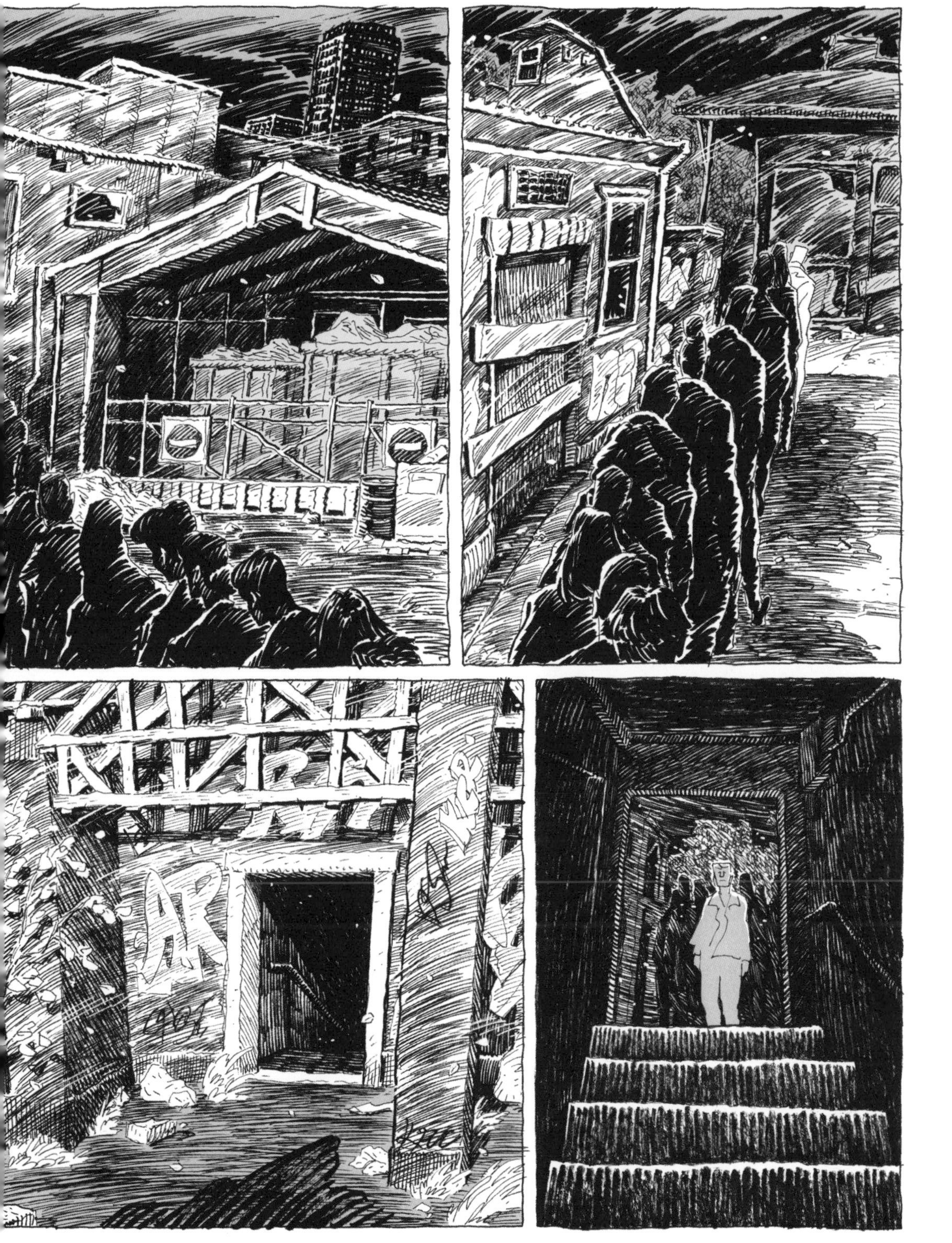

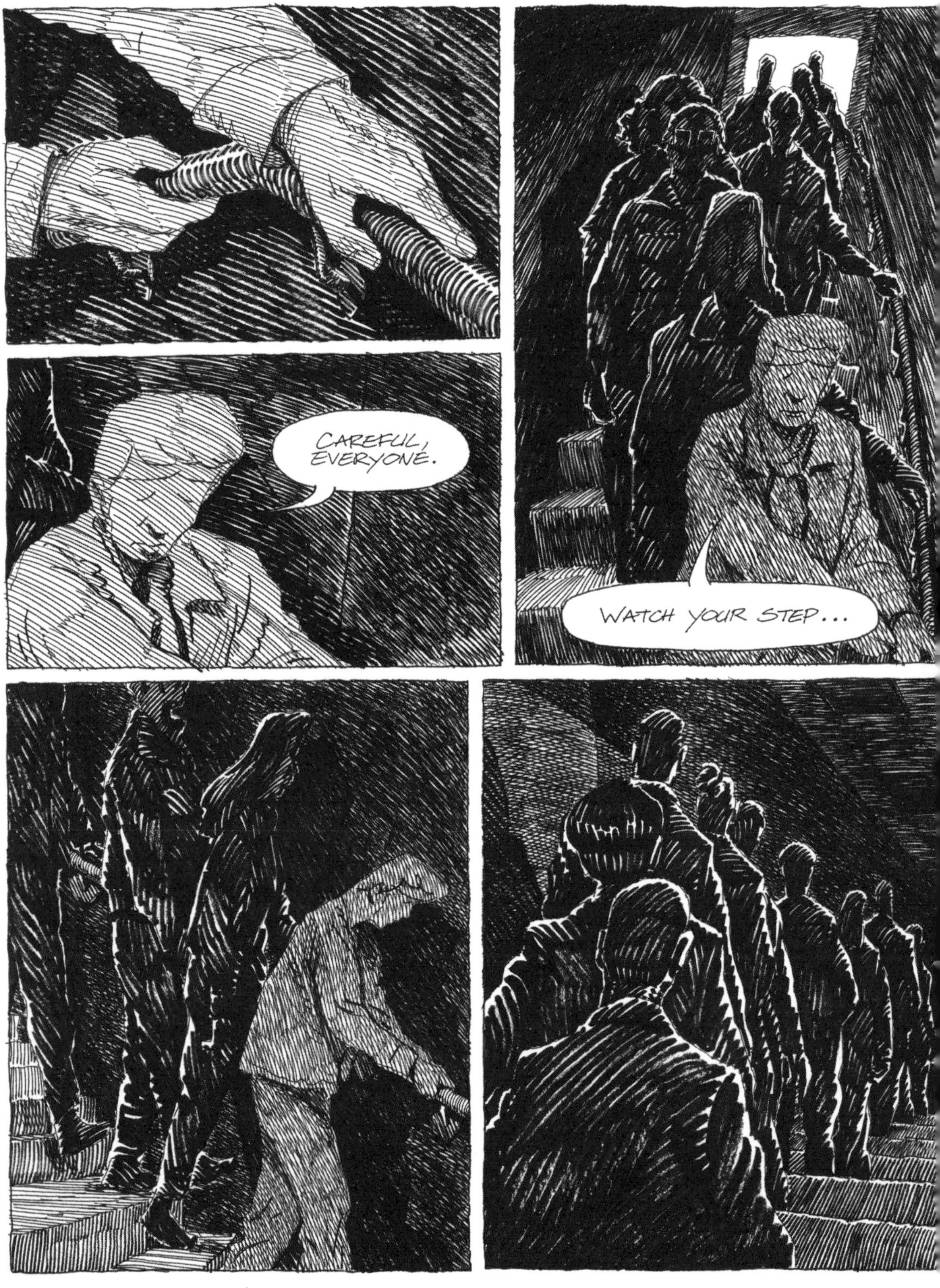
CAREFUL, EVERYONE.
WATCH YOUR STEP...

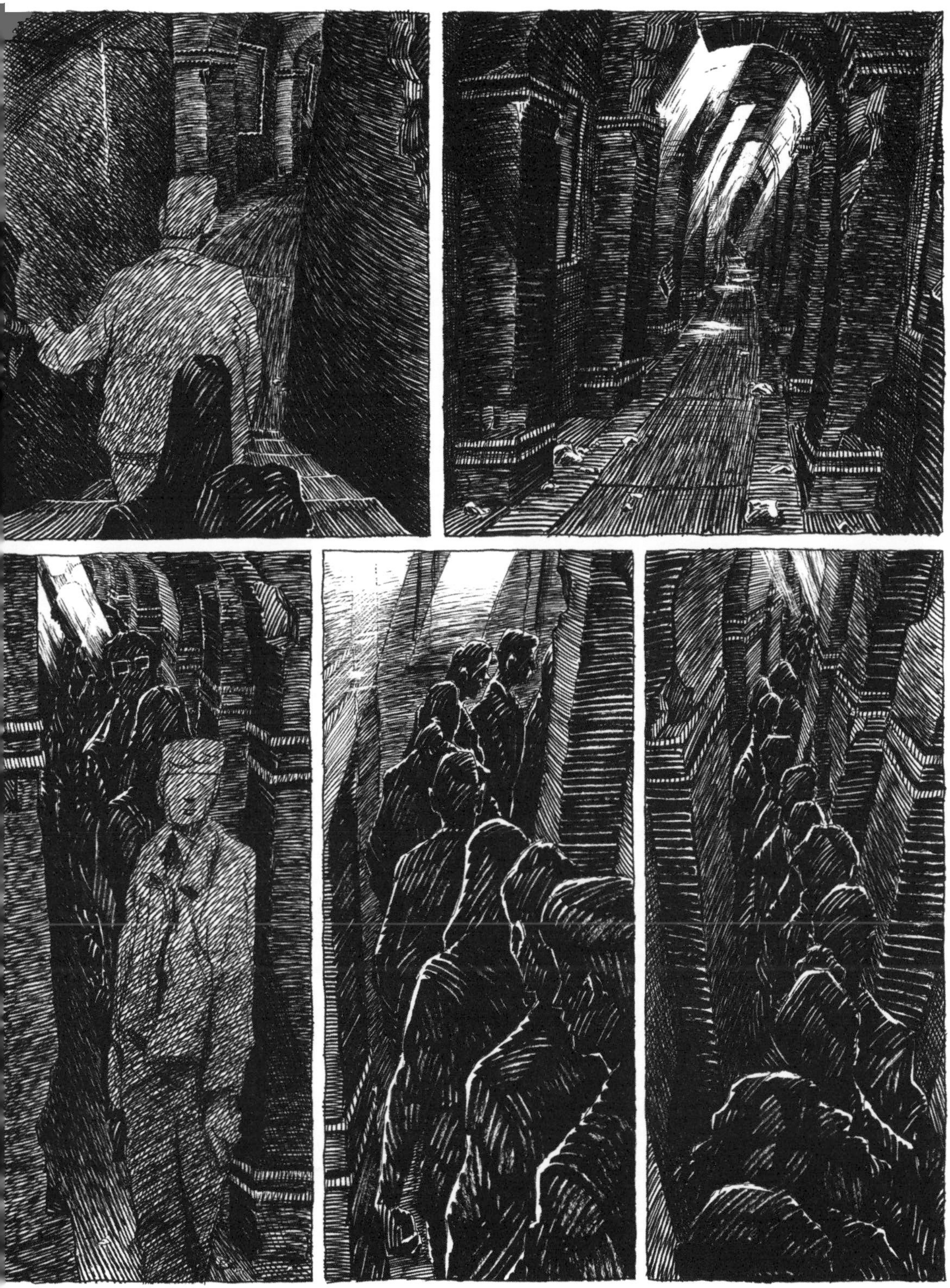

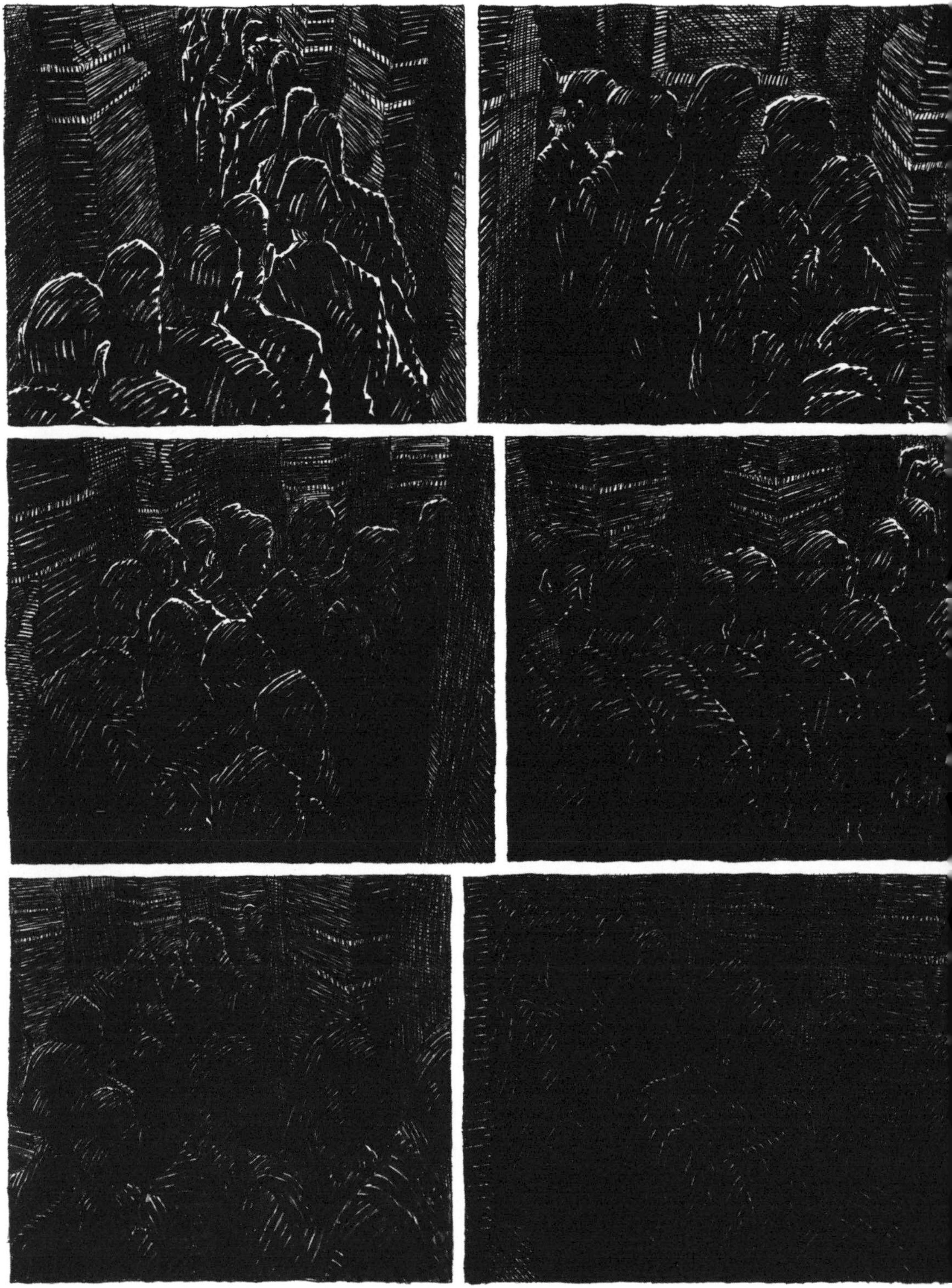

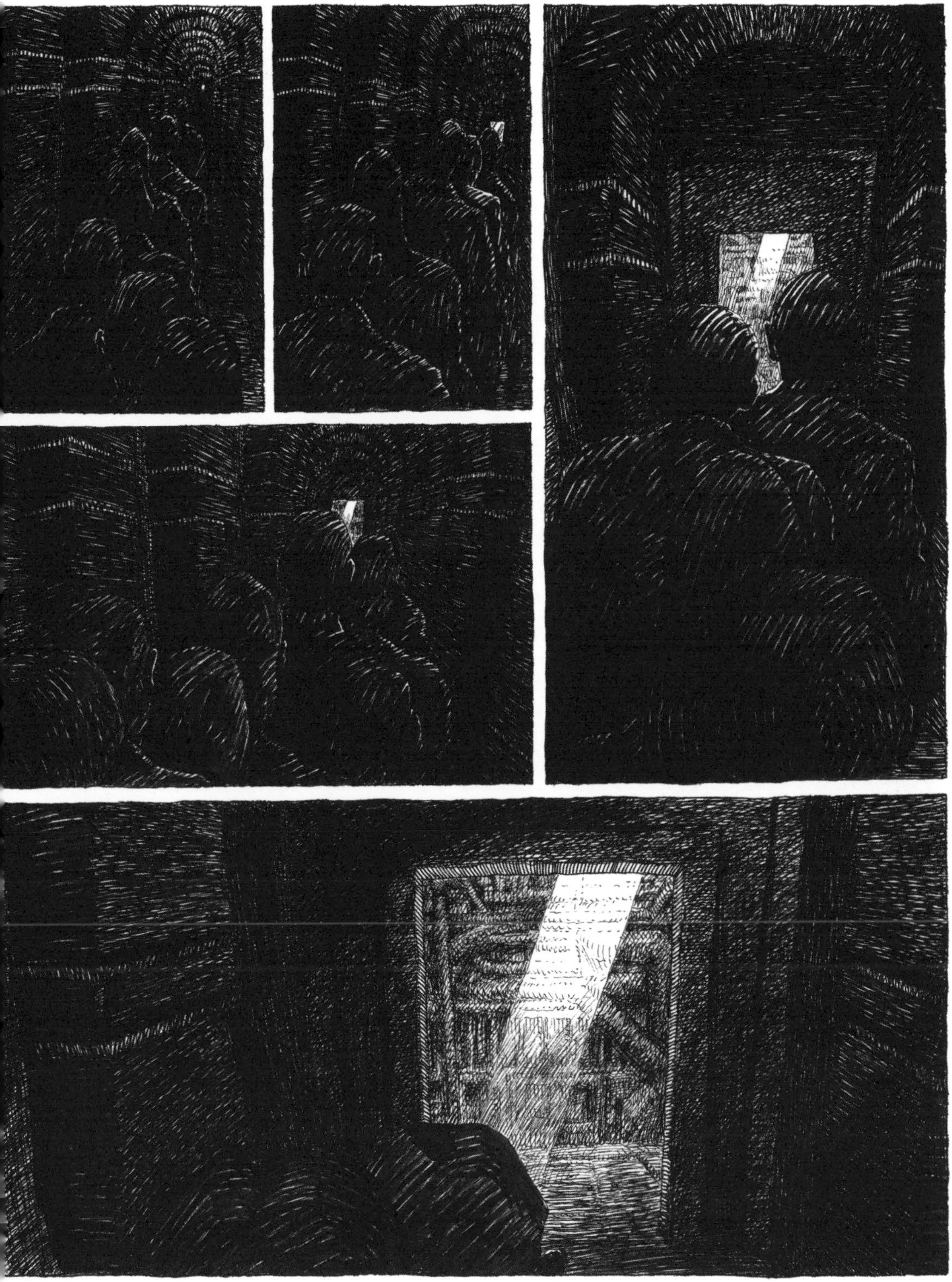

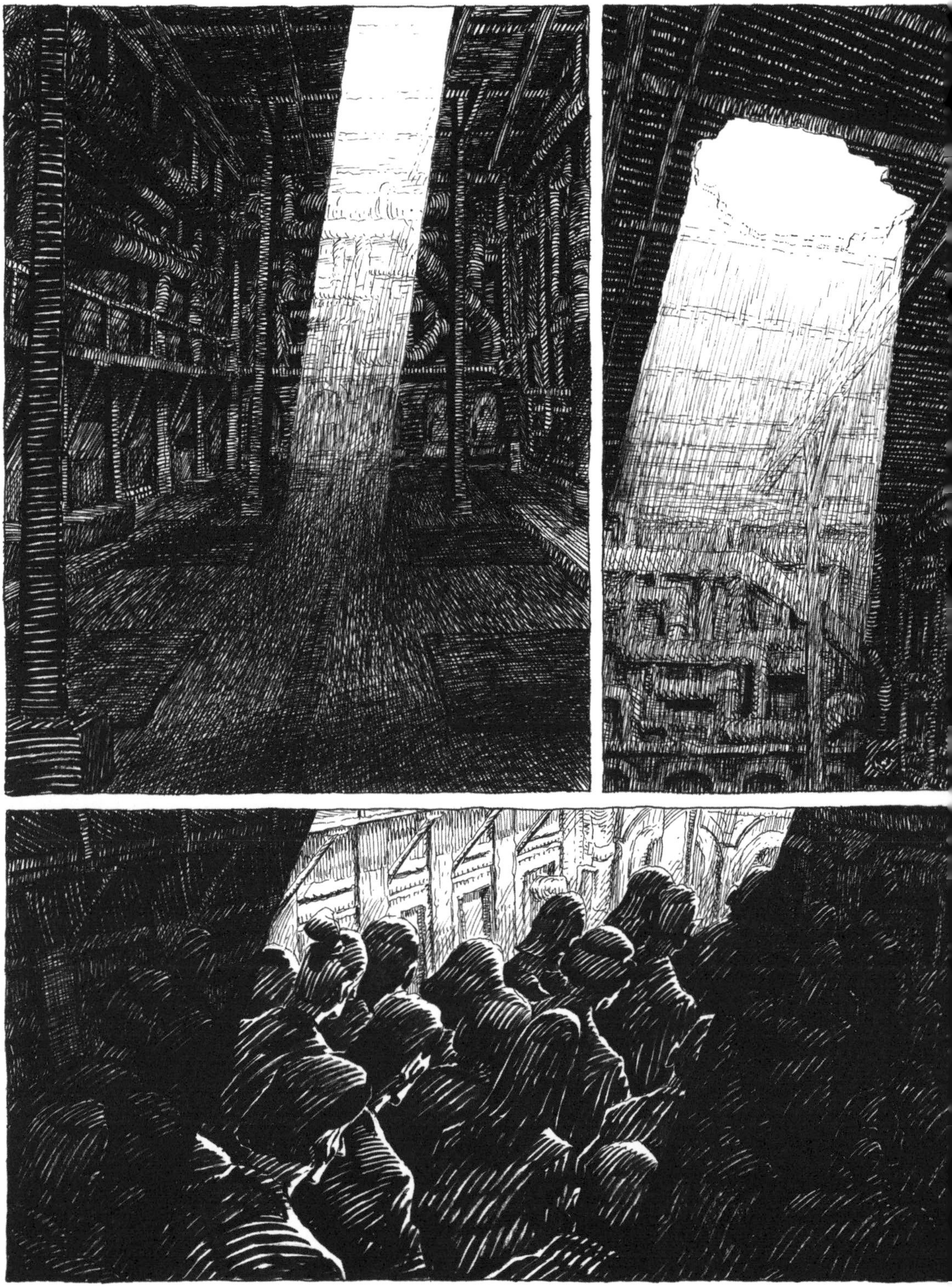

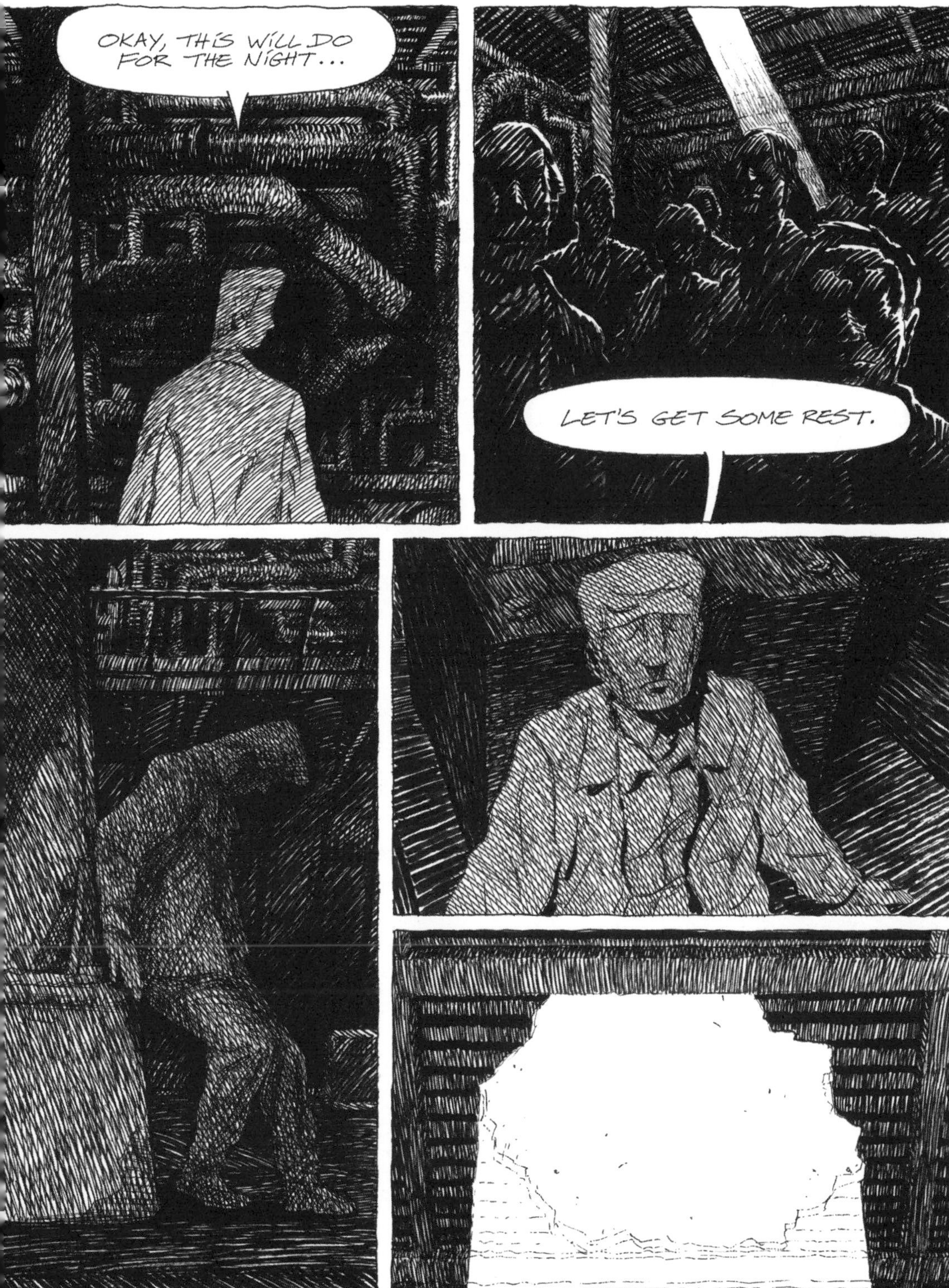
OKAY, THIS WILL DO FOR THE NIGHT...
LET'S GET SOME REST.

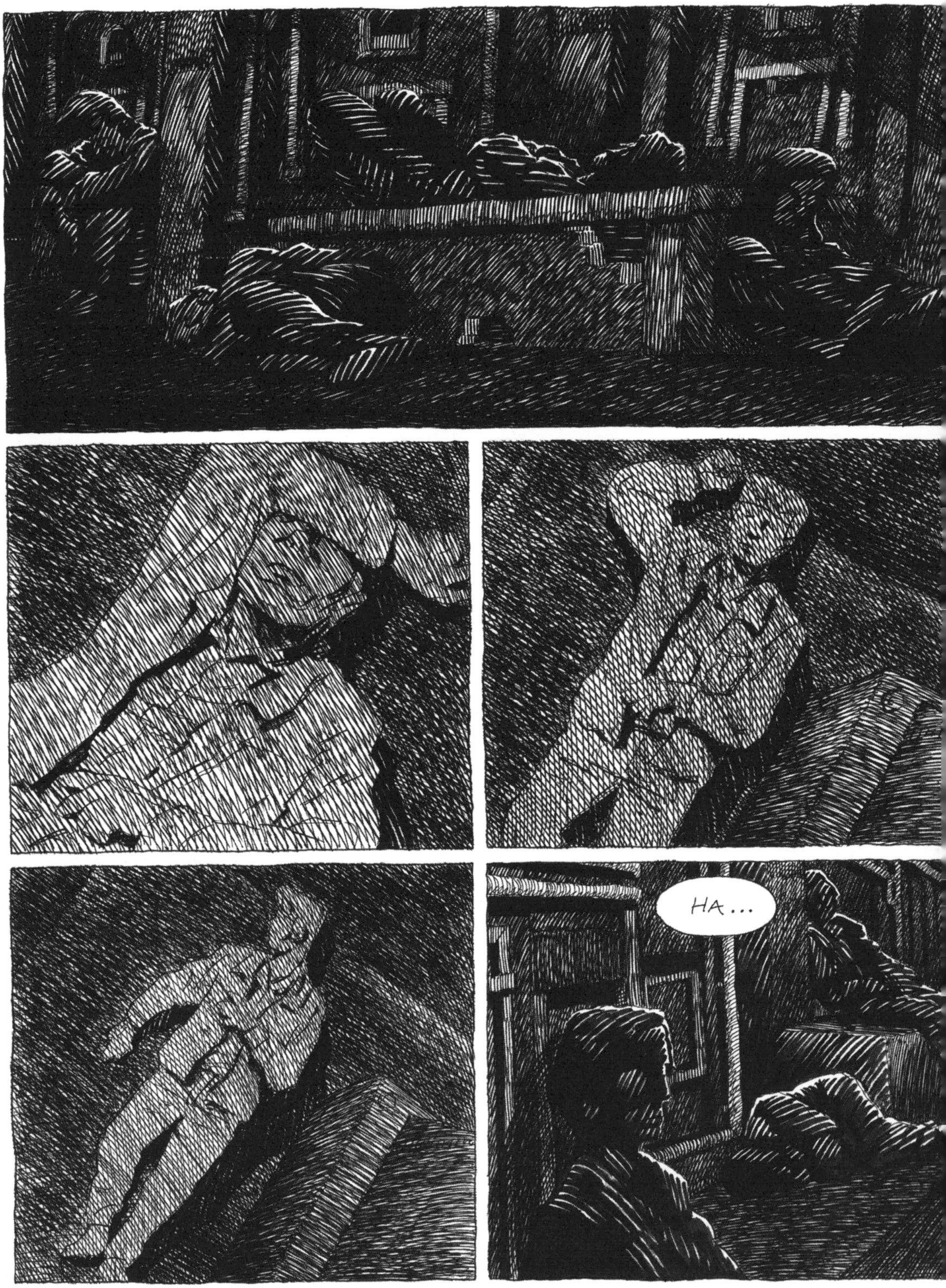
HA...

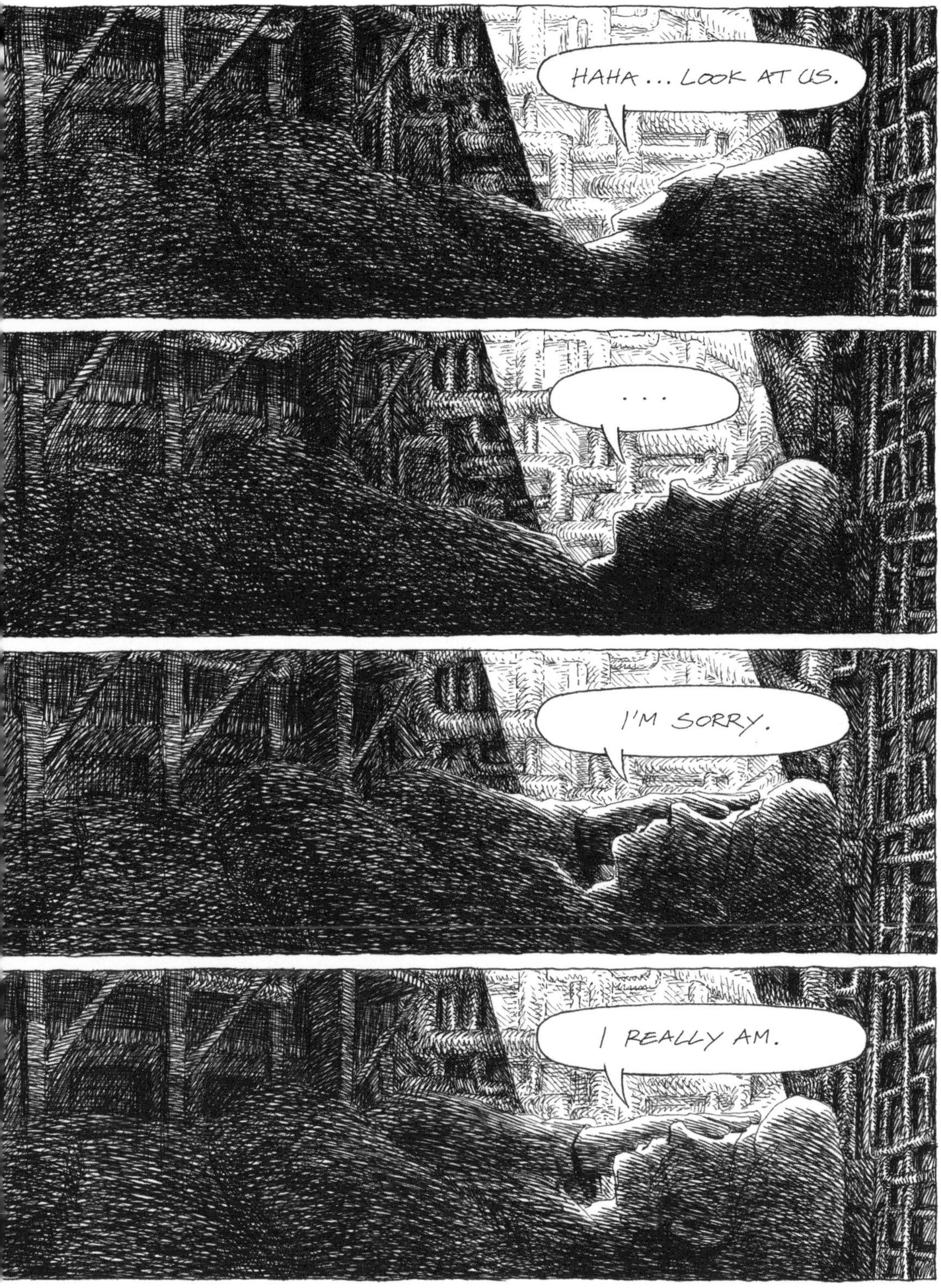
HAHA ... LOOK AT US.
. . .
I'M SORRY.
I REALLY AM.

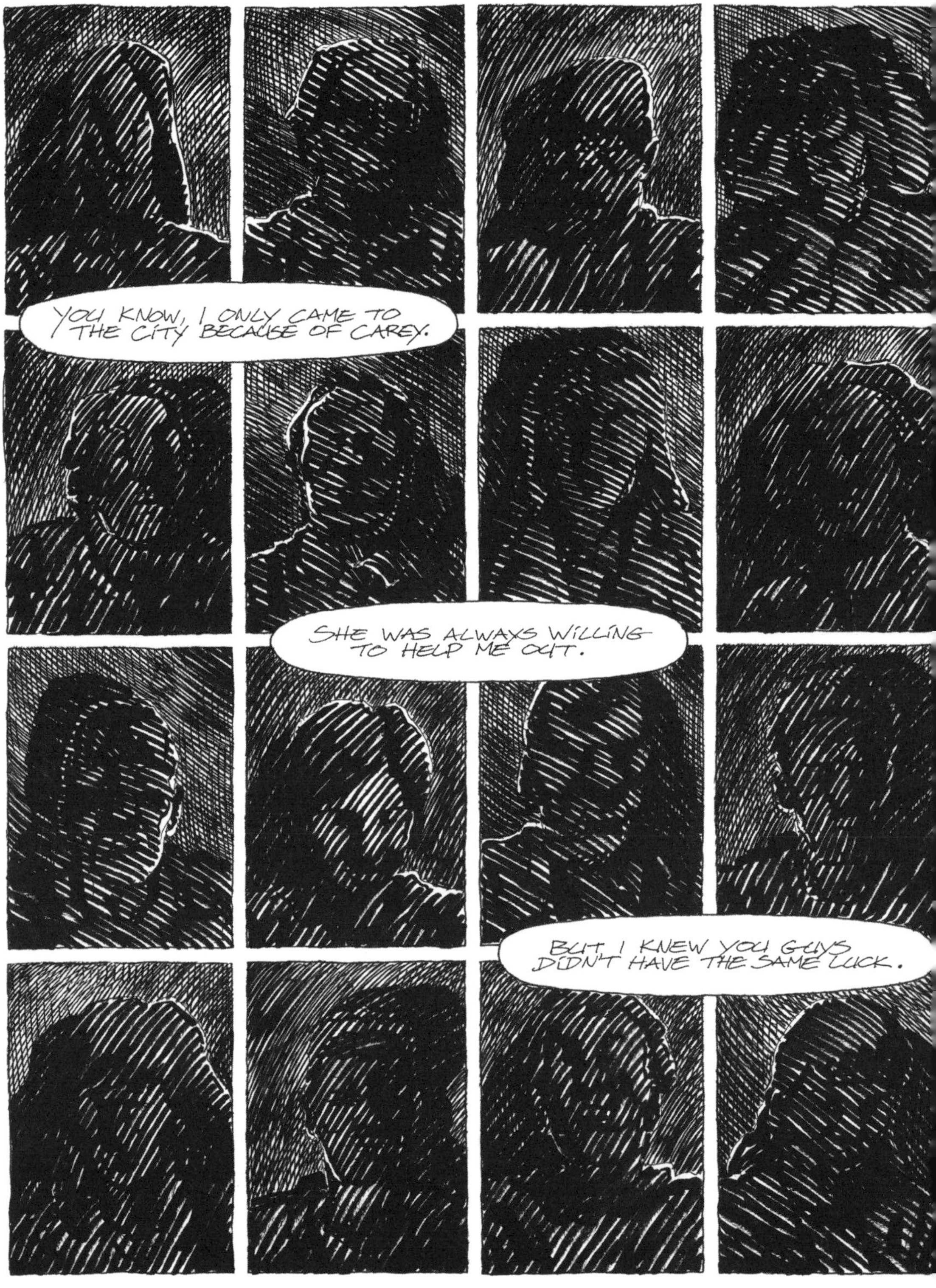
YOU KNOW, I ONLY CAME TO THE CITY BECAUSE OF CAREY.
SHE WAS ALWAYS WILLING TO HELP ME OUT.
BUT I KNEW YOU GUYS DIDN'T HAVE THE SAME LUCK.

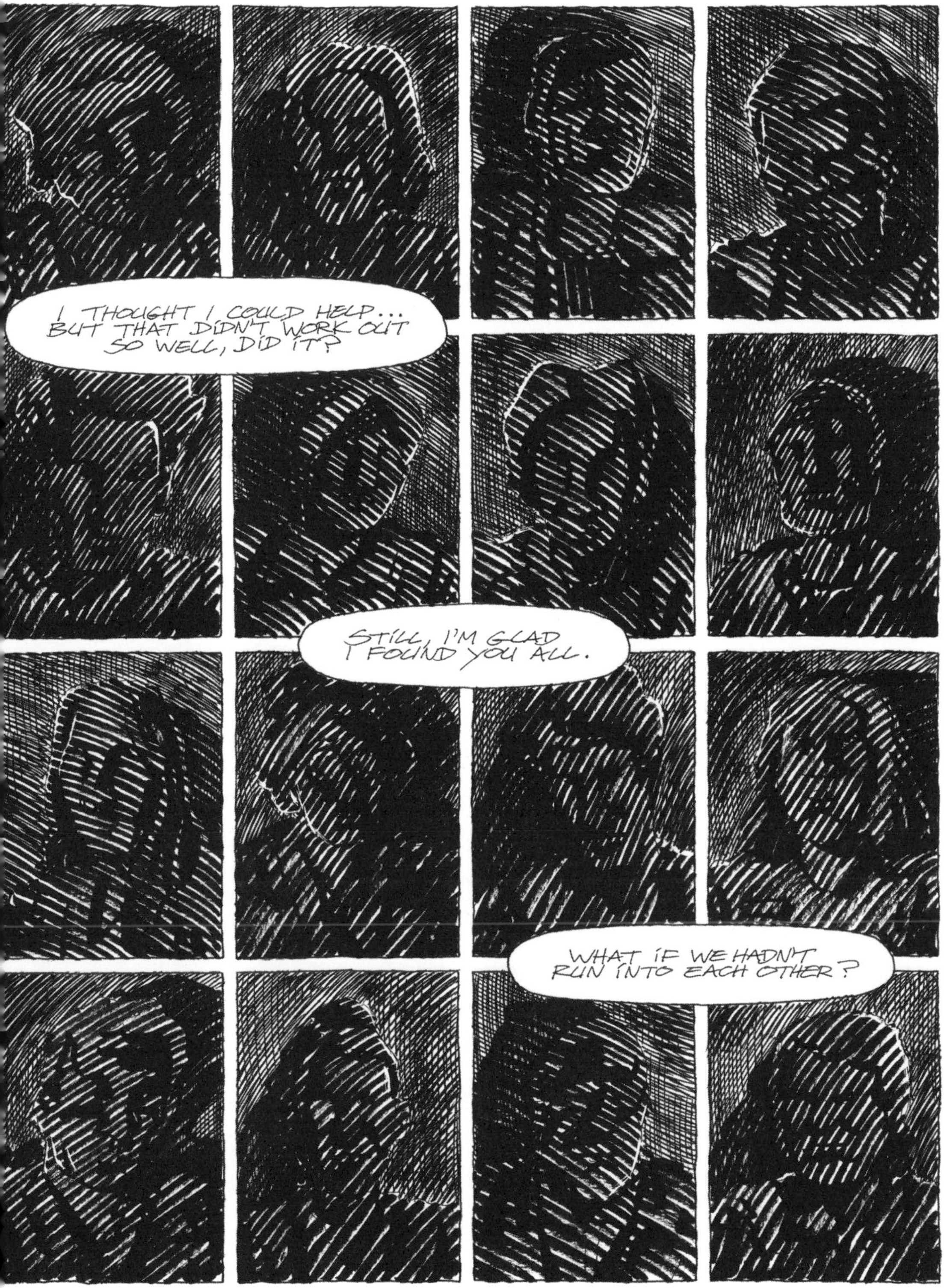
I THOUGHT I COULD HELP... BUT THAT DIDN'T WORK OUT SO WELL, DID IT?
STILL, I'M GLAD I FOUND YOU ALL.
WHAT IF WE HADN'T RUN INTO EACH OTHER?

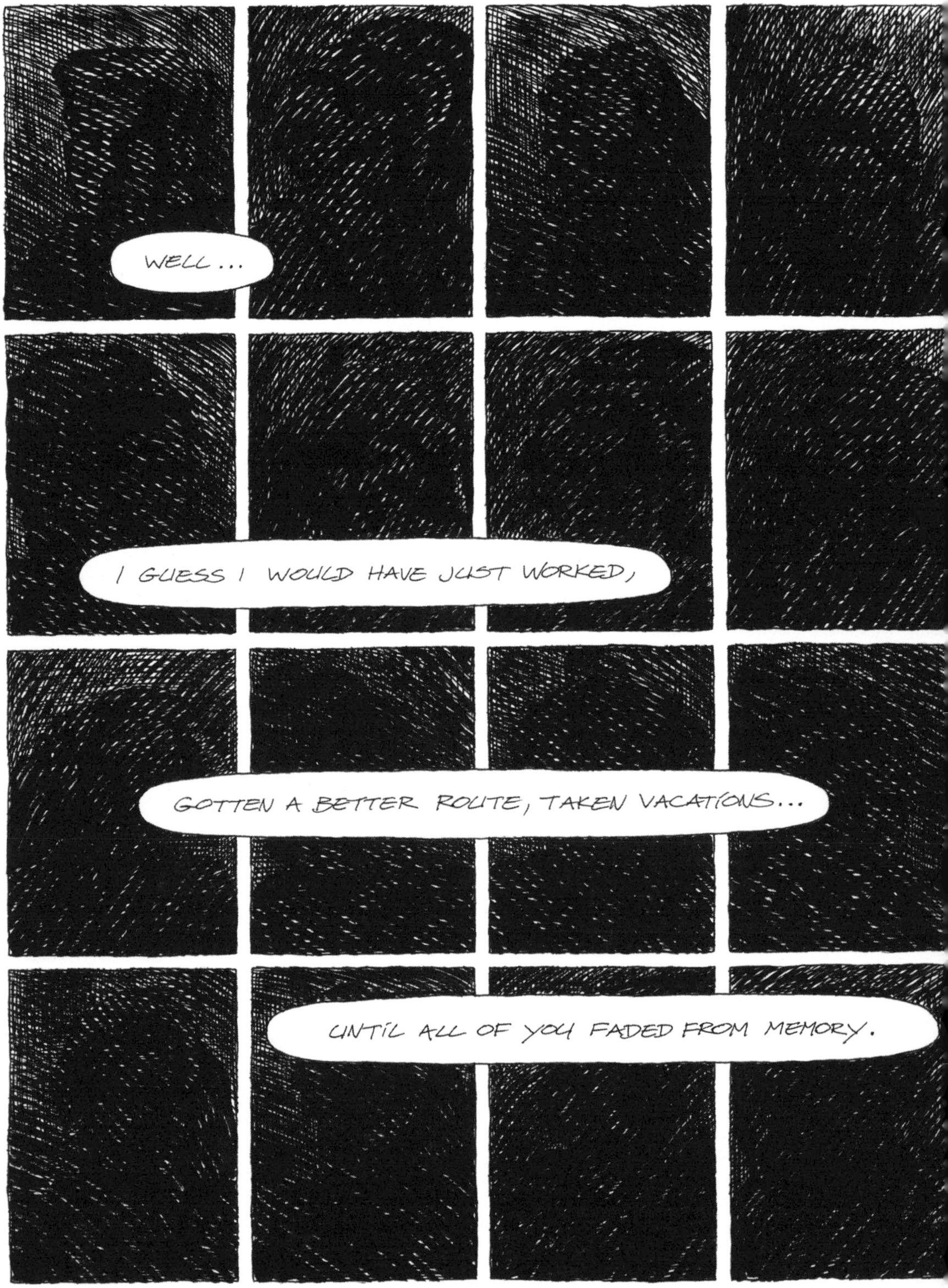
WELL...
I GUESS I WOULD HAVE JUST WORKED,
GOTTEN A BETTER ROUTE, TAKEN VACATIONS...
UNTIL ALL OF YOU FADED FROM MEMORY.

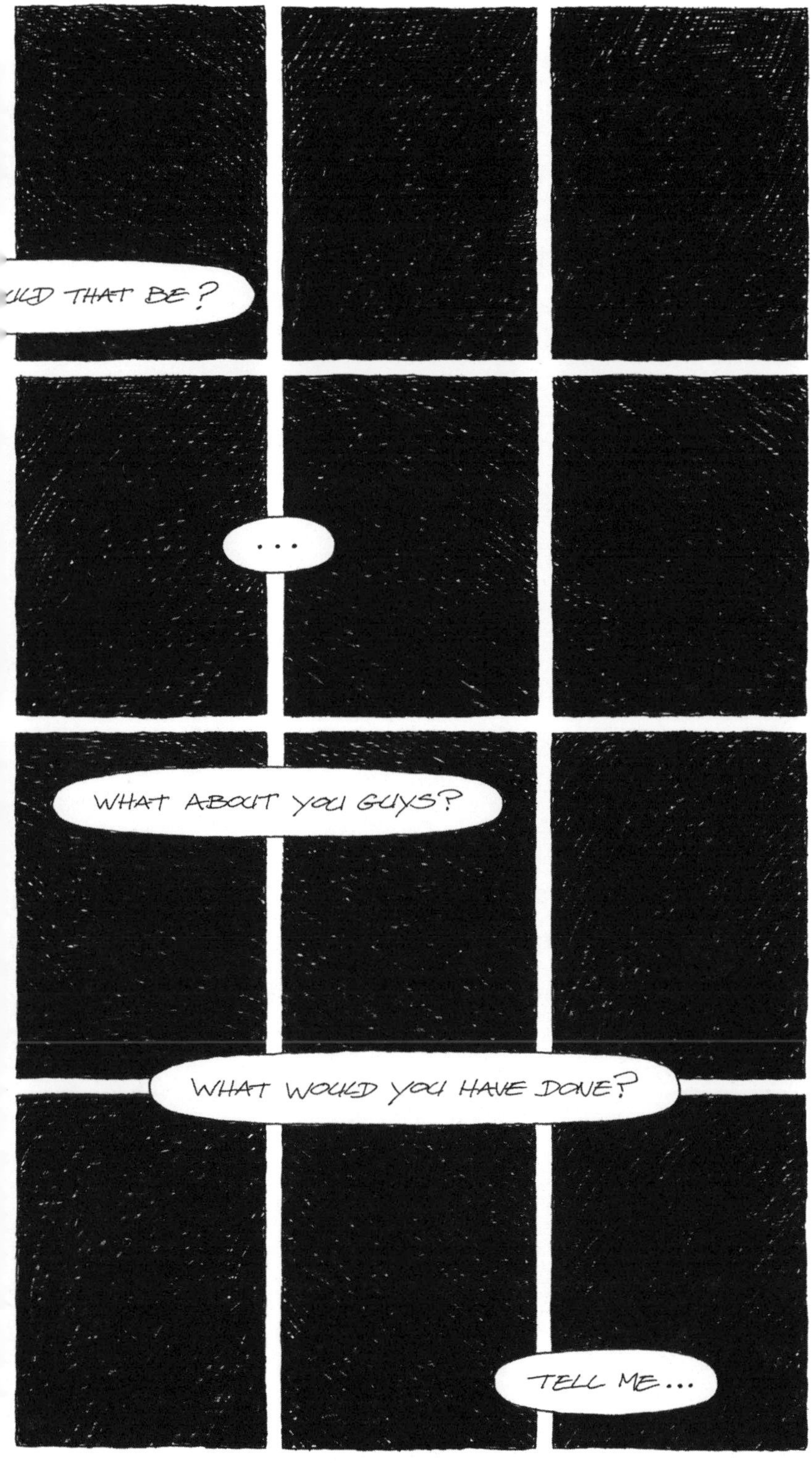
ULD THAT BE?
...
WHAT ABOUT YOU GUYS?
WHAT WOULD YOU HAVE DONE?
TELL ME...

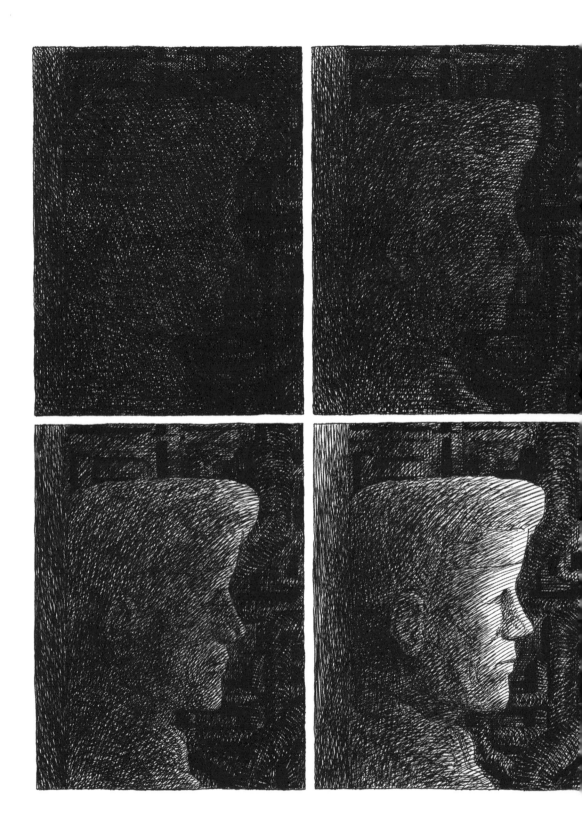

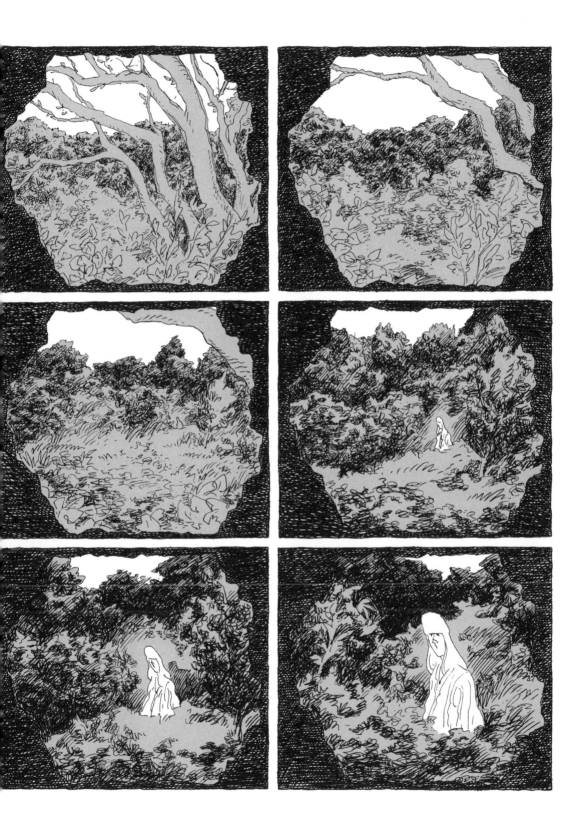

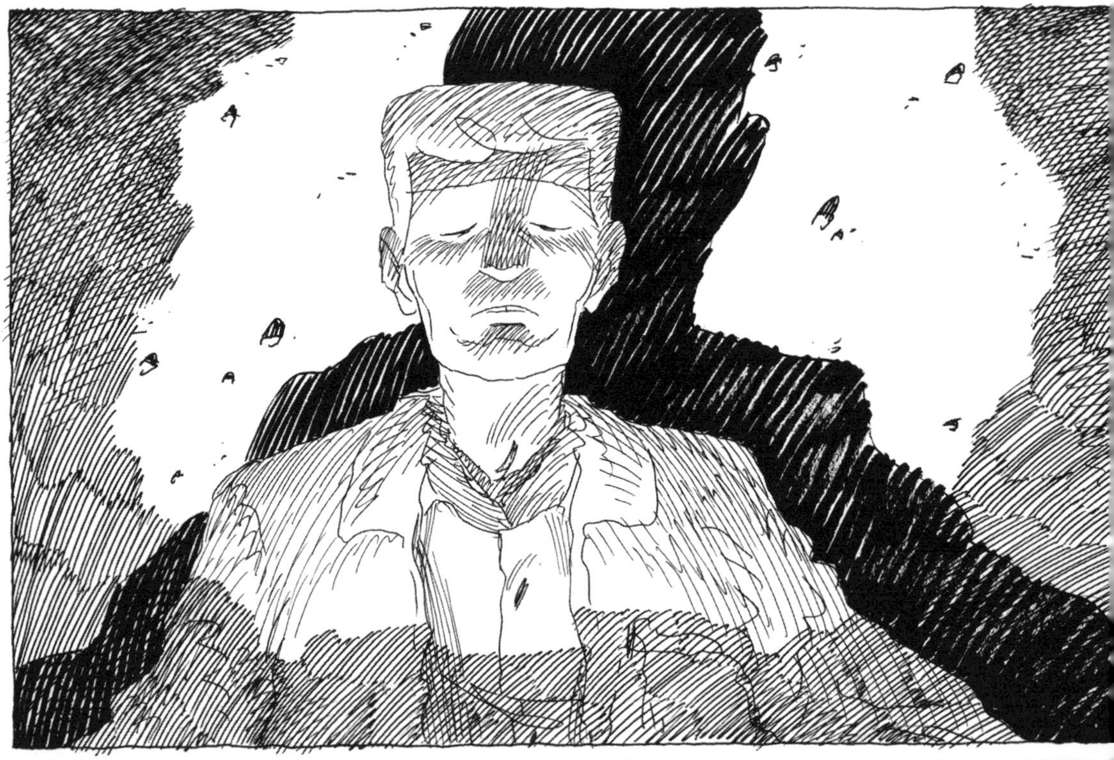

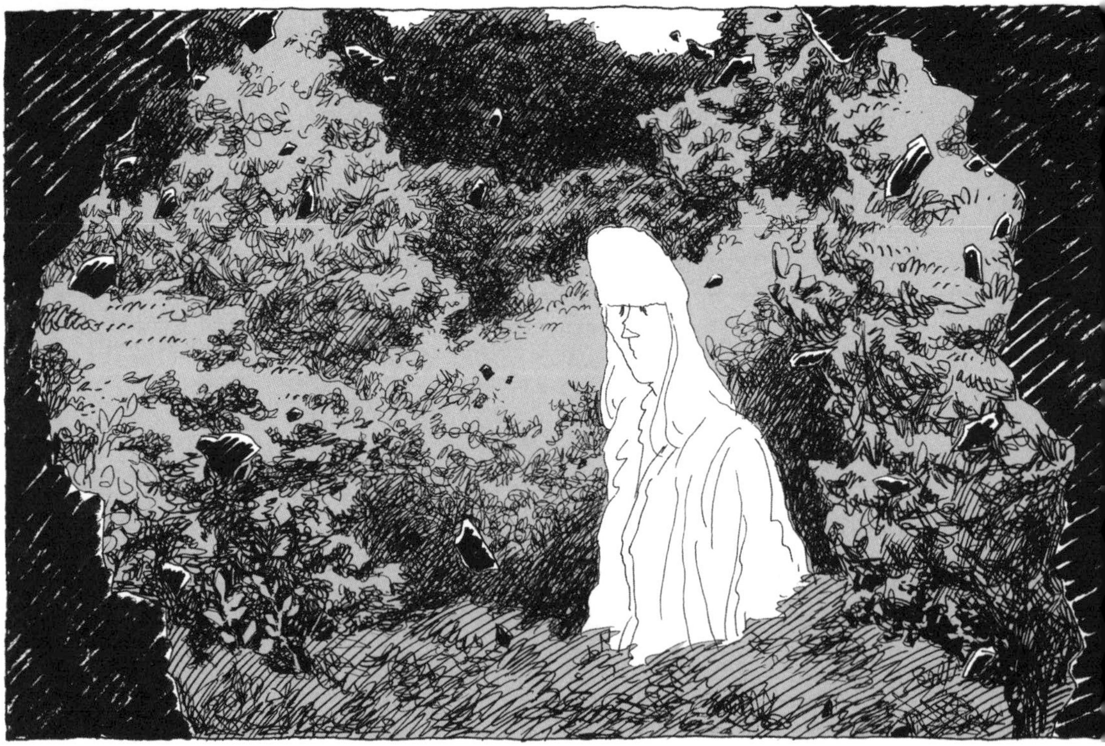

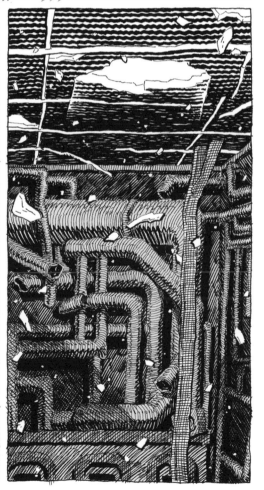

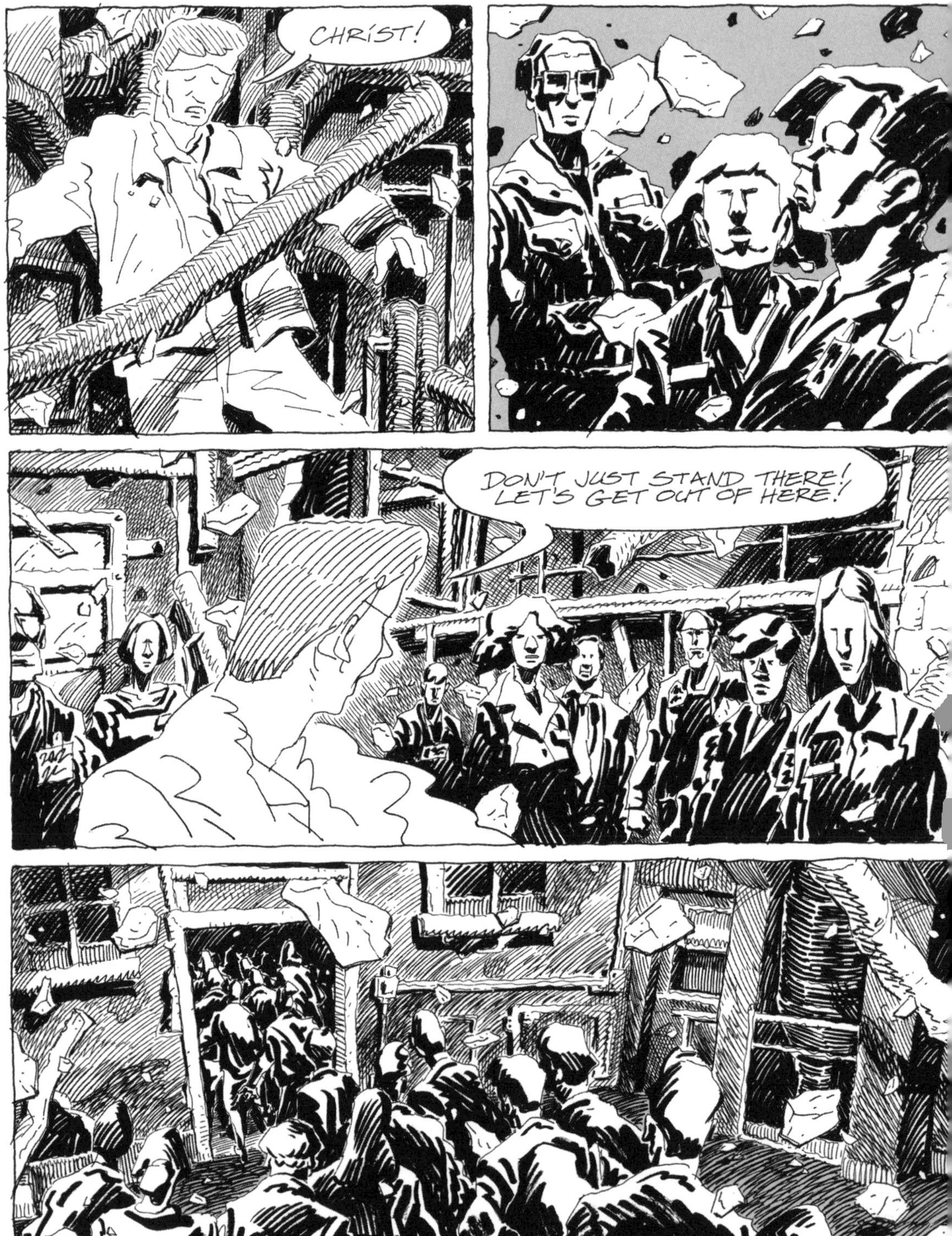
CHRIST!
DON'T JUST STAND THERE! LET'S GET OUT OF HERE!

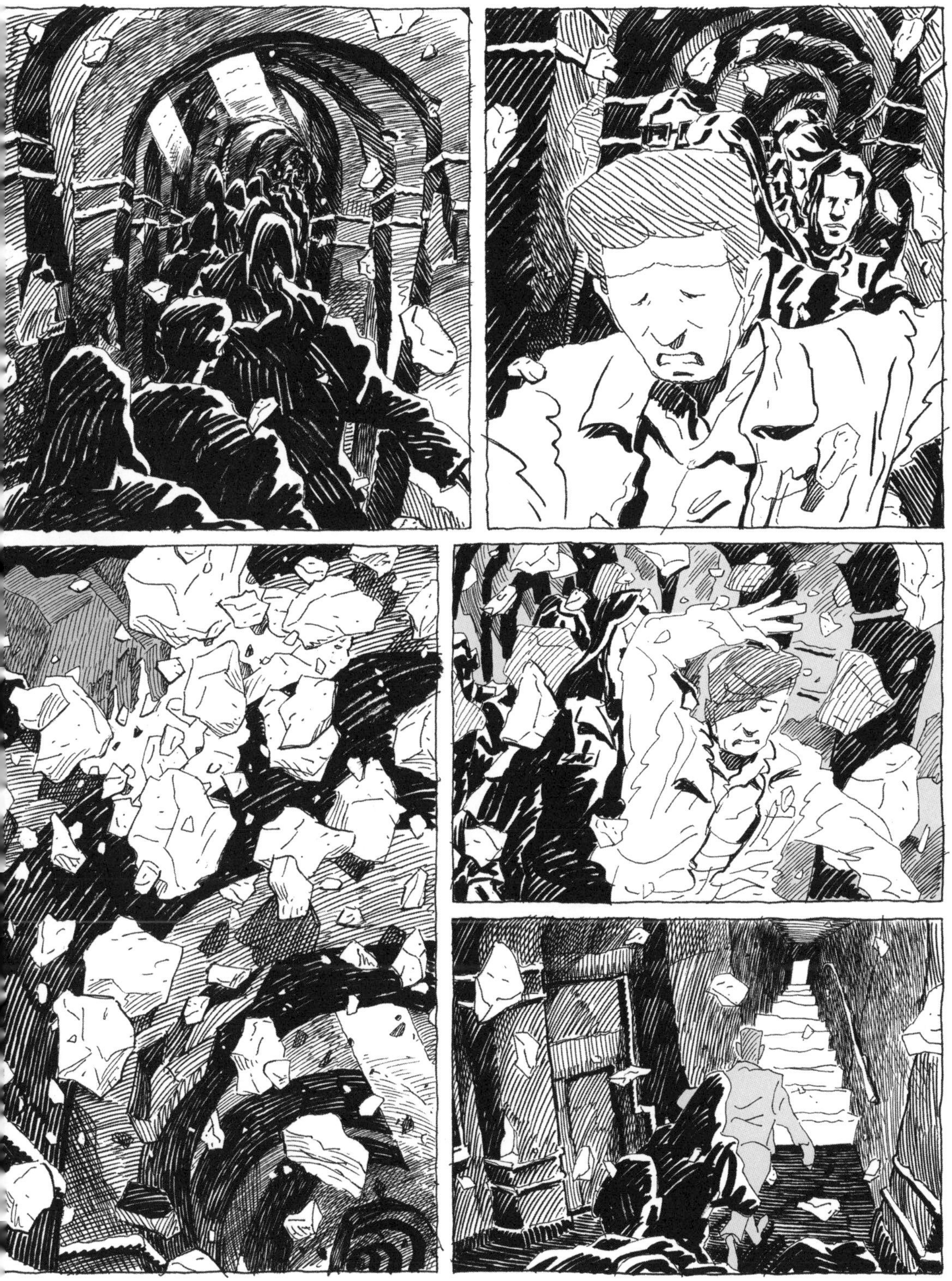

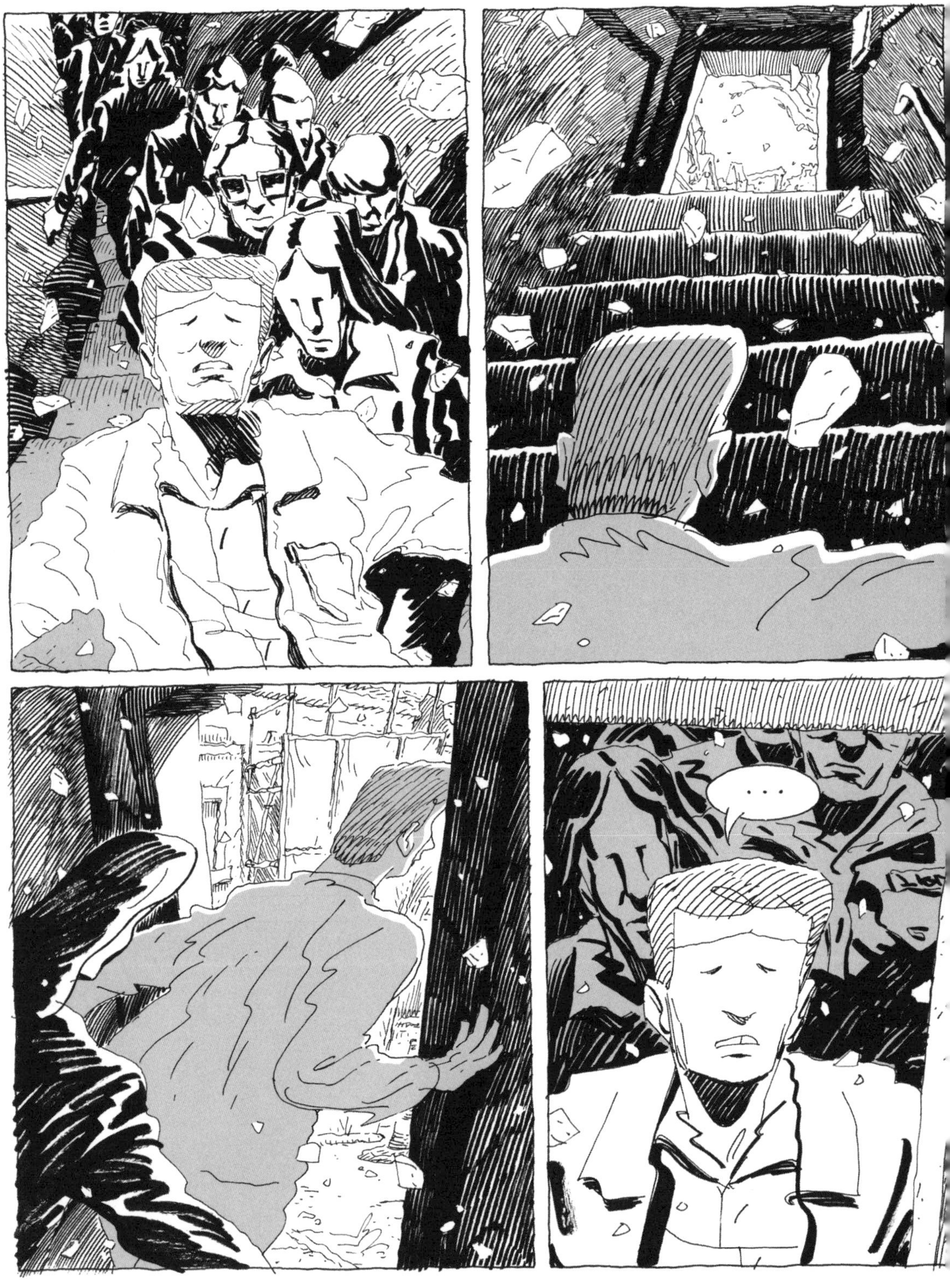
. . .

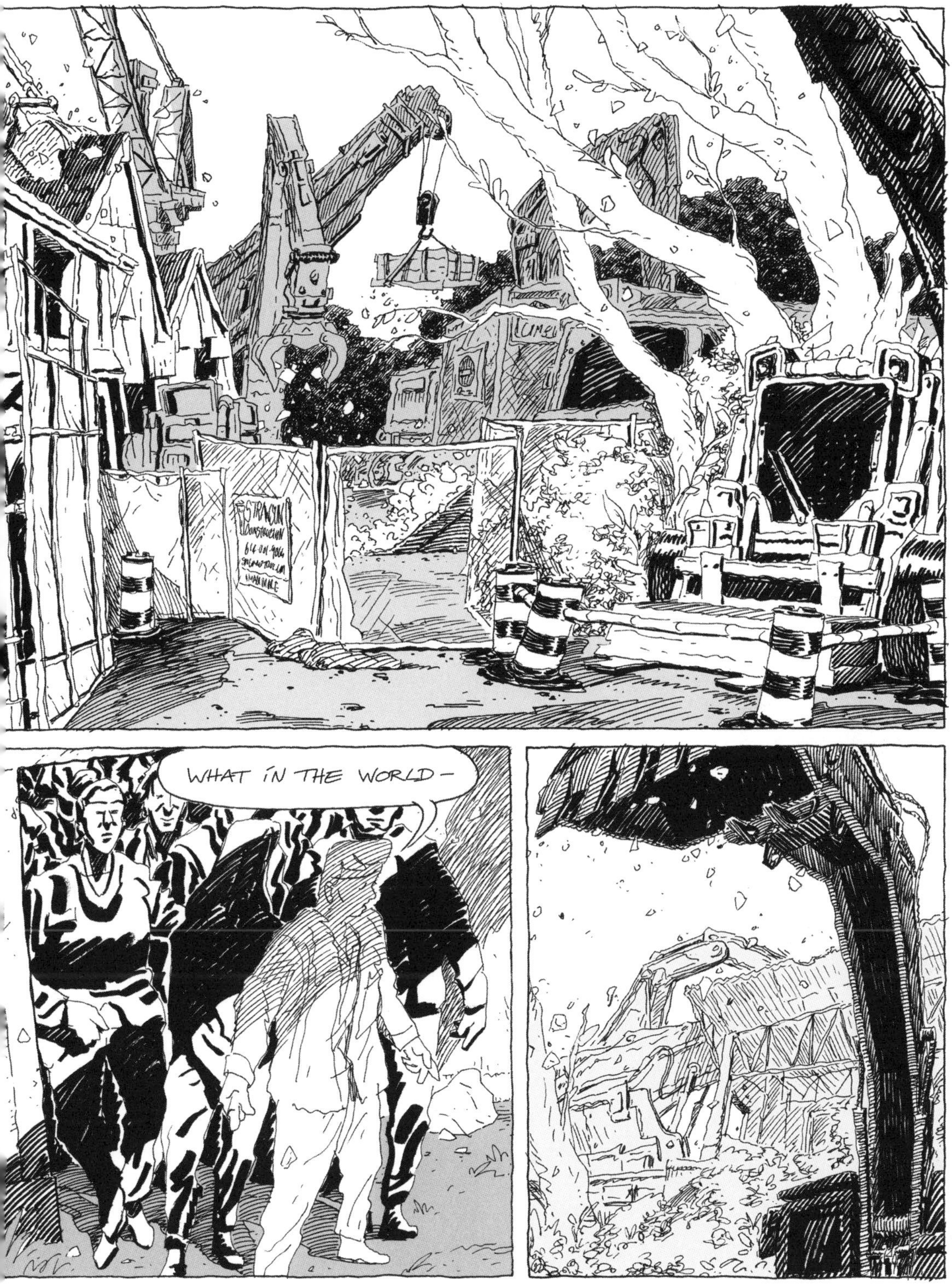
WHAT IN THE WORLD –

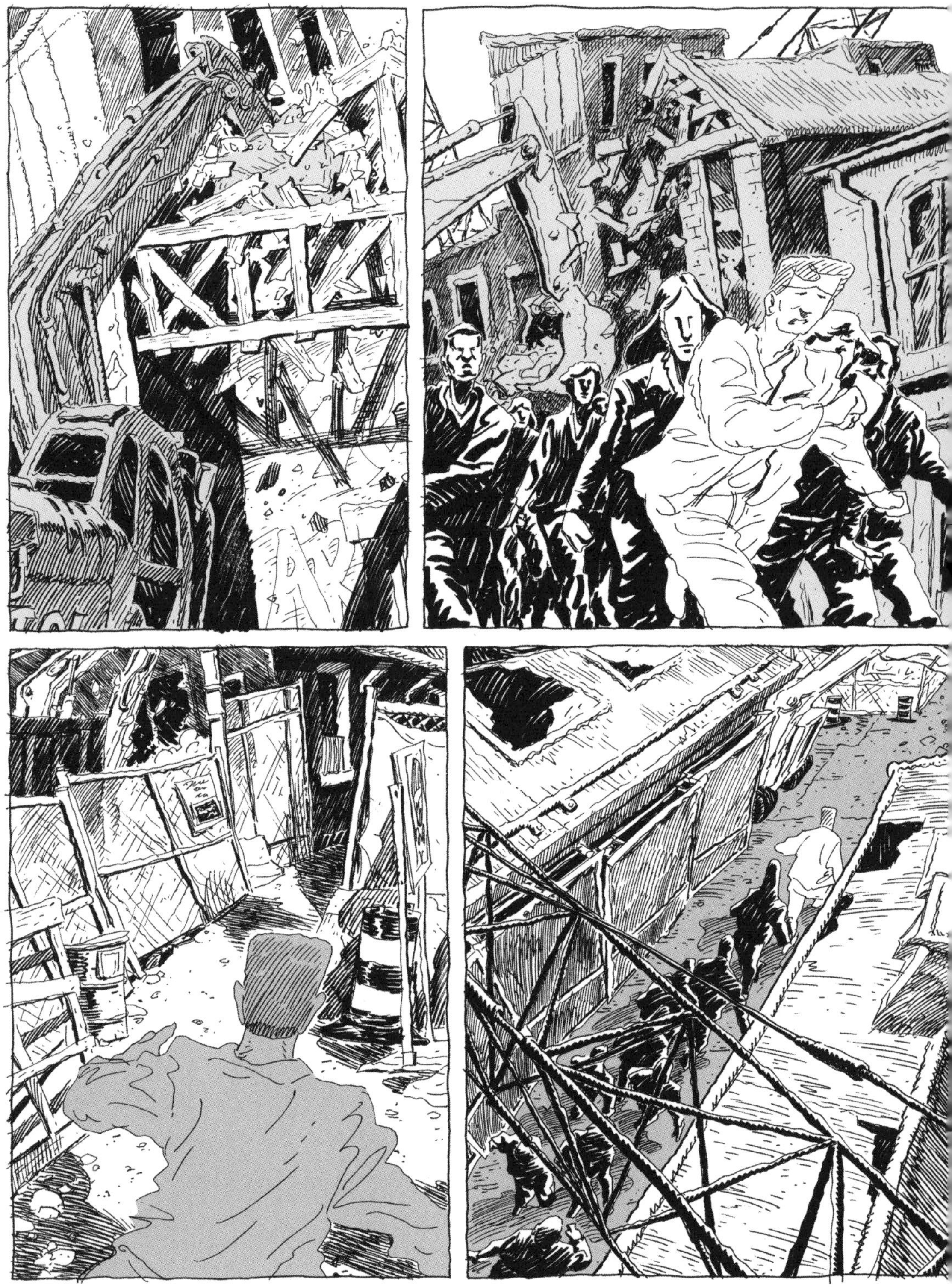

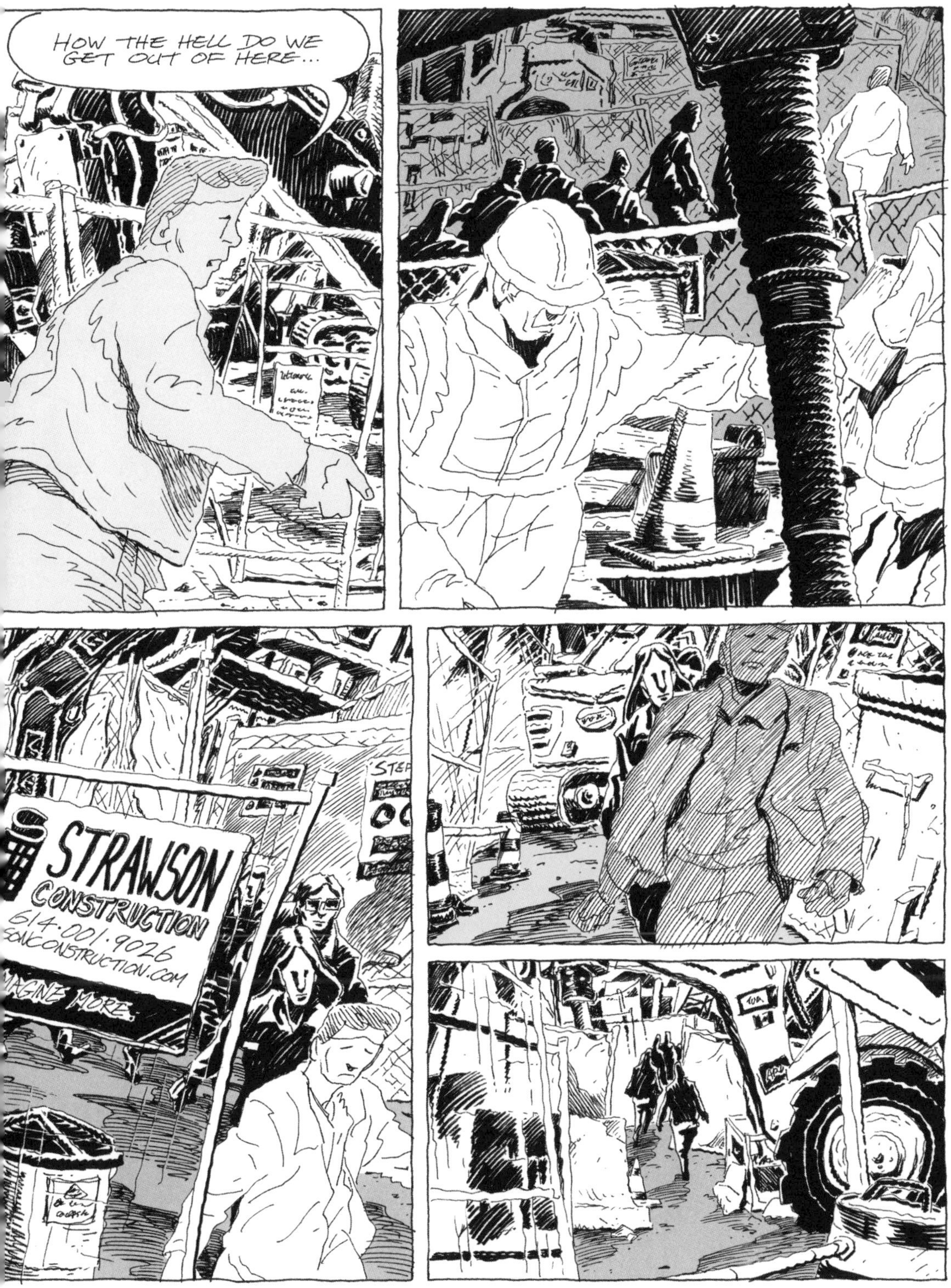
HOW THE HELL DO WE GET OUT OF HERE...
STRAWSON
CONSTRUCTION
614·001·9026

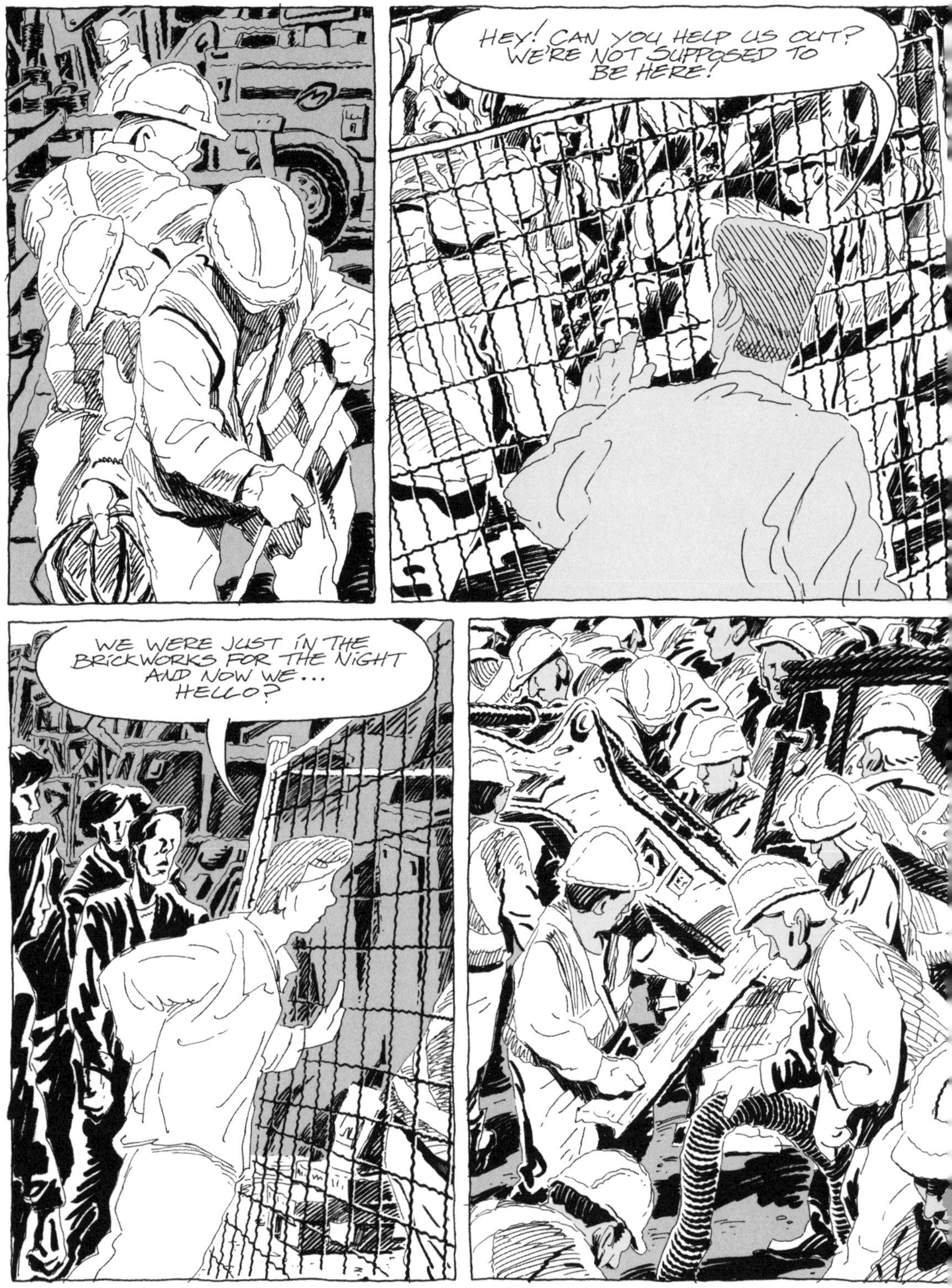
HEY! CAN YOU HELP US OUT? WE'RE NOT SUPPOSED TO BE HERE!
WE WERE JUST IN THE BRICKWORKS FOR THE NIGHT AND NOW WE... HELLO?

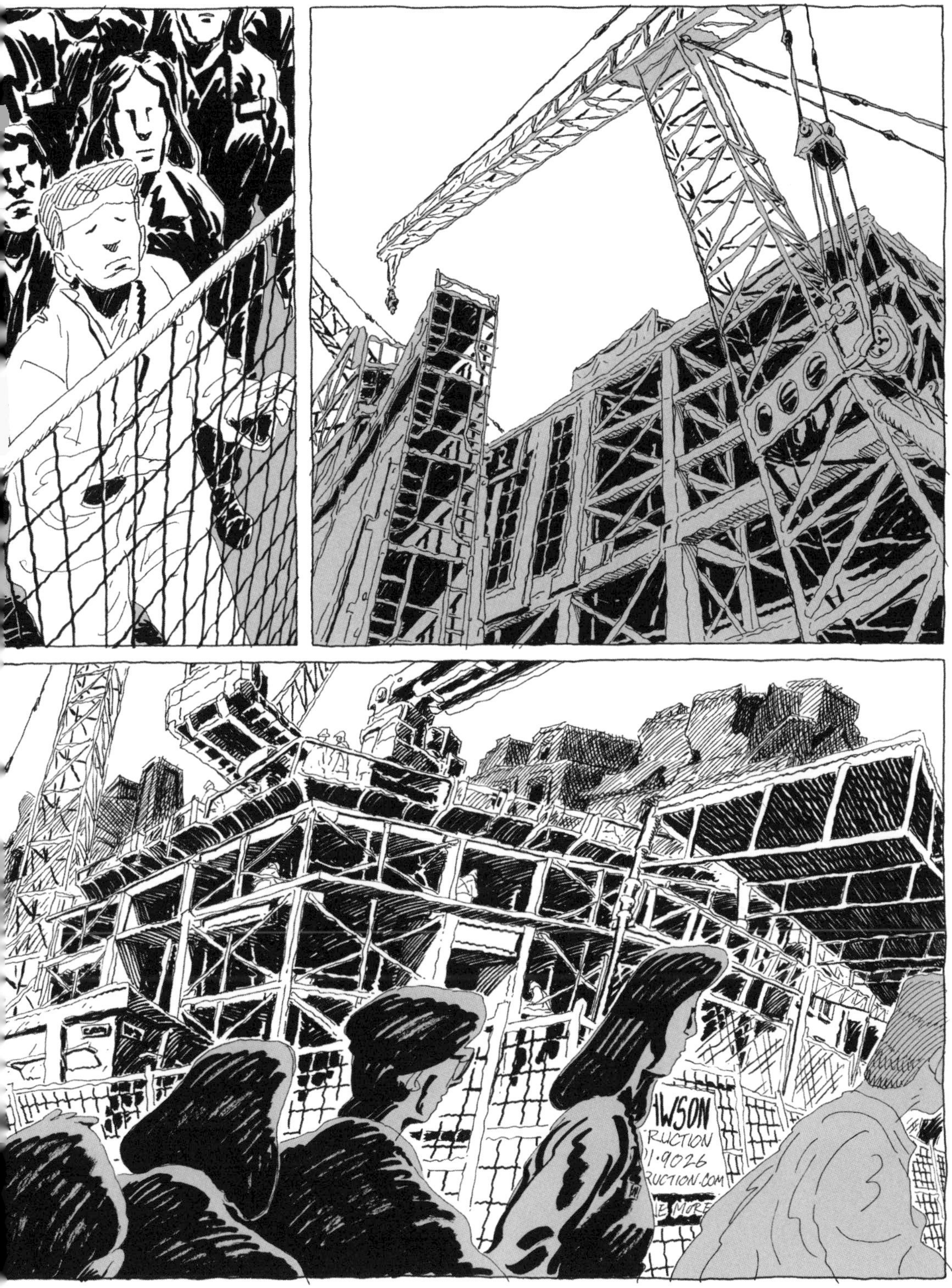
WSON
RUCTION
1·9026
RUCTION·COM
E MORE

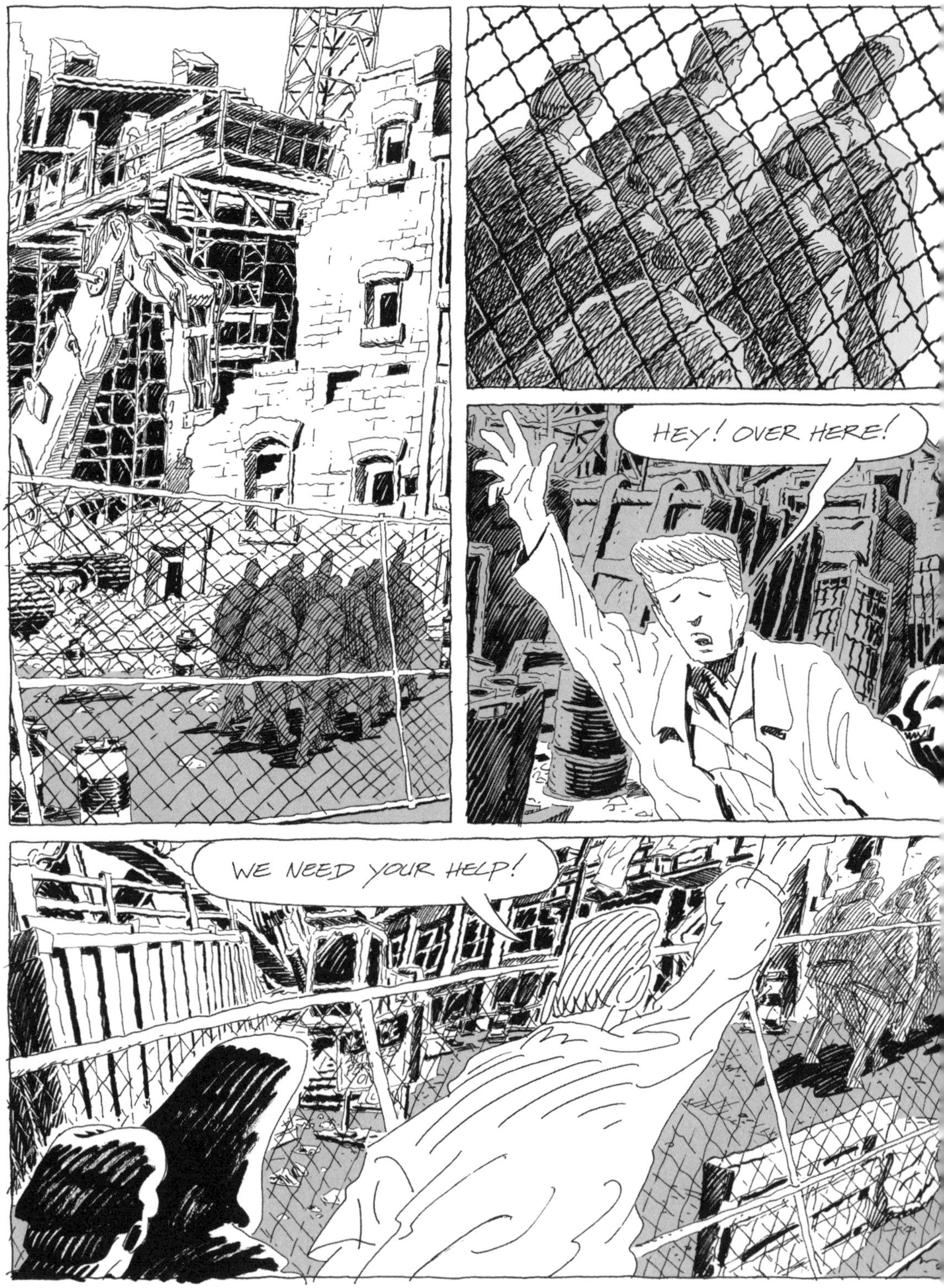
HEY! OVER HERE!
WE NEED YOUR HELP!

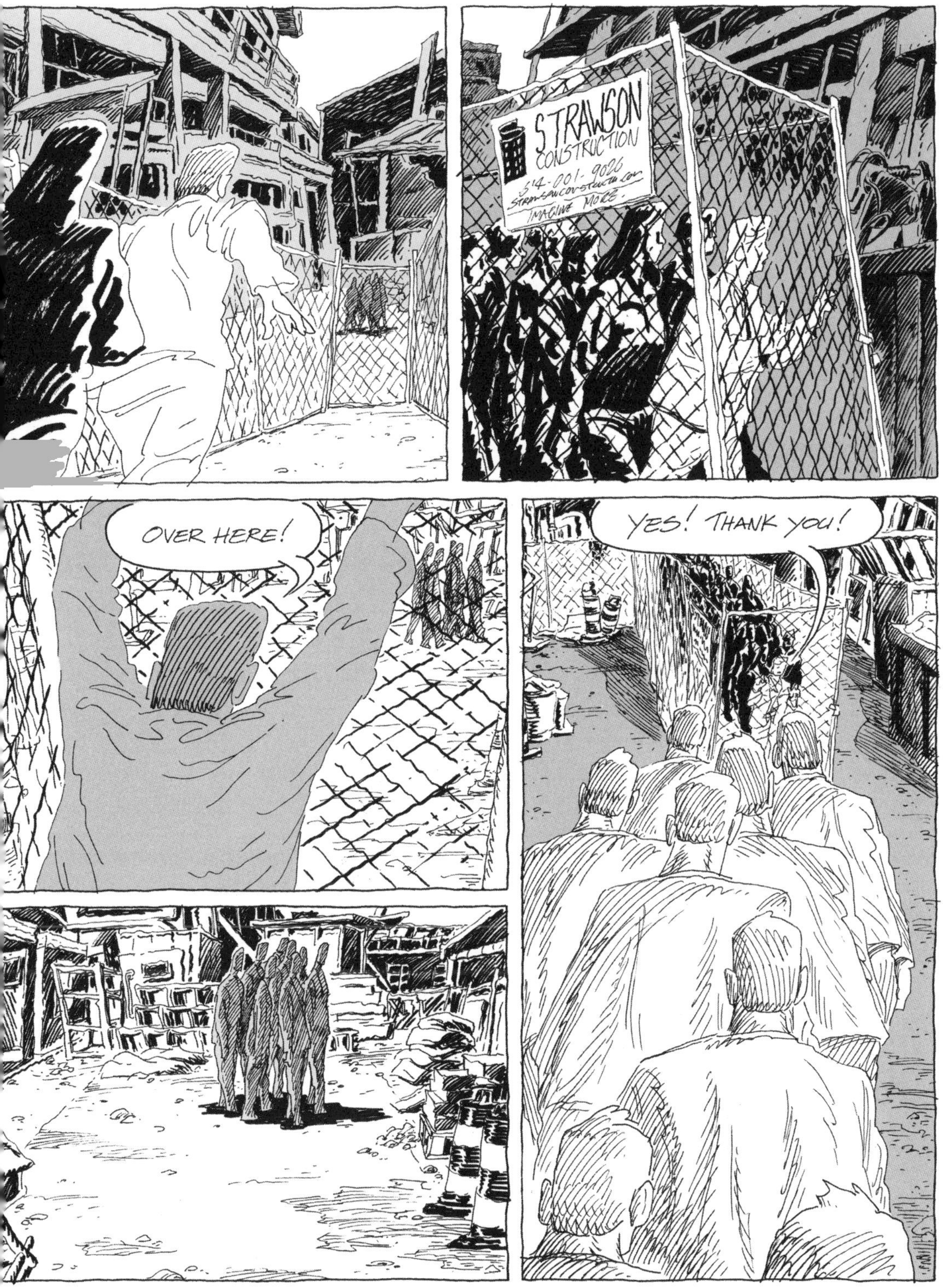
STRAWSON
CONSTRUCTION
514-001-9026
IMAGINE MORE.
OVER HERE!
YES! THANK YOU!

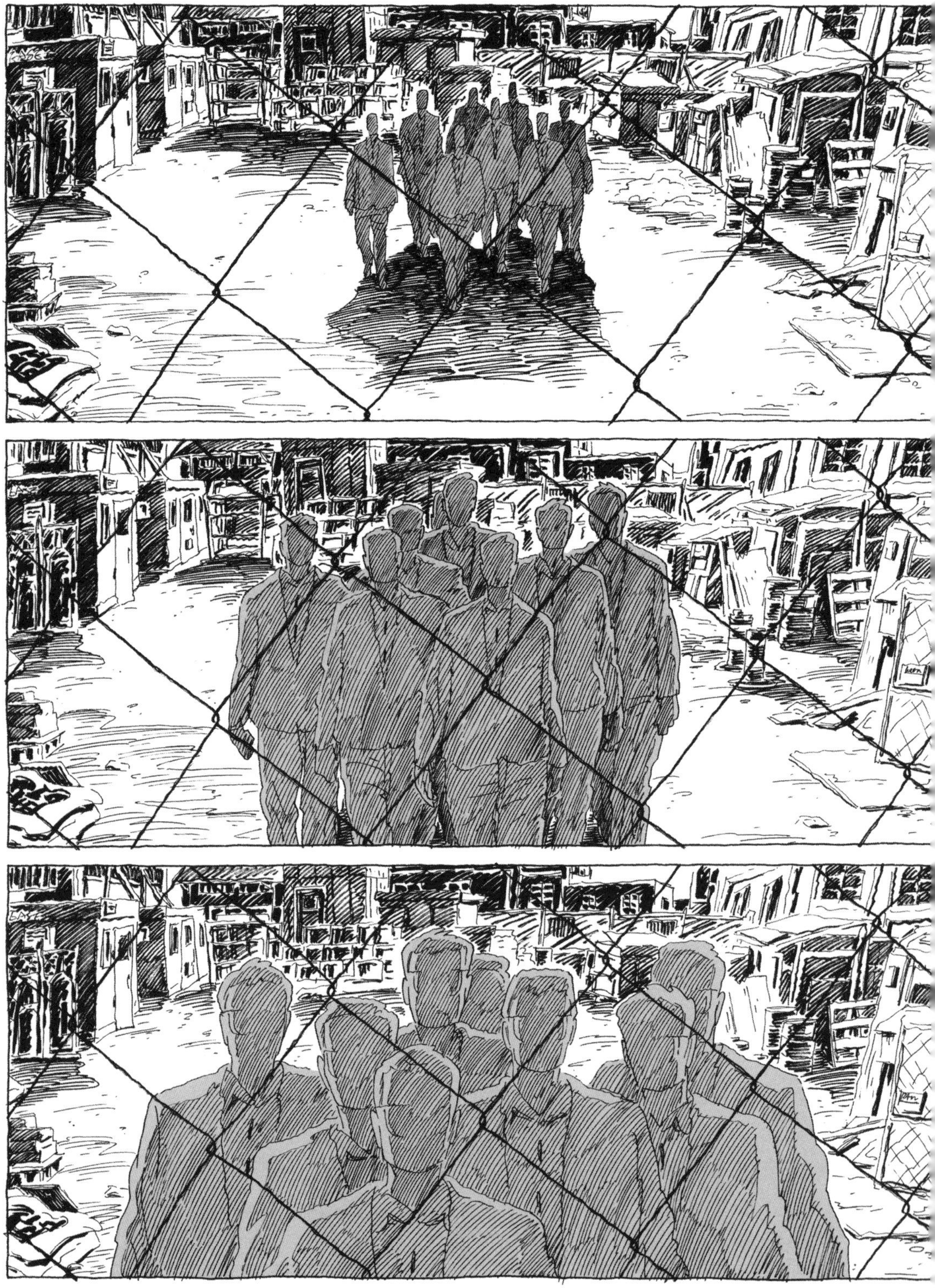

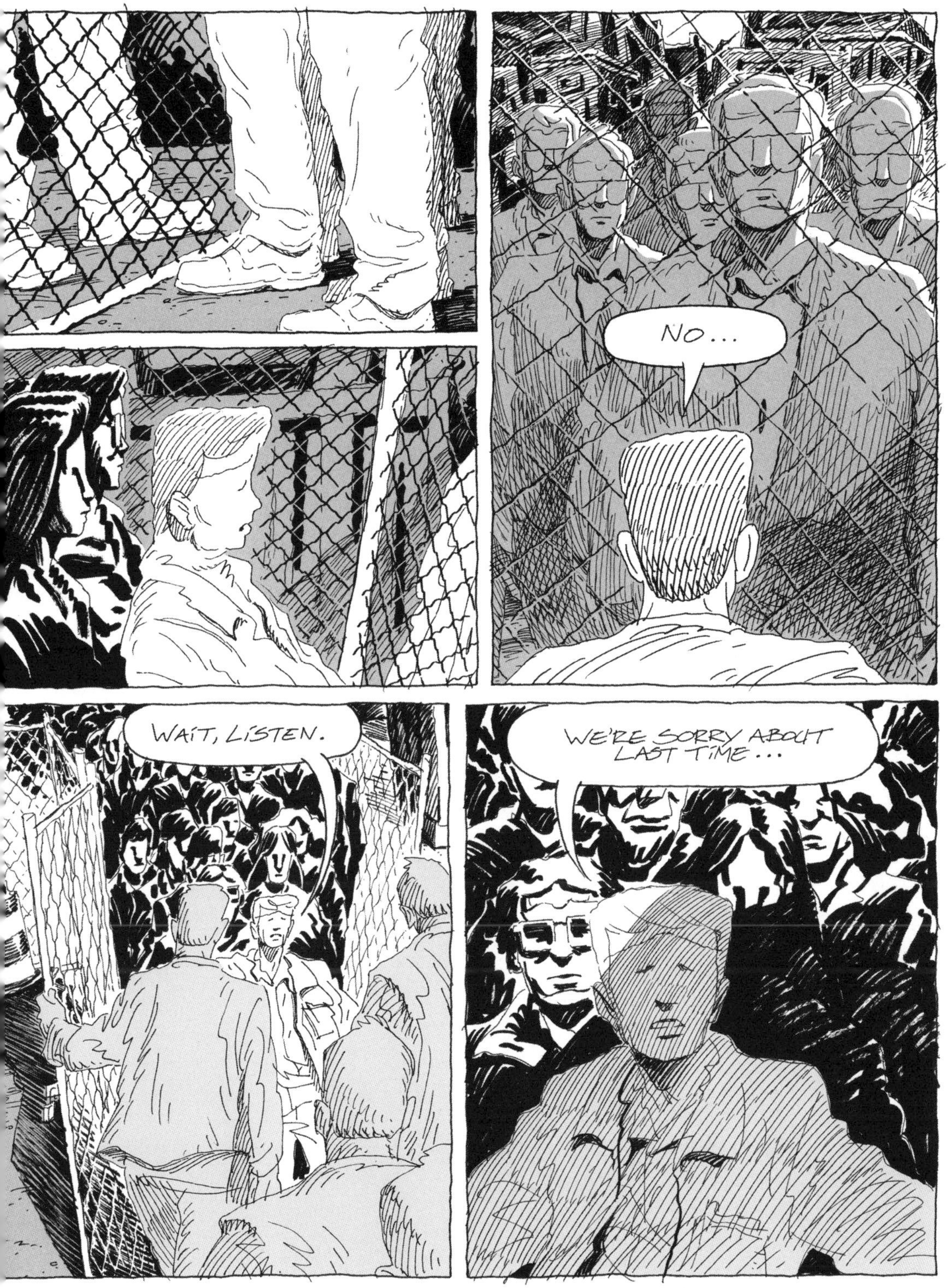
NO...
WAIT, LISTEN.
WE'RE SORRY ABOUT LAST TIME...

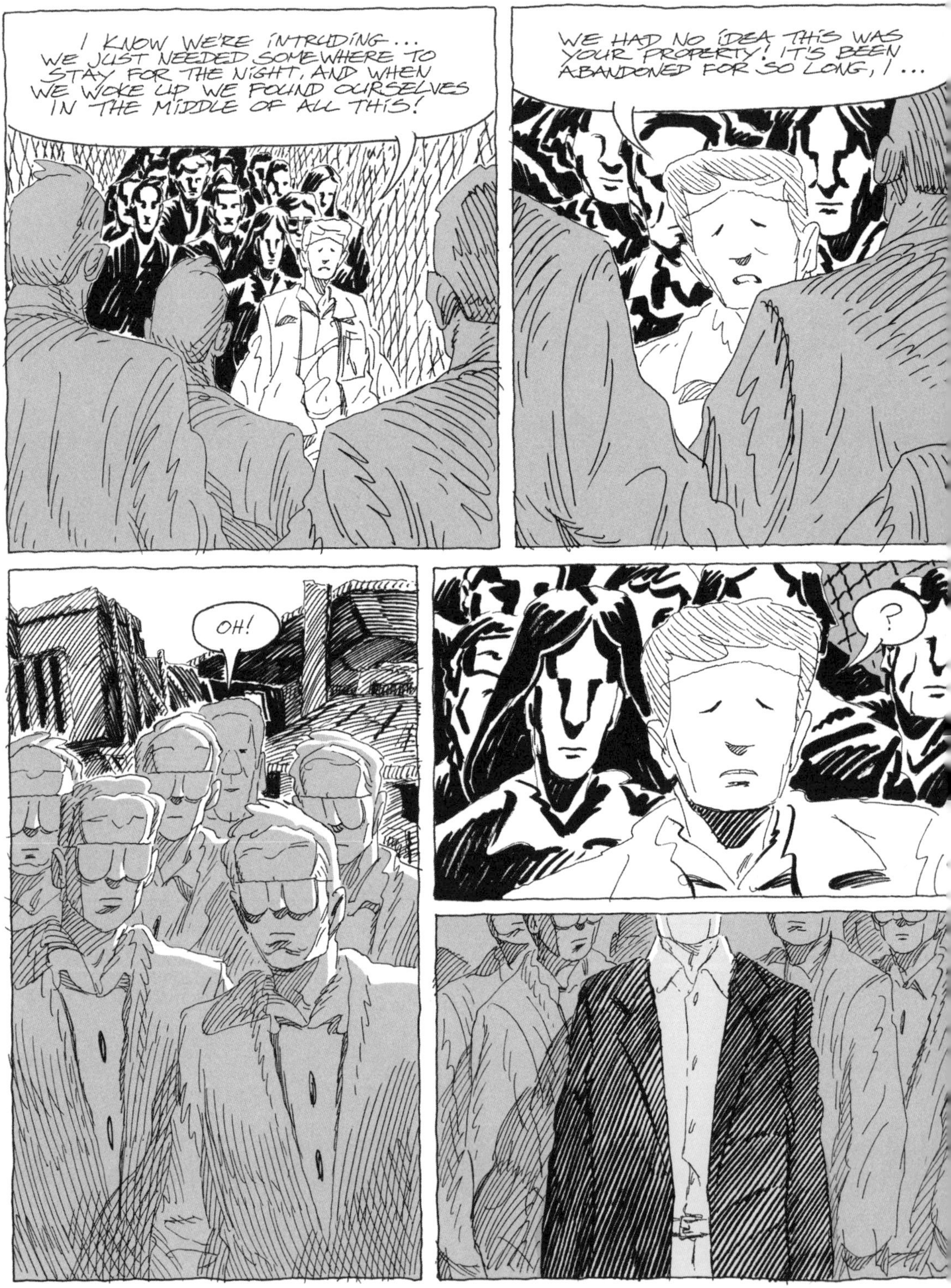
I KNOW WE'RE INTRUDING... WE JUST NEEDED SOMEWHERE TO STAY FOR THE NIGHT, AND WHEN WE WOKE UP WE FOUND OURSELVES IN THE MIDDLE OF ALL THIS!
WE HAD NO IDEA THIS WAS YOUR PROPERTY! IT'S BEEN ABANDONED FOR SO LONG, I...
OH!
?

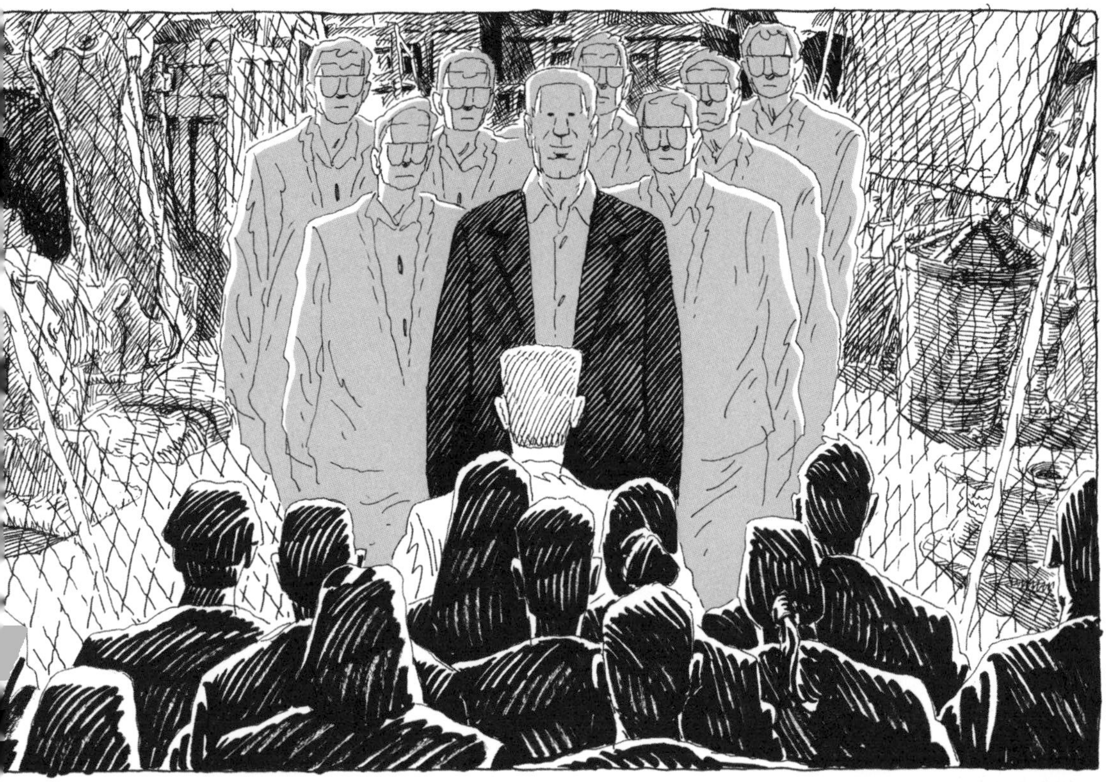

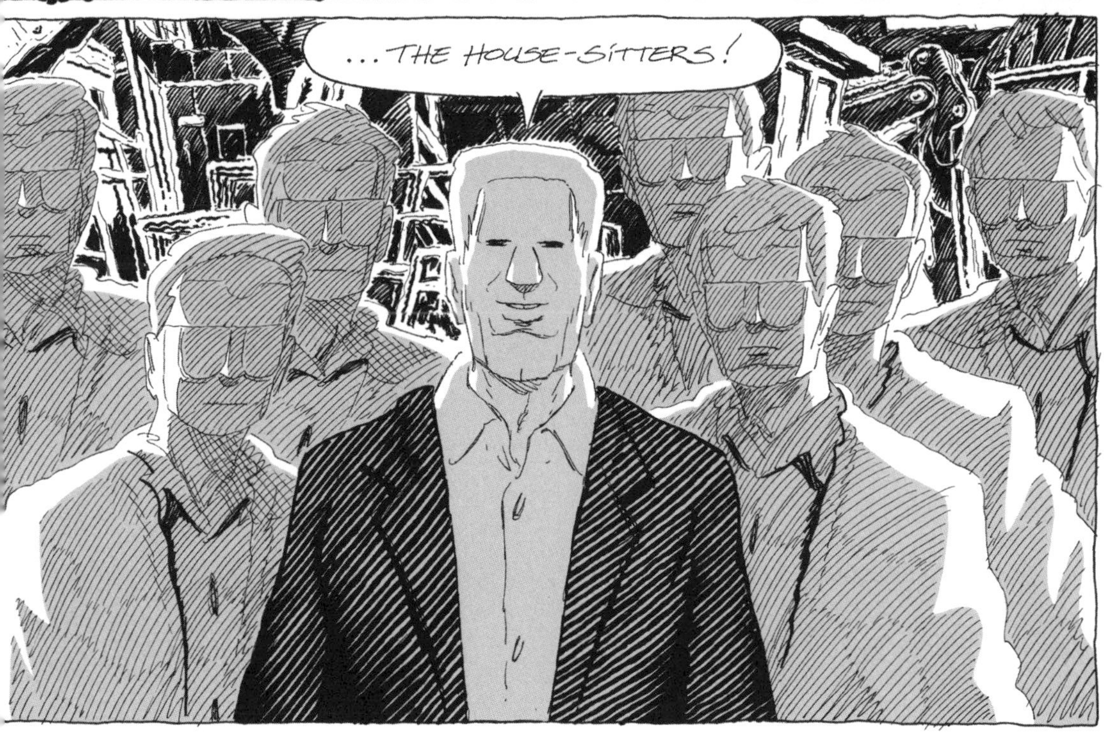
... THE HOUSE-SITTERS!

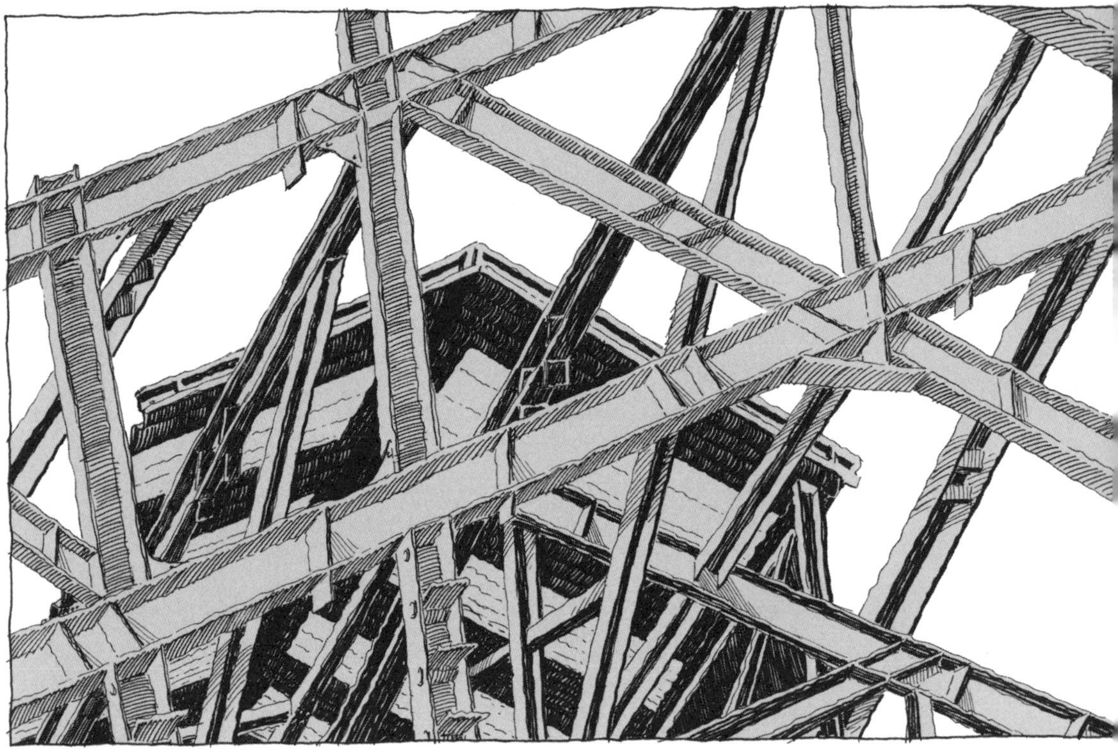

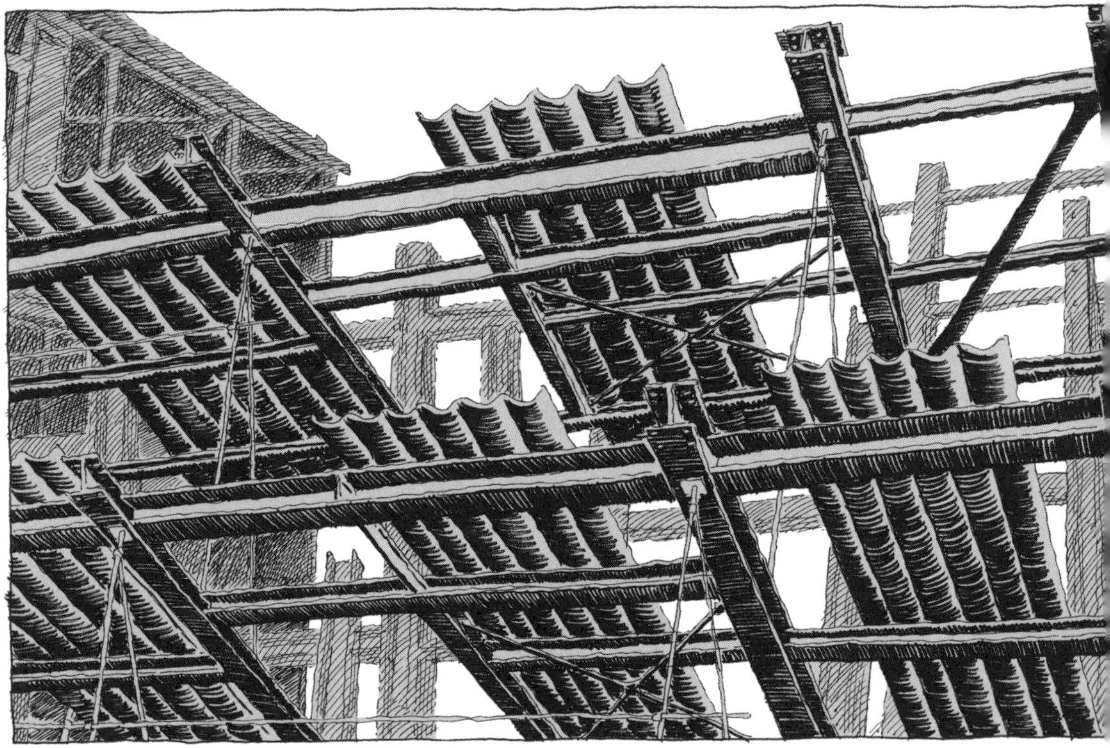

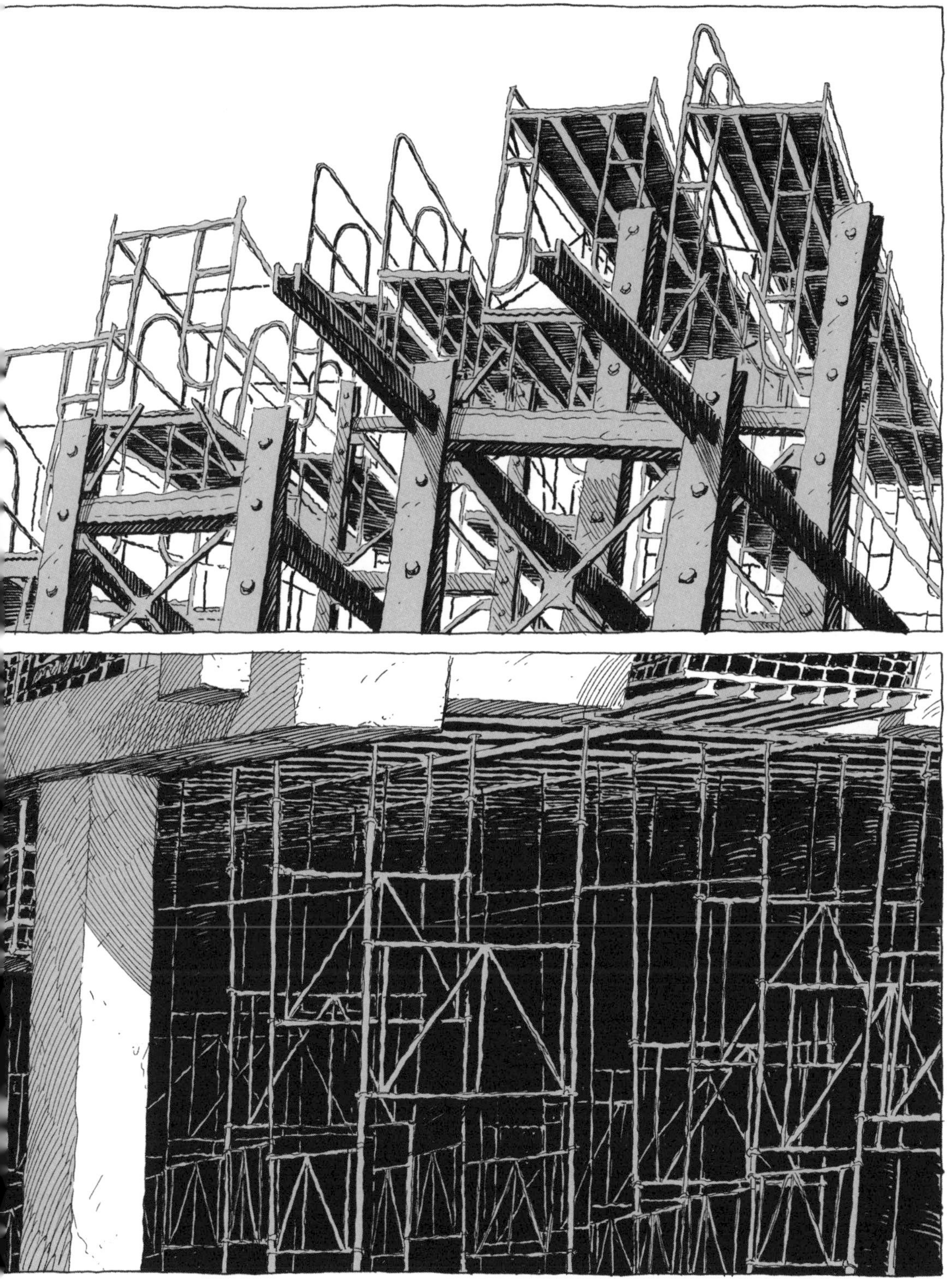

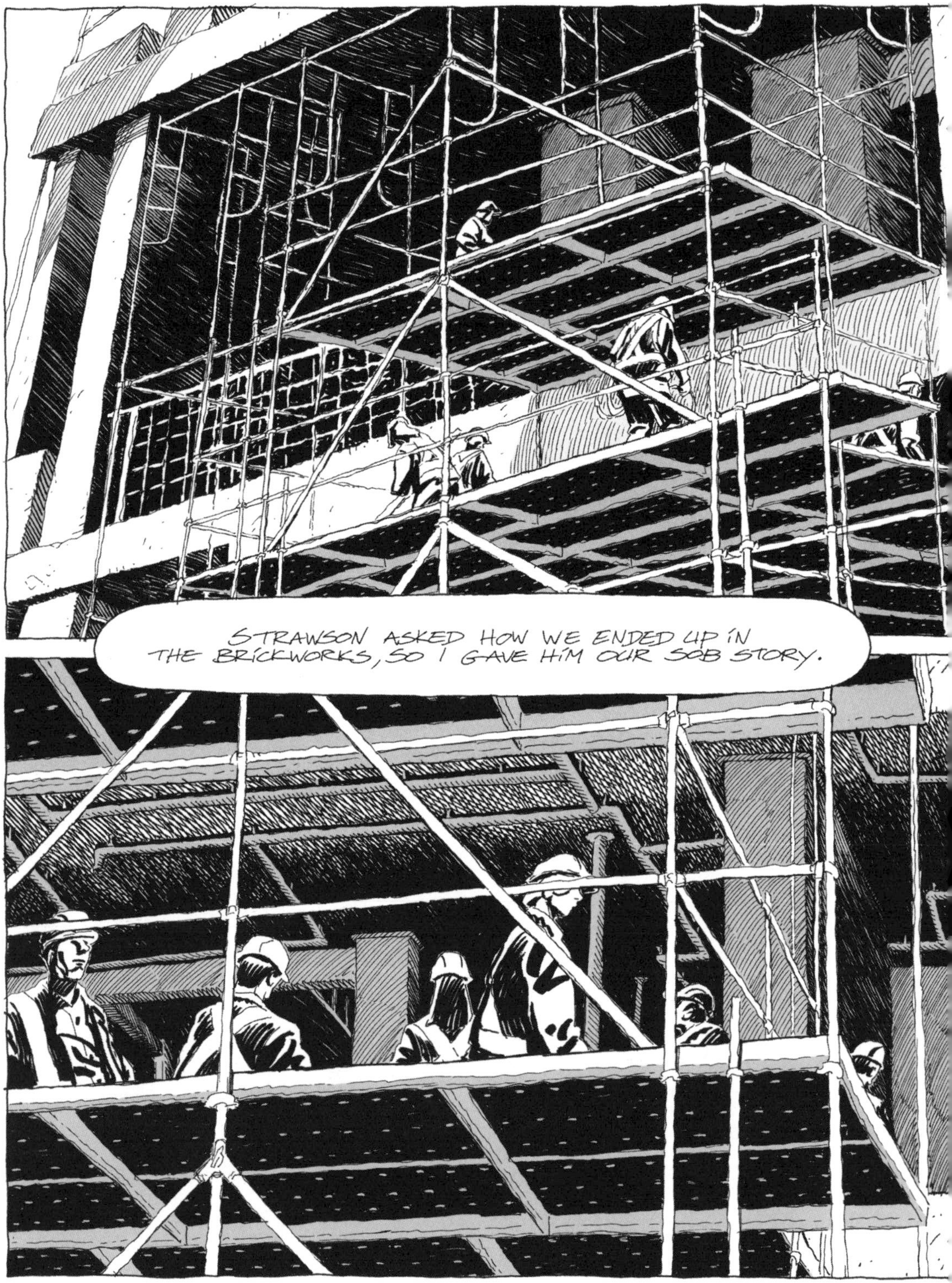
STRAWSON ASKED HOW WE ENDED UP IN THE BRICKWORKS, SO I GAVE HIM OUR SOB STORY.

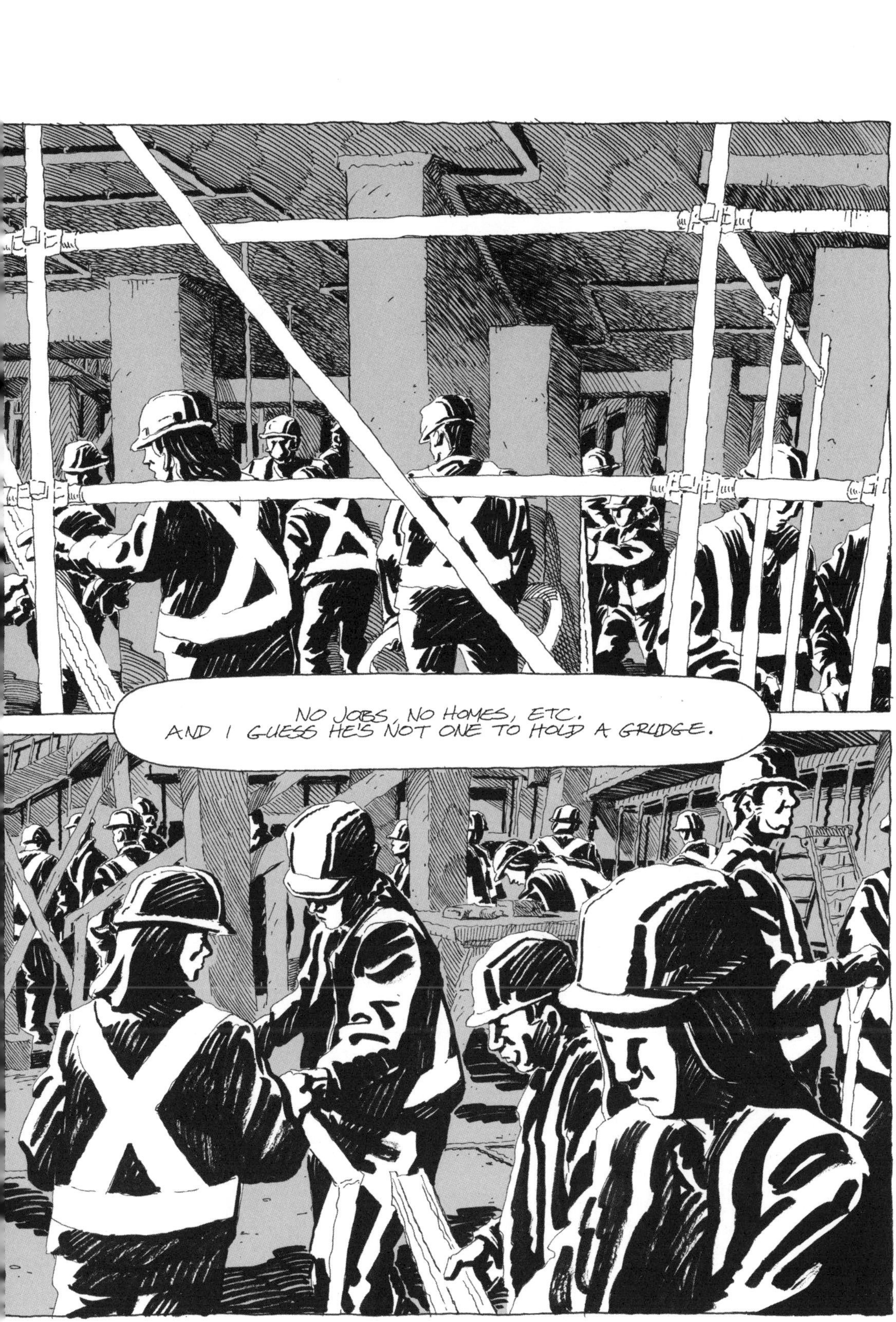
NO JOBS, NO HOMES, ETC.
AND I GUESS HE'S NOT ONE TO HOLD A GRUDGE.

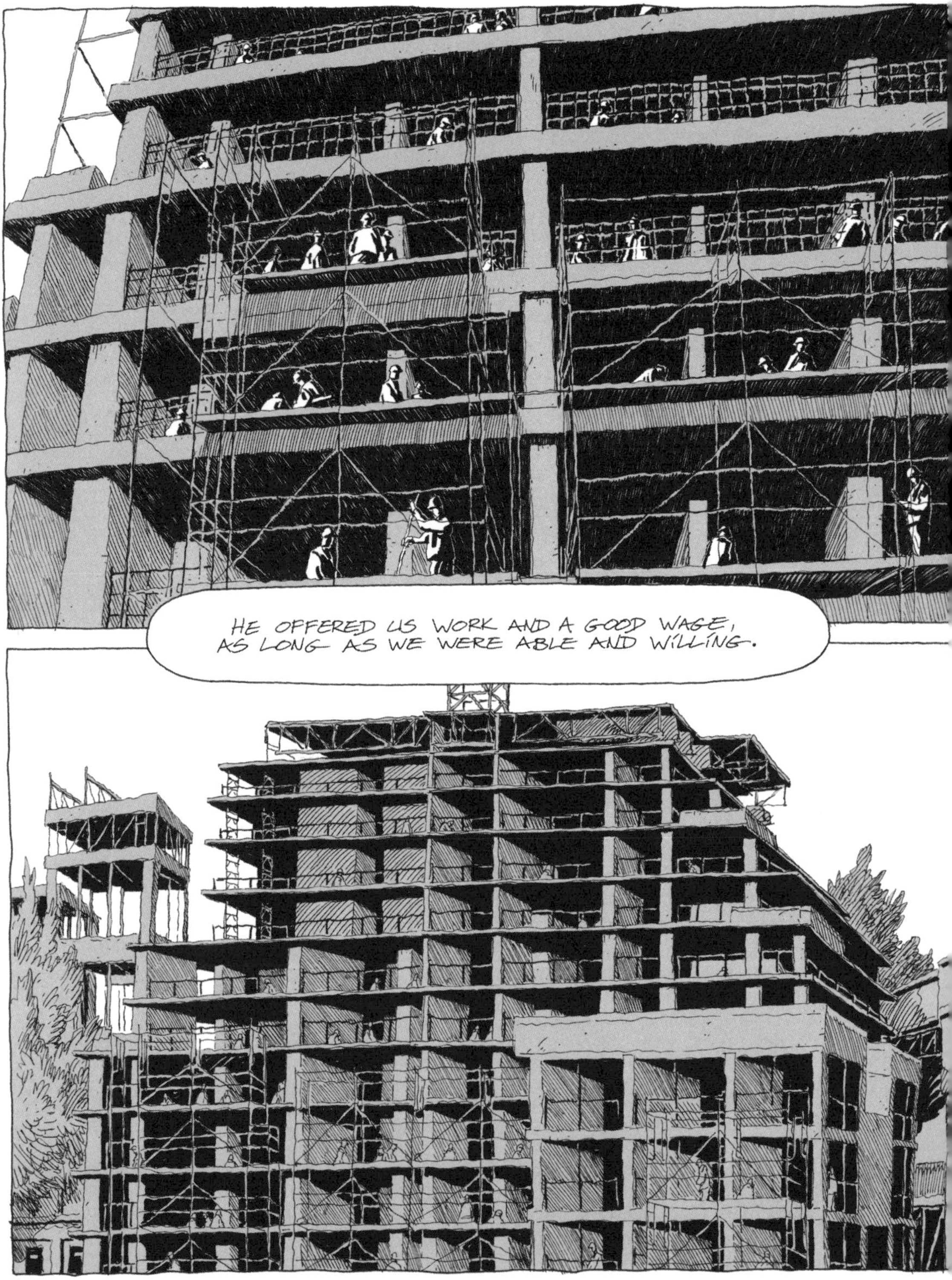
HE OFFERED US WORK AND A GOOD WAGE, AS LONG AS WE WERE ABLE AND WILLING.

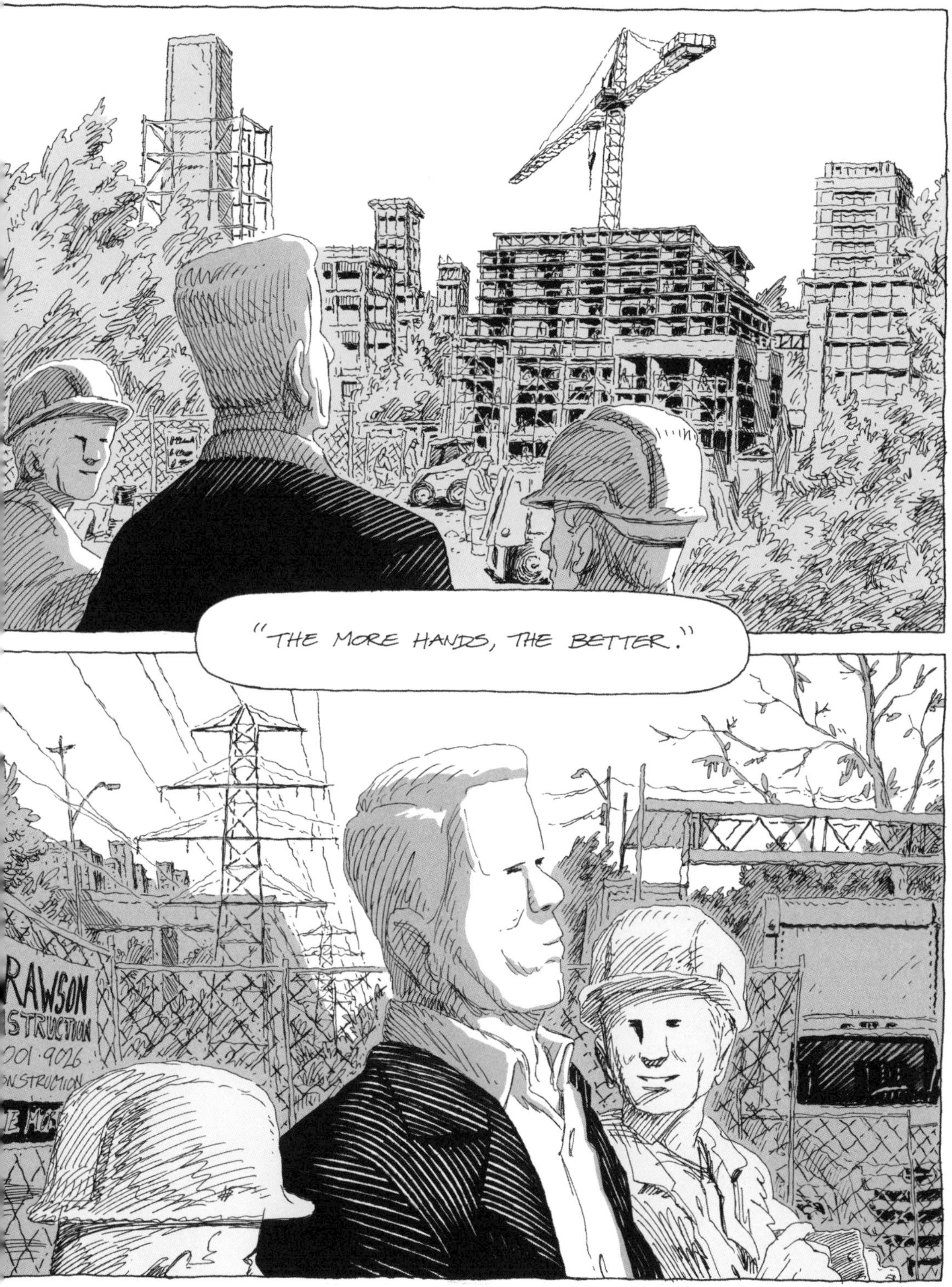
"THE MORE HANDS, THE BETTER."
RAWSON

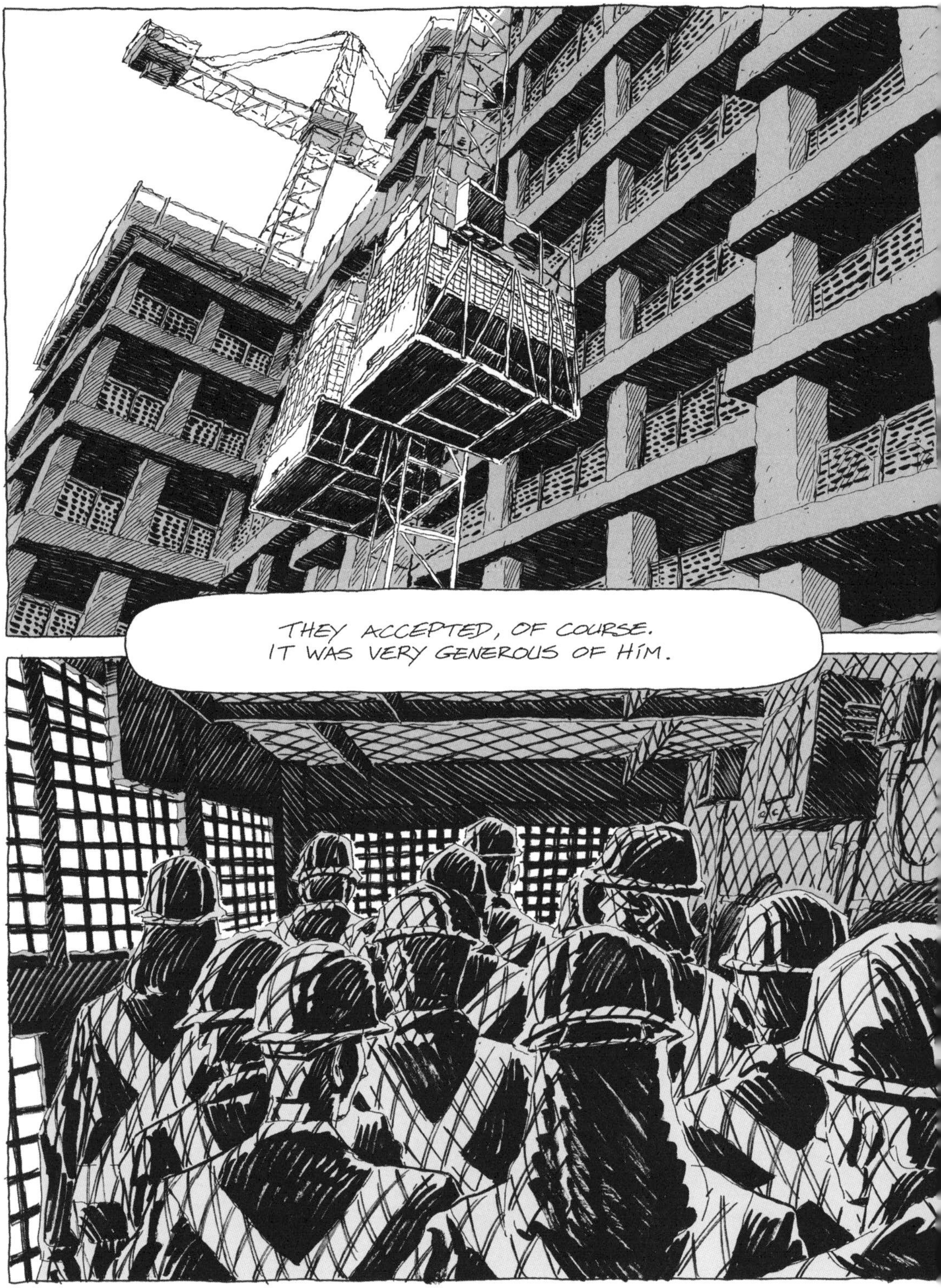
THEY ACCEPTED, OF COURSE.
IT WAS VERY GENEROUS OF HIM.

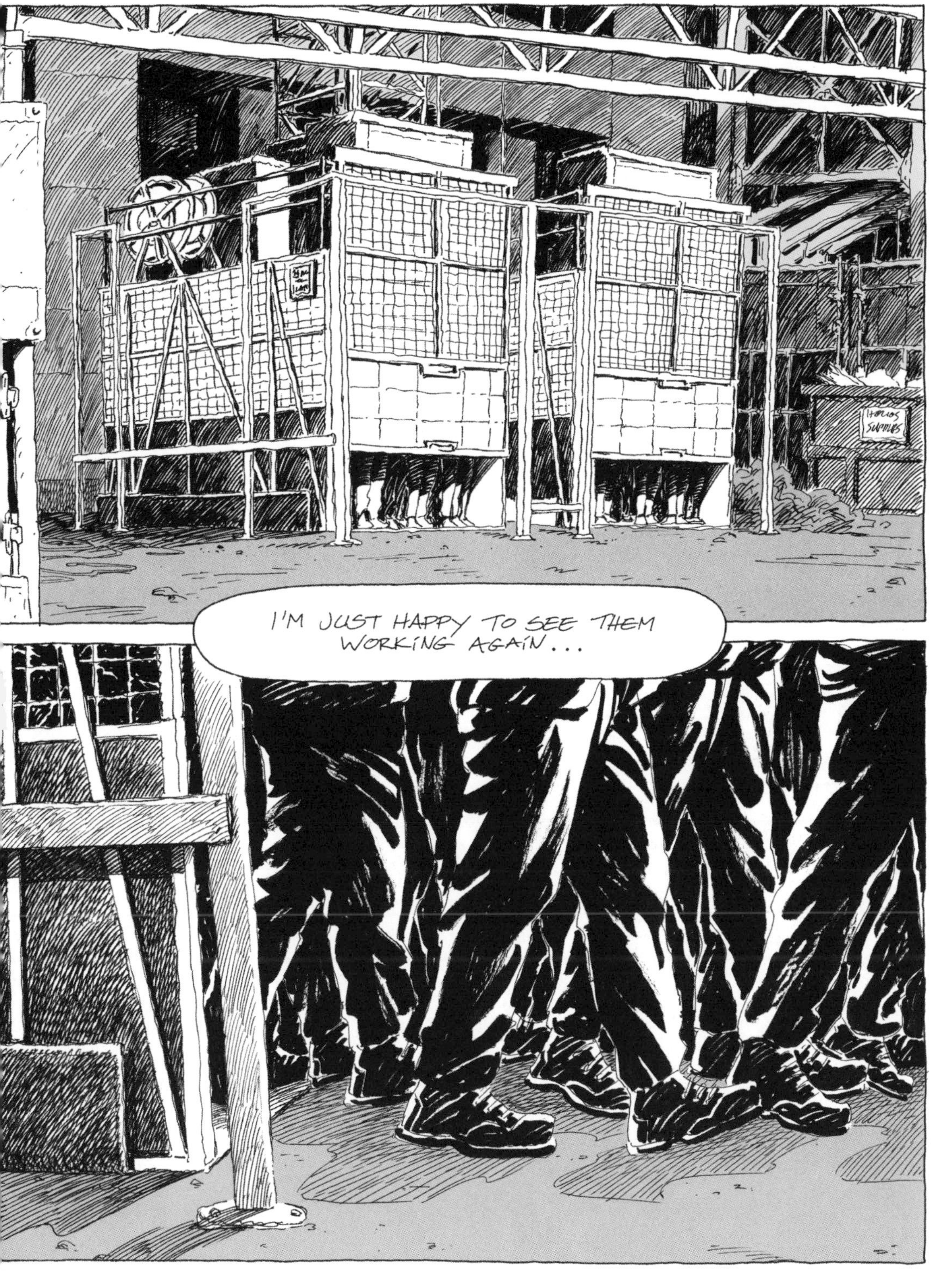
I'M JUST HAPPY TO SEE THEM WORKING AGAIN...

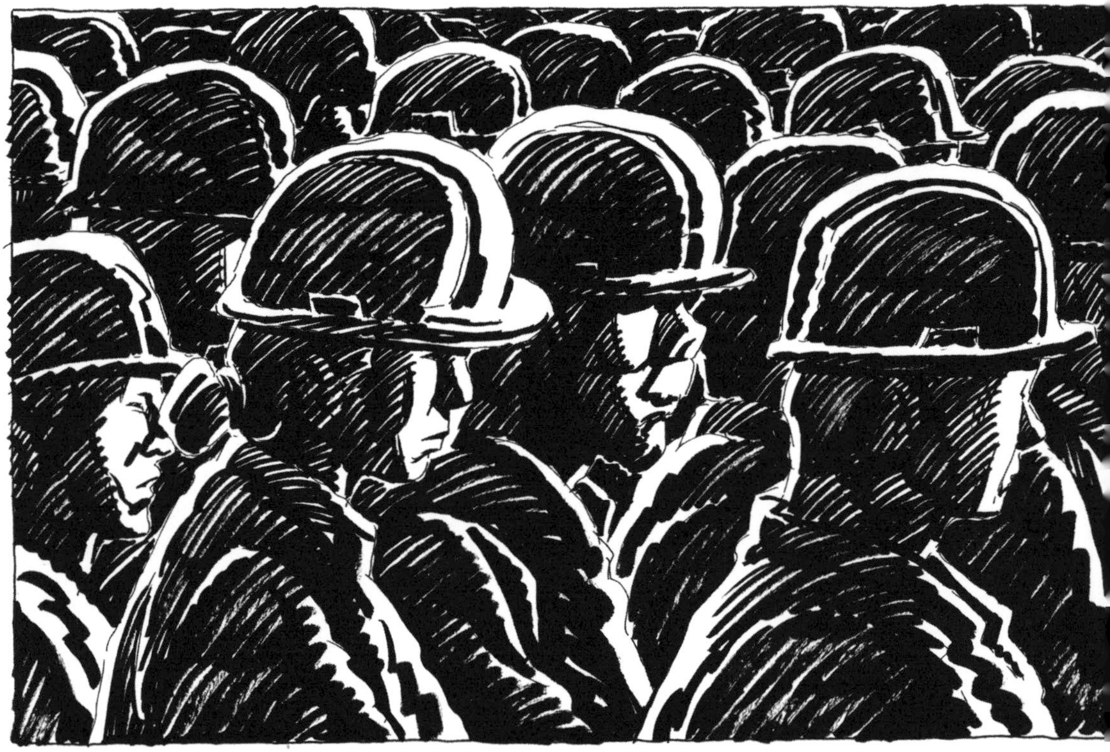

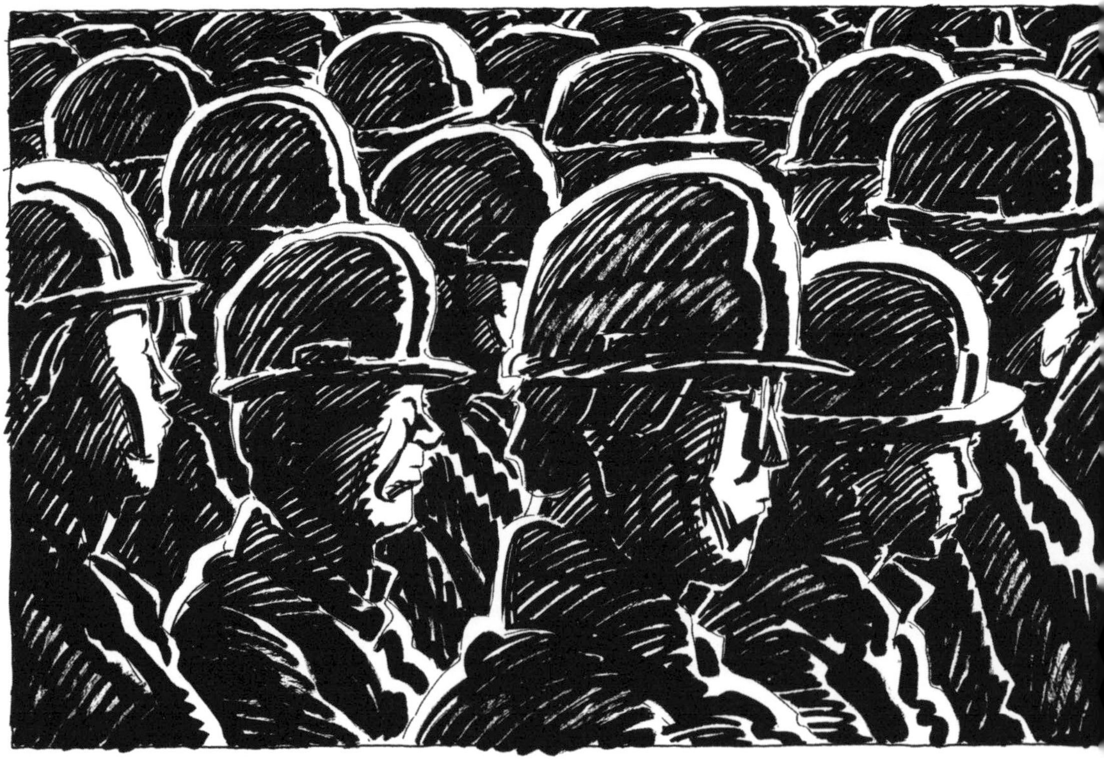

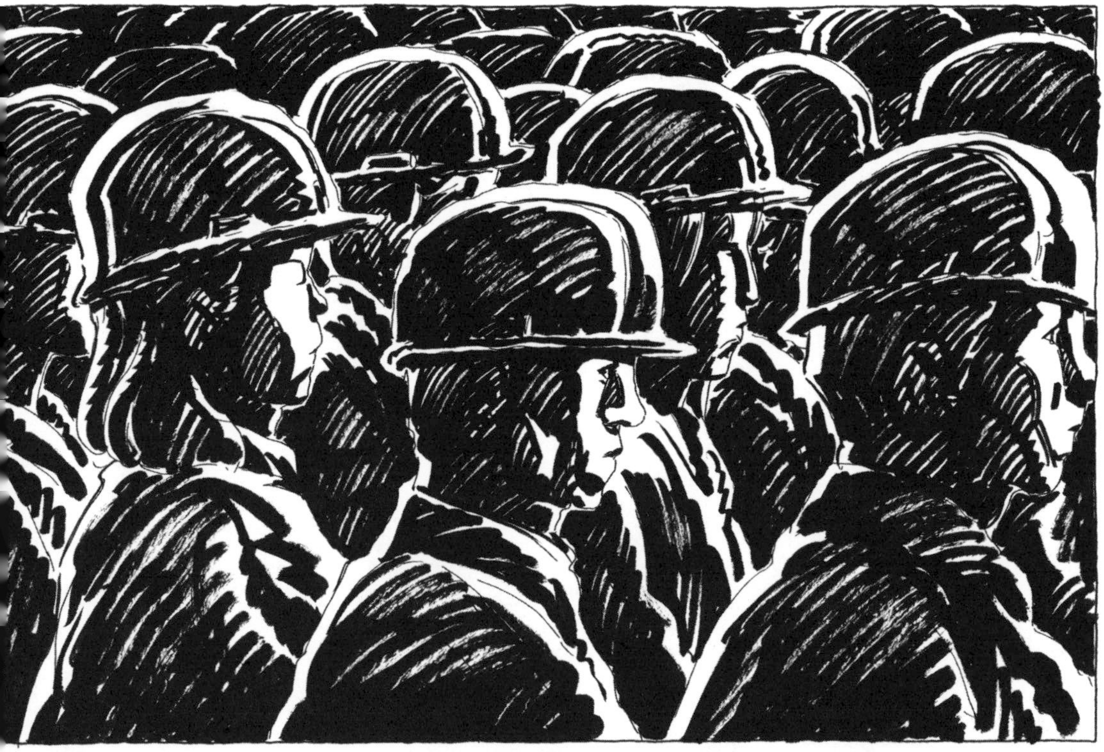

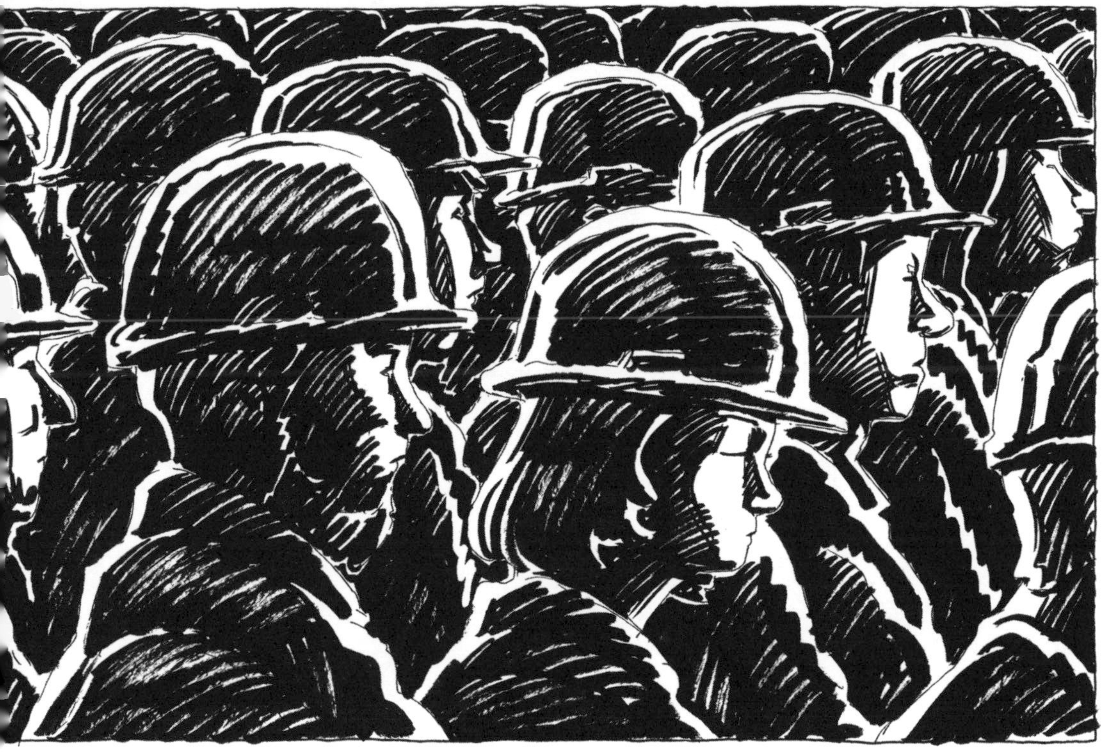

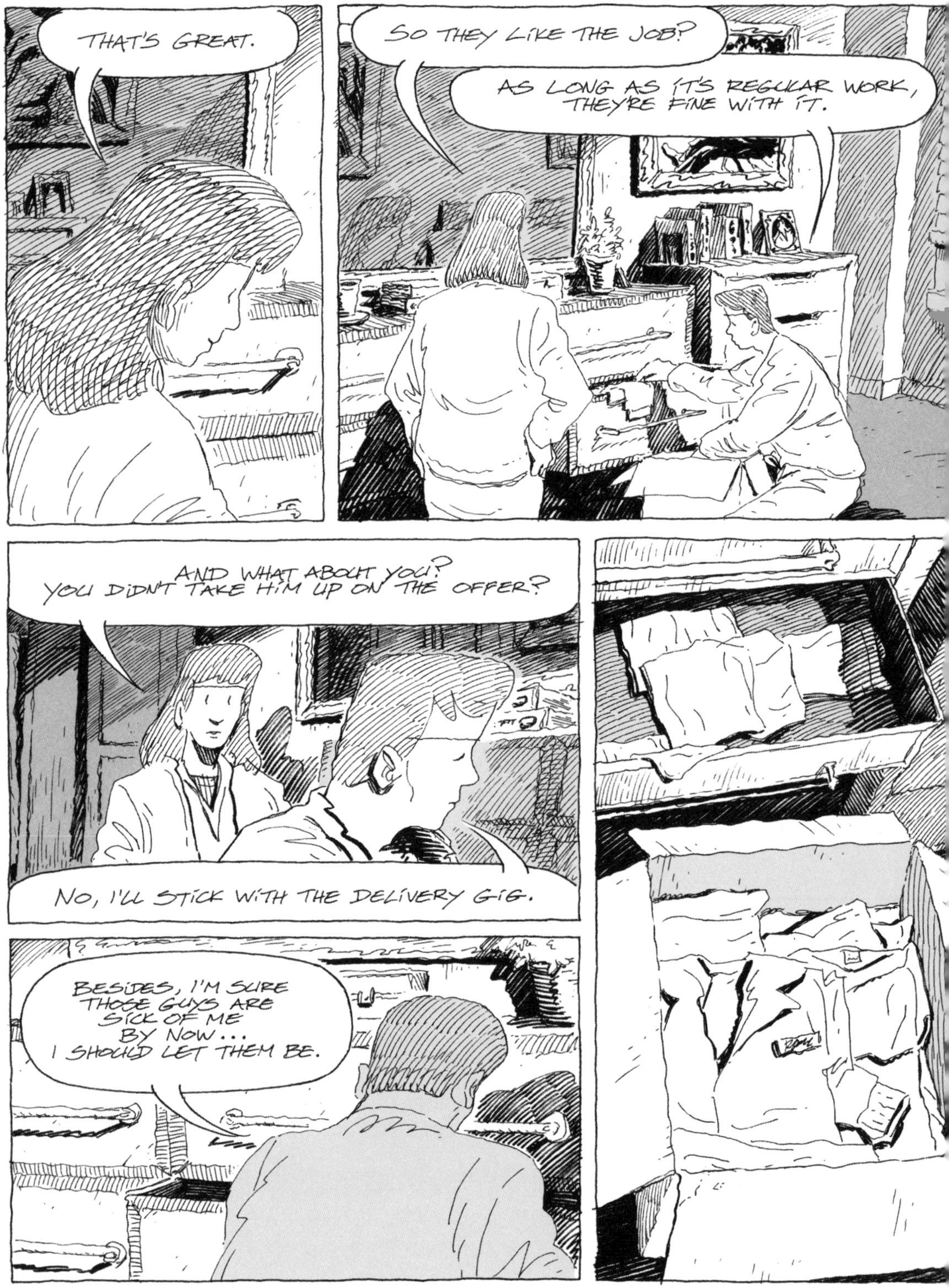
THAT'S GREAT.
SO THEY LIKE THE JOB?
AS LONG AS IT'S REGULAR WORK, THEY'RE FINE WITH IT.
AND WHAT ABOUT YOU? YOU DIDN'T TAKE HIM UP ON THE OFFER?
NO, I'LL STICK WITH THE DELIVERY GIG.
BESIDES, I'M SURE THOSE GUYS ARE SICK OF ME BY NOW... I SHOULD LET THEM BE.

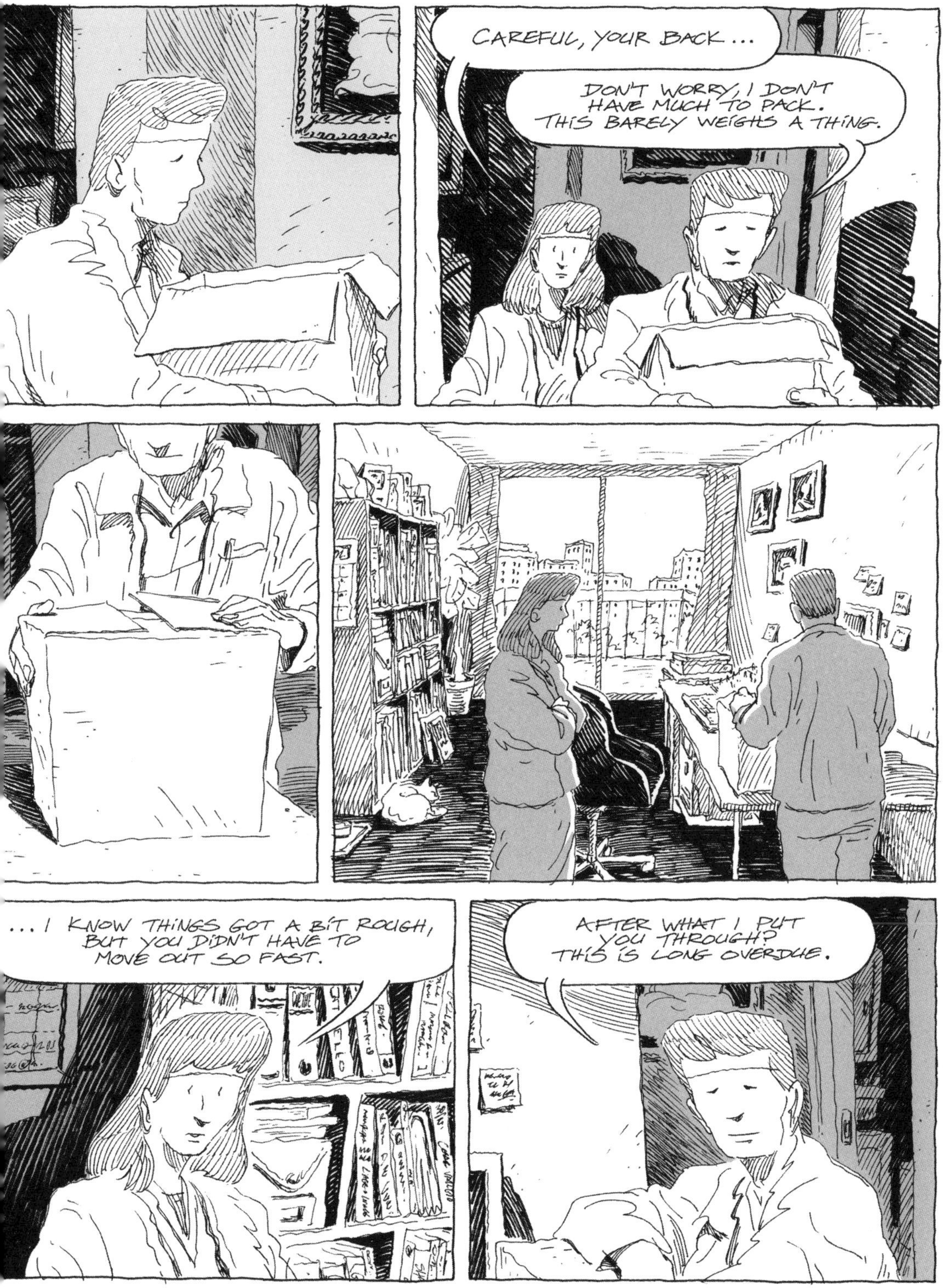
CAREFUL, YOUR BACK ...
DON'T WORRY, I DON'T HAVE MUCH TO PACK. THIS BARELY WEIGHS A THING.
... I KNOW THINGS GOT A BIT ROUGH, BUT YOU DIDN'T HAVE TO MOVE OUT SO FAST.
AFTER WHAT I PUT YOU THROUGH? THIS IS LONG OVERDUE.

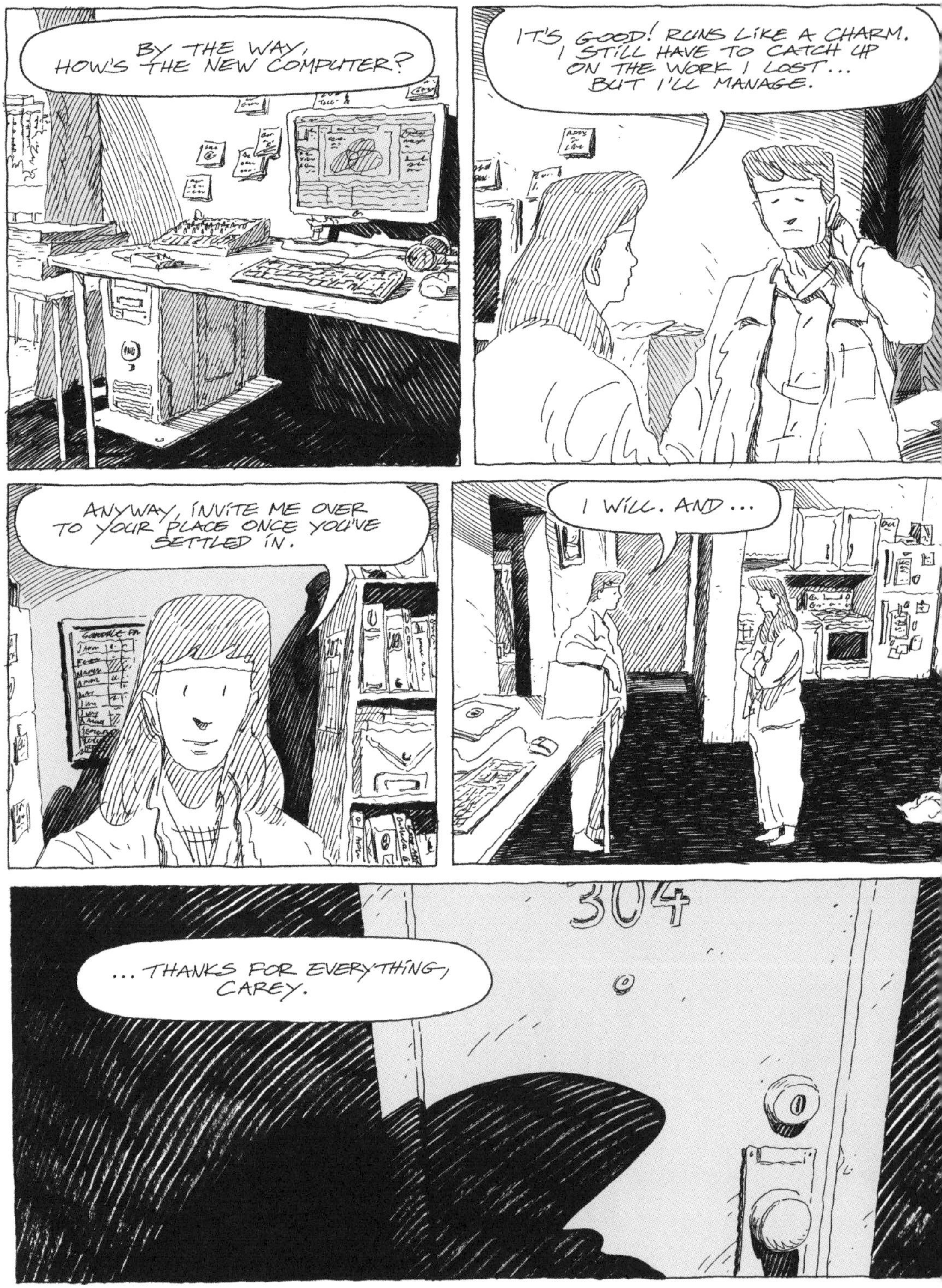
BY THE WAY, HOW'S THE NEW COMPUTER?
IT'S GOOD! RUNS LIKE A CHARM. I STILL HAVE TO CATCH UP ON THE WORK I LOST... BUT I'LL MANAGE.
ANYWAY, INVITE ME OVER TO YOUR PLACE ONCE YOU'VE SETTLED IN.
I WILL. AND...
304
... THANKS FOR EVERYTHING, CAREY.

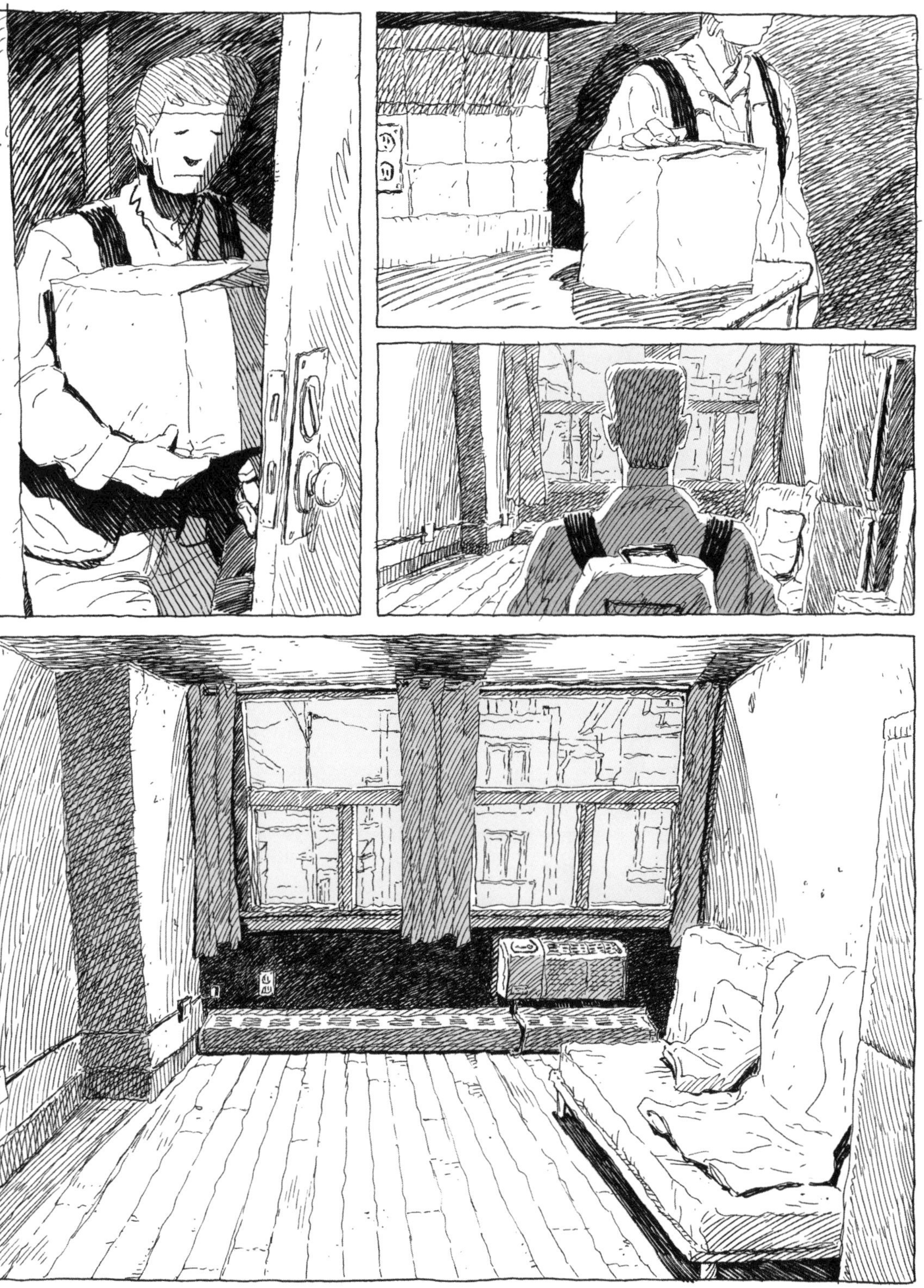

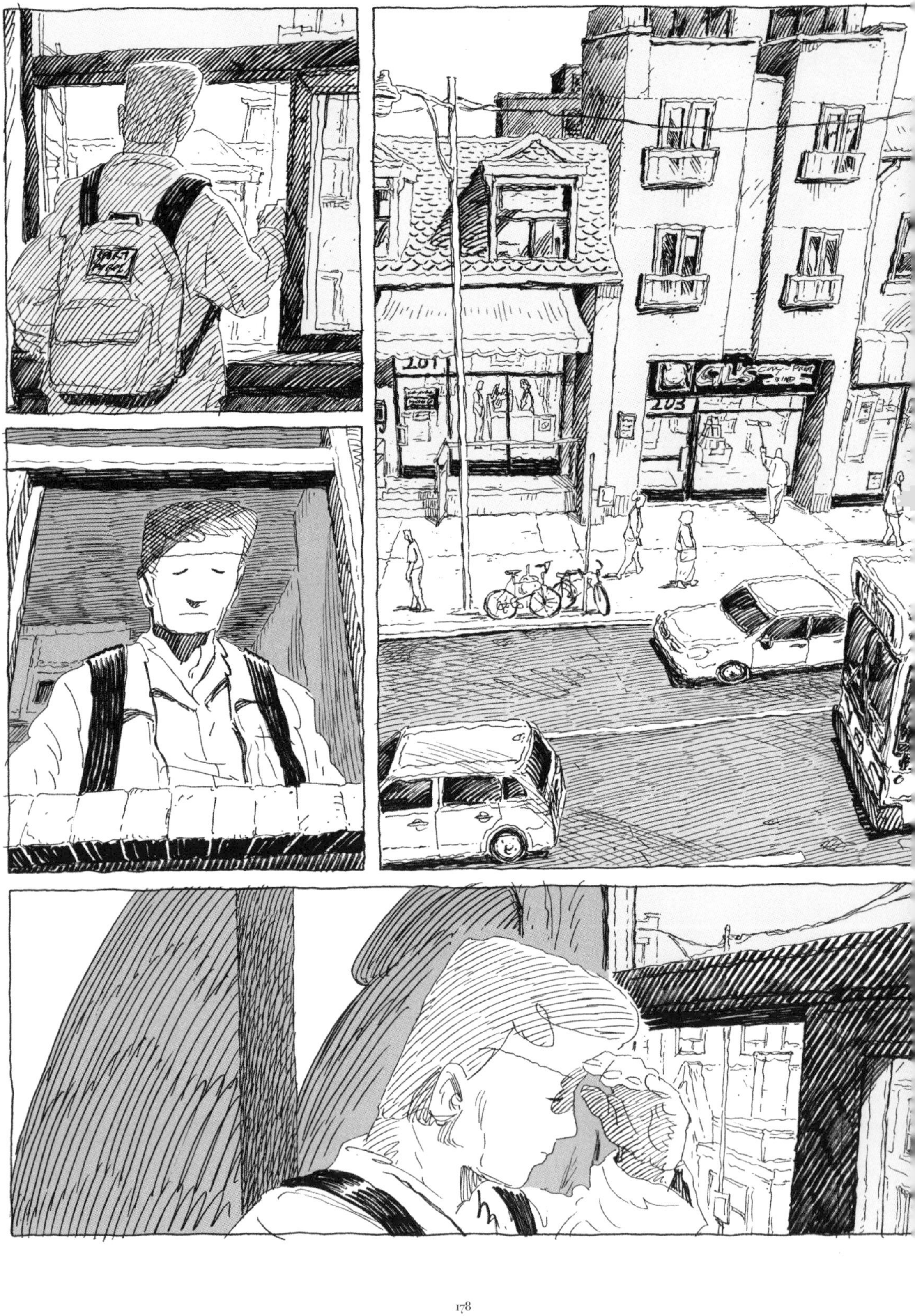
201
GIL'S COPY - PRINT - BIND
203

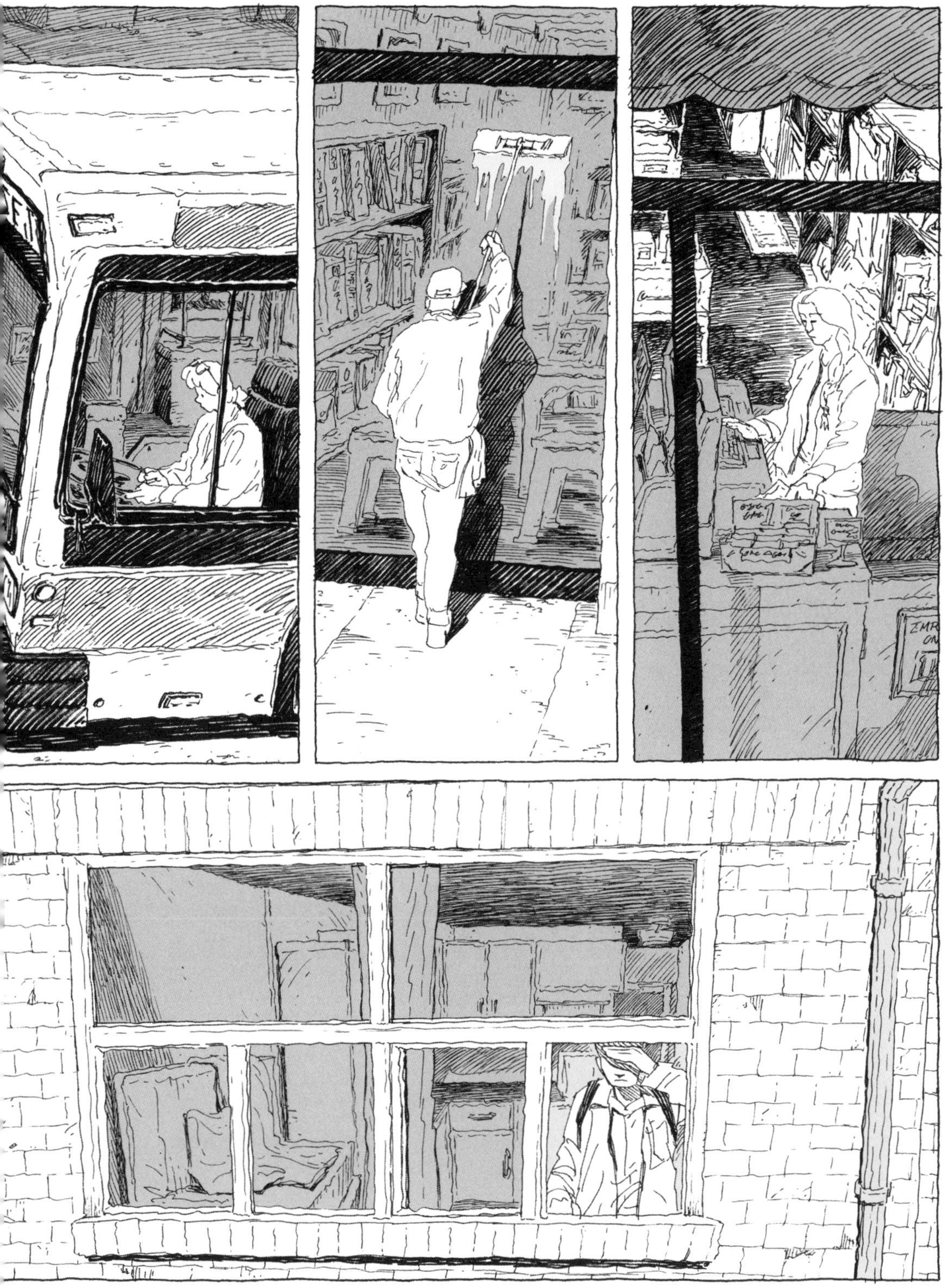

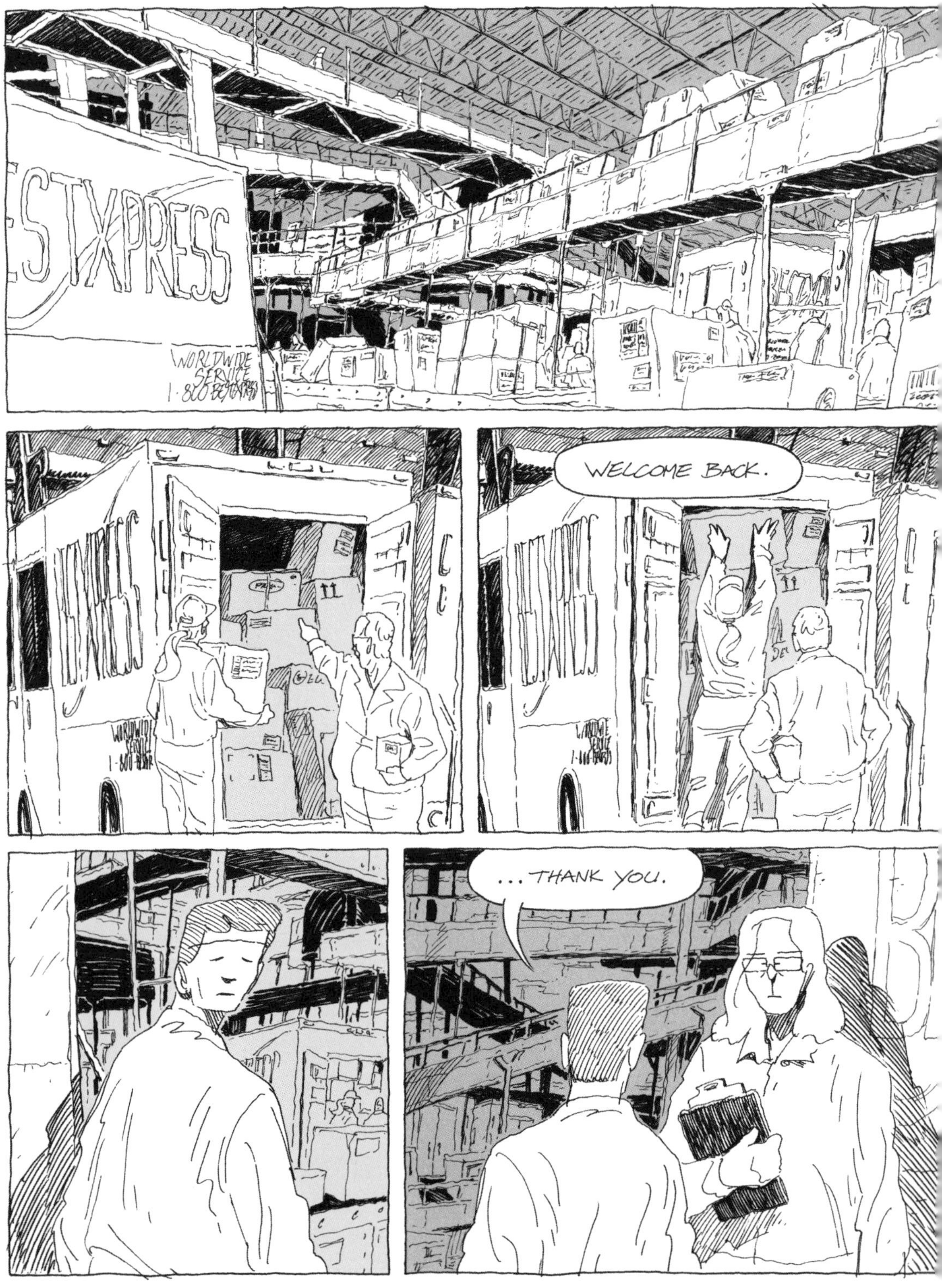
BESTXPRESS
WORLDWIDE SERVICE
1-800-BESTXPRESS
WELCOME BACK.
...THANK YOU.

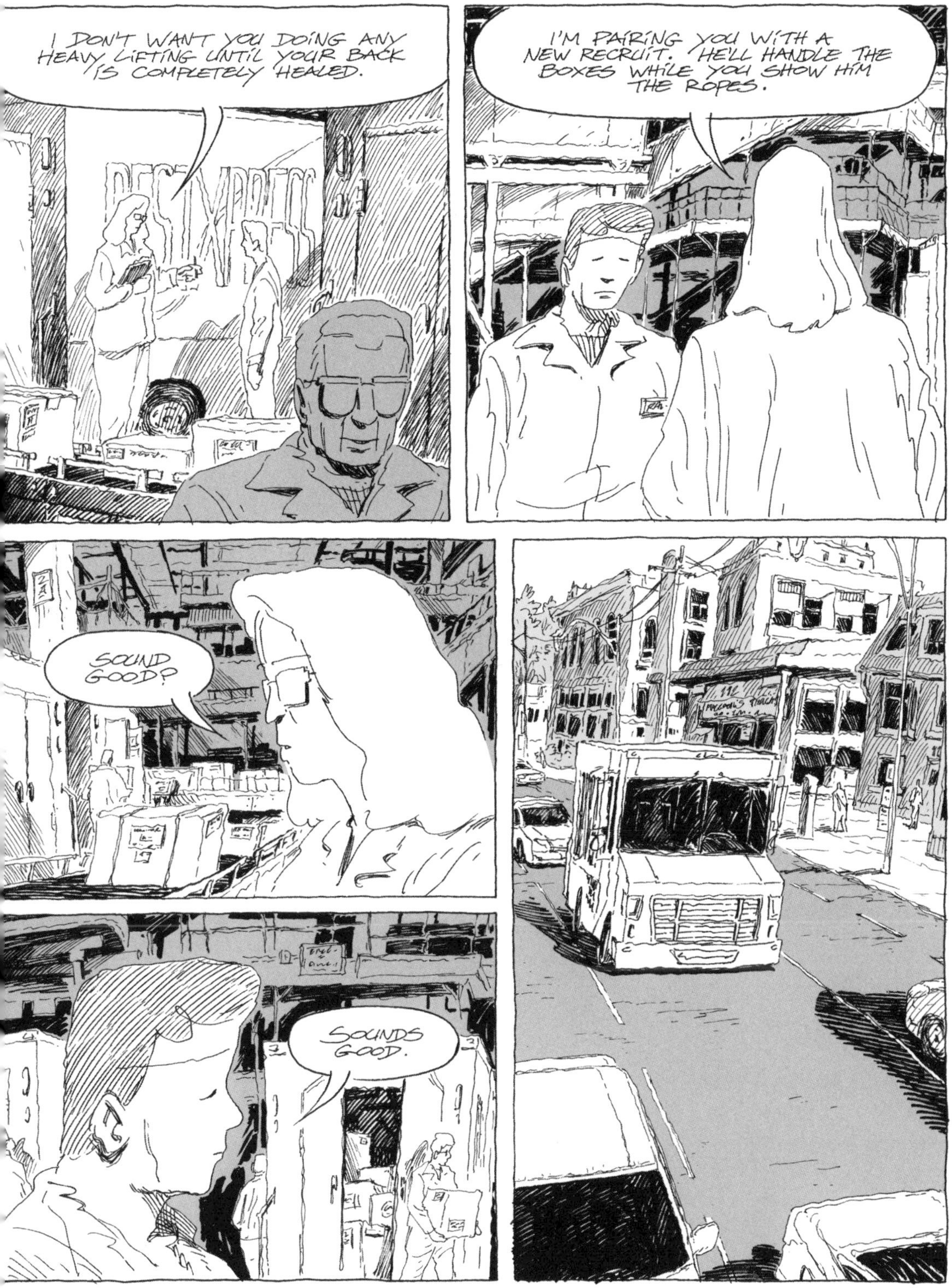
I DON'T WANT YOU DOING ANY HEAVY LIFTING UNTIL YOUR BACK IS COMPLETELY HEALED.
I'M PAIRING YOU WITH A NEW RECRUIT. HE'LL HANDLE THE BOXES WHILE YOU SHOW HIM THE ROPES.
SOUND GOOD?
SOUNDS GOOD.

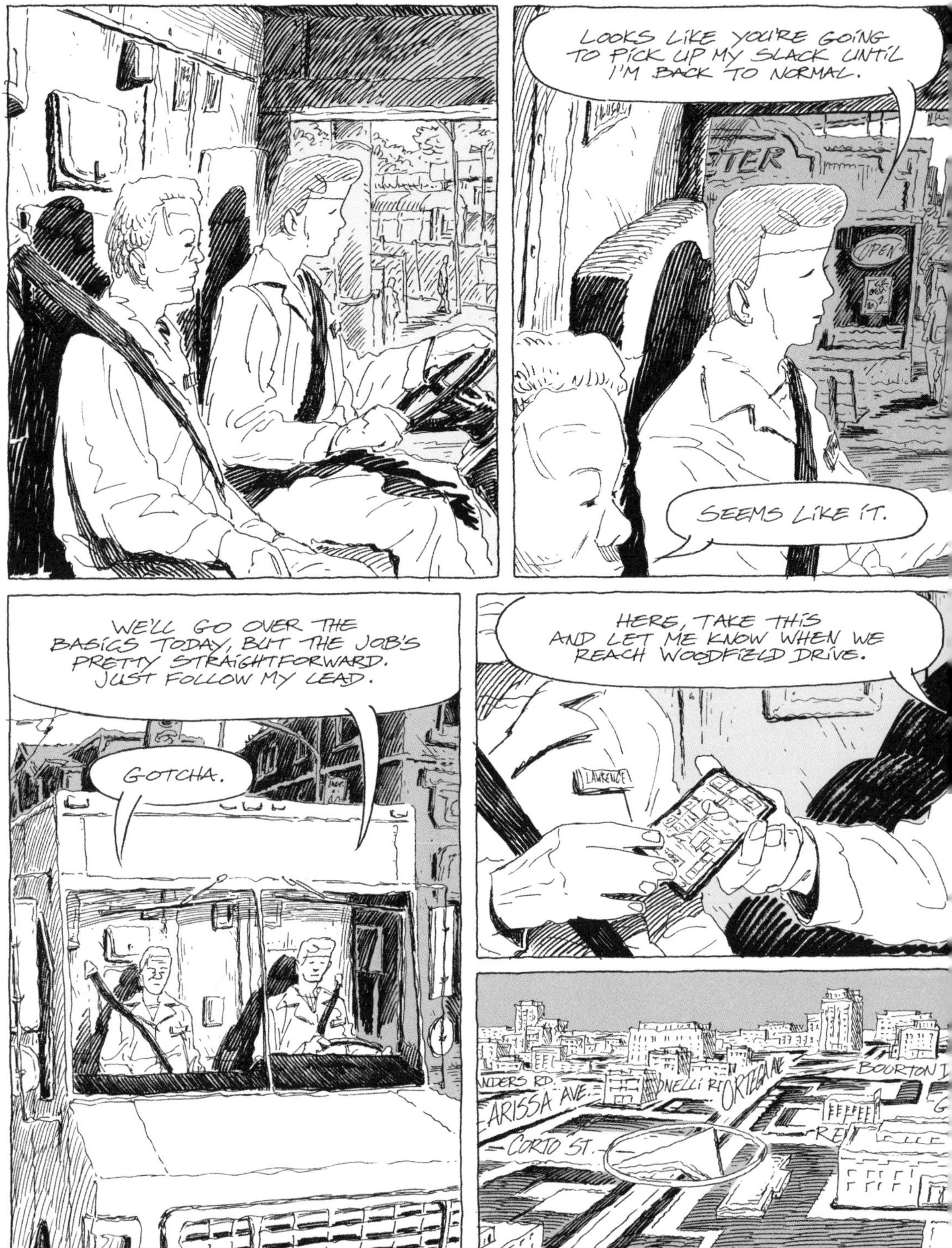
LOOKS LIKE YOU'RE GOING TO PICK UP MY SLACK UNTIL I'M BACK TO NORMAL.
SEEMS LIKE IT.
WE'LL GO OVER THE BASICS TODAY, BUT THE JOB'S PRETTY STRAIGHTFORWARD. JUST FOLLOW MY LEAD.
GOTCHA.
HERE, TAKE THIS AND LET ME KNOW WHEN WE REACH WOODFIELD DRIVE.
LAWRENCE
ORTEGA AVE
BOURTON
CORTO ST.

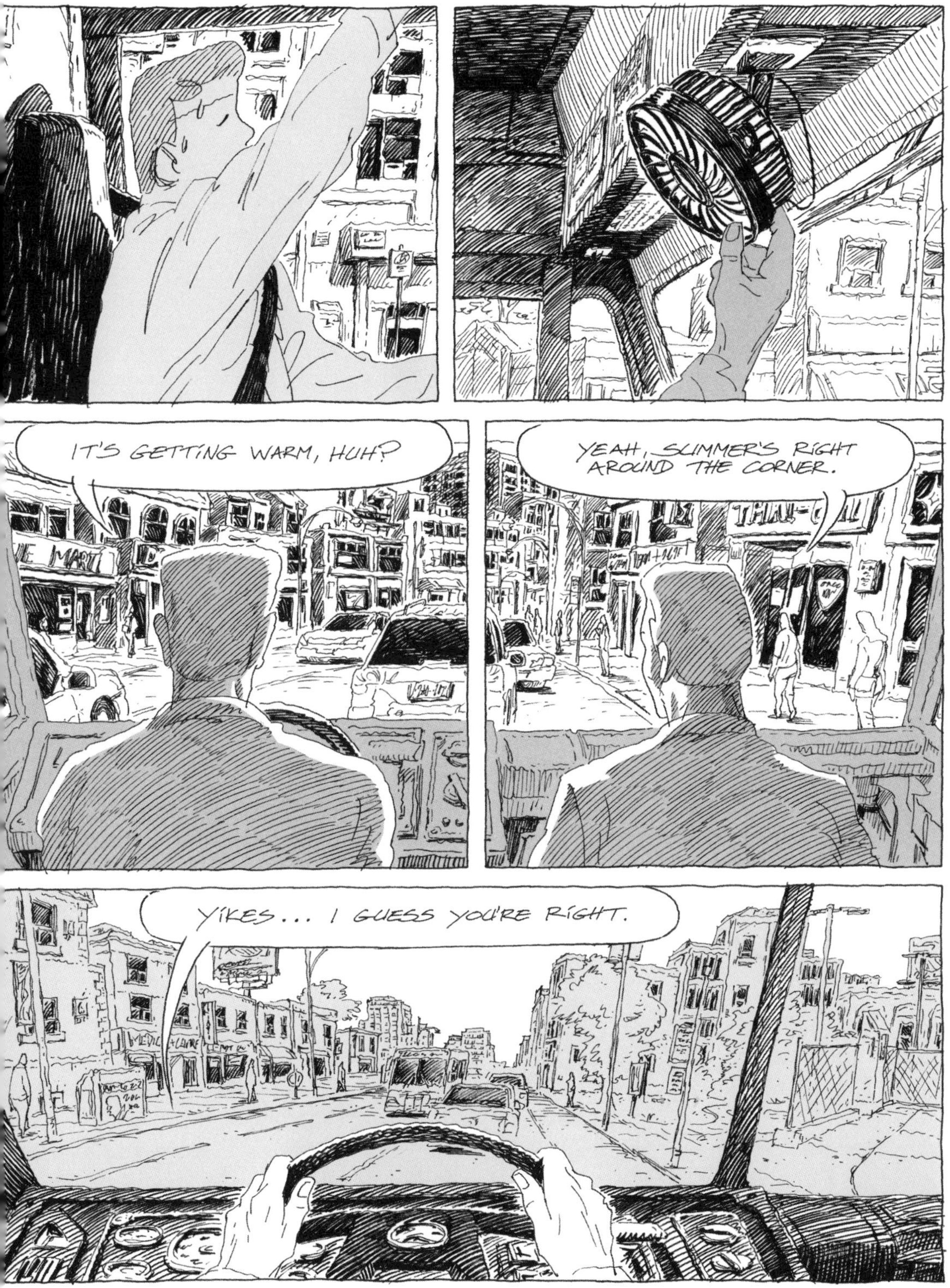
IT'S GETTING WARM, HUH?
YEAH, SUMMER'S RIGHT AROUND THE CORNER.
YIKES... I GUESS YOU'RE RIGHT.

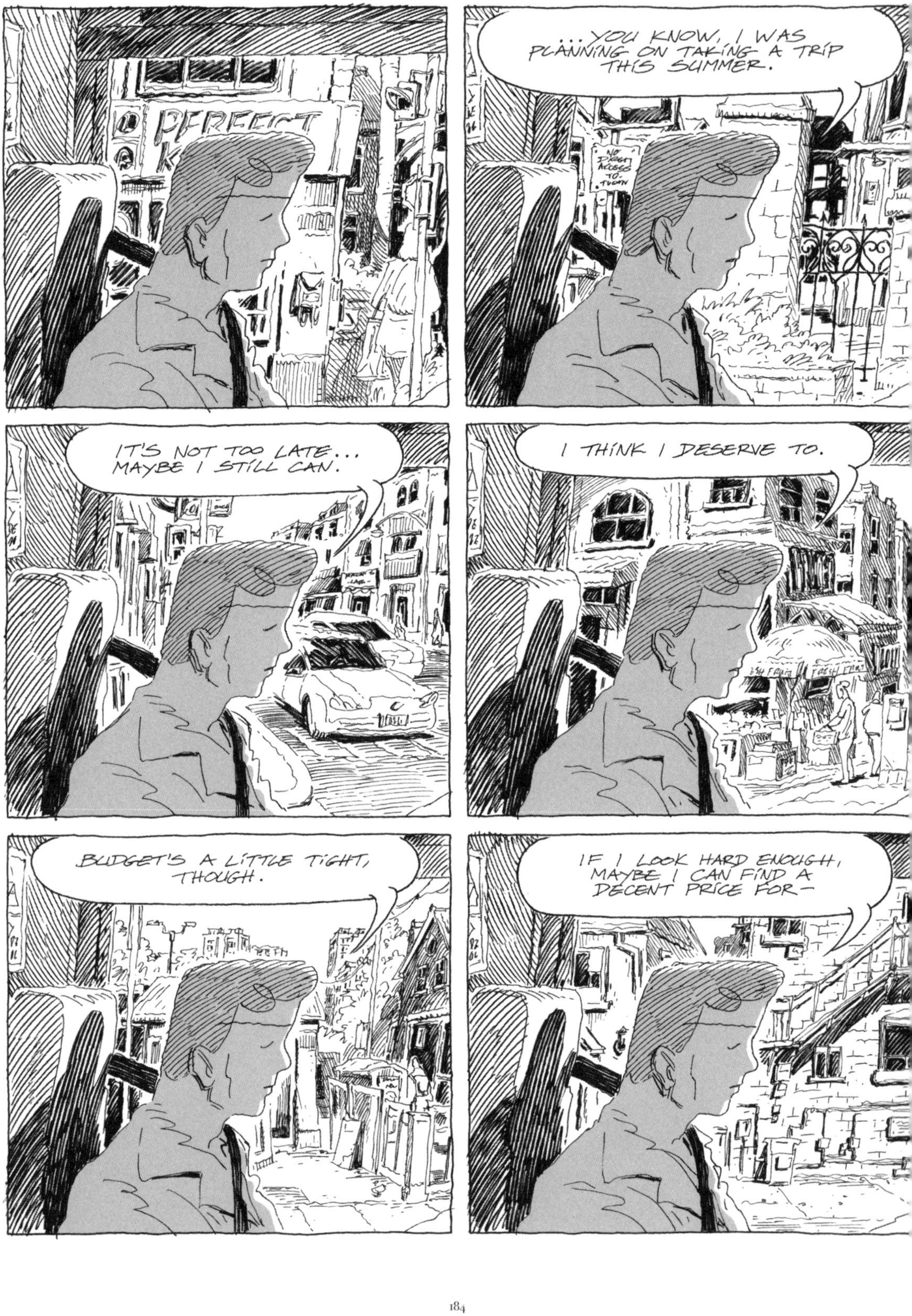
PERFECT
...YOU KNOW, I WAS PLANNING ON TAKING A TRIP THIS SUMMER.
IT'S NOT TOO LATE... MAYBE I STILL CAN.
I THINK I DESERVE TO.
BUDGET'S A LITTLE TIGHT, THOUGH.
IF I LOOK HARD ENOUGH, MAYBE I CAN FIND A DECENT PRICE FOR—

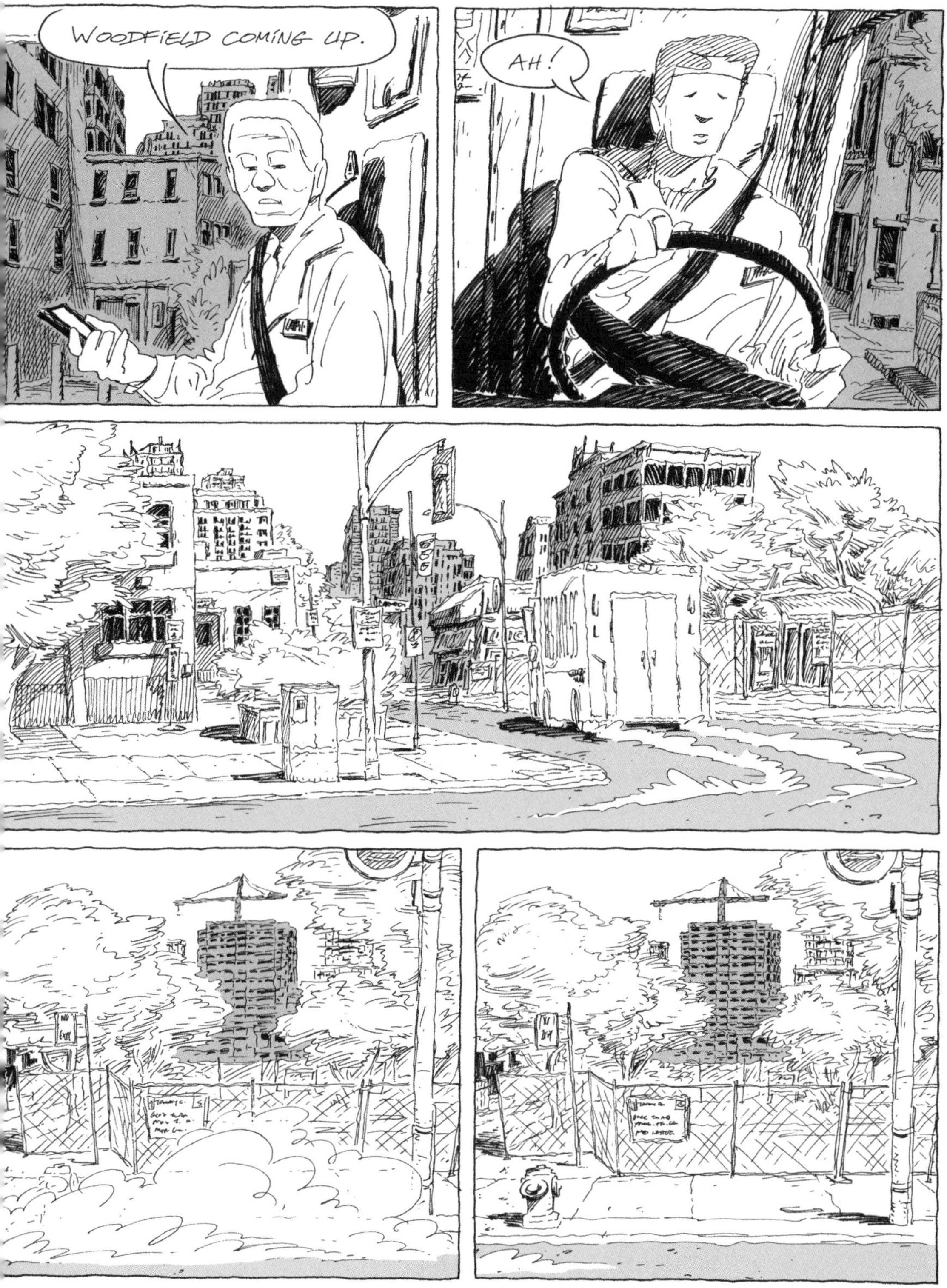
WOODFIELD COMING UP.
AH!

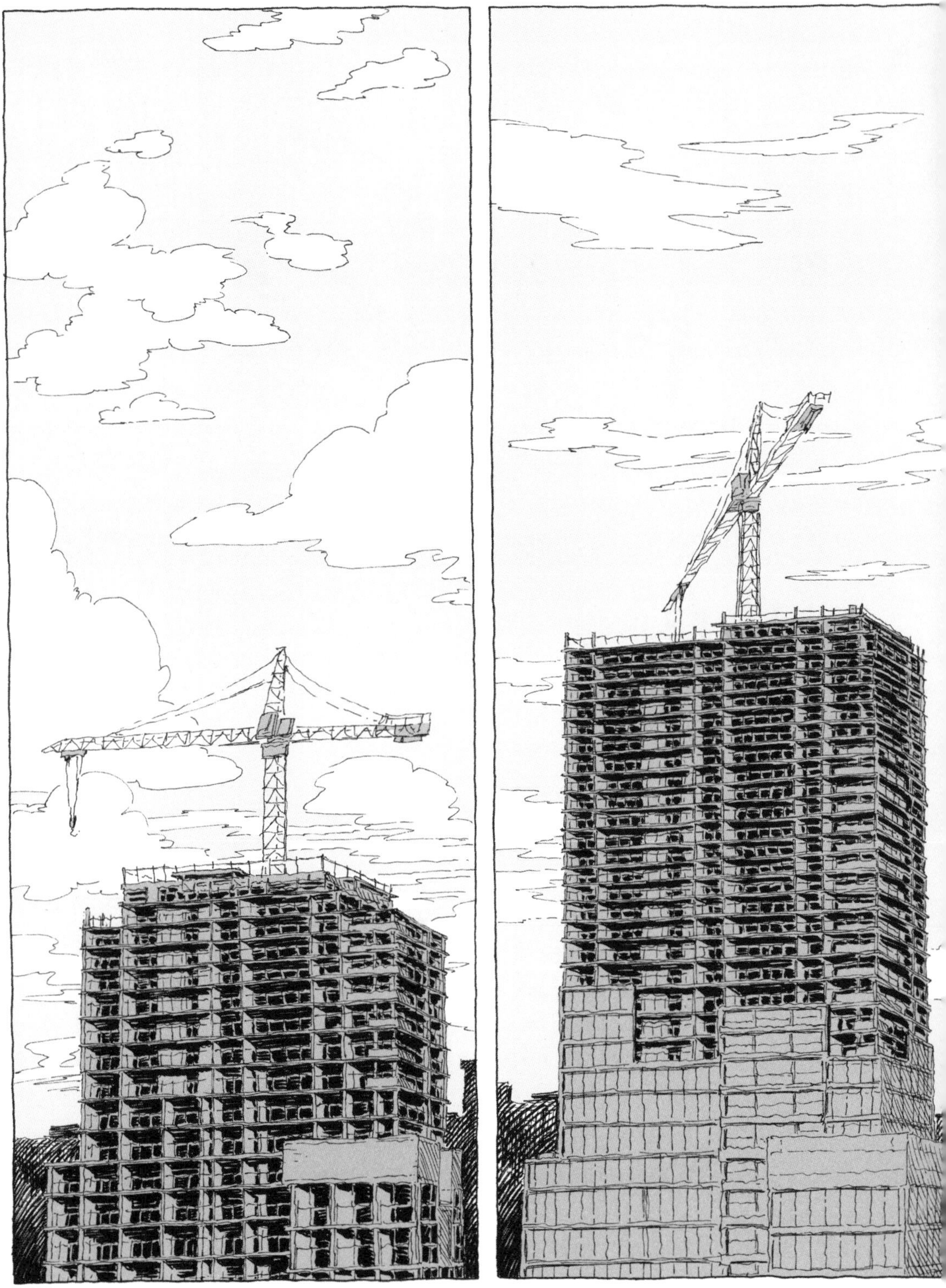

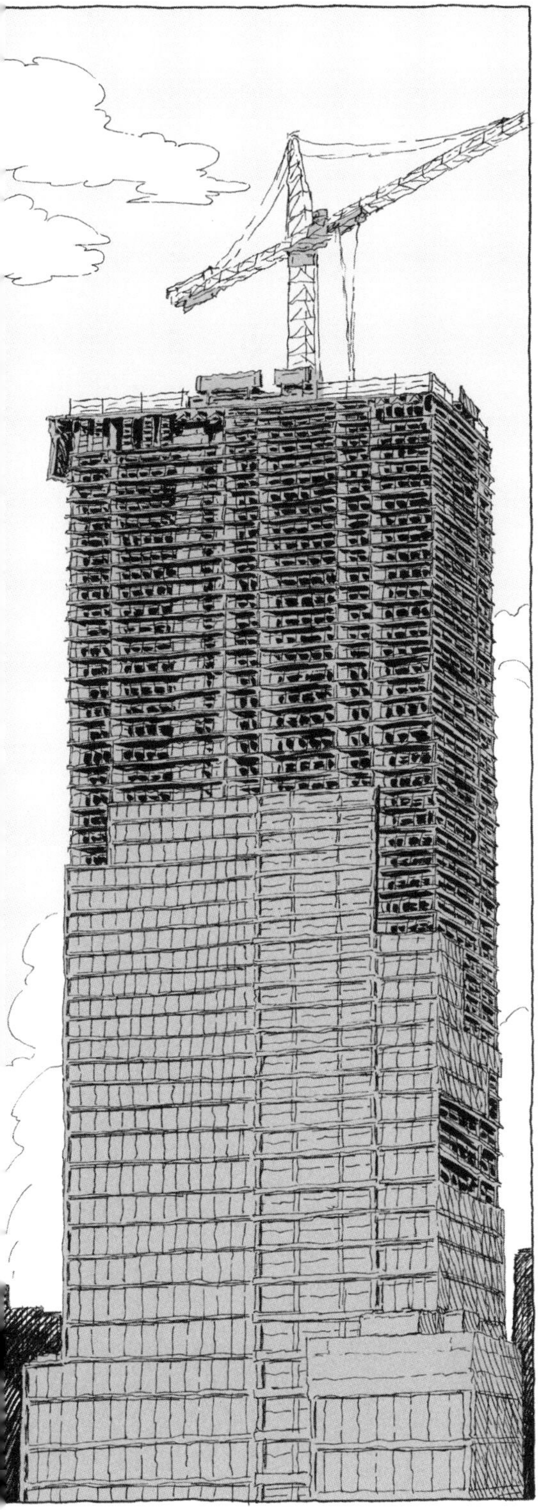

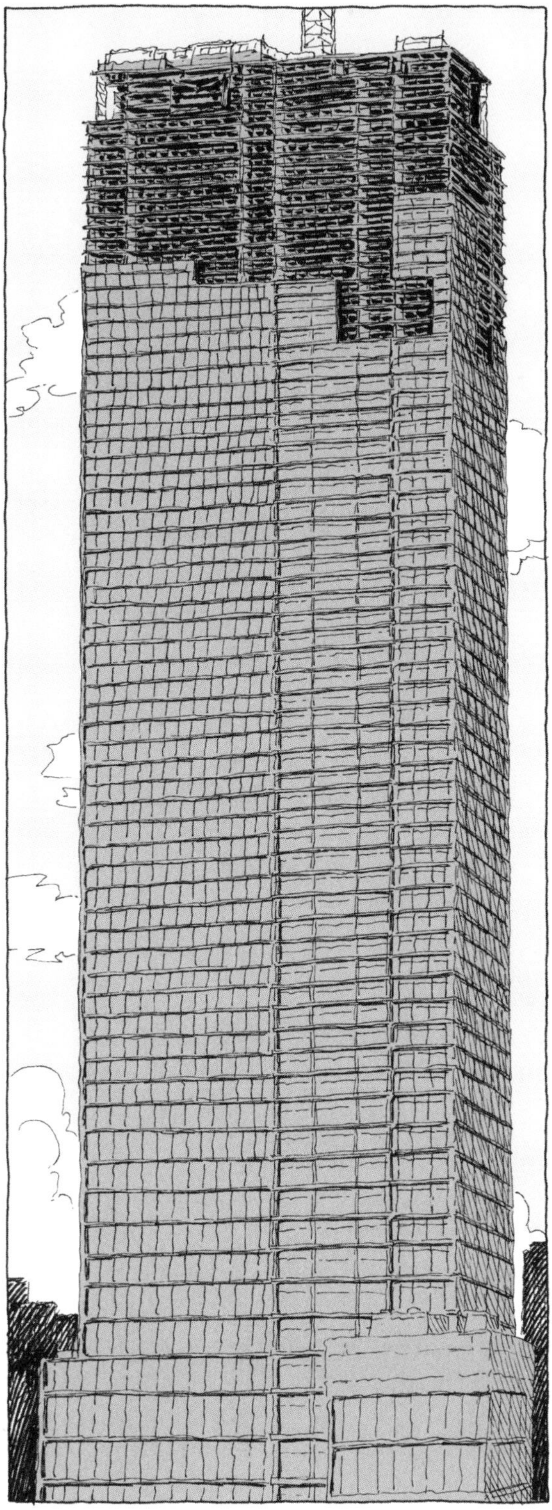

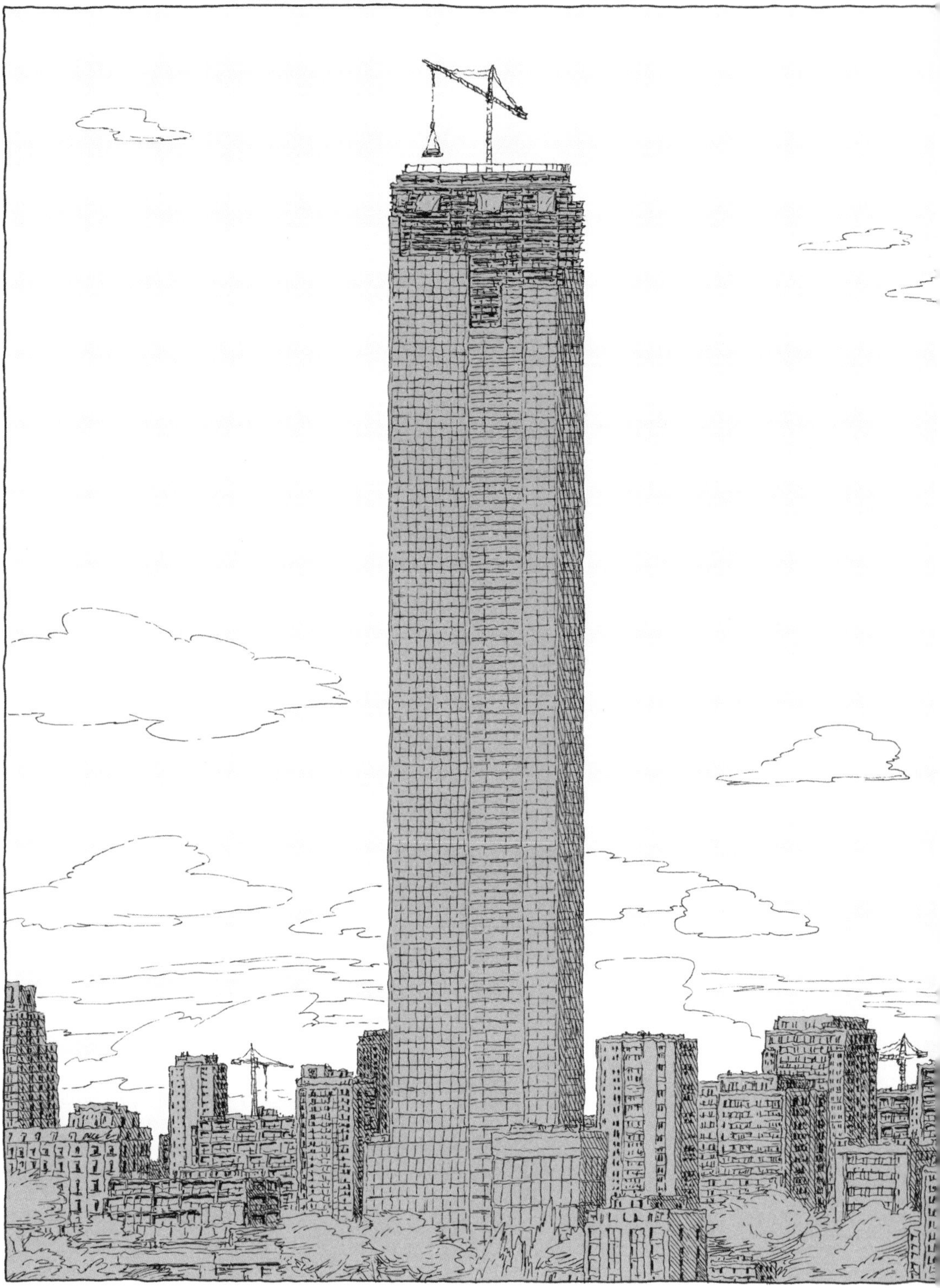

CHRIS W. KIM
is a comics artist
and illustrator.

A graduate of OCAD
University in Toronto,
his clients include *The
New York Times* and
The Hollywood Reporter.
Herman by Trade
(SelfMadeHero, 2017)
was his first graphic novel.
Strays is his second.